T0355389

THE I TATTI
RENAISSANCE LIBRARY

James Hankins, General Editor

MANETTI

AGAINST THE JEWS
AND THE GENTILES

BOOKS I–IV

ITRL 79

GIANNOZZO MANETTI

✦ ✦ ✦

AGAINST THE JEWS AND THE GENTILES

BOOKS I–IV

EDITED BY

STEFANO U. BALDASSARRI

AND

DANIELA PAGLIARA

TRANSLATED BY

DAVID MARSH

THE I TATTI RENAISSANCE LIBRARY

HARVARD UNIVERSITY PRESS

CAMBRIDGE, MASSACHUSETTS

LONDON, ENGLAND

2017

Series design by Dean Bornstein

Library of Congress Cataloging-in-Publication Data

Names: Manetti, Giannozzo, 1396–1459, author. | Baldassarri, Stefano Ugo,
editor. | Pagliara, Daniela, editor. | Marsh, David, 1950 September 25–
translator. | Container of (expression): Manetti, Giannozzo, 1396–1459.
Adversus Iudaeos et Gentes. | Container of (expression): Manetti, Giannozzo,
1396–1459. Adversus Iudaeos et Gentes. English.
Title: Against the Jews and the Gentiles / edited by Stefano U. Baldassarri
and Daniela Pagliara ; translated by David Marsh.
Other titles: I Tatti Renaissance library ; 79.
Description: Cambridge, Massachusetts : Harvard University Press, 2017. |
Series: I Tatti Renaissance library ; 79 | Text in Latin with English translation
on facing pages ; introduction and notes in English. | Includes bibliographical
references and index. Contents: Volume 1. Books 1–iv.
Identifiers: lccn 2016048603 | isbn 9780674974975 (alk. paper)
Subjects: lcsh: Christian philosophy. | Jewish philosophy. | Philosophy,
Ancient.
Classification: lcc B785.M2443 A38 2017 | ddc 195—dc23 lc record available at
https://lccn.loc.gov/2016048603

Contents

꽃§?꽃

Introduction

꙰ꙊꙉꙊ꙰

Giannozzo Manetti (1396–1459) is among the more remarkable figures of Florentine humanism in the fifteenth century—a wealthy merchant, an active statesman, a profound scholar, a secular philosopher and theologian, and a learned Christian Hebraist. Although we have little record of his success in business, his numerous activities both public and private are amply documented throughout his long career.[1] As an official representative of the Florentine republic, he has left funeral orations for Leonardo Bruni and Giannozzo Pandolfini as well as a considerable corpus of public speeches in both Latin and Italian. As a humanist scholar, he wrote important dialogues and treatises, including the celebrated *On the Dignity and Excellence of Man*, which many consider a central manifesto of the new Renaissance philosophy.[2] As a secular philosopher, he undertook the translation (or at least the critical revision) of Aristotle's ethical treatises. As a precursor of Protestant theology, he translated the Greek text of the New Testament into Latin. And as a Hebraist, he studied and mastered Hebrew, and not only evaluated texts central to the Judeo-Christian tradition but also translated the Psalms into Latin—a layman scholar's response to the canonic work of St. Jerome.

Giannozzo Manetti was born in Florence on June 5, 1396, the son of the merchant Bernardo Manetti and Piera Guidacci.[3] In the early years of the new century, Bernardo's fortunes were on the rise: according to the 1427 *catasto*, Florence's first public tax assessment, he was the tenth wealthiest man in the entire city of Florence and the second wealthiest man in the Santo Spirito district.[4] The Manetti family had owned property in this area since the late Trecento and built their *palazzo*, now Via Santo Spirito 23, in the early decades of the Quattrocento.[5]

By family tradition, Giannozzo was destined to a mercantile career, in which he soon prospered. At the same time, Florence in the early Quattrocento was a vibrant center of innovation in classical studies, and Giannozzo was inspired to pursue higher learning. Much of our information about Manetti's life and works comes from three biographical works written by the Florentine bookseller Vespasiano da Bisticci.[6] It is Vespasiano, for instance, who informs us that Manetti began at the age of twenty-five to study the *trivium* of Latin grammar, logic, and rhetoric, as well as philosophy and theology, at the Florentine Studium (or university). His teachers were the friars Girolamo of Naples and Evangelista of Pisa, and he participated in the activities of the Academy of Santo Spirito, near his home. He also joined the circle of the Camaldulensian friar Ambrogio Traversari, a noted translator of Greek texts, who may have encouraged Manetti to study Hebrew as well as Greek.

Manetti's business affairs allied him with two of the most powerful of Florence's major guilds. By 1425 he belonged to the banking guild (the *Arte del Cambio*), and from 1433 onward he also belonged to the silk-making guild (the *Arte della Seta*). In 1427, Manetti married Alessandra di Tommaso di Giacomino Tebalducci, who bore him seven children.

From an early age Giannozzo's name was routinely chosen by lot from among the select Florentine citizens who had passed the initial "scrutiny" for officeholding, and from the later 1420s onward he held an impressive variety of offices on behalf of the commune. As a prominent citizen, Manetti also served numerous times on major civic committees, apparently recommended in part by his substantial financial qualifications. His first public office, in 1429, was as a member of one of the two principal boards, the "Twelve Good Men" (*Dodici Buonuomini*), that advised the governing board of the city (the Priors of the Guilds and People of Florence). In the next twenty-five years he served in more than a dozen posi-

tions, and he governed three of the Tuscan towns ruled by Florence: Pescia, Pistoia, and Scarperia.

Despite his incessant activity as a private merchant and a public servant, Manetti was a prolific writer in both Latin and Italian. As a Florentine official capable of making impromptu speeches in both languages, Manetti is known to have delivered more than a dozen public orations, including two encomia of Genoa, which marked the beginning of his career as an ambassador.[7] He also composed funeral orations for Leonardo Bruni (1444) and Giannozzo Pandolfini (1456).[8] Besides his Latin encomia celebrating Genoa, he wrote a history of Pistoia, a city he had governed on behalf of Florence.[9] His friendship with the Spanish humanist Nuño de Guzmán inspired him to compose a defense of liberal studies but also motivated two biographical works: a biography of Guzmán's mother and the compilation *On Famous Men of Great Age*. Manetti's continued interest in biography led to lives of Dante, Petrarch, and Boccaccio; lives of Socrates and Seneca; and the numerous biographies and hagiographies included in his tract *Against the Jews and the Gentiles*.[10] Having enjoyed the patronage of Pope Nicholas V (1447–55), Manetti wrote a Latin biography of the humanist pope in three books, titled *De vita ac gestis Nicolai quinti*.[11] The work is notable for its celebration of the pope's building projects; since the reconsecration of the Florence cathedral in 1436, Manetti had taken a keen interest in the cultural importance of architecture.[12]

Since his twenties Manetti had pursued the study of philosophy, embracing both ethics and physics. When his four-year-old son Antonino died in 1438, he composed a Ciceronian *Dialogus consolatorius* portraying a philosophical debate about grief, written first in Latin and then translated into Italian. Some years later, he translated the three principal Aristotelian ethical treatises, the *Magna Moralia*, *Eudemian Ethics*, and *Nicomachean Ethics*. He

also composed the celebrated treatise *On the Dignity and Excellence of Man*, a work considered emblematic of Renaissance humanist ideals. Later, when Naples was struck by a catastrophic earthquake in 1456, Manetti responded by composing three books on the natural history of earthquakes and related theological issues (*De terremotu*).[13]

Manetti's wealth and success inevitably aroused the envy of his fellow Florentines. Medici partisans seem to have been responsible for the increasing taxes that finally drove him from the city in the 1450s. As a friend of Pope Nicholas V, Manetti first moved to Rome, where he was knighted and employed as a papal secretary; after the pope's death he joined the court of Alfonso of Aragon, the king of Naples.

Giannozzo Manetti died in Naples early in the morning of October 27, 1459. The following year, his son Agnolo managed to bring his remains back to Florence in a crate that, appropriately, was purportedly filled with books! The remains were destined for interment in Santo Spirito, the parish church of the Manetti family, and the family asked the learned Augustinian Guglielmo Becchi to deliver a funeral oration. Unfortunately, Cosimo de' Medici intervened and forbade the ceremony.[14] In 1490 Paolo Cortesi composed a Latin dialogue *On Learned Men* (*De hominibus doctis*) in which he paired Manetti and Alberti as the most learned men of their generation.[15] He noted, however, that Manetti's fame had suffered an eclipse in his own time; his explanation was that Manetti's mastery of many disciplines brought him less renown than supremacy in a single field might have done.

As a devout Christian, Manetti demonstrated his knowledge of Greek by translating the New Testament into Latin—the first scholar to do so since Jerome.[16] He even learned Hebrew and translated the Psalter in a version that he defended in the historical and philological treatise called *Apologeticus*.[17] Manetti's manu-

script of the Vulgate, which survives in the Palatine fondo of the Vatican Library as Pal. lat. 18, contains marginalia that suggest he used this text in preparing both his Psalm translation and his treatise *Against the Jews and the Gentiles*.[18] The two works seem to be closely linked. Negative response to his Latin version of the Psalms moved Manetti to write the defense called *Apologeticus*.

Manetti's humanist approach to religion began early. Together with Tommaso Parentucelli (the future Nicholas V), Manetti — as noted above — studied in Florence with the Camaldulensian friar Ambrogio Traversari, who may have inspired his personal faith. Manetti's Latin treatise *Adversus Iudaeos et Gentes* (*Against the Jews and the Gentiles*) offers a polemical defense of the Christian religion, originally planned in twenty books, although only ten were completed. Its title places it squarely in a tradition of Christian apologetics that begins with the Latin *Adversus Iudaeos* of Tertullian (ca. 160–ca. 225) and the Greek *Kata Ioudaiōn* (a cycle of eight sermons) by John Chrysostom (ca. 347–407) — a tradition with a long and notorious history.[19]

According to Vespasiano's life of Manetti, the author revised the work in Naples (1456–59) but presumably began to compose it nearly a decade earlier. In a letter to Nicholas V of May 4, 1448, Manetti mentions a manuscript of Philo Judaeus that he needs in writing his "extensive books against the Jews" (*nonnulla ingentia adversus Hebreos volumina*).[20]

Manetti's work was conceived as a more ambitious project of universal and encyclopedic dimensions, modeled in part on the fifteen-book *Preparation of the Gospel* by the Greek scholar Eusebius (263–339 CE), a work translated into Latin by Manetti's contemporary George of Trebizond.[21] Just as Eusebius' work seeks to demonstrate the superiority of Christianity over pagan religions and philosophies, in the conclusion of Book 1 Manetti styles his own work a *praeparatio evangelii*, echoing Eusebius' title. Yet whereas Eusebius strove to sanction Jewish tradition, Manetti

emphatically rejects the beliefs and practices of the Jews and pagans alike.

As a synopsis of the books will make clear, the ten extant books may be divided into two parts. In the first four books, presented in this volume, Manetti surveys human history from the Creation to the life, teaching, and resurrection of Christ. In the last six books, he offers a pageant of great Christians who demonstrated the excellence of their religion.

Book 1 begins with the creation and fall of man in the biblical account. There follows a long digression *adversus gentes* (the Gentiles, i.e., pagans), which both reviews central points of ancient Greek and Roman philosophy and religion and censures the ancients for their senseless doctrines and bloody rites. Manetti then returns to the Jews, whose beliefs and practices are praised from Abraham to Moses. During their centuries of "true" piety, Manetti calls the chosen people "Hebrews." But from the time of the Exodus onward, he censures them as "Jews," because they observe the absurd and cruel practices of Pentateuchal legislation, which he views as analogous to pagan rites. Manetti stresses several themes in Jewish history: the early development of the concept of righteousness, the Exodus, the Mosaic Law and its inadequacy — thus providing a "preparation for the Gospel" in Eusebius' sense.

The next three books provide a synoptic biography of Jesus in three stages. Book 2 describes the life of Christ up to the raising of Lazarus; Book 3 relates his teaching, and Book 4 offers an account of Christ's passion, death, and resurrection. Naturally, Manetti's principal source for these books is the Gospel, which he had translated from Greek into Latin, but he also draws on Eusebius, Jerome, and — to a lesser extent — the Greek Church Father John Chrysostom. In Book 2, Manetti, the practicing Christian, relates various events of the Gospel narrative to specific festivals of the contemporary Church, such as the Feast of the Visitation (2.20), Epiphany (2.42), and Candlemas (2.49). There are occasional for-

ays into historical criticism, as when Manetti clarifies the legal context of the Virgin Mary's marriage to Joseph, discards implausible legends, settles apparently conflicting reports, or, following Josephus, explains the history and politics of the Herodian kingdom at the time of Christ. Etymological explanations of Greek and Hebrew words are frequently inserted. As we would expect in a work of Christian apologetics, Manetti regularly points out parallels and typological prefigurings in the Old Testament of events in the New and refines arguments for the truth of various events in the Gospels, especially Christ's miracles. Overall, we get a mildly critical retelling of Jesus Christ's story from the point of view of a pious Christian, weaving together the four Gospel accounts with reflections on liturgy, theology, and language, all written in an elegant neoclassical Latin.

Again in a classical vein, Manetti enriches his narrative with poetic citations from the ancient Christian poet Juvencus' *Gospels*, a four-book epic written in sub-Vergilian hexameters, and most of all from the *Easter Poem* (*Carmen paschale*) by the fifth-century Christian poet Sedulius. In this Manetti follows the example of Cicero, who embellishes his philosophical works with poetic quotations drawn from both Latin and Greek literature. Manetti is not averse to adducing parallels from Roman history: for example, he compares Jesus' crucifixion to that of Gabinius (actually Gavius) as described in Cicero's speech against Verres (4.51), and the fates of Christ's accusers to those of Julius Caesar's assassins (4.71–72).

In the second part of this massive treatise, Manetti assembles a vast series of biographies of illustrious Christians, grouped by categories. Book 5 treats sacred authors, relying principally on Jerome's *On Illustrious Men* (*De viris illustribus*), supplemented by Gennadius' *Church Writers* (*De scriptoribus ecclesiasticis*) and by Gregory the Great's *Dialogues*. Book 6 treats secular authors from late antiquity to Manetti's own day. Here he mainly draws on *Famous*

Latin Writers in Eighteen Books (*Scriptorum illustrium latinae linguae libri XVIII*) by the north Italian humanist Sicco Polenton (1375–1447) and on the *Famous Florentines* (*De viris illustribus florentinis*) by Filippo Villani (fl. 1360–1400). In Book 7, Manetti narrates the lives of more than two hundred confessor-saints, striking a balance between the Eastern monks of Egypt and Syria—based on the various sources that constitute the *Lives of the Desert Fathers* (*Vitae Patrum*)—with predominantly Italian bishops and monks from St. Benedict to San Bernardino of Siena—drawn principally from Gregory the Great. Book 8 arranges various martyrs in chronological order, while Book 9 treats them less systematically; finally, Book 10 narrates the lives of virgins. While derived from various Latin martyrologies, these often shadowy lives are largely based on the *Martyrologium Romanum*, supplemented at times by Greek sources.

Gianfranco Fioravanti has characterized Manetti's treatise as a compilation with few humanistic elements, but the same could be said of an analogous work written in the next generation, Platina's *Lives of the Popes*.[22] Indeed, what critical or even reliable sources could the humanist use in narrating the lives of confessor-saints and virgins? Moreover, as Fioravanti observes, Manetti does not cite the traditional Christian argument that the Jews were responsible for Jesus' death.[23] Clearly, the most original part of this massive compilation lies in Book 1, in which Manetti reviews the ancient history and culture of the Jews and the "gentiles," that is, the non-Christian Greeks and Romans of the ancient world.

As an accomplished orator and the eulogist of Leonardo Bruni, Manetti preferred praise to blame; and his command of Hebrew often makes him a sympathetic interpreter of Jewish history. Thus, he writes that after the tower of Babel had dispersed humankind into different peoples with different languages, only the Jews remained true to the ideal of monotheism. In Manetti's view, the history of the Jews is divided by the figure of Moses. Before the

coming of Moses, the Jews were called Hebrews (*Ivrim*), either after an ancestor of Abraham called Heber (Genesis 10:21) or from the verbal root *avar* (to cross over). In any case, they lived exemplary lives without relying on laws and scriptures. By contrast, after Moses, the Jews were called Jehudith, after Judah; but despite their having received the Ten Commandments and the Bible from their leader, they lived corrupt lives.

The modern reader may perhaps be troubled by one aspect of Manetti's often unprejudiced openness to diverse texts and their cultural context. His *Apologeticus* contains several passages of polemical denunciation of the Jews. He writes that they envy the Christians' knowledge of Latin and Greek and are lacking in knowledge of the liberal arts and natural sciences; and since they rely on diacritical marks, they can read no Hebrew texts but the (Masoretic) Bible.[24] In defense of Manetti's assertions, Christoph Dröge notes that the humanist may have felt constrained to reprove the Jews in order to demonstrate his own orthodoxy.[25] If he risked censure for pursuing Hebrew studies, his treatise *Against the Jews and the Gentiles* clearly displays his Jewish erudition as marshaled in defense of the Christian faith. All the same, Manetti follows Jerome in applying his knowledge of Hebrew and Greek. He had already translated the New Testament and the Psalms, and — as noted earlier — had written a defense of his undertaking.

Despite his announced intention of confuting the Jews, Manetti defines them as a people blessed with unique divine favors. Unlike the Church Fathers, he reads the Old Testament as a historical narrative rather than as a typological and allegorical anticipation of Christianity. The life of Moses is narrated according to the biographical categories of the classical tradition, so that the Jewish leader plays his role in history as a commander, an orator, and a historian. Manetti's "attacks" on the Jewish tradition are in fact indirect — as when he asks why the genealogy of Joseph is cited when his paternity is explicitly denied — and are limited to the

Bible, making no reference to either the Talmud or the Kabbalah.[26]

A final comment is in order concerning Manetti's prose style. As a practiced orator capable of improvising speeches in Latin, Manetti relies on a large arsenal of lexical and rhetorical weapons, a classical repertoire that facilitates copious and voluble composition. Most notably, he unrelentingly employs pairs of synonyms — both nouns and verbs — which lend a certain amplitude, at times cumbersome, to his Latin syntax. (A trace of this semantic habit survives in English legal doublets, such as "cease and desist.") Since the present translation seeks to render Manetti's prose faithfully, it may at times seem verbose, but the reader, it is hoped, will benefit from greater fidelity to the original.

The Latin text and apparatus are the work of Stefano Ugo Baldassarri and Daniela Pagliara; the English translation is by David Marsh, who relied on annotation by Stefano Ugo Baldassarri for many of the Notes to the Translation. This introduction is the work of David Marsh. The editors and translator wish to thank Professor Andrew R. Dyck for his thorough comments and corrections on the Latin and the English texts, and Professor James Hankins for his generous guidance and advice in preparing this edition.

NOTES

1. See now Vieri Mazzoni, "Nuovi documenti su Giannozzo e la famiglia Manetti," *Bullettino dell'Istituto Storico Italiano per il Medio Evo* 117 (2015): 339–56.

2. Manetti, *De dignitate et excellentia hominis*, ed. Leonard. On the treatise, see Martin Schmeisser, *"Wie ein sterblicher Gott": Giannozzo Manettis Konzeption der Würde des Menschen und ihre Rezeption im Zeitalter der Renaissance* (Munich: Wilhelm Fink Verlag, 2006). A translation of the work is

scheduled to appear as a future volume in this I Tatti Renaissance Library series.

3. Foà, "Manetti, Giannozzo.". For a brief biographical sketch, see Manetti, *Biographical Writings*, ed. and trans. Baldassarri and Bagemihl, vii–xi.

4. Martines, *Social World*, 131–38, 176–91, and 365–78; Nicholas A. Eckstein, *The District of the Green Dragon: Neighbourhood Life and Social Change in Renaissance Florence* (Florence: Leo S. Olschki, 1995), 23–24 and 165–67.

5. Manettis also lived in the district of San Frediano, at Via del Fondaccio (now Borgo San Jacopo 2): see Martines, *Social World*, 131–38.

6. For Vespasiano's prose *Vita* and *Comentario*, see Vespasiano, *Vite*, ed. Greco. He may also be the author of an anonymous biography in tercets: see Stefano Ugo Baldassarri and Bruno Figliuolo, *Manettiana: La biografia anonima in terzine e altri documenti inediti su Giannozzo Manetti* (Rome: Roma nel Rinascimento, 2010).

7. See Wittschier, *Das Corpus der Orationes*. For the Genoese orations, see Manetti, *Elogi dei Genovesi*, ed. and trans. Balbi; and cf. Martelli, "Profilio ideologico di Giannozzo Manetti," 5–8.

8. Wittschier, *Das Corpus der Orationes*, 70–78 (Bruni); 139–41 (Pandolfini). On the Bruni oration, see Paolo Viti, "Giannozzo Manetti e l'orazione funebre per Leonardo Bruni," in Baldassarri, *Dignitas et excellentia hominis*, 311–32. On the Pandolfini oration, see Stefano Ugo Baldassarri and Brian J. Maxson, "Giannozzo Manetti's *Oratio in Funere Iannotii Pandolfini*: Art, Humanism and Politics in Fifteenth-Century Florence," *Interpres* 33 (2015).

9. Manetti, *Historia Pistoriensis*, ed. Baldassarri, Aldi, and Connell. There is also an Italian translation of this text by Stefano Ugo Baldassarri with notes by William J. Connell (Alessandria: Edizioni dell'Orso, 2011 and 2014).

10. See Manetti, *Biographical Writings*; and Baldassarri, "Scolastica e umanesimo." On the life of Socrates, see James Hankins, "Manetti's Socrates and the Socrateses of Antiquity," in Baldassarri, *Dignitas et excellentia hominis*, 203–19.

11. Manetti, *De vita ac gestis Nicolai Quinti summi pontificis*, ed. and trans. Modigliani; Anna Modigliani, "Il testamento di Niccolò V: la rielaborazione di Manetti nella biografia del Papa," in Baldassarri, *Dignitas et excellentia hominis*, 321–29.

12. See Smith and O'Connor, *Building the Kingdom*.

13. Manetti, *De terremotu*, ed. Pagliara.

14. Riccardo Fubini and Wi-Seon Kim, "Giannozzo Manetti nei resoconti biografici di Vespasiano da Bisticci," *Humanistica* 5 (2010): 35–49 at 48–49.

15. See Paolo Cortesi, *De hominibus doctis*, ed. and trans. Maria Teresa Graziosi (Rome: Bonacci Editore, 1973).

16. The Gospel passages translated in *Adversus Iudaeos et gentes* often differ both from the Vulgate and from Manetti's later complete translation: see Baldassarri, "Riflessioni preliminari." A critical edition of Manetti's New Testament is now available in Den Haan, *Manetti's New Testament*.

17. Manetti, *Apologeticus*, ed. De Petris; Manetti, *A Translator's Defense* (*Apologeticus*), ed. McShane and trans. Young.

18. Dröge, *Manetti als Denker und Hebraist*, 37–38.

19. The following studies, suggested by my colleague Stefano Ugo Baldassarri, may serve as a useful introduction to contextualize Manetti's approach to this topic and highlight the main sources at his disposal: Gerhardt B. Ladner, "Aspects of Patristic Anti-Judaism," *Viator* 2 (1971): 355–63; Amos Funkenstein, "Basic Types of Christian Anti-Jewish Polemics in the Later Middle Ages," *Viator* 2 (1971): 373–82; the essays collected in *Essential Papers on Judaism and Christianity in Conflict. From Late Antiquity to the Reformation*, ed. Jeremy Cohen (New York: New York University Press, 1991), especially Rosemary Radford Ruether, "The 'Adversus Judaeos' Tradition in the Church Fathers: The Exegesis of Christian Anti-Judaism," 174–89, and Jeremy Cohen, "Scholarship and Intolerance in the Medieval Academy: The Study and Evaluation of Judaism in European Christendom," 310–41; Yvonne Friedman's introduction to her critical edition of Peter of Blois, *Adversus Iudeorum inveteratam duritiem* (Turnholt: Brepols, 1985), vii–xxv; and Gianna Gardenal, *L'antigiudaismo*

nella letteratura cristiana antica e medievale (Brescia: Morcelliana, 2001). More in general, on the condition of Jews in medieval and Renaissance Italy, see now the following study by Riccardo Calimani and the rich bibliography reported therein: *Storia degli Ebrei italiani. I: Dalle origini al XV secolo* (Milan: Mondadori, 2013).

20. Wittschier, *Das Corpus der Orationes*, 44–45.

21. For an introduction to the work, besides Dröge, *Manetti als Denker und Hebraist*, see Charles Trinkaus, *In Our Image and Likeness*, 2:726–34; De Petris, "L'*Adversus Judaeos et Gentes*"; Fioravanti, "L'apologetica anti-giudaica"; Baldassarri, "Conferme e novità." A critical edition of Trebizond's translation by John Monfasani is in preparation.

22. See Platina, *Lives of the Popes*, vol. 1.

23. Fioravanti, "L'apologetica anti-giudaica," 29.

24. Trinkaus, *In Our Image and Likeness*, 2:593; Dröge, *Manetti als Denker und Hebraist*, 59.

25. Dröge, *Manetti als Denker und Hebraist*, 62–64.

26. Ibid., 75–77.

IANNOZII ⟨MANETTI⟩
ADVERSUS IUDAEOS ET GENTES
AD ALFONSUM
CLARISSIMUM ARAGONUM
REGEM

GIANNOZZO MANETTI
AGAINST THE JEWS AND THE
GENTILES
TO ALFONSO,
THE ILLUSTRIOUS KING OF
ARAGON

LIBER PRIMUS[1]

⟨*De praeparatione evangelica*⟩

1 Cum omnipotens Deus ac pius et misericors Dominus ex immensa quadam atque infinita eius bonitate mundum ab initio creasset, tandem hominem constituit, cuius gratia cuncta quaeque alia antea creaverat. Unde cum eius causa omnia fecisset, id maxime convenire ac decere videbatur, ut ipse ceteris operibus suis dignior atque excellentior conderetur. Quocirca cum angelicos spiritus intelligentes incorporeosque paulo ante constituisset, ad maiorem quamdam totius universi pulchritudinem ac decorem aliam naturam corpoream intellectusque capacem instituere atque condere voluit, quam ex corpore animaque compactam 'Adam' hebraice appellavit, quod latine 'hominem' significat.

2 Hunc igitur, cum omnibus animi et corporis dotibus mirabiliter exornasset, cunctis operibus suis iam antea creatis praeesse ac praedominari disposuit decrevitque; sed ut melius ea ipsa gubernare regereque ac per hunc modum probe gubernata beneque recta in utilitatem suam convertere valeret, illi rectam, callidam et sagacem mentem largitus ⟨est⟩. Et quamquam ipsum omnibus, ut diximus, naturae muneribus corroborasset munivissetque et in paradiso quoque voluptatis collocasset, ne tamen laberetur huic legi naturali, quacum ab origine ornaverat, admirabile quoddam terribileque praeceptum adhibuisse videtur, quo quidem plane et aperte admonebatur ut si quando transgrederetur morte — ut Sacra inquit Scriptura — moreretur.

3 At vero ipse, sive humana fragilitate sive ambitione quadam sive diabolicis illecebris temptationibusque illectus, divinum illud mandatum temere nimis ambitioseque admodum transgressus est. Ex

BOOK ONE

Preparation for the Gospel[1]

After Almighty God, our pious and merciful Lord, had in his immense and infinite goodness created the world from the beginning, at last He made man, for whose sake He had already created all other things.[2] Since He had made everything for his sake, it seemed most suitable and appropriate that man should be made more worthy and excellent than all his other works. As a result, having just established angelic spirits, both intelligent and incorporeal, to enhance the beauty and loveliness of the entire universe, he chose to found and fashion another nature, corporeal and endowed with intelligence.[3] He gave this combination of body and soul the Hebrew name *Adam*, which means the same as human being in Latin.[4]

Then, having ennobled man with every endowment of mind and body, He ordained and decreed for him to be leader and lord over all the works that had already been created. But so that man would better be able to govern and rule them, and in this way derive profit from whatever was rightly governed and well ruled, He bestowed on him an upright, ingenious, and insightful mind. Now, God had strengthened and fortified man with all the gifts of nature, as I said, and had placed him in a "paradise of pleasure."[5] Nevertheless, to prevent his lapsing from the natural law bestowed on him from the beginning, God imposed a strange and terrifying injunction warning him clearly and explicitly that, if he ever disobeyed, he would die, as Holy Scripture tells us.[6]

Yet that man all too rashly and quite arrogantly disobeyed the holy commandment—whether out of human frailty, or arrogance, or seduced by diabolical enticements and temptations.[7] And by

1

2

3

3

hac ergo tam miserabili tamque infelici transgressione non solum se ipsum sed etiam universum humanum genus, quod ex eo in perpetuum propagandum erat, miserabiliter calamitoseque damnavit. Qui ergo post multa saecula nati sunt homines ea primaevae transgressionis labe infecti paulatim in tantam ac tam flagitiosam libidinem dilapsi sunt ut per ducentos duos et quadraginta supra bina annorum milia usque ad tempora Noe—tantum namque intervalli inter primum hominem et hunc consolatorem (sic enim hoc nomen hebraice interpretatur) virum innocentem—intercessisse creditur. Deus demum, ingentibus et intollerandis flagitiis supra quam dici potest infensus, totum hominum genus una cum ceteris terrestribus et aereis animalibus—Noe insonte ac iusto et filiis atque uxoribus suis et aliis quoque animantibus quae in archa illa celeberrima ac famosissima salvata sunt dumtaxat exceptis—illo universali diluvio ad internicionem usque deleret.

4 Noe itaque cum tribus filiis et eorum uxoribus ob innocentiam suam, quemadmodum diximus, ex generali submersione salvato nonnulla salubria praecepta de multiplicatione generis humani, de abstinentia a commestione sanguinis cum carne cautioneque ab homicidiis ac latrociniis et ceteris huiusmodi malis facinoribus, ne forte sicut primus homo in ruinam laberetur, tribuisse traditur. Per quadraginta deinde duos supra noningentos annos—tantum enim intervalli inter praedictum diluvium et Abrae nativitatem intercessisse scribitur—qui nati sunt homines plerumque viam rectam, paucis labentibus, secuti sunt.

5 Nato igitur Abraha—a quo salus humani generis, quod iam dudum primi parentis praevaricatione damnatum fuerat, oriunda erat—eadem ut superius causa adductus aliud de circumcisione infantium adiunxit, ut hoc hominum genus ab eo electum, apud quod solum verus et pius Dei cultus (ceteris gentibus ad idolatriam conversis) remansurus et unde humano generi salus proventura fore videbatur, per hoc circumcisionis in carne praeputii signum ab aliis quibuscumque populis discerneretur. Post

this wretched and unhappy disobedience, he miserably and disas-
trously condemned not only himself, but also the entire human
race that would spring from him in unbroken succession. Thus,
the people born after many generations, tainted by the infection of
that primeval disobedience, gradually lapsed into such great and
scandalous lust that 2,242 years passed before the age of Noah.[8]
(So great an interval is thought to separate the first man from the
blameless Noah, the "comforter," which is the meaning of his name
in Hebrew.)[9] At last, unspeakably enraged at their enormous and
intolerable sins, God sent the famed universal flood to wipe out
and destroy the entire human race together with the other creatures of the land and air. God spared only the innocent and just
Noah with his sons and their wives and the other animals, which
were saved in the celebrated and famous ark.[10]

Thus, by their innocence Noah, his three sons, and their wives 4
had been saved from the general deluge, as I said. And tradition
credits him with a number of salutary precepts concerning human
reproduction and abstaining from meat mixed with blood, as well
as a warning against murder, robbery, and such crimes—lest he
fall into ruin, just like the first man.[11] The people born thereafter
largely followed this straight path—only a few of them lapsed—
for 942 years, which is recorded as the interval between the flood
and the birth of Abraham.[12]

After the birth of Abraham, who brought salvation to the hu- 5
man race that had originally been damned by the transgression of
our first father, he was moved for the same reason as Noah before
him to add another rule for the circumcision of infants. In this
way, this chosen race of God, who alone were to preserve His true
and devout worship (since the other peoples had turned to idolatry), and were to be the source of the salvation of the human race,
would be distinguished from all other peoples by the sign of their

vigintiquinque supra quadringentos annos Moysi apud Aegyptios orto, Deus—eisdem quibus superius rationibus motus—novam legem duabus lapideis tabulis divino digito conscriptam tradidit ac naturali primae legi et novis quoque mandatis quae Noe et Abrahae praedictis iustis piisque hominibus exhibita fuerant demum superaddidit. Cuius quidem divinae legis praecepta, ut ad unguem servarentur, plane aperteque edixit, et ne homines forte transgrederentur transgressoribus ipsis cuncta quaeque maledictionum et exsecrationum genera se illaturum terribiliter minatus est; servatoribus, versa vice, omnes benedictionum ac prosperitatum species sese daturum pollicebatur.

6   Et quoniam omnia quae servatoribus ipsis promittebantur humanum genus—primi, ut diximus, parentis praevaricatione damnatum—nec redimere nec salvare poterant, nec etiam ipsi generi humano nondum a sua damnatione redempto aeternam vitam offerri ac polliceri posse videbantur, post mille quingentos circiter annos plenitudine temporis—ut inquit apostolus—adventante misit Deus filium suum ut humanum genus redimeret novamque ac perfectam et evangelicam legem traderet, cuius servatores non caducis et momentaneis praemiis sed caelorum regno ac sempiterna vita donabantur, praevaricatores vero, versa vice, intollerandis cruciatibus ac perpetua morte damnabantur. Et quia Christus humani generis salvator ab Hebraeis oriri debebat—quem ipsi hebraice 'Messiam' nuncuparunt, qui graece 'Christus,' latine idcirco 'Unctus' interpretatur, quoniam ipse in regem tamquam verus omnium rex atque in sacerdotem tamquam verus pontifex oleo exsultationis iuxta suas de unctione regum sacerdotumque traditiones ungendus erat—apud illos dumtaxat eloquia Dei credita fuere. Soli namque ex omnibus populis prophetas habuere, quibus spiritus sanctus solemnia quaedam de creatione mundi ac devotione gentium et de adventu Messiae et alia[2] huiusmodi mysteria revelavit, et verus quoque omnipotentis Dei cultus, cum ceterae omnes gentes ad

circumcised foreskins. Some 425 years later, Moses, born in Egypt, was moved by the same reasons as his predecessors, and handed down a new Law written by God's finger on two stone tablets, as an addition to the first natural law and the new commandments that Noah and Abraham had revealed to just and pious men. In order to assure that the commandments of this divine Law were scrupulously observed, God clearly and openly proclaimed them. Lest the people transgress, He uttered terrible threats that he would afflict transgressors with every kind of curse and malediction, while He promised, contrariwise, to give every kind of blessing and prosperity to those who observed the Law.

Yet since all the things promised to the observant could not re- 6
deem or save the human race — which, as noted, had been damned by the transgression of our first parent — they still seemed unable to offer and promise eternal life to a human race not yet redeemed from its damnation. After some 1,500 years, and with the approach of the "fullness of time" (as the Apostle says),[13] God sent His Son to redeem the human race and to pass down a new, perfect, and evangelical law. Those who observe it received not fleeting and momentary rewards, but the Kingdom of Heaven and everlasting life, whereas transgressors on the other hand were condemned to intolerable torments and perpetual death. Since Christ the savior of mankind was to spring from the Jews, it was they alone who believed the words of God. He was called "Messiah" in Hebrew, "Christus" in Greek, which is rendered *unctus* in Latin, since, as true King of all and true priest, he had to be anointed as a king and priest with the "oil of exaltation"[14] according to the Hebrew traditions for the anointing of kings and priests. The Hebrews alone of all peoples had prophets to whom the Holy Spirit revealed solemn mysteries concerning the creation of the world, the faith of the nations, and the coming of the Messiah and other such matters. It is also said that they preserved the true worship of omnipotent God when all the other nations

idolatriam converterentur, servatus esse traditur. Quod ut clarius atque evidentius elucescat a primi hominis origine paulo altius repetemus.

7   Primus igitur homo, quamquam in iustitia[3] originali — ut theologico verbo utamur — ab omnipotenti Deo conditus et constitutus esset, distincta tamen conditoris sui cognitione idcirco caruisse creditur quoniam ipsum numquam nec adorasse nec invocasse legitur, tum etiam quia de Enos (Seth filio, nepote suo) in hoc modo[4] sacris litteris scribitur: 'Sed et Seth natus est filius quem vocavit Enos,' quod ex Hebraeo in Latinum idioma interpretatum proprie 'virum' significat; 'iste coepit invocare nomen Domini.' Noe deinde paucis praetermissis, licet vir iustus esset, nec tamen ipse nec filii sui usque ad Abraham distinctam Dei notitiam iure habuisse existimantur.

8   De eo namque apud Eusebium Caesariensem in libro *De temporibus* sic scriptum fuisse comperimus: 'Primo omnium prophetarum Abraham verbum Dei, cum in figura apparuisset humana, vocationem gentium pollicetur, quam in nostro tempore sermo Christi deduxit ad finem per evangelicam in omnes gentes praedicationem.' Cum igitur non multo post generalem illam primi diluvii inundationem humanum genus — quod tunc dumtaxat labi videbatur — in varias multiplicum gentium nationes ob confusionem linguarum per novam illius altissimae atque celeberrimae turris, quam merito a confusa rerum consecutione 'Babel' hebraice vocaverunt, aedificationem divinitus ac mirabiliter subsecutam diffunderetur, factum est ut sicut diversae hominum linguae in propatulo diversis sonitibus apparebant ita pariter primo de origine mundi, de principiis deinde rerum naturalium ac postea de anima et, quod ad mores attinet, de summo deinceps bono et an virtus per se sola sufficiat an aliquo alio adiumento ad bene beateque vivendum indigere videatur et utrum unum solum vel plura sint bonorum genera et tandem de religionibus diversae hinc inde opiniones vulgarentur.

turned to idolatry. In order to make this shine forth more clearly and distinctly, I shall retrace events from the origin of the first man in somewhat greater detail.

Now the first man, although created and made by God in 7 original righteousness, to use a theological term, is thought to have lacked any distinct knowledge of his Creator, for we nowhere read that he worshiped or invoked God. Instead, Enos, the son of Seth and Adam's grandson,[15] is described in the Holy Scriptures as follows: "To Seth also was born a son, whom he called Enos" (which, translated from Hebrew into Latin, properly means "man"); and "Enos began to call upon the name of the Lord."[16] Afterward, to omit a few people, neither Noah, though he was a just man, nor his sons can rightly be thought to have had a distinct conception of God before Abraham.

In the *Chronicle* of Eusebius of Caesarea, we read concerning 8 him: "The Word of God, which appeared in human form in Abraham, the first of all the prophets, promises the calling of the Gentiles. In our time, the word of Christ has brought this calling to completion through the preaching of the Gospel among all nations."[17] Now, not long after the universal inundation of the first flood, the human race, which at that time seemed merely to be going astray, was scattered into various nations of different peoples by the confusion of tongues. This was the divine and miraculous result of the building of that high and famous tower which in Hebrew they justly called "Babel" because of the chaos that ensued.[18] As humankind was scattered, it happened that just as people's different languages were clearly distinguished by different sounds, in the same way different opinions were spreading, first concerning the origin of the world, next the principles of nature, and finally the soul; and what relates to ethics, [namely] the highest good, and whether virtue alone is sufficient for the good and happy life, or requires assistance, and whether there is a single good or several kinds of goods;[19] and finally concerning religions.

9

9   Nam primae duae inter ceteras celebratae de mundo ipso opiniones fuisse perhibentur. Alii namque, cum mundum ingenerabilem
atque incorruptibilem putavissent, genus hominum animaliumque
aeternum esse asseverarunt. Alii vero, cum ipsum generabilem atque corruptibilem opinarentur, homines quoque et alia animalia
partim certis ab hac nostra aetate remotissimis temporibus, ut per
quadraginta septuaginta annorum milia incepisse affirmarunt, ceu
Cicero in primo *De divinatione* philosophos quosdam sensisse scribit, partim vero longinquis sed nobis propinquioribus temporibus
uti per plura quam quinquaginta annorum milia, ceu Diogenes
Laertius in praefatione *De vita et moribus philosophorum* testari videtur. Alii quoque mundum, ut Plato et Aristoteles, divina providentia gubernari, alii autem, ut Democritus et Epicurus, fortuito ferri
regique propterea tradidere quoniam bonis viris mala, pravis vero
bona plerumque evenire cernebant. Quae quidem prisca philosophorum opinio usque ad tempora Ciceronis et Senecae perdurasse
videtur.

10   Cicero enim in tertio *De natura deorum* hanc antiquissimam
philosophorum opinionem explicare volens verba haec ponit: 'Cur
igitur duos Scipiones fortissimos et optimos viros in Hispania
Poenus oppressit? Cur Maximus extulit filium consularem? Cur
Marcellum Hannibal interemit? Cur Paulum Cannae sustulerunt?
Cur Poenorum crudelitati Reguli corpus est praebitum? Cur Afri-
canum domestici parietes non texerunt? Sed haec vetera et alia
permulta; propiora videamus. Cur avunculus meus, vir innocentis-
simus idemque doctissimus, P. Rutilius in exilio est? Cur sodalis
meus interfectus domi suae Drusus? Cur temperantiae pruden-
tiaeque specimen ante simulacrum Vestae pontifex maximus Q.
Scaevola trucidatus?[5] Cur ante et tot[6] civitatis principes a Cinna
interempti? Cur omnium perfidiosissimus C. Marius Q. Catulum

Two early opinions among the rest concerning the world are   9
regarded as the most celebrated. Some thought that the world
knew neither generation nor decay, and hence pronounced the race
of men and animals eternal. But others, regarding the world as
subject to both generation and decay, asserted that people and
other animals had arisen at a fixed time remote from our age, as
for instance some philosophers traced this origin to 470,000 years
in the past, as Cicero writes in Book 1 of *On Divination*;[20] others
thought that it arose in distant times but closer to ours, for instance more than 50,000 years ago, as Diogenes Laertius seems to
attest in the preface to his *Lives and Characters of the Philosophers*.[21]
Some philosophers, like Plato and Aristotle, thought that the
world is governed by Divine Providence, while others, like Democritus and Epicurus, described it as guided and ruled by chance
because they noted that bad things often happen to good men,
and good things to bad men. This early opinion of the philosophers seems to have survived until the age of Cicero and Seneca.

Expounding this ancient opinion of the philosophers, Cicero in   10
Book 3 of *On the Nature of the Gods* writes as follows: "Why, therefore, was the Carthaginian in Spain suffered to destroy those best
and bravest men, the two Scipios? Why did Maximus bury his
son, the former consul? Why did Hannibal kill Marcellus? Why
did Cannae deprive us of Paulus? Why was the body of Regulus
delivered up to the cruelty of the Carthaginians? Why did the
walls of his house not protect Africanus from violence? But these
are ancient instances, and there are many others; let us examine
some more recent ones. Why is Publius Rutilius, my uncle, a man
of the greatest virtue and learning, now in banishment? Why was
my boon companion Drusus assassinated in his own house? Why
was Scaevola, the high priest, that pattern of moderation and prudence, butchered before the statue of Vesta? Why, before that,
were so many leading citizens put to death by Cinna? Why had C.
Marius, the most perfidious of men, the power to order the death

praestantissimum[7] dignitate virum mori potuit iubere? Dies defi-
ciat si velim numerare quibus bonis male evenerit nec minus si
commemorare quibus improbis optime. Cur enim Marius[8] septimum consul domi suae senex est mortuus? Cur omnium crudelis-
simus tam diu Cinna regnavit?'

11   Et Seneca quoque, cum hanc ipsam opinionem temporibus suis
invalescere intelligeret, particularem quemdam librum scribere non
dubitavit, cuius titulus est *Quare bonis viris mala accidant cum sit
providentia*, de quo Lactantius in quinto suarum *Institutionum adversus gentes* ita scribit: 'Si quis volet scire plenius cur malos et iniustos
Deus potentes, beatos, divites fieri sinat, pios contra humiles, miseros, inopes esse patiatur, sumat eum Senecae librum cui titulus
est *Quare bonis viris multa mala accidant cum sit providentia*, in quo
multa ille non plane imperitia saeculari sed sapienter ac paene divinitus elocutus est. "Deus," inquit, "homines pro liberis habet, sed
corruptos ac vitiosos luxuriose ac delicate patitur vivere quia non
putat emendatione ⟨sua⟩[9] dignos; bonos autem, quos diligit, casti-
gat saepius et assiduis laboribus ad usum virtutis exercet, nec eos
caducis et mortalibus bonis corrumpi ac depravari sinit."'

12   Alii insuper unum solum alii plures alii innumerabiles mundos
existimaverunt. De principiis deinde naturalibus primi philosophi
et qui postea secuti sunt inter se maxime dissenserunt. Quippe ut
a primorum philosophorum origine paulo altius repetamus, duo
apud Graecos, ceu Eusebius Augustinusque testantur, philosophorum genera fuisse traduntur: unum Italicum ab ea Italiae parte
quae quondam Magna Graecia dicebatur et hodie vulgo Calabria
vocatur, alterum Ionicum in his regionibus ubi vera et re et nomine Graecia nuncupatur. Italicum genus auctorem habuit Py-
thagoram Samium, quem primum philosophi nomen invenisse

of Q. Catulus, a man of the greatest dignity? But there would be no end of enumerating examples of good men who fared badly and wicked men who prospered. Why did that Marius die an old man at his own house in his seventh consulship? Why did that monster Cinna enjoy so long a reign?"[22]

Seneca, too, observing that this same opinion was gaining strength in his day, did not hesitate to write a specific treatise entitled *Why Bad Things Happen to Good Men if Providence Exists*.[23] In Book 5 of his *Institutions Against the Gentiles* Lactantius writes of it: "But if anyone shall wish to know more fully why God permits the wicked and the unjust to become powerful, happy, and rich, and, on the other hand, suffers the pious to be humble, wretched, and poor, let him pick up the book of Seneca titled *Why Bad Things Happen to Good Men if Providence Exists*, in which he wrote a good deal, clearly not from ignorance of this world, but with wisdom and almost divine inspiration. 'God,' he says, 'regards men as His children, but He permits the corrupt and vicious to live in luxury and comfort, because He does not think them worthy of His correction. But He often chastises the good men, whom He loves, and trains them for the practice of virtue through continual labors; nor does He allow goods that die and decay to corrupt and deprave them.'"[24]

Now, some believed in one world, some in several worlds, and others in countless worlds. And concerning the principles of nature the first philosophers and their successors were in complete disagreement. If we delve into them further, beginning with the first philosophers, we learn from Eusebius and Augustine that there were two schools of philosophers among the Greeks.[25] One was the "Italian" school, so called from the part of Italy that was known as Great Greece and is now commonly named Calabria; the other the "Ionic" school, in those regions where the true Greece is so designated in fact and in name. The founder of the Italian school was Pythagoras of Samos who, they say, first coined

11

12

ferunt. Nam cum antea sapientes appellarentur hi qui altissimarum rerum contemplationi vacare videbantur, iste interrogatus
quid profiteretur 'philosophum' se esse respondit, id est studiosum
vel amatorem sapientiae, quoniam sapientem profiteri arrogans
nimis superbumque putabat. Et quia Pythagoras ipse et eius discipuli ad numeros omnia referebant, ita obscure de rebus tum naturalibus tum moralibus disseruisse perhibentur ut nulla vel pauca
rerum suarum monumenta reliquerint et illa ita obscura atque
confusa sunt ut vix intelligi posse videantur.

13   Idcirco Italis philosophis omissis ad Ionicos accedamus, quamquam Pythagoras deum animum per universas mundi partes per
omnemque naturam commeantem atque diffusum diffiniverit, ex
quo omnia quae nascerentur animalia vitam caperent. Ionici generis princeps fuit Thales Milesius, unus eorum septem qui sapientes appellabantur. Sex autem alii a ceteris hominibus quos
humana et communis conversatio tulit et sanctimonia vitae et
probitate morum et nonnullis insuper ad vivendum utilibus praeceptis distinguebantur. Thales vero, naturam rerum scrutatus, ut
successores propagaret disputationes suas litteris mandavit max-
imeque ideo admirabilis visus est quod astrologiae numeris com-
prehensis defectus solis et lunae, quos Graeci 'eclipsis' vocant,
multo ante praedixit atque aquam rerum omnium principium et
sensit et voluit.

14   Huic successit Anaximander, eius auditor, qui infinitum, quod
Graeci 'apyron' dicunt, rerum omnium generationis ac corruptionis
causam existimavit. Hic Anaximenem discipulum ac successorem
reliquit, qui aerea principium omnium opinatus est. Anaxagoras et
Diogenes, eius auditores, a praeceptore suo et a se invicem dissenserunt; nam Anaxagoras harum rerum omnium quas videmus divinum animum censuit atque omnia ex infinita materia confici af-
firmavit, quae ex similibus inter se particulis constaret; Diogenes
vero cunctarum rerum materiam ⟨aerem⟩ esse dixit, e qua omnia
fierent.

the term "philosopher." Earlier, those who took time to ponder the highest subjects were called wise men. But when Pythagoras was asked what his profession was, he said he was a philosopher, a student or lover of wisdom, since he thought it overhaughty to profess wisdom.[26] Pythagoras and his pupils conceived everything in terms of numbers, but they discussed nature and morality so obscurely that they left no records of their doctrine, or only a few so obscure and confused that they are nearly incomprehensible.

Leaving the Italians, then, let us turn to the Ionic philosophers. 13 (All the same, Pythagoras defined God as a soul diffused and moving through all parts of the world and all of nature, from whom all animals receive life when they are born.)[27] The head of the Ionic school was Thales of Miletus, who was one of the seven who were called Wise Men. While the other six were distinguished from the other men produced by common human society by their pious lives and upright behavior, and by teachings useful for living, by contrast Thales examined nature, and wrote down his findings in order to spawn successors. He inspired the greatest wonder when his astronomical calculations allowed him to predict well in advance those darkenings of the sun and moon that in Greek are called eclipses. He also thought and maintained that water is the basis of everything in nature.[28]

He was succeeded by his student Anaximander, who regarded 14 the infinite — in Greek called *apeiron* "boundless" — as the cause of the generation and decay of all things. He in turn left as his student and successor Anaximenes, who regarded air as the basis of all things. His students Anaxagoras and Diogenes disagreed with their teacher and with each other. Anaxagoras thought there was a divine mind causing all visible phenomena, and asserted that everything is made of boundless matter composed of particles that are homogeneous.[29] By contrast, Diogenes said that air was the matter of all things.

15   Anaxagorae successit eius auditor Archelaus, qui eamdem de particulis inter se similibus opinionem secutus est. Xenophanes nec corruptionem nec generationem ullam esse contendit; esse namque simile quicquid est. Parmenides, Xenophanis auditor, universum sempiternum atque immobile esse censet. Melissus omnia tantummodo unum et illud pariter immobile opinatur. Democritus universum infinitum esse atque ex atomis, quas corpuscola individua appellavit, constare inquit. Epicurus, maiestati omnipotentis Dei detrahere conatus, nihil ex eo quod non est fieri asserit ac semper universum sic se habuisse nec aliquid novi fieri praeter id quod tempore infinito iam factum est corpusque universum non solum immutabile verum etiam infinitum esse testatur.

16   Empedocles, qui res naturales apud Graecos Graecis sicut Lucretius apud nos Latinis versibus mandavit, quattuor elementa ponit: ignem, aerem, aquam, terram, ex quibus omnia conficiantur. Metrodorus universum sempiternum non tamen sicut Parmenides immobile esse confirmat. Socrates, cum nihil sciri posse academicorum more arbitraretur, de altioribus sublimiorisque rebus nequaquam disserebat; unde, moralibus dumtaxat studiis utpote ad intelligendum facilioribus contentus, opinationibus dumtaxat suis ibidem acquiescere videbatur. Plato, Socratis discipulus, licet praeceptoris sui vestigia imitaretur, formis tamen—quas 'ideas' appellavit—multa et quidem praecipua privilegia tribuit, cum ex ipsis in materia impressis omnia constare voluerit. Aristoteles, Platonis auditor, a praeceptore suo plerumque ita dissensit ut plurima ac paene omnia opinionibus suis vel contraria vel saltem dissimila et dicat et sentiat. Tria namque, quantum ad praesens propositum spectat, naturalium rerum principia (materiam, formam ac privationem) esse censuit. Theophrastus denique ac Menedemus, duo celebratiores ex omnibus Aristotelis discipulis, praeclara praeceptoris sui vestigia imitati eadem sicut[10] ille nobilitatis eorum scriptis approbaverunt.

Anaxagoras was succeeded by his student Archelaus, who em-   15
braced the same doctrine of homogeneous particles.[30] Xenophanes
argued that there is neither decay nor generation, since everything
that exists is homogeneous. His student Parmenides judges that
the universe is eternal and immobile. Melissus regards everything
as a unity which is also immobile. Democritus says that the universe is infinite and composed of "atoms," as he called the indivisible particles.[31] Epicurus, who attempted to diminish the majesty
of almighty God, asserts that nothing springs from a nonexistent,
that the universe has never changed, that nothing new arises except what existed for an infinite time, and that the universe is a
body both immutable and infinite.[32]

Empedocles, who among the Greeks wrote about nature in   16
Greek verse just as among us Lucretius wrote in Latin,[33] posits
four elements, of which everything is composed: fire, air, water,
and earth. Metrodorus affirms that the universe is eternal, but not
immobile, as Parmenides holds. Socrates, who in the Academic
manner believed that nothing can be truly known, never dis-
coursed on nature's higher and more sublime elements. Content to
study ethics as more easily understood, he merely seemed to accept as his own others' suppositions in this field.[34] Socrates' pupil
Plato followed in his teacher's footsteps, but assigned many important features to the forms that he called ideas, asserting that everything is composed of matter bearing their stamp. Plato's student
Aristotle often disagrees with his teacher, holding and expressing
views that nearly all contradict, or at least differ from, his opinions. Thus, as regards our present subject, he judged that there are
three principles in nature: matter, form, and privation. The two
most famous of Aristotle's pupils, Theophrastus and Menedemus,[35] followed in the illustrious footsteps of their teacher, and
embraced his doctrines in their distinguished writings.

17   Ceterum de anima quam variae quamque diversae philosophorum opiniones exstiterint difficile dictu est. Alii namque ipsam
immortalem, alii vero eam una cum corpore interire putaverunt.
Quid porro esset ipse animus aut ubi aut unde magna dissensio
erat; aliis enim cor ipsum animus videbatur ac quoque exinde
'excordes' 'vecordesque' dicebantur. Empedocles animum censebat
cordi suffusum sanguinem; alii partem quamdam cerebri animi
principatum tenere opinabantur, aliis nec cor ipsum placebat nec
cerebri quamdam partem esse animum, sed alii in corde alii in ce-
rebro dicebant animi esse sedem et locum. Zenoni stoico animus ignis apparebat. Aristoxenus musicus idemque philosophus
animum armoniam esse diffiniebat. Xenocrates animi figuram et
quasi corpus negabat esse. Plato triplicem fingebat animum, cuius
principatum, id est rationem, in capite sicut in arce ponebat et
duas partes separabat: iram in pectore, cupiditatem subter praecordia locabat. Aristoteles animum 'endelecheiam' novo quodam et
antea inusitato nomine appellabat, quae perfectionem quamdam
significare videbatur. In quo quidem Theophrastus et Menedemus,
duo praeclari eius discipuli, a magistro suo nequaquam dissentire
ac dissidere audebant.

18   At cum has de mundo et de principiis rerum naturalium et de
anima priscorum philosophorum opiniones supra recitaverimus,
reliquum est ut quidnam de summo bono et de virtutibus senserint parumper videamus. Multas philosophorum sectas fuisse manifestum est sed de celebratioribus nonnulla breviter attingemus,
quas quattuor dumtaxat stoicorum, academicorum, peripatetico-
rum, epicureorum exstitisse non dubitamus. Stoici namque, qui a
Zenone profluxerunt, solum id summum bonum fore putaverunt
quod honestum decorumque esset. Academici et veteres et novi
more suo de omnibus dubitantes nihil certi de felicitate opinionibus suis attulerunt. Verum peripatetici, quorum princeps Aristoteles — magister omnium — fuisse traditur, summum bonum in

As for the soul, it is hard to summarize the various and dif- 17
ferent opinions of the philosophers. Some thought it immortal,
but others that it perishes with the body. The exact nature of
the mind, its location, and its origins caused major disagreement. Some thought the heart (*cor*) itself was the mind, which is
why certain people were called *excordes* "senseless" and *vecordes* "de-
mented." Empedocles regarded the mind as blood suffused in the
heart.[36] Some thought that a part of the brain controlled the
mind, others refused to allow that the mind was the heart itself or
a part of the brain, while some placed its seat and site in the heart,
and others in the brain. Zeno the Stoic thought the mind was
fire,[37] and Aristoxenus the musical theorist and philosopher defined the mind as a sort of harmony.[38] Xenocrates denied that the
mind has a shape or sort of body.[39] Plato imagined a three-part
mind. He placed its guiding part, reason, in the head as if in a
citadel; and he separated the other two parts, situating anger in
the breast and desire beneath the midriff (*praecordia*).[40] Coining a
new and previously unheard-of word, Aristotle called the mind
endelecheia, which apparently denoted a certain perfection.[41] His
two famous pupils Theophrastus and Menedemus dared not disagree with or dissent from their teacher in this matter.

We have now expounded the ancient philosophers' opinions 18
about the world, the principles of nature, and the soul. It remains
for us to take a quick look at their views of the virtues and the
highest good. Clearly, there were many philosophical sects, but we
shall only touch briefly on the most celebrated, which beyond
doubt are merely four: the Stoics, Academics, Peripatetics, and
Epicureans. The Stoics, whose school began with Zeno, believed
that only what is honorable and decorous is the highest good. The
Academics of both the Old and New Schools, practicing their
usual doubt about everything, taught nothing certain as their own
opinion concerning happiness. The Peripatetics, however, whose
traditional founder is Aristotle, the universal master, seem to place

operatione secundum virtutem perfectam et quidem non impedita constituisse et collocasse videntur. Aristoteles enim, eius sectae princeps atque inventor, ut quodam loco ait Cicero, virtutis usum cum vitae perfectae prosperitate coniunxit. Sed epicurei et Aristippus et Cleantes et Eudoxus et Metrodorus nescio quis id ipsum in voluptate posuerunt, propterea quod omnia animalia eam appetere cernebant. Aristoteles enim in decimo *Ethicorum* de voluptate loquens verba haec ponit: 'Eudoxus voluptatem propterea summum bonum esse censebat quod cuncta animalia tam rationalia quam irrationalia eam appetere cernebat.' Et qui in voluptate summum bonum constituerunt atque versa vice maximum malum in dolore posuerunt ab invicem dissenserunt; partim enim in voluptate corporis partim in voluptate animi partim in utrisque felicitatem, in contrariis vero miseriam collocabant.

19   Aristippus enim et Cleantes tantum corporeae voluptati tribuebant ut eam ipsam in tabula quadam pictam effingerent pulcherrimo vestitu et ornatu regali in solio sedentem et praesto esse virtutes ut ancillas quae nihil aliud agerent, nullum suum officium ducerent nisi ut voluptati ministrarent atque ei in auribus dicerent: 'Nos quidem virtutes sic natae sumus ut tibi serviremus. Aliud negotii nihil habemus.' Epicurus insuper interdum in voluptate corporis interdum in voluptate animi interdum in utrisque felicitatem suam collocabat. Hieronymus praeterea summum bonum in vacuitate doloris, quam maximam voluptatem existimabat et 'indolentiam' appellabat, fore opinabatur.

20   Nonnulli denique, praeter allegatas philosophiae sectas, philosophi fuisse perhibentur qui partim in primis naturae, hoc est in his quae suapte natura appetebantur, ut Carneades, partim vero in scientia et cognitione rerum altissimarum, quales Aristo, Herillus Pyrrhoque fuere, summum bonum existimavere. Hi namque tres tantum cognitionis et scientiae amorem nobis innatum esse videbant ut nemo iure dubitare posset quin ad eas res humana

and locate the supreme good in unimpaired action according to perfect virtue. As Cicero writes in a certain passage,[42] the Peripatetics' founder and creator Aristotle linked the practice of virtue with the prosperity of perfect living.[43] By contrast, the Epicureans, Aristippus, Cleanthes,[44] Eudoxus, and a certain Metrodorus placed the highest good in pleasure, because they noted that all animals seek it. Thus, in Book 10 of his *Ethics* Aristotle says the following about pleasure: "Eudoxus deemed pleasure to be the highest good since he observed that all creatures both rational and irrational desire it."[45] In addition, those who placed the highest good in pleasure and the greatest evil in pain differed in their views. Some placed happiness in pleasure of the body, some in pleasure of the mind, and some in both; and they placed unhappiness in their opposites.

Aristippus and Cleanthes attributed such power to bodily pleasure that they depicted her as a woman in a painting dressed in finery and royal garments and seated on a throne attended by virtues as handmaids who did nothing else and considered it their sole duty to serve Pleasure and whisper in her ear: "We virtues were born to serve you, and have no other occupation."[46] Epicurus, moreover, placed happiness sometimes in the pleasure of the body, sometimes of the mind, sometimes of both. Hieronymus thought that the highest good lay in the absence of pain, which he considered the greatest pleasure and called "nonsuffering" (*indolentia*).[47]   19

Besides the schools already mentioned, there are said to have been some philosophers who assigned the highest good to the primary natural needs (that is, whatever is desired by its own nature), such as Carneades, and others who assigned it to the knowledge and understanding of the most lofty subjects, such as Aristo, Herillus, and Pyrrho.[48] These three philosophers saw that we are born with such love of knowledge and understanding that human nature is undoubtedly attracted to it without the inducement   20

21

natura, nullo emolumento invitata, raperetur. Callipho[11] adiunxit ad honestatem voluptatem, Diodorus ad eamdem honestatem addidit vacuitatem doloris.

21   Quid de virtutibus dicemus? Quibus nonnulli tantum tribuebant ut nullo extrinseco vel corporis ⟨vel⟩ externarum rerum adiumento ad bene beateque vivendum indigere viderentur, ut stoici quin immo eos qui virtutes haberent atque cunctis aliis corporis et externis sive commodis (ceu ipsi) sive bonis (ceu appellant peripatetici) carerent nimirum beatos et felices — etiam si corporis, quod profecto mirabilius atque incredibilius est, doloribus vehementer angerentur et in rota et in Phalaridis tauro[12] crudeliter torquerentur — existimare et nuncupare non dubitarunt. Verum enimvero cum omnia sicut promisimus iam ut potuimus singillatim recensuerimus, nunc ad religiones accedamus.

22   De priscis antiquissimarum gentium religionibus impresentiarum breviter tractaturi, de singulis populis pauca quaedam ceteris digniora attingentes, de Aegyptiorum religione, velut aliis omnibus vetustiore, initium sumemus. Cum Aegyptii primi omnium in caelos oculos sustulissent, motum, ordinem et quantitatem caelestium corporum ita admirati sunt ut solem et lunam deos putarent, ac solem quidem Osirim, lunam vero Isin nuncuparunt. Nec ab re huiusmodi nomina illis caelestibus corporibus indiderunt. Nam si quis verba haec in Latinam linguam interpretari voluerit Osirim 'multoculum' interpretari poterit. Radios enim suos quasi oculos ad res multas immittit quibus omnia prospicit. Isin vero latine 'priscam' dicere possimus, quod nomen lunae propterea convenire videtur, quoniam sempiterna priscaque sit. Religioni vero sacra faciebant non ex myrtis aut casiis[13] (nam haec longe postea inventa fuere) sed nonnullas herbas virides, quasi productivarum terrae virium primitias, manibus sumentes offerebant. Arbores enim priusquam animalia terra produxerat, herbas autem multo antequam arbores. Ex herbis ergo integras quasdam sumentes cum foliis radicibusque ac fructibus cuncta simul commiscentes concremabant

of any reward. To what is honorable, Callipho added pleasure; whereas Diodorus added freedom from pain.[49]

What shall we say about the virtues? Some philosophers attrib-   21
uted so much power to them that they seemed sufficient for living well and happily, requiring no outside aid from either the body or external things. The Stoics did not hesitate to think and call those who possess virtues and lack all bodily or external "benefits," as they call them, or "goods," as the Peripatetics say, blessed and happy, even when (more surprisingly and incredibly) they are afflicted with the most awful physical pains, tortured on the wheel or in Phalaris' bull. Having now expounded, as promised, so far as we could, all these philosophies one by one, let us now proceed to religions.

We shall briefly treat the early religions of the most ancient na-   22
tions, touching upon a few notable aspects of distinct peoples. And we begin with the religion of the Egyptians, as being older than all the others. When before all others the Egyptians raised their eyes to the heavens, they were so amazed by the motion, order, and number of heavenly bodies that they thought the sun and moon were gods, and called the sun Osiris and the moon Isis. They assigned such names to the heavenly bodies with good reason. Thus, if we wish to translate these names into Latin, we may render Osiris as "many-eyed." For the sun directs its rays on many things, like eyes by which it views all things. But Isis we could call "ancient" in Latin, a name that seems to suit the moon as being eternal and ancient. They performed the rites of their religion not with myrtle and cassia—which were discovered much later—but instead offered up certain green herbs, plucked by hand, as the firstfruits of the earth's productive power. For the earth produced trees before animals, and herbs well before trees. Hence, they gathered whole herbs—with leaves, roots, and fruits—and mixing

et hac exalatione ac huiusmodi fumo caelestibus litabant. Ignem quoque accensum in templis, utpote caelestibus simillimum, semper et sine intermissione servabant; et quod omnium pessimum simul ac turpissimum videbatur cocodrillum[14] aut ibin[15] aut pelen aut Apim, sanctissimum illum bovem suum, venerabant,[16] quae quidem animalia bruta ac spurca ipsi deos effinxerant pro diisque colebant. Phoenices, serpentem et accipitrem (ecce alia crassa, insana et intolleranda fatuitas!) deos putabant ventosque pro diis adorabant atque herbis quibusdam pro sacrificiis atque cerimoniis utebantur.

23 Phryges Maeona antiquissimum apud eos regem fuisse asseruerunt, de quo nata est Cibele, quae fistulam invenerat quam 'siringam' dixere, et 'montana mater' appellabatur. Hunc suum regem, purum mortalemque hominem, pro deo coluere. Graeci iuxta seriem temporum sequuntur. Graecorum religio a Cadmo, Agenoris filio, initium sumpsisse videtur, quem Moyse posteriore⟨m⟩ exstitisse manifestum est, unde per multa saecula absque ulla religione vixisse creduntur. Cadmum namque ex Phoenicia patria ad quaerendum Europam sororem suam, quae a Iove rapta fuerat, ab Agenore patre transmissum fuisse dicunt, qua non inventa ipse in eodem proposito perseverans quaerendi gratia tandem in Boetiam venit atque illic Thebarum urbem condidit idque sedes suas fixit. Cumque Harmoniam Veneris filiam in uxorem suscepisset ac Semelem ex ea generasset, postea ex Iove et Semele natum Dionysum ferunt, qui vitis et vini usum homines docuit, unde propterea inter deos connumeratus est. Postremo, cum corpora caelestia deos esse arbitraretur, ad Graecos postea hanc de sideribus opinionem traduxit.

24 Atlantiorum religio adventat, quam cum huiusmodi esset prisci illi populi acceperunt: Atlantem enim regem apud se primum regnasse tradunt, qui quadragintaquinque filios habuisse perhibetur, quorum cum decem et octo Ops uxor sua genuisset propterea in

them all together, they burned them, propitiating the heavenly beings by their vapors and smoke. In their temples, they also kept a
fire lit always and without interruption for its evident similarity to
the heavenly beings. Further, whatever beast seemed most evil and
foul they worshiped — the crocodile, the ibis, the falcon, and Apis
their sacred bull: these crude and filthy animals they had imagined
to be gods and worshiped as such.[50] The Phoenicians regarded the
snake and the hawk as gods — behold another coarse, insane, and
intolerable folly! — and they worshiped the winds as gods, using
certain herbs in their sacrifices and rites.

The Phrygians declared that Maeon was their earliest king; he   23
had a daughter named Cybele, who invented the reed pipe that
was called a syrinx, and who was called the Mountain Mother.
This king, who was a blameless but mortal man, they worshiped
as a god. The Greeks follow next in the succession of ages. The
Greeks' religion seems to have originated with Cadmus, the son of
Agenor; but he was clearly born later than Moses, so that the
Greeks are thought to have lived for many centuries with no religion. Now, it is said that Cadmus was sent by his father Agenor
from his Phoenician homeland to find his sister Europa, who had
been seized by Jupiter. But not finding her, he continued his mission, and in his search came at length to Boeotia, where he
founded the city of Thebes and established it as his residence. He
took to wife Harmonia, the daughter of Venus, and by her begat
Semele; later, they say, to Jupiter and Semele was born Dionysus,
who taught mankind the use of vines and wine, for which he was
later counted among the gods. Finally, since he thought the heavenly bodies were gods, Cadmus introduced this notion of the stars
to the Greeks.

Next there arrived the religion of the Atlantes, which those   24
early peoples understood to be of this kind: they say that Atlas
reigned as their first king, and had forty-five sons. Of these, his
wife Ops bore eighteen and is hence thought to have joined the

dearum numerum relata creditur. Atque has diversas religiones ac plures et varios deos apud praedictas nationes antequam Roma conderetur exstitisse prodidere. Romani denique accesserunt, qui post Romam conditam, priusquam imperium suum longe lateque amplificarent, plures deos pluresque antiquos ritus a Troianis priscis maioribus suis susceperunt, ut auguria, oraculorum responsa, varias somniorum interpretationes, vaticinationes ac divinationes et cetera huiusmodi. Post vero ingentem quamdam imperii amplificationem tantam deorum turbam in religionem suam traduxerunt ut diis deabusque omnia replevisse videantur. Nam ut a deabus incipiamus, quarum plena sunt omnia, et Cluacinam et Volupiam, a voluptate, et Libertinam, a libidine, et Cuninam, quae cunas infantium administraret eos instituisse scribunt; nec his deabus contenti, ruribus Rusinam,[17] collibus Collatinam, vallibus Valloniam praefecerunt. Nec segetibus unam deam sufficere arbitrati, sata frumenta—cum sub terram essent—praepositam voluerunt habere deam Seiam; cum vero iam essent super terram et segetem facerent, deam Segeam, frumentis vero collectis ac reconditis, ut tute servarentur, deam Tutilinam praeposuerunt. Proserpinam frumentis germinantibus, involumentis folliculorum deam Volutinam; cum folliculi patescunt, ut spica exeat, deam Patelenam, cum segetes novis aristis aequantur, quia veteres aequare 'ostire' dixerunt, deam Ostilinam, florentibus frumentis deam Floream,[18] maturescentibus deam Maturam, cum runcantur, id est a terra auferuntur, deam Runcinam. Atque omnibus his particularibus deabus Cererem, tamquam cunctarum commemoratarum maximam, praeesse voluerunt, quae universis frumentis, segetibus ac messibus praesideret. Cardinibus Cardeam, mari Salaciam praefecerunt atque in terra ipsa aliud Terram, aliud Tellurem, aliud numen Tellumonem esse putaverunt. Vestem praeterea ac Nationem[19] adhibuerunt, 'cui,' ut quodam loco sic de ea inquit Cicero, 'cum fana circuimus in agro Ardeati rem divinam facere

number of the gods. The different religions and many varied gods are said to have existed among these nations before Rome was founded.[51] Next, the Romans arrived. After founding Rome, but before they had expanded their rule far and wide, they inherited from their early ancestors the Trojans many gods and many ancient rites — such as auguries, oracular responses, various interpretations of dreams, prophecies and divinations, and other such things. Later, after the huge expansion of their rule, they introduced into their religion such a crowd of gods that they seemed to have filled all the world with gods and goddesses. Let us begin with the goddesses, with whom "all things are filled."[52] It is written that the Romans created Cluacina,[53] Volupia (from *voluptas* "pleasure"), Libertina (from *libido* "lust"), and Cunina, who watches over babies' cradles (*cunae*). Not content with these goddesses, they gave dominion to Rusina over the countryside (*rus*), to Collatina over hills (*colles*) and to Vallonia over valleys. Thinking that a single goddess did not suffice for their fields of crops, they chose to place the goddess Seia in charge of grain sown when it was under the ground; the goddess Segea in charge of grain sprouting above ground; and the goddess Tutilina in charge of storing harvested grain safely (*tute*). They had Proserpina preside over budding grains, Volutina over seed husks (*involumenta*), Patelena over seeds that open (*patescunt*) to release the ear of corn, Ostilina when the grain is level with the new spikes (from an archaic verb *ostire* "to be level"), Florea over the flowering grain, Matura over the maturing crop, and Runcina over the grains that are plucked from the earth (*runcantur*). And they wanted Ceres to be above all these particular goddesses, as the greatest of all those mentioned, so that she would have oversight of all grains, crops, and harvests. They placed Cardea over hinges (*cardines*), and Salacia over the sea. As for the earth, some thought the deity was Terra, some Tellus, and some Tellumo. They also called upon Vesta, and Natio, "to whom," Cicero somewhere writes, "when we visit the temples of

solemus; quae quia partus matronarum tueatur a nascentibus Natio[20] nominata est.'

25   Quid vero de diis maribus dicemus? Nonne Romani, rerum
domini, masculis diis sicut deabus feminis omnia referserunt?
Nam et Vaginatum qui infantum vagitibus et Iugarnium qui montium iugis et Nodutum qui geniculis nodisque, Culmorum ⟨qui
culmis⟩[21] et Lactinium qui lactescentibus frumentis et Forculum
qui foribus et Limentinum qui ostiorum liminibus praesiderent
temere nimium et insane admodum excogitarunt.

26   Atque haec de minutorum, ut ita dixerim, deorum dearumque
turba dicta sufficiant. Nunc quid de maioribus deabus diisque
senserint parumper videamus, ne forte in istis maximis vera sensisse putentur cum in minutissimis praedictis insanorum, fanatico-
rum ac furiosorum hominum more tantopere ac tam turpiter
aberraverunt. A feminis incipientes, tres inter ceteras et quidem
maximas deas fore putaverunt: Venerem, quam libidinibus et amoribus ac coniugiis, Minervam, quam sapientiae et artibus et aliis
ingeniosis operibus, Iunonem, quam divitiis et opibus ac reg-
nis praeesse voluerunt. Deos vero quosdam magnos censuerunt,
siquidem Saturnum temporibus, Iovem eius filium tamquam ceterorum omnium principalissimum cunctis rebus maximis, unde
'Iupiter Optimus Maximus' proprio cognomine appellabatur, Nep-
tunum mari, unde a natando quidam ipsum nomen assecutum
fuisse asseruere, Plutonem inferno, Martem bellis, Vulcanum igni-
bus, Mercurium eloquentiae, Apollinem et Esculapium medicinae,
Liberum denique Dionysum et Bac⟨c⟩hum vino vitibusque praeposuerunt.

27   Ac non solum haec et huiusmodi inter se varia et diversa sed
etiam contraria singulae nationes, ut dictum est, quin immo etiam
summi philosophi — qui philosophiae studiis, ceteris posthabitis,
assiduam operam navabant — ita temere stulteque senserunt, ut

the land around Ardea, we usually make a sacrifice, for since she safeguards mothers' deliveries, she is named Natio after the newborns."[54]

What shall we say about male divinities? Didn't the Romans, the masters of the world, also fill the world with gods as well as goddesses? They dreamed up gods with the rashness of insanity: Vaginatus to preside over the crying (*vagitus*) of babies, Iugarnius over mountain ridges (*iuga*), Nodutus over nodes and knots, Culmorus over stalks (*culmi*), and Lactinius over milky (*lactescentes*) grains, Forculus over doors (*fores*), and Limentinus over the thresholds (*limina*) of doorways.[55]

Let this suffice for the crowd of what we may call the lesser gods and goddesses. Now let us look briefly at what the Romans thought about the greater gods and goddesses, lest they be thought to have held true views about these greatest deities, although regarding the lesser ones they so badly and basely erred like mad, fanatical lunatics! To begin with the goddesses, they thought that the three greatest among them were Venus, goddess of lust, love, and marriage; Minerva, goddess of wisdom, the arts, and other ingenious works; and Juno, goddess of wealth, riches, and kingdoms. They regarded the following as the greatest gods: Saturn the god of ages; his son Jupiter, as the head of all the other gods, the god of the greatest of matters (hence he bore the special title of "Jupiter best and greatest"); Neptune the god of the sea (some say his name comes from swimming [*natando*]);[56] Pluto the god of the underworld; Mars the god of wars; Vulcan the god of fire; Mercury the god of eloquence; Apollo and Aesculapius gods of medicine; and Liber or Dionysus or Bacchus the god of wine and vines.[57]

Not only did particular nations hold these various and different, even mutually contradictory, opinions, as we have said; but even the most eminent philosophers—who above all else assiduously gave priority to the search for wisdom—held such opinions

Cicero in primo libro *De natura deorum* (cum diversas inter se contrarias Thaletis, Anaximandri, Anaximenis, Anaxagorae, Alcmaeonis, Pythagorae, Xenophanis, Parmenidis, Empedoclis, Prothagorae, Democriti, Diogenis, Platonis, Antisthenis, Speusippi, Aristotelis, Xenocratis, Heraclidis, Theophrasti, Zenonis, Cleanthis, Chrysippi, Epicuri de conditionibus deorum opiniones recitaverit) ita demum inquit: 'Exposui fere non philosophorum iudicia sed delirantium somnia; nec enim multo absurdiora sunt ea quae poetarum vocibus fusa ipsa suavitate nocuerunt, qui et ira inflammatos et libidine furentes induxerunt deos feceruntque ut eorum bella, proelia, pugnas, vulnera videremus, odia praeterea, discidia, discordias, ortus, interitus, querelas, lamentationes, effusas in omni ⟨in⟩temperantia²² libidines, adulteria vincula' luce, ut dicitur, meridiana clarius conspiceremus.

28   Sed inter cetera nefanda, flagitiosa ac scelesta praedictorum deorum gesta plures de reliquis diis pharetrati Cupidinis, Veneris filii, triumphos commemorant et Iovem denique ante quemdam aureatum commemorati Cupidinis triumphantis currum catena aurea, magna semideorum deorumque comitante caterva, alligatum inducunt. Non enim insulse quidam poeta, ut ait Lactantius, triumphum Cupidinis scripsit, quo in libro non modo potentissimum deorum Cupidinem sed etiam victorem facit. Enumeratis namque amoribus singulorum quibus in potestatem Cupidinis dicionemque venissent, instruit pompam in qua Iupiter cum ceteris diis, ut diximus, ante currum triumphantis ducitur catenatus; et cum humano quoque genere concubitus miscuisse mortalesque ex immortalibus procreatos carminibus suis fuisse testantur.

29   Cum hoc autem poetarum errore coniungere licet portenta Magorum Aegyptiorumque in eodem genere dementiam, tum etiam vulgi opiniones quae in maxima quadam veritatis ignorantia²³ ver-

rashly and foolishly. Cicero writes in the first book of his *On the Nature of the Gods* (where he rehearses the varied and contradictory views of the nature of the gods held by Thales, Anaximander, Anaximenes, Anaxagoras, Alcmaeon, Pythagoras, Xenophanes, Parmenides, Empedocles, Protagoras, Democritus, Diogenes, Plato, Antisthenes, Speusippus, Aristotle, Xenocrates, Heraclides, Theophrastus, Zeno, Cleanthes, Chrysippus, and Epicurus): "I have been setting forth the ravings of madmen, not the judgments of philosophers. In fact, the utterances poured forth by poets, the very attractiveness of which has caused harm, are not much more absurd when they introduced gods inflamed with anger and raging with desire, and made us see their wars, battles, fights, and wounds, and behold more clearly than the midday sun, as they say, their enmities and feuds and discords, their births and deaths, their complaints and lamentations, their lusts carried far beyond bounds of restraint, their adulteries, and their imprisonments."[58]

Now, among the other horrible, scandalous, and wicked deeds   28
of these gods, they record the many triumphs over other gods of Cupid, the son of Venus, with his quiver of arrows. They even imagine Jupiter bound by a golden chain, moving before the gilded chariot of triumphant Cupid and attended by a great crowd of gods and demigods. As Lactantius tells us, one witty poet wrote a "Triumph of Cupid," in which he makes Cupid not only the most powerful of the gods but even their conqueror.[59] Listing all the affairs of the individual gods who had fallen under Cupid's power and jurisdiction, the poet arranged a parade in which Jupiter was led, as we said, in chains with the other gods, in front of the triumphal chariot. In their poems, the poets note that Jupiter also had intercourse with the human race, and that mortals thus sprang from immortals.[60]

To this delusion of the poets, we may add the portents of the   29
Magi and the Egyptians' kindred insanity as well as the beliefs of the masses that involve an utter ignorance of truth.[61] In addition,

santur; praeterea deos ipsos humanam habere formam stultissime simul atque insulsissime censuerunt. Cicero enim paulo post in eodem libro verba haec ponit: 'A natura habemus omnes omnium gentium speciem deorum nullam aliam nisi humanam; quae enim forma alia occurrit umquam aut vigilanti cuiquam aut dormienti? Nam quae praestantissima natura sit—vel quia beata est vel quia sempiterna—convenire videtur eamdem esse pulcherrimam. Quae enim compositio membrorum, quae conformatio lineamentorum, quae figura, quae species humana potest esse pulchrior? Quod si omnium animantium formam vincit hominis figura, deus autem animans est, ea figura profecto est quae pulcherrima sit omnium. Et quoniam deos beatissimos esse constat, beatus autem esse sine virtute nemo potest nec virtus sine ratione constare nec ratio usquam inesse nisi in hominis figura, humana esse deos specie confitendum. Nec tamen ea species corpus est sed quasi corpus, nec sanguis sed quasi sanguis.'

30 Atque haec et alia huiusmodi de diis deabusque figmenta Romani—tunc rerum, ut diximus, domini, qui cum omni doctrinarum genere tum prudentia ac reliquis virtutibus et potentatibus ceteris totius terrarum orbis gentibus longe praestitisse videntur—insulse admodum ac stulte reppererunt. Nam inter cetera insania stultitiaque plenissima illud de diversitate eiusdem sexus, mea quidem sententia, maximum est. Nam si dii sunt, ⟨ut⟩ in opinionibus suis plane aperteque testantur, profecto immortales et aeterni sunt. Quid igitur opus est sexibus nisi ut generent? Sed ipsa progenie quid opus est cum successione non egeant qui semper futuri sunt? In hominibus quippe ceterisque animantibus diversitas sexus et coitio et generatio nullam aliam rationem habere videntur nisi ut omnia genera viventium, quoniam sunt condicione mortalitatis obitura, mutua possint successione servari. Deo autem, qui est sempiternus, neque alter sexus neque successio necessaria.

they thought in their extreme folly and stupidity that the gods themselves had human form. In the same book, soon after the passage quoted, Cicero adds: "All of us of every nation have from nature no other form for the gods except a human one, for under what other shape do they ever present themselves to anyone, whether waking or asleep? [. . .] Now the nature that is outstanding—whether because it is blessed or eternal—is the most beautiful. What disposition of parts, shaping of lines, what shape or form can be more beautiful than the human? [. . .] If the human form surpasses that of all living things, and god is a living thing, he possesses that form which is the most beautiful of all. Since, moreover, it is understood that the gods are supremely blessed, and since no being can be blessed without virtue, and virtue cannot exist without reason, or reason be found anywhere except in a human form, it must be admitted that the gods have the human form, though this form is not body, but quasi-body, and does not contain blood, but quasi-blood."[62]

Such were the fantasies about the gods and goddesses that were   30
quite stupidly and foolishly invented by the Romans, who were yet the masters of the world, as I said, and seem to have far excelled all the other peoples of the world in all branches of learning, in prudence, and in the other virtues and powers. In my opinion, the greatest insanity and folly of all lay in the different sexes of their divinities. For if gods exist, as Roman beliefs clearly and openly declare, they must be immortal and eternal. Why, then, do they need sexes, unless to reproduce? And why do they need offspring to succeed them when they will always exist? Now, in human beings and other animals, the different sexes, intercourse, and reproduction seem to have no other purpose than that all the living species, since they are subject to mortality, may be preserved by succeeding one another. But God, who is everlasting, needs neither a second sex nor a succession.

31   Quocirca si Romanos, ceteris totius mundi nationibus prudentiores, de cultu divino frivola quaedam et inania et falsa, ut superius plane aperteque ostendimus, sensisse constat, quid de reliquis
gentibus, ne forte particularem quamdam mentionem faciamus,
coniectura augurari possumus? Nonne eadem et forte tanto peiora
et inaniora omnes alios sensisse putandum est quanto illis ingenio
prudentiaque eos ipsos inferiores fuisse cognoverimus? Carthaginenses, ut de eis antea praetermissis dumtaxat aliqua brevissime
attingamus, cum de imperio orbis terrarum cum populo Romano,
omnium gentium victore, per multos annos continuis bellis ac
structis aciebus dimicarent, plures et varios cum plebeios tum
magnos deos promiscue finxerunt illosque ab eis turpiter cultos et
adoratos fuisse comperimus. Omnes itaque gentes — praeter Hebraeos dumtaxat, apud quos solos verus et pius omnipoten⟨ti⟩s Dei
cultus idcirco reservabatur, quoniam exinde Christus, humani generis redemptor, oriundus erat — ad idolatriam convertebantur.
Eos namque deos esse putabant quos vel maximos ac potentis-
simos reges fuisse vel aliqua humanarum artium inventione cla-
ruisse noverant eorumque memoriam divinis cultibus conse-
crabant.

32   Unde factum est ut privatim singuli populi gentis aut urbis suae
conditores, seu viri fortitudine insignes essent seu feminae castitate mirabiles, summa veneratione colerent, ut Aegyptus[24] Isidem,
Mauri Iubam, Macedones Cabirum, Poeni Uranum, Latini Fau-
num, Sabini Sanc[t]um,[25] Romani Quirinum eodemque modo
Athenae Minervam, Samos Iunonem, Paphos Venerem, Vulcanum
Lemnos, Liberum Naxos, Apollinem Delphos pro diis adoraverunt. De quo si quis forte dubitaret, res eorum gestas et facta
consideret, quae universa tam poetae quam historici veteres prodidere. Omnes namque deos quos gentilitas adorabat flagitia, stupra,
virginum corruptelas, adulteria et incestus commisisse ac perpetrasse testantur. Si enim poetas atque historicos veteres Graecos
pariter ac Latinos paulo accuratius legerimus, profecto neminem

Hence, if it is clear that the Romans, who were wiser than the 31
other nations of the entire world, held frivolous, worthless, and
false opinions about the worship of the gods — as we clearly and
openly showed above — what can we conjecture about other nations, without citing some particular instance? Shouldn't we think
that they held the same or even worse and more worthless beliefs,
since we recognize that they were inferior to the Romans in wit
and wisdom? To briefly touch upon those previously omitted, for
many years the Carthaginians fought against the world-conquering
Roman people in continual wars and pitched battles: they imagined many different gods, both common and great alike, whom
(we read) they basely worshiped and adored. Thus, with the sole
exception of the Jews, who alone were granted the true and pious
worship of almighty God, for Christ, the redeemer of the human
race, was to be born among them, all the nations turned to idolatry. For they regarded as gods either those they knew to have been
the greatest and most powerful kings or the famed inventors of
human arts, and they made their memory sacred by means of divine cult.

As a result, the different peoples each worshiped with extreme 32
devotion the founders of their race or city, or any men noted for
their bravery, or any women of outstanding chastity. So the Egyptians worshiped Isis as a god; the Moors, Juba; the Macedonians,
Cabirus; the Phoenicians, Uranus; the Latins, Faunus; the Sa-
bines, Sancus; and the Romans, Quirinus; so, too, Athens worshiped Minerva as their god; Samos, Juno; Paphos, Venus; Lemnos, Vulcan; Naxos, Bacchus; and Delphi, Apollo.[63] If anyone
doubts this, let him consider their exploits and deeds, all of which
have been recorded by the poets and the historians. For they bear
witness that all the gods that were worshiped in the gentile world
committed and perpetrated disgraceful acts, rape, seduction of
virgins, adultery, and incest. Indeed, if we carefully read the ancient poets and historians, both Greek and Latin, we shall find

deorum humanarum vel potius inhumanarum libidinum ac luxu-
riarum expertem reperiemus. Nam Hercules, Iovis ex Alcmena filius, quem ob virtutum suarum excellentiam inter deos connume-
rabant, nonne orbem terrae quem peragrasse atque expugnasse
narratur stupris, adulteriis, libidinibus inquinavit? Nam, ut de ceteris eius flagitiis sileamus,[26] nonne Omphale, impudicae mulieri
Eurysthei regis filiae, cuius insanis amoribus deperibat, ita turpiter inservivit ut ipsum mulieribus vestibus indueret atque ad pedes suos sedentem ac pensa facientem et in calathis collocantem
constitueret?

33   Quid Apollo? Nonne Aesculapium flagitio genuit? Nonne ob
amorem quo in Admeti[27] regis filium flagrabat turpissime gregem
suum pavit? Nonne Damnem[28] virginem supra omnem humanum
modum dilexit? Nonne formosum puerum quem adamabat turpiter violavit ludensque occidit? Castor et Pollux, gemelli fratres,
dum alienas sponsas rapiunt esse gemini desierunt. Nam Idas
magnis eorum iniuriiis lacessitus ita concitatus est ut alterum gladio transverberaret atque interimeret. Mars insuper nonne Calydoniam[29] virginem mirum in modum deperiit? Nonne cum Venere
adulterium commisit, unde Vulcanum iratum[30] dicunt? Pluton
Proserpinam, Mercurius Hersen, Neptunus Coronidem usque
adeo amaverunt, ut primus dilectam suam rapere atque ad infernum, habitationis suae locum, traducere cogeretur; secundus quoque suam ita dilexit ut relicto caelo terras aliquamdiu habitaret;
tertius similiter suam nimium in modum deperisse traditur.

34   Quid horum omnium pater Iuppiter, qui in solemni⟨bu⟩s hym-
nis — ut diximus — Optimus Maximus nominabatur? Nonne totam vitam suam in stupris, adulteriis incestibusque consumpsit?
Omitto virgines quas quotidie vitiabat: Io, Inachi filiam, Nonacri-
nam Semelem, Europam, Damnem.[31] Has enim duas ultimas usque adeo dilexit, ut pro Europa formam tauri et pro Damne im-
bris aurei figuram impudenter admodum induere auderet, ut per
illa pulchra involucra ac decora tegmenta puellas illas deciperet

none of their gods innocent of human, or rather inhuman, lust and licentiousness. Take Hercules, the son of Jupiter by Alcmena, whom they counted among the gods for his surpassing virtues. Did he not pollute the entire world, which he is said to have traveled and conquered, by his acts of rape, adultery, and lust?[64] To omit his other disgraceful acts, in his crazed passion did he not so basely serve Omphale, the shameless daughter of king Eurystheus, that she dressed him in feminine garments and placed him at her feet, sitting and spinning wool and putting it in baskets?[65]

What about Apollo? Did he not beget Aesculapius in a scan- 33 dalous union?[66] Did he not burn with love for the son of king Admetus and therefore feed his flock most basely?[67] Did he not love the virgin Daphne beyond any human limit?[68] Did he not rape a beautiful boy whom he basely loved, and kill him in sport?[69] The twin brothers Castor and Pollux ceased to be twins when they ravished the brides of other men. For Idas was so stung by their massive insults that he plunged a sword through one of them and killed him.[70] Did Mars, too, not burn with love of the Calydonian virgin?[71] Did he not commit adultery with Venus, by which they say Vulcan was angered?[72] Pluto loved Proserpina so much that he was compelled to seize her and bear her to his dwelling in the underworld.[73] Mercury so loved Herse that he left heaven for a while to dwell on earth.[74] And Neptune likewise loved Coronis so much that he is said to have burned with extraordinary passion.[75]

What about Jupiter, the father of them all, who is called best 34 and greatest in solemn hymns, as we said?[76] Did he not spend his entire life in acts of rape, adultery, and incest? I say nothing of the virgins whom he daily violated: Io the daughter of Inachus, Semele of Arcadia, Europa, and Danae. He was so enamored of the last two that for Europa he shamelessly dared to take the form of a bull, and for Danae that of a golden shower. By such fair disguises and fine camouflage he deceived the maidens, and by decep-

deceptasque cognosceret; de quo Ovidius in tertio *Methamorpho-
seos*, nimia praedictorum flagitiorum impudentia superatus, car-
mina haec canere non dubitavit:

> Non bene conveniunt nec in una sede morantur
> maiestas[32] et amor: sceptri gravitate relicta,
> ille pater rectorque deum, cui dextra trisulcis
> ignibus armata est, qui nutu concutit orbem,
> induitur faciem tauri mixtusque iuvencis
> mugit et in teneris formosus obambulat herbis.

Atque haec de Europa et dixit et sensit.

35   Terentius vero de Damnis amoribus in *Eunucho* loquens verba
haec ponit:

> Suspectans tabulam quamdam ubi inerat pictura haec, Iovem
> quo pacto Damne misisse aiunt quondam in gremium imbrem
> aureum.
> Egome⟨t⟩ quoque id spectare coepi, et quia luserat
> iam olim ille ludum impendio magis animus gaudebat mihi,
> deum sese in hominem convertisse atque per alienas tegulas
> venisse clanculum per incoloratum impluvium[33] fucum factum
> mulieri.
> At quem deum! Qui templa caeli summa sonitu concutit!
> Ego homuncio hoc non facerem? Ego vero illud ita feci ac
> lubens!

36   Missas facio maritatas Alcineam[34] Iunonemque, quas impu-
dice nimis cognoscebat; nonne Ganymedem, formosissimum ac
regium puerum, ut sibi in poculis ministraret atque in secretiori-
bus cubiculis obsequeretur in deliciisque haberetur, ad manifestum
quoddam et apertum et non celatum et occultum stuprum rapuit?
Atque quod ceterorum omnium flagitiosissimum et impudentissi-
mum videbatur, omnes puellas, matronas puerosque quos quasve
turpiter cognoverat ob stupra et adulteria aeternis praemiis afficie-

tion knew them carnally.[77] Ovid was overwhelmed by the gross shamelessness of these disgraceful acts, and in Book 3 of his *Metamorphoses* he did not scruple to write these verses:

> Royalty and love do not sit well together. So the father and ruler of the gods, who is armed with the three-forked lightning in his right hand, whose nod shakes the world, setting aside his royal scepter, took on the shape of a bull, lowed among the other cattle, and strode, a beauty to behold, in the tender grass.[78]

This is what Ovid thought and wrote about Europa.

Now, Terence in his comedy *The Eunuch* describes the seduction 35 of Danae in these words:

> She was looking up at a certain painting, which showed how Jove is said once to have sent a golden shower into the bosom of Danae. I began to look at it myself, and as he had once played this game, I felt extremely delighted that a god had changed himself into a man, and secretly come through the roof of someone else's house, to play a trick on a woman. But what a god! He shakes the lofty temples of heaven with his thunder. Would I, a poor mortal, not do the same? Certainly, I did it, and gladly.[79]

I won't mention Alcmena and Juno, wives whom he so shame- 36 lessly seduced. Didn't he snatch up Ganymede, a handsome and royal boy, and openly rape him with no attempt to hide or cover up, just so the lad would serve as his cupbearer and do his bidding in his private chambers and be his love?[80] And what seemed to be the most disgraceful and shameless of all his deeds, on the maidens, matrons, and boys that he had basely seduced he bestowed eternal rewards for their rape and adultery, and he placed them in

bat atque in caelis collocabat ac deas deosque efficiebat. De quo Iuno apud poetam tragicum conquerens ita inquit:

> Soror Tonantis, hoc enim mihi
> nomen solum relictum est, semper alienum Iovem
> ac templa summi vidua deserui aetheris
> locumque caelo pulsa pelicibus dedi;
> tellus colenda est, pelices caelum tenent,

et reliqua huiusmodi ita prosequitur, ut per plura violatarum puellarum matronarumque celebrata exempla caelum pelicibus a Iove cum aliarum dearum numero in praemium vitiationis constitutis plenum referctumque ostenderit. Quae quidem stupra, adulteria, flagitia nedum diis convenire videantur, sed a cunctis etiam leviusculis hominibus plebeis et infimis et ab ipsa insuper humana natura vel maxime discrepare et abhorrere noscuntur.

37   Ac quemadmodum omnes gentes in falsa quadam et frivola ac insulsa plurium deorum institutione decipiebantur ita etiam in diversis libationibus, immolationibus et sacrificiis mirabiliter aberrabant, siquidem Aegyptii inter sacrificandum nonnullas odoriferas herbas cum earum radicibus cremabant et his exalationibus talibusque fumis diis suis litabant. Phrygii quotannis Cybelae, deorum matri, sacra crudelissimis certaminibus faciebant. Rhodii hominem vivum Saturno deo suo sacrificabant. In Salamina insula Diomedi, quem deum putabant, homo sic immolabatur: a nonnullis enim adolescentibus ter circum aram ducebatur ac postea a sacerdotibus quibusdam hasta percutiebatur et rogo tandem superimpositus comburebatur. Apud Chios Dionyso cognomine Omadio, hunc enim pro deo colebant, homines inhumana quadam crudelitate hinc inde discerpti sacrificabantur. Lacedaemonii Marti, bellorum deo, homines immolabant. Phoenices ad amovendas impendentesque bellorum pestilentiarumque miserandas calamitates viros probos diisque gratos et acceptos immolare solebant

the heavens and made them gods and goddesses. In the tragedian's verse, Juno complains of this, saying:

> The sister of the Thunderer (for this name alone is left to me), I have abandoned Jove, always another's lover; widowed, I have left the spaces of high heaven empty and, banished from the sky, have given up my place to harlots; I must dwell on earth, for harlots hold the sky.[81]

And she continues in this vein to show, by numerous celebrated examples of maidens and matrons violated, that heaven is filled with harlots counted among the goddesses as a reward for their deflowering. Such rapes, adulteries, and enormities would seem not just unsuited to the gods, but inconsistent and incompatible with all the untrustworthy people of the base and lower classes, and even with human nature itself.

Just as the gentile nations were deceived by the false, frivolous, and absurd doctrine of multiple gods, so they also entertained astonishing delusions in various libations, immolations, and sacrifices. Thus, in their sacrifices the Egyptians burned certain aromatic herbs with their roots, and supplicated their gods with their vapors and smoke. The Phrygians made yearly sacrifices to Cybele, mother of the gods, with bloody battles. The people of Rhodes used to sacrifice a living man to their god Saturn. On the island of Salamis a man was slaughtered to Diomedes, whom they thought a god, in this way: he was led thrice around the altar by young men, then transfixed by priests with a spear, and placed on a pyre and burned. The inhabitants of Chios tore humans apart with inhuman cruelty as a sacrifice to Dionysus, whom they worshiped by the name Omadius, for they worshiped him as a god.[82] The Spartans sacrificed human beings to Mars, the god of war. In order to forestall impending misfortunes of terrible wars and plagues, the Phoenicians used to sacrifice men of good character who were pleasing and acceptable to the gods; and they even cut

atque demum dilectissimum quemque ex filiis principis sui in convenientem quamdam earum calamitatum redemptionem iugulabant. Curetes in Creta insula Saturno—omnium deorum, ut ipsi arbitrabantur, maximo—formosos pueros lactentesque infantes sacrificare consueverant, atque ipso in Latio etiam eodem sacrificii genere colebatur. Carthaginenses insuper ei ipsi humanas hostias immolabant et cum victi essent ab Agatode[35] Siculorum rege ut deum diligentius placarent, quem sibi in bello iratum fuisse putaverant, ducentos nobilium civium filios sacrificaverunt. In Laodicea Syriae Palladi, artium inventrici, virgo immolabatur. Arabes singulis annis singulos pueros litantes sub aris sepeliebant.

38   Omnes Graecorum populi priusquam in bella expeditionesque prodirent diis suis vivos homines immolabant, quod de Iphigenia—licet Agamemnonis Argivorum regis filia esset—bello tamen Troiano factum fuisse legimus. Athenienses—cum propter Androgei filii Minois, Cretensium regis, necem, quem simul cum Megarensibus per invidiam (quoniam ceteros in palaestra superabat) crudelissime interemerant, ingenti quadam ac maxima fame pro iusta et divina ultione agitarentur—necessarium fuit ut ad auxilia deorum confugerent. Quocirca consultus Apollo iussit ut singulis annis septem mares totidemque feminas in Cretam sacrificandos mitterent. Scythae quoscumque advenas capiebant Dianae statim immolare non dubitabant. In Pelle quadam Thessaliae provinciae civitate hominem Achivum Pelleo et Chironi, quos deos putabant, quotannis litabant. Iunonem et Apollinem propterea quod decima hominum ab Italis sibi immolata non fuerat, usque adeo adversus illos indignatos fuisse ferunt ut multis eos calamitatibus praemerent, quarum una—ceteris omissis—erat quod nullus in arboribus fructus ad maturitatem usque perducebatur.

39   Romani, quamquam in tantam immolandorum hominum insaniam inhumana quadam crudelitate immanique saevitia non prosiliissent, ut diis suis quorum turba utriusque sexus ingens ac maxima erat homines sacrificarent, multis tamen turpibus obsce-

the throats of their ruler's most beloved sons as a suitable redemption from those misfortunes. On the island of Crete, the Curetes were accustomed to sacrifice handsome boys and nursing infants to Saturn, whom they regarded as the greatest god, and who was worshiped in Latium itself with the same kind of sacrifice.[83] The Carthaginians also sacrificed human victims to Saturn; and after their defeat by Agathocles, a king of Sicily, they sacrificed two hundred sons of nobles in order scrupulously to placate the god, whom they thought was angry with them during the war.[84] In Laodicea, a virgin was sacrificed to the Syrian Pallas, the inventor of the arts. Every year the Arabs buried a single boy under their altar as an offering.

Before departing for wars and campaigns, all the peoples of   38
Greece used to sacrifice living victims to their gods, as we read they did in the Trojan War concerning Iphigenia, even though she was the daughter of Agamemnon, king of Argos. After the Athenians, envious of his athletic victory, had conspired with the Megareans to cruelly slay Androgeus, son of the Cretan king Minos, because of his death they were afflicted with vast and dire famine by just and divine retribution, and were forced to seek the aid of the gods. When Apollo was consulted, he bade them send seven boys and seven girls each year to Crete as a sacrifice. The Scythians did not hesitate to sacrifice at once to Diana any wayfarers that they captured.[85] In Pella, a city in the region of Thessaly, they yearly sacrificed a Greek to Peleus and Chiron, whom they thought were gods. It is said that Juno and Apollo were so angered at the Italians for not sacrificing a tithe of human victims to them that they afflicted them with many disasters; one of these (not to mention the others) was that their trees produced no ripe fruit.

Although the Romans did not rush to such a pitch of insanity   39
for immolating people with horrendous cruelty and savagery that they sacrificed them to their gods, who formed a vast crowd of both sexes, they did employ foul and obscene rites in their sacri-

nisque ritibus in sacrificiis suis utebantur. Qualia fuisse dicunt ut cum Libero patri sacra fierent pudenda virilia cum magno totius populi honore omniumque gentium applausu celebrabantur atque plastellis quibusdam per urbem vehebantur; et inter vehendum sacerdotes pro precibus et orationibus ac litaniis quae diis ab humano genere propria debentur verbis flagitiosissimis atque obscenissimis utebantur, donec illud membrum per forum transveheretur atque ad consuetum mansionis suae locum transferretur, ubi mater quaedam familias deligebatur—honestate morum et vitae sanctimonia praedita—quae illi membro tam flagitioso tamque obsceno publice coronam e frondibus contextam imponeret. Bacchanalia deinde eidem Libero patri, quem Bacchum Iacchumque variis ob diversas causas nominibus appellabant, autumnalibus temporibus turpiter nimis ac sceleste admodum facere consueverant. Quippe nudi viri—nudati[s] omnia membra—mulieribus, matronis ac virginibus promiscue ad peragenda sacra conveniebant, quae non nisi nocturna erant; omnes namque capita atque femoralia et pudenda viri pariter ac mulieres pampinis et uvarum racemis incincti et hinc inde saltantes discurrebant.[36] Alii uvarum racemos manibus tenebant et tumultuario invicem commixti coetu in sublime saltabant variique et obscenis gesticulationibus brachia, cervicem caputque movebant ac carmen huiusmodi inconditum atque obscenum 'Heu hoe io Bache' laeti alacresque cantabant atque easdem voces crebris clamoribus conditas saepenumero repetebant; nec prius huius saltationis[37] talisque incantationis modus adhibebatur quam defatigati et toto corpore vacillantes hi qui sacrificiis praeerant partim resupinarentur cruribus inherentes partim in pavimentum fanatici amentesque procumberent.

40 Berecyntiae insuper, ut ipsi fingunt deorum matri, in solemnibus sacrificiis ludibria quaedam ac ridicula faciebant. Simulacrum enim suum ingens quoddam tympanum ambabus manibus gestabat; plurimas quoque turres in capite habebat. Unde Virgilius:

fices. Such were, they say, the rites performed for father Liber (Bacchus) when male genitals were celebrated with great honor by the whole people and to the applause of everyone. They were carried on small carts through the city, and during the procession, priests recited scandalous and obscene words rather than the prayers and supplications that are properly owed to the gods by the human race. Then, after the member had been carried across the forum and transferred to its customary resting place, a matron was selected, possessing honorable morals and a saintly life, to publicly place a crown woven of leaves on the scandalous and obscene member. In the autumn, they used to celebrate most shamefully and wickedly their Bacchanalia, in honor of the same father Liber, whom for several reasons they also variously called Bacchus or Iacchus. For naked men mingled indiscriminately with women, both matrons and maidens, baring their entire bodies in order to celebrate the rites, which were always performed at night. All of them, both men and women alike, their heads, thighs, and genitals girded by vine shoots and grape clusters, ran leaping in all directions. Some clutched grape clusters in their hands and made high leaps amid the chaotic throng, and moved their arms, necks, and heads with obscene gestures, singing gladly and gleefully the coarse and obscene song "Evoe! Io Bacche!" They often repeated these words, shouting them continuously, and there was no end of the dancing and chanting until the leaders of the sacrifices, exhausted and staggering, either fell backward, their legs immobile, or fell forward to the ground, frantic and distracted.

They also acted absurdly and ludicrously in their solemn rites 40 for the Berecynthian goddess, whom they imagined to be the mother of the gods.[86] Her immense statue held a tambourine with both hands, and she wore several towers on her head, so that Ver-

'Qualis,' inquit, 'Berecyntia mater invehitur /curru Phrygias turrita per urbes.' Ei igitur simulacro Galli sacerdotes molliter turpissimeque serviebant et cum post eam sese iactarent cymbalorum sonitus diversorumque ferramentorum hinc inde iactorum strepitus simul cum manibus plagentibus fiebat atque usque[38] ad caelum extollebatur. Postremo Priapo, ortorum deo, obscena sacra quotannis facere consueverant.

41   Atque haec ipsa quae supra recitavimus partim crudelia et impia partim insulsa et vana partim furiosa et insana fuisse novimus, quae quidem si paulo latius refellere et uberius confutare vellemus latissimus nobis ad pervagandum campus ostenderetur. Quod de industria vitavimus, veriti ne prolixiores efficeremur quam crassa quaedam tantarum rerum indignitas et intolleranda feritas exigere et postulare videretur, praesertim cum confutationum capita ac refellendi argumenta luce, ut dicitur, meridiana clariora omnibus (vulgo nedum doctis hominibus) pateant.

42   Quid enim aut crudelius aut certe inhumanius esse excogitarive potest quam in anniversariis deorum sacrificiis infantes, pueros, adolescentes et cuiuscumque aetatis homines de more iugulari, mactari, trucidari? In quo quidem sacrificatores ipsi immanitatem omnium bestiarum sua humana vel potius inhumana feritate superabant, quae fetus suos amant. Unde celebrata illa Ciceronis sententia exstat: 'Si ferae partus suos diligunt qua nos indulgentia in liberos nostros esse debemus?' Aut quid illis dii sui facere amplius peiusve possent si adversus eos essent iratissimi quam faciunt propitii cum cultores suos parricidiis inquinant, crudelitatibus mactant, humanis sensibus spoliant? Quid enim sancti an religiosi talibus immolatoribus esse potest aut quid in profanis locis facerent cum inter aras deorum summa scelera quotannis perpetrant ac scelesta facinora committunt, quae profecto a civilibus et

gil writes: "The Berecynthian mother rides her chariot turreted through the Phrygian cities."[87] Her priests, the Galli, effeminately and shamefully served that statue; and as they paraded behind it, the sound of their cymbals and the clanging of their metal instruments bursting out hither and yon, accompanied by the clapping of hands, rose up to the heavens. And finally, each year the Romans used to perform obscene rites to Priapus, the god of gardens.

We know that the acts related above were in part cruel and 41 impious, in part absurd and futile, and in part crazed and insane. If we wished to refute them somewhat more fully and confute them in greater detail, we would find a vast field to explore. But we have intentionally avoided doing this, fearing that we would become more prolix than is demanded or required by the gross indignity and intolerable savagery of such practices, especially since the points that confute, and arguments that refute them are, as they say, clearer than the noonday sun to everyone — even to the masses, let alone men of learning.

For what more cruel or inhuman act could be conceived than to 42 mark the annual sacrifices of the gods by the custom of slaying, slaughtering, and butchering infants, children, adolescents, and adults of every age? In this way, those who made sacrifice by their human, or rather inhuman, savagery surpassed the brutality of all animals, who love their offspring. This is the source of Cicero's famous statement: "If beasts love their newborns, what kindness do we owe our children?"[88] If their gods were angry at them, what worse or more extreme punishment could they inflict on their devotees than when, though propitiated, they pollute them with acts of parricide, torment them with acts of cruelty, and deprive them of human feelings? What could be either holy or religious to those who sacrifice in this way? What would they do in profane places when before the gods' altars they annually commit the most wicked acts and crimes, deeds that civil and secular laws, not to

saecularibus—nedum a sacris et divinis legibus—gravissime plec-
tuntur ac severissime vindicantur? Aut quis alia nempe non crudelia, non impia, non inhumana at certe vana et insulsa ac ludibria
sacrificia non videat, cum videat homines tamquam furiosos et ceu
insania hebrios et velut mente captos ea serio facere quae si quis
inter ludendum faceret porro lascivorum omnium lascivissimus atque cunctorum ineptorum ineptissimus videretur?

43   Haec itaque et multa alia huiusmodi partim flagitiosa et scelesta partim vana et frivola partim crudelia et impia opera omnes
cunctarum gentium populi in quotidianis eorum sacrificiis quae,
ne nimii essemus, brevitatis causa omittendo curavimus, quotidie
factitabant. Ceterum Hebraei dumtaxat ad verum et pium omnipotentis Dei, ut supra diximus, cultum convertebantur. Soli namque illi pia sanctaque consideratione primum elementa et ea quae
ex elementis componebantur (solem similiter et lunam ac ceteras
stellas et caelum ipsum) non modo deos non esse, verum etiam
insensata quaedam inanimataque iudicabant. Et cum totum mundum diversorum generum animalibus refertum viderent, id non
absque providentia divina provenire potuisse intelligebant atque a
magnitudine et pulchritudine creaturarum ob puritatem mentis
creatorem omnium immortalem ipsum atque invisibilem cognoscebant. Unde illa Pauli apostoli celebrata sententia post tot saecula
emanasse videtur quam ad Romanos scribens his verbis expressit:
'Invisibilia Dei per ea quae facta sunt a creatura mundi intellecta
conspiciuntur.' Hominem quoque singularem quamdam totius
universi particulam existimaverunt atque animam scilicet verum et
interiorem hominem praecipuam eius partem, corpus autem quasi
hominis indumentum putaverunt. Unde tanto maiorem curam ad
cultum animarum quam corporum attulerunt ut corpora contem-
nerent, animas vero, quia ad similitudinem Dei creatae erant,

mention sacred and divine ones, most gravely punish and most severely avenge? Wouldn't anyone regard such sacrifices as cruel, impious, inhuman, futile, absurd, and ludicrous, when he sees people acting as if crazed, drunk with madness and out of their minds, and doing things in earnest that, if done in jest, would make someone seem the most licentious of libertines and most foolish of fools?

In their daily sacrifices, all the peoples of all the gentile na- 43 tions practiced these and many other such rites — some sinful and wicked, some futile and frivolous, some cruel and impious — but so as not to be tiresome, we have chosen to omit them for the sake of brevity. Now, the Hebrews alone (as noted above) turned to the true and devout worship of almighty God. For they alone with their holy and devout contemplation judged that the elements and the bodies they form — the sun, moon, and the other stars, and even the heavens — not only were not gods, but were things without sense or soul. But when they saw that all the world was filled with animals of every kind, they understood that this could not have happened without divine providence, and from the magnitude and beauty of the creatures, by virtue of their purity of mind, they recognized that the Creator of all things was both immortal and invisible. This seems to be the source from which flowed, centuries later, the apostle Paul's famous statement, which he thus expressed in writing to the Romans: "The invisible works of God are seen clearly, being understood through the things that have been made since the creation of the cosmos."[89] They considered the human being to be a special part of the entire universe, and the soul, that is, the true and inner person, to be his special part, but the body only a sort of garment of the person. Hence they dedicated so much more care to the cultivation of the soul than of the body that they despised their bodies, but magnified their souls, as created in the likeness of God, magnifying them so much

usque adeo magnificerunt ut summum hominis bonum Dei cognitionem arbitrarentur.

44   Hac igitur pietate veraque in creatorem religione Dei altissimi
sacerdotes genus electum atque regium et gens sancta appellabatur
atque his et aliis similibus appellationibus digni habebantur. Hac
inquam pietate ac vero et immaculato Dei cultu armati multi ex eis
ad tantum et tam sublime cunctarum virtutum culmen ascenderunt ut angelorum visione divinisque oraculis, non syllogismis
nec coniecturis neque aliis huiusmodi humanis argumentis, divinitus uterentur; atque ita a Deo instituerentur ut quae futura erant
plerumque gratia Domini repleti ea quasi praesentia viderent. Atque haec antequam Graecorum nomen esset in terris, primo vero
etiam ante Moysen et ante Iudaeorum gentem, priscis illis Hebraeis veris et piis omnipotentis Dei cultoribus caelitus innotesce-
bant. Iudaei enim post Moysen a Iuda, Hebraei vero ab Hebere, a
quo Abraham originem traxit, appellati fuere.

45   Hac denique pietate ducti, hac dominica gratia adiuti, multis
ante Moysen saeculis absque aliqua lege scripta pie sancteque vivebant et absque ulla divinarum legum, quae nondum late fuerant,
doctrina solis oraculis mentisque acumine puram quamdam altissimarum rerum veritatem mirabiliter consequebantur. Primus
namque apud eos Moyses, sancto ac divino spiritu afflatus, cogitationes suas litterarum monumentis memoriaeque mandavit. Hic
enim antequam leges ferret plures maiorum nostrorum vitas pro-
bosque mores in suo *Geneseos* libro viventium et posteriorum
animis impressit atque per hunc modum ⟨piorum⟩ praemiis et
impiorum suppliciis ad amplexandam virtutem impietatemque fu-
giendam plurimum et vivos et posteros exhortaretur. Divinas tandem leges in medium protulit et ne forte Iudaeis difficillima earum

that they recognized the knowledge of God as the highest good of man.

Thus by this piety and true devotion to the Creator the priests 44 of God on high were called an elect and royal race and a holy nation, and were considered worthy of these and other similar titles. Armed with piety, then, and the true and stainless worship of God, many of them rose to such great and lofty heights of all virtues that not by syllogisms, inferences, and other such human arguments, but by divine power they experienced the vision of angels and divine prophecies. And God trained them in such a way that, filled by the Lord's grace, they often beheld future events as if present. These things became known by divine power to these ancient Hebrews, the true and pious worshipers of almighty God, before the Greeks had any fame on earth, and even before Moses and the nation of the Jews. For after Moses the Jews were named for Judah, while the Hebrews were named for Heber, an ancestor of Abraham.[90]

Guided by this piety and aided by the Lord's grace, for many 45 centuries before Moses they lived pious and holy lives without any written law and without any teaching of divine laws, which had not yet been enacted, and they amazingly achieved the pure truth of the highest matters, using only their learning, divine prophecies, and the keenness of their minds. Now, among the Jews the first to commit his thoughts to the memory and record of written documents was Moses, who was inspired by God's holy and divine spirit. Before he enacted any laws, in his book of Genesis he imprinted on the minds of contemporaries and posterity many holy lives and upright morals of our ancestors. In this way, by citing the rewards of the pious and punishments of the wicked, he exhorted both the living and posterity to embrace virtue and to flee impiety. Finally, he published his divine laws; and so that the precepts of the laws being handed down to them would not seem difficult to the Jews and they therefore recoil from them, he wished to set

legum quae eis tradebantur praecepta viderentur, ac propterea ab
illis resilirent, digna quaedam priscorum virorum exempla coram
eis proponenda curavit et voluit. Unde Enos primum verum hominem suis designationibus conscripsit; Enos enim vocatus est qui
latine 'verus homo' interpretatur. Hebraei enim neminem verum
hominem praeter eum esse putabant, qui verum Deum mente cognosceret pieque coleret; alios vero nihil a mutis pecoribus differre
arbitrabantur. Horum alios lupos, alios canes, alios equos, alios
porcos, alios asinos, alios serpentes varia quadam diversorum brutorum similitudine sancta Iudaeorum scriptura appellare consuevit, quemadmodum communiter totum hominum genus commo-
dissima appellatione Adam significavit, quo nomine 'de terra natus'
propterea designatur quia primus homo de terra conspersa — quae
'adama' hebraice, unde 'adam,' 'humus' vero latine dicitur, unde
hominem dictum volunt — divinitus factus esse scribitur.

46   Primus iustorum Enos fuisse traditur, qui ante alios omnes nomen Domini Dei invocare coepit. Hunc Enoch postea imitatus,
cum Deo ambulavit; proinde in terris non inveniebatur, quia Deus
ob virtutes suas eum in caelum transposuerat. Is namque perfectus
homo in Deo reperitur, qui periculosa et frivola multorum hominum colloquia fugit. Is hominibus invisibilis est nec ab ipsis facile
invenitur qui Deo caritate coniunctus ab eo solo cognoscitur.
Hunc Hebraei Enoch appellarunt, quod nomen latine interpretatum 'gratiam Dei' significare videtur, qua ita refulsit ut primus
omnium prophetaverit. Iudas enim in sua epistola verba haec ponit: 'Prophetavit autem de his septimus ab Adam Enoch, dicens:
"Ecce venit Dominus in sanctis milibus suis,"' et reliqua. Noe tertius in iustitia vir praestans et eximius fuisse perhibetur, cuius
quantae qualesque virtutes exstiterint ex eo cognosci vel maxime
potest, quod cum universum hominum genus multis flagitiorum
specibus inquinaretur inquinatumque paene totum irretiretur irre-
titumque comprehenderetur, solus Noe vir iustus et innocens in

before them worthy examples of ancient men and took care to do so. Hence, he wrote that Enos was by his name the first true human being, since he was called Enos, which in Latin translates as "true human being."[91] For the Hebrews regarded as a true human being only a person who knows the true God in his mind and piously worships Him; but they regarded all others as no different from dumb sheep. The Holy Scriptures of the Jews often called such people wolves, dogs, horses, pigs, asses, or snakes according to different analogies with various beasts.[92] By the same token, they called the entire human race together by the apt name of Adam. By this name he is described as "born of earth," because it is written that the first human being was divinely fashioned from moistened earth, which in Hebrew is called *adama*, whence "Adam," or *humus* in Latin, from which some believe derives *homo* (human being).[93]

Enos is said to have been the first just man, since he before all others began to invoke the name of the Lord God.[94] Enoch, who imitated him, walked with God; and then he was no longer found on earth, for God had borne him up into heaven on account of his virtues. For that person is found perfect in God who shuns the dangerous and frivolous talk of many people. And that person is neither visible to others nor easily found by them who is joined to God in love and only known by Him. The Hebrews called him Enoch, which translated into Latin seems to mean "God's grace," by which he was so resplendent that he was the first to prophesy.[95] In his epistle Jude writes these words: "And Enoch, the seventh from Adam, prophesied of these saying, 'Behold, the Lord comes with thousands of his saints,'" and what follows.[96] Third in righteousness, Noah is cited as an excellent and outstanding man. The quantity and quality of his virtues can be best understood from the fact that when the entire human race was defiled by every sort of sin and, having been defiled, was ensnared and, having been ensnared, was captured, Noah alone in that generation of men was

46

eo hominum genere repertus est. Unde ipse ceteris hominibus
aquarum inundationibus submersis una cum filiis suis simul atque
nuribus mirabili quodam modo per arcae illius famosissimae fabri-
cationem quasi unicum futuri humani generis seminarium conser-
vatus est.

47   Atque hi tres ante diluvium vixisse narrantur. Post diluvium
vero Melchisedech, quo nomine 'rex iustus' apud Hebraeos designabatur, apud quos nec circumcisionis ulla nec mosaycae legis
mentio habebatur, vir iustissimus ac praestantissimus fuit. Qua re
ne Iudaeos (posteris enim hoc nomen inditum fertur) neque gentiles, quoniam non ut gentes pluralitatem deorum opinabantur,
sed Hebraeos potius et expressius nuncupamus aut ab Hebere, ut
dictum est, aut, si verius appellamus, quia id nomen hebraice
'transituros' significabat. Soli quippe Hebraei a creaturis naturali
ratione ac lege non scripta sed nata ad cognitionem veri Dei
transire potuerunt et voluptatibus corporis contemptis ad rectam
vivendi viam pervenerunt, cum omnibus praedictis praestantibus
viris clarissimus ille — totius generis sui origo — Abraham nume-
randus est, quem sacra scriptura admirabilem quamdam Dei cognitionem incredibilemque iustitiam, quam non a mosayca lege
(septima enim post Abraham generatione Moyses nascitur) sed
naturali vi ac ratione consecutum fuisse summa cum laude his
verbis manifestissime attestatur: 'Credidit Abraham Deo et reputa-
tum est ei ad iustitiam.' Qua re multarum gentium patrem divino
oraculo futurum atque in ipso benedicendas omnes gentes claris et
apertis vocibus hoc videlicet ipsum cecinerunt, quod nos iam diu
penitus et omnino impletum fuisse videmus, cuius iustitiae perfectionem non mosayca lege sed Dei cognitione ac sincera fide conse-
quebatur.

48   Hic vir perfectus post multas invisibilis Dei visiones legitimum
genuit filium, quem primum — divino persuasus oraculo — in carne
praeputii circumcidit et ut ceteris qui ab eo nascerentur idem facerent mandatum praebuit. Abrahae Isaac filius in vera pietate suc-

found to be just and innocent.[97] So when the rest of humankind was submerged by flood waters, he, together with his sons and daughters-in-law, was miraculously saved by constructing the famous ark as the sole nursery of the future human race.[98]

These three men are recorded as living before the flood. And 47 after the flood, there lived the most just and excellent Melchizedek, by which name he was designated as "just king" by the Hebrews,[99] among whom we find no mention of circumcision or Mosaic Law. We shall therefore call these people neither Jews (the name given to their descendants) nor Gentiles (since they did not, like the Gentiles, believe in a multitude of gods). Rather, we shall call them more precisely Hebrews, either from Heber, as noted above,[100] or more truly because in Hebrew the noun means "about to cross over."[101] For the Hebrews alone among the creatures were able to cross over to the knowledge of the true God by natural reason and law, unwritten but innate in them; and despising bodily pleasures, they attained the right way of living. Illustrious Abraham, the source of all his race, must be counted among all the excellent men mentioned above.[102] He achieved a marvelous knowledge of God and incredible justice, not by the Mosaic Law (for Moses was born in the seventh generation after Abraham) but by his natural power and reason, as Holy Scripture bears manifest witness with the highest praise in these words: "Abraham believed in God, and He reckoned it to him as righteousness."[103] Hence divine prophecies sang with clear and unambiguous words that he would be the father of many nations, and that all nations would be blessed in him; which we have long since seen completely fulfilled; and he achieved the perfection of this righteousness not by the Mosaic Law, but by the knowledge of God and by sincere faith.

After many visions of invisible God, this perfect man begat a 48 lawful son; and obeying a divine prophecy, he circumcised him first in the flesh of his foreskin, and left as a commandment to others born from him that they do the same.[104] Isaac succeeded

cessit, hac ista felici hereditate a parentibus accepta. Rebeccae uxori coniunctus, cum Esau et Iacob geminos genuisset pudicitiae et castitatis amore demum ab uxore abstinuisse perhibetur. Iacob patris sui (Esau omisso; non enim dignus est ut in hoc sanctorum virorum cathalogo ⟨memoretur⟩)[39] vestigia imitatus postmodum Israhel cognomen accepit. Iacob namque praeter 'supplantatorem'—sic enim apud Hebraeos vere interpretatur—'athletam' latine dicere possimus, quam appellationem primum habuit cum actuosis, ut ita dixerim, operationibus multos pro pietate ac vera religione labores ferebat. Cum vero iam victor luctando evasisset ac speculationis tranquillitate frui videbatur, tunc Israhel appellatus est, quod quidem praeter 'luct⟨tat⟩orem cum angelo'—ceu in Latinum eloquium transferri consuevit—'per contemplationem' quoque 'videns Deum' appellari potest.

49   Ab hoc praestantissimo viro duodecim patriarchae profecti sunt, de quibus singillatim pauca dicemus atque a Ruben, omnium primogenito, incipiemus. Hic etsi adolescentiae suae tempora pulchra quadam muliere fortuito visa in fornicationis crimine temere incidisset, tanta tamen huius flagitii poenitentia ductus est, ut per septem continuos annos a vino et carnibus se penitus abstineret, quo quidem in tam diuturno tempore numquam lacrimis pepercisse deprehenditur. Magna deinde iustitia in gestis suis utebatur; non modo enim ius suum unicuique tribuebat, sed iniuriam etiam ab aliis quod poterat propulsare conabatur, quod in persona Iosephi germani sui vel maxime declaravit, quando ipsum ceteri fratres ob invidiam—communem quamdam excellentium virorum labem

50   ac perniciem—interimere voluerunt. Nam illos a scelesta eius nece magna cum industria revocavit. Quippe cum eis ab initio impium adversus fratrem suum facinus dissuadere non posset, in siccum quemdam puteum demittere plurimum hortabatur, quid de eo agendum foret paulo post maturius consulturi⟨s⟩;[40] intempesta deinde nocte ad praedictum puteum illum eruendi[41] causa reversus,

his father Abraham in true piety, having received this happy inheritance from his parents. He married Rebecca; but after begetting twin sons, Esau and Jacob, he is said to have abstained from his wife for love of modesty and chastity. Jacob followed in his father's footsteps and later received the name Israel. (I leave out Esau, who is not worthy to be mentioned in this list of holy men.) Now, we may call Jacob both "substitute," as the name is truly translated in Hebrew,[105] and "athlete" in Latin: for he first acquired this name when he sustained many labors of piety and true devotion by what may be called his "active" works. Then, after he had emerged victorious from his wrestling match and enjoyed the peace of contemplation, he was called Israel, which can mean both "the wrestler with the angel," as we usually say in Latin, and "the one seeing God through contemplation."[106]

From this excellent man sprang twelve patriarchs, whom we will individually describe in a few words, beginning with Reuben, the first born.[107] During his adolescence, he chanced to see a beautiful woman, and rashly committed the crime of fornication; but moved by great remorse for this sin, he completely abstained from wine and meat for seven whole years; and during this long time, he was always seen shedding tears.[108] Then he showed great righteousness in his actions, both rendering to everyone what was their right and attempting to protect them, insofar as he could, from others' injustice. He demonstrated this most clearly in the case of his brother Joseph, when his other brothers sought to kill him out of envy, the common stain and ruin of excellent men. For with great diligence he kept them from wickedly murdering Joseph. Unable to dissuade them at the outset from this impious crime against their brother, he urged them to lower him into a dry well, to take counsel later about how to deal with him. Then he returned to the well in the dead of night to lift him out, but could not find him. For in his absence, when he had returned to his

49

50

eum reperire non potuit, quoniam reliqui fratres ipso absente (nam interim ad sua pascua contenderat) eum Ismahelitis mercatoribus in Aegyptium contendentibus vendiderant.

51   Secundus in ordine Simeon, vir robustissimus ac fortissimus, fuit. Una enim cum Levi fratre suo, ob stuprum Dinae eorum sorori illatum, adversus Sichimitas — quorum princeps praedictam Dinam violaverat — ita se gessit ut armis repente susceptis plurimos cives interemerit ac postea munita urbis suae moenia funditus everterit. Cum plura deinde in vita sua egregie iusteque peregisset, demum gravi quadam aegritudine oppressus ad filios in unum convocatos brevem orationem habuit, quam litteris postea mandatam testamentum suum nuncuparunt. In hac oratione paulo post moriturus primum detestabile invidiae vitium gravissime exsecratus atque acerrime insectatus est. De Levi deinde ac Iuda, duobus fratribus suis, mirabilia quaedam vaticinatus ad oboedientiam eorum germanos ceteros adhortatur. De quibus quidem futura quaedam memoratu digna, quasi iampridem evenissent, tanto ante praedixit. Inter cetera namque ex altero pontificem maximum oriundum, sicut postea evenit, manifestissime prophetavit; de altero vero regem quemdam descensurum hominem simul atque deum eadem persona futurum certissime exprimens praesagire ac praedicere non dubitavit. Et cum haec ista ita plane et aperte explicasset, ut nullam posteris ambiguitatem relinqueret, paulo post deum in terris humana forma appariturum et cum hominibus conversaturum subiunxit, a quo genus humanum ex peccatis suis redimendum ac salvandum fore videbatur. Atque haec ipsa et alia quaedam huiusmodi de Christo Domino nostro post multa tunc saecula de virgine nascituro quonam modo clarius exprimi atque apertius explicari possent non sane intelligo.

52   Tertius Levi accedit, qui probitate morum ac vitae sanctimonia apprime floruit. Huic enim optimo atque integerrimo viro nonnulla divina mysteria per angelos sibi crebro apparentes divinitus revelata sunt. Inter cetera namque de baptismate et de certa

pastures, his other brothers had sold him to some Ishmaelite merchants who were traveling to Egypt.

Second in order was Simeon, a mighty and courageous man. 51
Together with his brother Levi, he battled the men of Shechem, whose ruler had raped their sister Dinah: swiftly taking up arms, he succeeded in killing many of their citizens, and then completely toppled the walls fortifying their city.[109] After many outstanding and righteous accomplishments, he was stricken with a serious illness; and gathering his sons together, he made a short speech, which was later written down and called his testament. In this deathbed speech, he first solemnly cursed and bitterly inveighed against the detestable vice of envy.[110] Then he made wondrous prophecies about Levi and Judah, his two brothers, and exhorted the other brothers to obey them.[111] And he foretold well in advance memorable events concerning them, as if they had already occurred. Among other things, he clearly prophesied that a high priest would spring from one of them, as later happened. And he did not hesitate to presage and predict, speaking with conviction, that a king, both human and divine in the same person, would descend from the other. Once he had expounded these points clearly and manifestly, leaving nothing ambiguous for posterity, he added that soon thereafter God would appear on earth in human form and converse with men, and by Him the human race would be saved and redeemed from their sins.[112] I do not understand how these and other such similar prophecies about our Lord Christ, destined to be born of a virgin many centuries later, could have been more clearly expressed or more openly expounded.

Third came Levi, who was greatly distinguished by his honor- 52
able behavior and pious life.[113] To this excellent and upright man several divine mysteries were revealed by angels who often wondrously appeared to him. Among other things, he miraculously prophesied about baptism, about the certain and indubitable

quadam et indubitata Christi Domini nostri pro salute humani generis crucifixione de futuroque iuditio mirabiliter vaticinatus est. De quibus omnibus nonnullisque aliis similibus mysteriis, utpote absque ulla dubitatione futuris, in oratione quam incolumis revelata sibi mortis suae die ad tres filios simul congregatos habuit et testamentum eius appellatur admonere et eos certiores reddere non dubitavit.

53   Quartus sequitur Iudas. Hic inter ceteras praecipuas corporis et animi sui dotes cursu ac robore plurimum valebat. Cursu quippe capreas cervosque, mirabile dictu, superabat; robore quoque adeo vigebat ut, haedo de ore leonis arrepto, feram ipsam resistentem repugnantemque interimeret. Ursum etiam per pedes capiens in praecipitium revolvebat atque apros hinc inde discerpens laniabat; uros ac silvestres boves per cornua apprehensos in girum conquassabat tenebrisque per assiduam quamdam revolutionem incussis demum interficiebat. Nec solum adversus immanes feras, ut dictum est, cursu roboreque praevalebat, sed in impios quoque reges et principes impetu facto superior evadebat. Nam et duos Cananeorum reges magnis quibusdam exercitibus suis praesidentes —incredibile dictu—inter dimicandum in proelio prostravit atque fugientes eorum acies hinc inde dispersit fugavitque. Postremo gigantem quemdam simul ac regem nomine Akhor,[42] ante et retro iuxta veterem Parthorum morem in equis sagittantem, obtrunca-

54   vit. Quid plura? Multos reges, complures principes plurimosque populos seorsum ipse et una cum fratribus suis—mirabile dictu— in bellis superavit. Haec et cetera huiusmodi ab eo praeclare gesta quamquam suapte natura mirabilia videantur et sint, admirari tamen desinemus si simul cum eo adversus acerrimos et impios divini nominis hostes in proeliis suis omnipotentis Dei angelum non dimicantem sed potius fulminantem fuisse animadverterimus. His igitur multisque aliis florenti aetate egregie peractis, filios suos dum aegrotaret ad se convocavit, quibus moribundus persuasit ut inter cetera vitia luxuriam et avaritiam maxime detestarentur. Quo

crucifixion of Christ our Lord for the salvation of humankind, and
about the future judgment.[114] Though he was in good health, he
gathered his sons together, and since the day of his death had been
revealed to him, he did not hesitate to inform them. He delivered
a speech—it is called his testament—describing all these matters
and other similar mysteries as undoubtedly impending.

    Judah follows as the fourth son. Among his other extraordinary 53
physical and mental gifts, he excelled in speed and strength.[115] In
running—wondrous to say!—he outstripped roe deer and stags;
and his strength was such that he could wrest a goat from a lion's
mouth and kill the beast itself when it fought back and resisted.
He also grabbed a bear by the hind paws and tossed him over a
cliff, tore boars apart,[116] and seized wild oxen and cattle by the
horns and swung them around until they lost consciousness from
the continual spinning, and finally killed them.[117] Not only did he
surpass fierce beasts in speed and strength, as we said, but he also
emerged victorious over impious kings and princes in battle. Incredible to relate, he defeated in battle two kings of Canaan leading great armies, breaking up their ranks and putting them to
flight.[118] Finally, he beheaded a giant king named Achor,[119] who
could ride on horseback shooting arrows in front and behind in
the manner of the ancient Parthians.[120] To be brief, by himself or 54
together with his brothers—wondrous to say!—he defeated many
kings, several princes, and numerous peoples in war. Although
these and similar excellent deeds appear by their nature miraculous, and in fact are, we may cease to be amazed when we note
that an angel of almighty God did not fight with him in battle, but
rather hurled thunderbolts against the fierce and impious enemies
of God.[121] Having achieved these and many other outstanding
feats in his vigorous years, he fell ill and summoned his sons,
whom on his deathbed he urged to detest self-indulgence and avarice above all other vices.[122] Next he advised them to cherish the

facto eos admonuit ut sacerdotium colerent cultumque regno in honore praeferrent, Dei nutu sic fieri oportere testatus, quod quidem temporibus nostris servari et impleri videmus. Ad extremum hominem quemdam post plura saecula nasciturum esse praedixit, qui genus humanum a peccatis redimeret atque ita redemptum mirabiliter salvaret.

55   Isachar deinceps quintus occurrit, vir simplex et rectus ac timens Deum et recedens a malo, ut de Iob quodam alienigena et peregrino homine sacris litteris scriptum fuisse legimus. Hunc Hebraei divinis altissimarum rerum contemplationibus, ceteris omnibus posthabitis, vacasse tradidere, quod breviuscula eius oratio paulo antequam moreretur ad filios habita plane et aperte declaravit, quam scriptam postea testamentum suum vocitarunt. In hac enim oratiuncula primum de operationibus virtutum, deinde de simplicitate cordis tanta efficacia et, ut graece expressius dixerim, *energia* verba facit ut plane appareat ipsum rectissimum quemdam simul ac iustissimum virum exstititisse. Et ne per singula vager sed brevissime sua gesta complectar, vigintiduos supra centum annos natus nullum anteactae vitae suae erratum recognoscit, quemadmodum ipse de se quattuor filiis suis, dum moreretur, testari concupivit et voluit.

56   Zabulon sextus ostenditur. Hic tanta probitate morum tantaque benignitate pollebat, ut cunctis inopia laborantibus totis viribus opitularetur. Si quando vero opem pauperibus et inopibus ferre ac favere non posset, usque adeo ob ingentes indigentium hominum calamitates intrinsecus commovebatur ut iuges exinde lacrimas effunderet. Ob hac igitur huiusmodi praecipuas quasdam virtutes suas nonnulla altissima omnipotentis Dei arcana et de Messiae adventu et de futura defunctorum hominum resurrectione percepire atque intelligere meruit. De quibus in oratione quam moriens ad filios habuit et testamentum suum dicitur divinitus prophetavit.

priesthood and to honor worship above kingship, testifying that by God's will it must so be done, which we see maintained and fulfilled in our day.[123] Finally, he predicted that after several centuries a man would be born who would redeem the human race from its sins and miraculously save it once it was redeemed.[124]

Next comes Issachar, the fifth son, a man "simple and upright, and fearing God and shunning evil," as the Holy Scriptures describe Job, who was a foreigner and of another race.[125] Tradition has it that Issachar abandoned all other studies to devote himself to the divine contemplation of lofty subjects, as he plainly and openly declared in the brief speech that he addressed to his sons before dying, and which, written down afterward, they called his testament. In this short speech, he first talks about devoting effort to the virtues, and then about simplicity of heart, with such efficacy and "energy" (to use a more precise Greek word) that it is plain that he was a most upright and righteous man.[126] Rather than entering into details, let me briefly summarize his actions by saying that at the age of 122 he could find no errors in all his previous life, as on his deathbed he desired and wished to attest concerning himself to his four sons.[127]

Zebulun appears as the sixth son. He was endowed with such great integrity and kindness that he did all he could to help anyone suffering from poverty.[128] If ever he was unable to offer aid and show favor to the poor and needy, he was so troubled by the enormous calamities of the indigent that he continually shed tears.[129] By such extraordinary virtues he deserved to foresee and grasp certain of almighty God's profound secrets, both the advent of the Messiah and the coming resurrection of the dead. He divinely prophesied about them in the speech which he made to his sons as he lay dying and which is called his testament.[130]

55

56

57   Dan in ordine septimus appropinquat. Hic profecto vir mitissimus fuit. Nam in omni vita sua non minus operibus quam verbis
iracundiam ac mendacium — duo illa magna ingentiaque vitia — vehementer exsecratus est neque eorum vitiorum in oratione sua,
quae testamentum vocitatur, oblitus ita detestatur exsecraturque
ut exinde multa scelera crudeliaque facinora iam dudum provenisse atque in posterum proventura plane et aperte demonstraverit
ac se virum optimum fuisse significaverit.

58   Octavus tum Nepthalim[43] integra atque optima probitate vitae
usus est atque pridie quam moreretur ad filios in unum congregatos piam quamdam orationem habuit, in qua inter cetera ne a timore et veneratione Domini recedere auderent, sed naturae bonitatem sequerentur diligenter admonuit.

59   Nonus post Gad usque adeo robore et fortitudine valuit ut cum
sibi a genitore suo nocturna gregis custodia iniungeretur, omnes
feras quae forte noctu proprium ac peculiarem gregem invade-
bant eo usque persequebatur quoad manu[44] apprehenderet appre-
hensasque per circuitum hinc inde revolveret, donec exanimatae
conciderent. Orationem quoque ad septem filios suos paulo antequam moreretur habuisse dicitur, quam litteris postea mandatam
testamentum eius nuncuparunt, ubi de vitando adversus proximos
odio dilectioneque erga eos magnopere prosequenda plurimum
versatus est.

60   Decimus procedit Aser, vir probus atque integritate vitae et
probitate morum excellens; quamquam enim adhuc nulla aegritudine teneretur, testamentum tamen suum verbis dumtaxat ac vocibus expressit atque sex filiis in unum convocatis sapientissime
instituit. Nam inter cetera de duabus hominum viis — una vitiorum altera virtutum — per quas ad baratrum tendunt in caelosque
ascendunt praecipue egregieque tractavit. De facienda insuper humani generis per baptismum a peccatis redemptione ac de futuro
Ihesu Christi Domini nostri adventu, qui cum hominibus oppor-

Next comes Dan, the seventh in order, who was the gentlest of   57
men. Throughout his life he fiercely execrated anger and lying—
those two great and enormous vices—in both his words and
deeds. Nor does he forget those vices in the speech that is called
his testament; rather, he detests and execrates them, showing
plainly and clearly that they have been and will always be the
source of many cruel villainies and crimes, and proving himself an
excellent man.[131]

The eighth son, Naphtali, practiced upright and virtuous hon-   58
esty in life, and on the day before he died he gathered his sons
together and gave a pious speech, in which he admonished them,
among other things, not to stray rashly from fear and reverence for
the Lord, but diligently to pursue the goodness of nature.[132]

The ninth son, Gad, possessed such might and courage that,   59
when his father placed him as night watchman over their flocks,
he would pursue any beasts that attacked his particular flock at
night until he laid hold of them and swung them around in his
grasp until they fell dead.[133] He too is said to have made a speech
to his seven sons just before he died, which, written down later, is
called his testament; in it he dwells upon avoiding hatred of one's
neighbors and pursuing love of them.[134]

Tenth comes Asher, an upright man of superior integrity and   60
moral character. Although he was not afflicted with any illness,
he summoned his six sons together, pronounced his testament
orally, and gave them wise instruction.[135] Among other things, he
discussed in an exceptional and outstanding manner the two paths
of men: the way of sins that leads them to hell, and the way of
virtue by which they ascend into heaven.[136] It is said that he
miraculously prophesied humankind's redemption from its sins
through baptism, and the future coming of our Lord Jesus Christ,

tuno tempore vivis conversaturis manducaret et biberet, mirum in modum prophetasse traditur.

61   Ultimo paene loco Ioseph omnibus naturae muneribus ornatus feliciter assurgit. Hic enim ille Ioseph qui et corpore formosissimus et mente aptissimus erat, quippe de eximia eius pulchritudine nonnulla mirabilia et vix credibilia narrantur. Hieronymus namque ipsum quodam loco usque adeo formosum fuisse testatur ut dum per vias transiret tota de muris et turribus ac fenestris puellarum Aegypti turba prospiciendi causa concurreret. Ex quo factum est ut mulier illa Aegyptia, cuiusdam praesidis pharaonis regis uxor, insanis quibusdam eius amoribus ita caperetur ut in ipsum, quando aliter cognoscere non poterat, manus turpiter inicere atque arroganter admodum violare auderet. Quod cum ipse aequo animo pati non posset, tum quia castus erat tum etiam ne domino suo — illius mulieris viro — tantam iniuriam contumeliamque inferret, eam qua apprehendebatur laciniam dimisit atque e vestigio

62   aufugit. Unde, cum de violatione quasi ipse mulierem violare voluisset falso ab ea insimularetur, captus ac carceri mancipatus est; ubi per ingenii sui excellentia⟨m⟩ ac praecipua⟨m⟩ qua⟨m⟩dam mentis acrimonia⟨m⟩ plura et quidem difficilia insomnia verissime interpretaretur, sicut postmodum pluribus evidentibus exemplis manifestissime apparuit, tantam et tam magnam pharaonis praedicti regis gratiam consecutus est ut eum toti regni sui gubernationi praeficeret. Et ne forte in laudatione sui nimii simus rem eius totam paucis perstringemus.

63   Hic est enim vir ille constantissimus qui etsi a formosissima muliere Aegyptii praesidis uxore totiens de adulterio enixe interpellaretur neque precibus tamen allici neque muneribus invitari neque minis exterreri ullo pacto potuit quominus adolescens in singulari quadam ac paene incredibili continentia temperantiaque perseveraret. Hic est ille qui ob admirabiles virtutes suas ex servo et ergastulo quidem damnato ad regale prope fastigium extolli et exaltari meruit. Hic est denique ille qui maximas et capitales

who would eat and drink in conversation with men living at the right time.[137]

Second to last comes Joseph, auspiciously endowed with all the gifts of nature.[138] This is the celebrated Joseph with his handsome body and clever mind: indeed, incredible miracles are related about his exceptional beauty. In a certain passage, Jerome attests that he was so handsome that as he walked in the street a whole crowd of Egyptian girls converged from the walls, towers, and windows to look at him.[139] This is why the infamous Egyptian woman, the wife of an official of Pharaoh the king, was so overcome by insane passion for him that, unable to approach him in any other way, she shamelessly laid hands on him and insolently dared to defile him. Joseph could not accept this: for he was chaste, and refused to commit such an insult and injury against his master, the woman's husband. So he abandoned the garment she clutched and instantly fled. Now, when he was falsely accused by the wife of attempting to rape her, he was arrested and put in prison. There, through his superior ingenuity and extraordinary mental acumen he was able to interpret accurately many difficult dreams, as was made clear later by multiple evident proofs. In this way, he won such great favor with Pharaoh the king that he was placed in charge of the entire kingdom. To avoid excessive praise of Joseph, we shall briefly summarize his story.

This was the steadfast man who, although assiduously and repeatedly solicited by a beautiful woman, the wife of an Egyptian captain of the guard, could in no way be enticed by entreaties, won over by gifts, nor frightened by threats; instead, this young man persevered in his exceptional and nearly incredible continence and self-control. This was the man who deserved by his outstanding virtues to be elevated and exalted from a slave and condemned prisoner to a nearly royal height. This, finally, was the man who

61

62

63

commemoratorum fratrum suorum iniurias—quae, permittente
Deo, pro salute eorum ne rei frumentariae inopia qua tota illa regio laborabat fame perirent contigisse videbantur, quamquam in
magno ac paene altissimo dignitatis et potentatus gradu constitutus esset—non modo ulcisci noluit, sed eos etiam tamquam veros
sicut erant fratres propterea unice adamavit, quoniam et ipsa iniuriarum suarum genera sibi pro salute patris et totius familiae suae
accidisse intellexerat. Qua propter Cassianus noster, in quodam
sanctarum collationum libro, ipsum 'ambidextrum' non iniuria appellavit, 'qui in prosperis'—ut eius verbis utar—'gratior patri, reli-
giosior fratribus, acceptior Deo, in adversis castus, domino fidelis,
carceri mitissimus, illatarum iniuriarum immemor, beneficus inimicis invenitur.'

64   Ultimus omnium Beniamin ob integram quamdam morum
suorum probitatem magnamque vitae suae sanctimoniam omnipotenti Deo ita gratus acceptusque fuit ut omnia fere paulo altiora
eius mysteria sibi divinitus revelata plane aperteque cognosceret.
Siquidem abstrusa quaedam et occulta incarnationis et passionis Salvatoris nostri simul atque resurrectionis mortuorum et ul-
timi denique iudicii arcana illa divina tanto ante praedixit. Haec
enim omnia et cetera huiusmodi in oratione quam ad filios simul
congregatos habuit et eius testamentum vocitatur plane et aperte
futura esse praenuntiavit.

65   Ioseph igitur a pharaone Aegyptiorum rege toti regno suo—
quemadmodum diximus—in gubernatione praepositus Iacob patrem una cum reliquis filiis et universa eius familia, cum ingenti
quadam et maxima atque extrema totius rei frumentariae caritate
praemerentur, in Aegyptum salutis causa accersivit; atque dum ibi
non multo tempore commorarentur, divina providentia operante
ita pullularunt ut in miraculum usque procederet. Nam plures
quam septuaginta animae fuerunt quae a Cananea abeuntes in
Aegyptum ingrederentur, ceu ex Hebraica veritate in principio
Exodi manifestissime exprimitur, quamquam in vulgata transla-

chose not to punish the great and deadly wrongs of his brothers, which (with God's permission) were evidently committed for their own salvation: for otherwise they might have starved because of the grain shortage that afflicted the entire area. Although placed in a great and nearly supreme position of dignity and power, he not only refused to take vengeance but loved them as the true brothers they were, because he saw that he had suffered such wrongs for the sake of the salvation of their father and his entire family. Hence, in one of his *Sacred Conferences*, our John Cassian rightly called him "ambidextrous" because (to cite his words) "in prosperity, he proved himself grateful to his father, loyal to his brothers, and acceptable to God; and in adversity, chaste, faithful to his master, humble in prison, oblivious to wrongs suffered, and generous to his enemies."[140]

Last of all was Benjamin, who for the upright morals and great   64
holiness of his life was so favored and loved by almighty God that he knew nearly all His higher mysteries, which were plainly and openly revealed to him by divine grace.[141] Thus he predicted far in advance certain abstruse and hidden secrets about the incarnation and passion of our Savior as well as about the resurrection of the dead and the Last Judgment. For he plainly and openly predicted that all these and other such things would happen in the speech that he made before his gathered sons, which is called his testament.[142]

Now Joseph had been placed, as we said, in charge of the entire   65
realm by the Pharaoh, king of Egypt. When his father Jacob, along with his other sons and his entire family, suffered from the great, enormous, and severe dearth of all grain, he summoned them to come to Egypt in order to survive. After they had dwelt there for a short time, they grew so numerous by God's providence that it seemed a miracle. For there were more than seventy souls that left Canaan for Egypt, as the Hebrew original states most clearly toward the beginning of Exodus,[143] although the Vulgate

tione nostra septuagintaquinque nominentur, quod unde provene-
rit ignorare me fateor. Et tamen ducentis circiter annis quo quidem tempore Aegyptiis usque ad suam ex Aegypto egressionem
sexcenta virorum milia, mirabile dictu, absque mulieribus et parvulis, per varias — ut fit — successiones pepererunt.

66   Cum itaque hoc praecipuum et peculiare Hebraeorum genus
apud Aegyptios mirum in modum propagaretur, factum est ut
appropinquante egressionis suae tempore duo peregregii infantes
germani ex ipso eodem Hebraeorum genere mirabiliter nascerentur, quorum alter maior natu nomine Aaron primus ex Hebraeis
sacerdos Dei institutus est, a quo deinceps totum Levitarum genus — quos dumtaxat sacerdotes constituebant — ex sacris litteris

67   plane ⟨et⟩[45] aperte profluxisse cognovimus. Hic profecto omnium
sui temporis vir eloquentissimus fuit; in omnibus enim divinis
mandatis quae vel pharaoni vel Hebraeorum populo Dei nomine
exponenda et referenda erant hic ipse utpote elegantior fratri suo
ministrabat. Multa quoque miracula coram ipso rege et coram
quoque populo suo mirabiliter operatus est, de quibus alibi for-
tasse opportunior dabitur enarrandi locus. Sed duo vel tria paulo
maiora, ceteris omissis, in hoc loco praetermittere non possum.
Virga enim illa mirabilis, qua plura et quidem ingentia miracula
fecerat, cum arida esset, incredibili dictu, repente floruit. Aaron
enim quamquam divino nutu in sacerdotio constitutus esset non
defuerunt tamen qui[46] id recte factum esse inficiarentur. Qua de re
contentionibus ortis, duo viri, qui ipsarum seditionum auctores
exstiterant, hiatu terrae primum absorti periere. Huius tantae rei
miraculo attonita et obstupescente plebe, cum nondum ortae seditiones cessarent, aliquot alii illius contentionis principes igne quodam caelitus in terras demisso comburuntur, ac per hunc modum

68   in cineres evasere. Sed cum neque ob haec tanta ac tam ingentia
miracula commotae seditiones adhuc sedarentur, divinitus mandatum est ut Moyses ipse singulas virgas, ex quibuscumque duodecim tribuum principibus nominibus superimpositis, acciperet

records seventy-five, for reasons that I do not understand.[144] All the same, in the two hundred years or so before his departure from Egypt some six hundred thousand men — not counting the women and children — wondrous to say! — were born, as happens, in successive generations.

When this extraordinary and special race of the Hebrews mi- 66
raculously increased among the Egyptians, it happened that, as the time of their departure approached, two outstanding brothers were marvelously born of the Hebrew race. Of the two, the older was named Aaron and was installed as the first priest of God from the Hebrews, and from him descended the entire tribe of the Levites — who were the only ones to be appointed as priests — as we learn plainly and unambiguously from the Holy Scriptures. In his 67
time, this man was the most eloquent of all, for he performed the service of explaining and relating all the divine commandments to the Pharaoh or the Hebrew people, since he was more eloquent than his brother. He marvelously wrought many miracles before the king and before own his people, which we will perhaps narrate more appropriately elsewhere. But leaving the rest aside, in this place I cannot pass over two or three great miracles. His marvelous staff, with which he wrought several major miracles, was dry, but — incredible to relate! — suddenly blossomed.[145] Although Aaron had been appointed to the priesthood with divine approval, there were some who denied that this had been done correctly. When disputes arose about this matter, the two men who had instigated the revolt died, swallowed up by a chasm in the earth.[146] While the masses were astonished and stupefied by such a great miracle, and before the revolts had ended, further chiefs of the rebellion were consumed by a fire that descended from heaven to earth and reduced them to cinders.[147] Yet when even these great 68
miracles did not extinguish the discord stirred up, it was divinely commanded that Moses would collect the single staffs from the leaders of the twelve tribes, each marked with a name, and would

atque in tabernaculo collocaret ac mox inde depromeret; si qua earum floruisset, is cuius florida virga exstitisset ad sacerdotium divino iussu delectus esse intelligeretur. Cum ergo Moyses, iuxta Dei mandatum, coram universo populo omnes e tabernaculo ipso virgas protulisset, sola fratris sui virga — ceteris arescentibus — germinasse conspecta est. Ex ea quippe turgentibus gemmis flores eruperant, qui foliis dilatati in veras et expressas amygdalas[47] formati videbantur.

69   Atque cum haec quae dicta sunt mirabiliter apparuissent, confestim in sacerdotio Dei — nemine discrepante — constituitur; ac per hunc modum sacerdos constitutus sacras vestes mirabiliter formavit formatasque vestivit. Et cum in singulari et praecipua quadam Dei gratia esset, nonnulla divina mandata utpote Dei sacerdos accipere meruit, quae ab eo ac posteris suis in perpetuum servarentur. Universam insuper Levitarum tribum, ut facilius divinis mysteriis vacaret, a bellis gerendis et re militari penitus et omnino segregavit; et ne forte ob inopiam rerum ad victum necessariarum a divino cultu vel impedirentur vel aliquatenus retardarentur, multis eam privilegiis muneribusque exornavit. Inter cetera namque memoratu digna sapienter pieque instituit ut decimae omnium quae e terrarum fructibus suscipiebantur ab universo populo sacerdotibus ipsis quotannis praeberentur, quod institutum per multa saecula sine intermissione servatum usque ad tempora nostra pervenisse conspicimus. Atque haec et alia multa memorabilia in vita sua gessisse traditur, quae ut ad Moysen fratrem suum divine legislatorem celerius accedamus omittenda curavimus.

70   Hic est enim Moyses qui in Aegypto natus per tres menses a parentibus idcirco occultatus est, ut saevum illud et inhumanum pharaonis regis de mactandis omnibus Hebraeorum infantibus mandatum evitarent. Sed ne post in flagranti, ut dicitur, crimine a quaesitoribus et exploratoribus ac satellitibus deprehenderentur,

place them in the tabernacle and then remove them. If any of them blossomed, all would know that the man with the blossoming staff had been chosen for the priesthood by divine command.[148] Now, when Moses, following God's command, brought forth the staffs from the tabernacle before all the people, only his brother's staff was seen to have sprouted, while the others were barren. And from the staff blossoms had burst forth with swelling buds, and their burgeoning leaves seemed to be shaped like real and distinct almonds.

After these signs had marvelously appeared, Aaron was at once 69 appointed to the priesthood of God, with no dissenters; and appointed as priest in this way, he marvelously fashioned sacred vestments, and dressed himself in them.[149] Living in the singular and extraordinary grace of God, as God's priest, he deserved to receive certain divine commandments to be observed by himself and his descendants forever. So that the entire tribe of the Levites would be free to devote themselves more readily to divine mysteries, he completely and utterly excluded them from warfare and military operations. And lest they be hindered or in some way inhibited from divine worship for lack of the necessities of life, he endowed them with many privileges and gifts. Among other notable things, he wisely and piously established that the entire people would each year offer the priests a tenth of all the fruit yielded by the land. We see that this arrangement has been observed for many centuries without a break and has survived to our day. It is recorded that he accomplished these and many other memorable things in his life, but we have intentionally omitted them in order to proceed more swiftly to his brother Moses, the divine lawgiver.

This Moses was born in Egypt and kept hidden by his parents 70 for three months in order to evade the savage and inhuman decree of Pharaoh the king to slaughter all the Hebrew infants.[150] But being rightly fearful lest they later be apprehended in flagrant crime, as the saying goes, by scouts, spies, and henchmen, they

non iniuria ambigentes ipsum more desertorum infantium va-
gientem infinitae omnipotentis Dei misericordiae ac fortunae suae
exposuerunt; ex quo paulo post divinitus factum est ut a filia pharaonis, dum per ripas Nili fluminis pedissequarum comitante caterva spatiaretur, fiscella quaedam — ex scirpis[48] in qua infans ille
fortunae suae exponebatur — fortuito reperiretur. Ubi cum infantem formosum, aptum atque elegantem inveniret in patris sui
regia educari curavit et voluit; grandiusculusque effectus, mirabilis
cuiusdam et potius divinae quam humanae indolis apparebat. Inter cetera enim admiranda quaedam perfectae indolis signa omnipotens Deus staturam suam triennem ita exstulerat ut omnes
praetereuntes ipsum admirabundi ad intuendum converterentur.
Unde ipsa regis filia, liberis carens, eum postea adoptavit.

71   Puerum igitur quemadmodum diximus adoptatum ad patrem
crebro ludendi causa baiulabat, ad quem semel — iam paulo gran-
diorem — delatum in manibus suis dimiserat. Ut vero rex ipsum
gremio suscepit regium diadema capiti suo imposuit, quod puer
statim ambabus manibus comprehendit in terramque prostravit
ac postremo, e regio gremio in terram descendens, pedibus
conculcavit pessumdavitque; quod quidem non temere et fortuito
ac pueriliter sed potius graviter ac mature et mystice adeo factum
manifestam quamdam regni sui eversionem, sicut postea evenit,
portendere videbatur.

72   Post nonnullos deinde annos, ubi egregius puer mirum in modum adoleverat, magna quaedam pro Aegyptiis adversus Aethiopes
belligerandi occasio — studioso sibi et iam litterarum studiis apprime dedito — divinitus occurrit. Aethiopes enim contra Aegyptios structis aciebus belligerantes, exercitibus eorum usque ad internicionem profligatis, illos pluribus iam proeliis, ut ad divina
oracula — rebus suis diffidentes et quodam modo de salute sua
desperantes — in posterum confugere cogerentur; a quibus crebro
admonebantur ut in tam magno et tam formiduloso rerum suarum
73   discrimine duce et fautore uterentur Hebraeo. Unde cum per

exposed him crying like an abandoned infant to God's infinite mercy and his own destiny. Not long after, it came about by divine grace that a daughter of the Pharaoh, who was walking along the banks of the Nile river accompanied by a group of maidservants, chanced to find the basket made of bulrushes in which the infant was exposed to his destiny. Finding the infant handsome, neat, and elegant, she resolved to raise him in her father's palace. When the child had grown bigger, he was seen to possess a marvelous nature, more divine than human. Among the other wondrous signs of his perfect nature, almighty God so increased his stature at age three that everyone who passed him would turn to look at him and marvel. Hence, the king's daughter, having no children, later adopted him.

Having adopted the boy, as we said, she often carried him to 71 play with her father, and once she brought the boy, now a bit older, and left him in his care. The king held him in his lap and placed a royal diadem on his head. But the boy at once grabbed it with both hands, hurled it to the ground, and jumping down from the king's lap, stamped on it with his feet, destroying it. Rather than reckless, fortuitous, or childish, this act was serious, mature, and mystical, and seemed to portend the clear destruction of his kingdom, as later happened.[151]

After several years, when the outstanding boy had wondrously 72 matured, and was quite studious and devoted to literature, heaven furnished him with a great opportunity for battling for the Egyptians against the Ethiopians.[152] For the Ethiopians were waging war against the Egyptians in pitched battles, and had completely routed their armies in several of them. Lacking faith in their fortunes and nearly despairing of their survival, the Egyptians were forced to turn to divine oracles for the future, and these repeatedly counseled them to adopt a Hebrew as their general and protector in this great and terrifying crisis. They interpreted the oracle's 73

antonomasiam, ut graece expressius ac brevius quam latine dicitur, sententiam oraculi interpretarentur ac propterea Moysen utpote ceteris omnibus sui generis praestantiorem intelligerent manifeste-que illum fore cognoscerent qui ab oraculo designabatur, a filia regis ipsum summis precibus efflagitarunt atque re patefacta rege-que consentiente impetrarunt. Aegyptii itaque de propriis illius virtutibus plurimum confidentes, eum dumtaxat exercitibus suis praefecerunt atque solum eorum imperatorem delegerunt.

74   Sed cum paratis novis peditum equitumque delectibus maximis postmodum in expeditionem proficisceretur atque terrestre iter ex magna quadam noxiorum cuiuscumque generis serpentum copia et abundantia hinc inde impeditum reperirent, novum quoddam machinationis genus prae ingenii acrimonia invenisse perhibetur, quod tali impedimento salubre remedium fuisse traditur. Ex peri-culoso enim et impedito ac paene avio itinere ad tutum quoddam et expeditum ac pervium, mirifico quodam inventionis acumine, redigisse creditur. Multas namque plectas ex papiro composuit ibibusque, quas vulgato verbo 'ciconias' dicimus, propterea refersit, quod licet huiusmodi animalia suapte natura mansueta videantur universo tamen omnium serpentium generi infestissima et haben-tur et sunt.

75   Ita per hunc modum iter ipsum ex Aegypto in Aethiopiam du-cens Aegyptiis exercitibus expeditum ac pervium et tutum mirabi-liter praebuit. Postea vero quam incolumis cum exercitibus suis praedictis in Aethiopiam venit, adversus Aethiopes ita strenue belligeravit ut superatis hostibus gloriosissimam victoriam reporta-verit. Nam non solum ex Aegyptiis antea ab Aethiopibus victis il-lorum victores effecit, sed plura quoque eorum oppida urbesque in dicionem suam redegit; in quarum numero civitas quaedam no-mine Saba, cum a Nilo flumine hinc inde circumdaretur, mirum in modum munita recensetur. Atque dum egregia quaedam strenui ducis simul atque fortissimi militis ibi facinora ederet, filiae regis Aethiopum — quem Tharbi[49] nuncupabatur — ita placuit itaque

meaning by *antonomasia* "metonymy," as the Greeks say more precisely and concisely than the Latins. Since they saw that Moses surpassed all the others of his race, and clearly recognized him as the one denoted by the oracle, they begged the princess for him with fervent supplications, and approval was granted after the matter was made known and the king had assented.[153] Thus, trusting greatly in his personal virtues, they placed him alone in charge of their armies and appointed him sole commander.

After assembling vast new troops of foot and horse, and setting forth on their campaign, they found their land march blocked by great numbers of different kinds of poisonous snakes. But Moses is said to have used his keen wits to devise a novel type of strategy, which was, they say, a salutary remedy for this obstacle. By a wonderful flash of inspiration, he is said to have led the army out of a dangerous, obstructed, and nearly impassable route to a safe, unobstructed, and passable one. For he constructed many baskets woven of papyrus, and filled them with ibises, which we commonly call storks. For although by nature these creatures appear tame, they are known to be the deadliest enemy of the entire race of all snakes.[154]

As he led the way from Egypt into Ethiopia, he thus miraculously afforded the Egyptian armies an unobstructed, passable, and safe march. Later, after arriving safely with his armies in Ethiopia, he so vigorously battled against the Ethiopians that he conquered the enemy and claimed a most glorious victory. Not only did he make the Egyptians conquerors of the Ethiopians, although they had previously been conquered by them, but he also reduced several towns and cities under his sway. Among them was the city named Saba which, surrounded by the Nile river on all sides, was found to be marvelously fortified. Having performed there the outstanding feats of a vigorous general and courageous soldier, he so pleased and won over the daughter of the Ethiopian king, who was called Tarbi, that she was seized by sudden passion

74

75

76   gratus et acceptus fuit ut subitis eius amoribus caperetur. Unde urbe illa in deditionem accepta postea uxorem duxit ac per hunc modum Aethiopibus superatis victor in Aegyptum triumphantis more remeavit; ubi non multum postea commoratus exinde recedere statuit, quoniam Aegyptum quemdam cum Hebraeo iurgantem interemerat. Proinde ex nimia arrogantia pharaoni regi infensus esse videbatur. Itaque regis iram fugiens in urbem Madian contendit, ubi opilio et gregis ovium pastor effectus in monte quodam, nomine Sinai,[50] fertili et herboso qui in Arabia situs erat pastoris officio fungebatur.

77   Hoc loco Deus ei in rubo apparuit atque ut in Aegyptum reverteretur, defuncto eo cui infensus fuerat rege, admonuit. Per hunc igitur modum ei ex Arabia in Aegyptum reverso paulo post Deus iniunxit ut nomine suo pharaoni novi regi (omnes enim Aegyptiorum reges sicut primo 'pharaones,' ita deinde 'ptolemaei' cognominati sunt) quoquo modo persuaderet quatenus Hebraeorum populo recedendi ex Aegypto licentiam largiretur, ut sibi in monte santo suo sacrificaret; sic enim ei imperaverat. Quo quidem divinae legationis officio dum Moyses diligenter et accurate fungeretur, ei omnibus modis persuadere conabatur ut id facere curaret quod sibi a Domino verbis suis iniungebatur. Sed ut libentius faceret id ipsum Deo gratum admodum futurum plane et aperte significavit; at vero si forte eos dimittere detrectaret eumdem Deum sibi et genti suae succensurum multiplicesque et ingentes plagas inflicturum manifestissime denuntiavit.

78   Ceterum etsi Moyses optimi et elegantissimi oratoris officio fungeretur atque ex parte omnipotentis Dei, cuius legatus erat, pharaoni loqueretur, usque adeo tamen durae cervicis et obstinati animi fuit, ut non modo Hebraeis abeundi licentiam non concederet sed sese eis ita infestiorem ostendit ut totum populum suum assiduis quibusdam diuturnis nocturnisque laboribus multo gravius vehementiusque opprimeret, quod Deus ferre ac tolerare

79   non potuit. Unde ex hac pharaonis regis inhumana in populum

for him.[155] Upon accepting the surrender of the city, he married   76
her, and having conquered the Ethiopians in this way, he made a
triumphant return to Egypt. After staying there briefly, he decided
to depart because he had killed an Egyptian who was quarreling
with a Hebrew.[156] As a result, his excessive arrogance made him
seem an enemy of the Pharaoh. Therefore, fleeing the king's anger,
he went to the city of Midian, where he became the shepherd of a
flock of sheep on the fertile, grassy mountain named Sinai located
in Arabia, and lived a shepherd's life.[157]

In this place God appeared to him in a bush and advised him to   77
return to Egypt, since his enemy the king had died.[158] When Moses then returned to Egypt from Arabia, God enjoined him to go
in His name to the new king, the Pharaoh (for all the kings of
Egypt were at first called Pharaohs, and later Ptolemies) and to
persuade him in any way possible to grant the Hebrew people
permission to depart from Egypt, so that Moses could sacrifice to
Him on His holy mountain; so He had commanded him.[159] In
carrying out this divine mission diligently and carefully, Moses
tried in every way to persuade Pharaoh to do what the Lord's
words had enjoined. To induce him to act more readily, Moses
plainly and openly indicated that this action would be very acceptable to God. But he also threatened him in no uncertain terms: if
he refused to let them go, God would be angry with him and
his people, and would inflict on them numerous and prodigious
plagues.

Now, although Moses discharged the role of orator in a most   78
excellent and eloquent way, and spoke to Pharaoh on behalf of almighty God, whose envoy he was, the king was so hard-hearted
and obstinate that not only did he refuse to allow the Hebrews to
depart, but showed greater hostility, even more severely and violently oppressing all their people with unremitting labors both day
and night, which God could not bear or tolerate.[160] Violently and   79
indescribably vexed by the king Pharaoh's inhuman cruelty toward

suum crudelitate supra quam dici potest vehementer irritatus universam Aegypti regionem decem illis celebratissimis notissimisque flagris parvo temporis intervallo mirum in modum afflixit. Primo namque, ut de singulis pauca quaedam brevissime attingamus, omnes quorumcumque fluviorum aquas in sanguinem mirabiliter convertit. Proinde Aegyptii de aquis in sanguinem per hunc modum conversis atque exinde putrefactis bibere non poterant. Post septem vero dierum spatium, cum pharao in eodem maligno proposito pertinaciter nimis[51] obdurasset, ubi aquas in pristinam naturam suam Moyse operante remeasse noverat, tantam ranarum copiam per universam provinciam illam immisit, ut tota terrae superficies cooperiretur, quarum tanta abundantia erat ut ex acervis illarum — per praeceptum Moysi mortuarum — hanc inde congregatis terra ipsa putrefieret. Pharaone deinde in pertinacia sua obdurante, tanta scinifum[52] turba e pulvere terrae aborta est ut exinde plerique homines plurimaque iumenta perirent. Hos scinifes[53] consecuta est tanta et tam ingens muscarum diversi generis multitudo, ut universa Aegypti provincia ab huiusmodi muscis circumquaque corrumperetur. Accessit deinde gravissima et saevissima pestis, quae omnia domestica animalia Latino nomine cicurum appellata, exceptis dumtaxat hominibus, in dies absumebat. Ecce insuper vulnera vesicarum turgentium homines pariter ac iumenta aggrediebantur. Quid de grandine dicemus, quam tanta⟨m⟩ ac tam magnam Sacra Scriptura fuisse testatur ut homines et iumenta ac cunctae agrorum herbae et omnes arbores exinde percussae vehementer laederentur? De locustis praeterea, mirabile dictu, et quarum multitudinem ita copiosam, ita ingentem, ita maximam in totam Aegyptum ex sacris litteris adventasse vel advolasse novimus ut innumerabiles viderentur. Quid plura? Tot tantaque locustarum agmina fuisse traduntur ut totam Aegypti terram cum herbis, pomis ac arboribus quae forte a praedicti grandine illesa remanserant penitus devastarent devorarentque. Quid de tenebris referemus, quas per totam Aegypti regionem ita spissas densasque exstitisse

His people, He miraculously afflicted the entire land of Egypt with the ten famous and renowned plagues in a short space of time.[161] Let us quite briefly touch on a few aspects of each. First, He wondrously turned all the waters of every river into blood, so that the Egyptians could not drink from waters that had turned to blood and then putrefied. After the space of seven days, when Pharaoh very stubbornly persisted in his spiteful policy, having learned that through Moses' work the waters had returned to their original nature, He released such a vast number of frogs into the entire region that all the surface of the land was covered. And such was the profusion of them that, when they died by Moses' command, the heaps of them collected everywhere caused the very earth to putrefy. When Pharaoh persisted in his stubbornness, 80 such a swarm of gnats arose from the dust of the land that many men and many beasts of burden perished. These gnats were followed by a multitude of different flies so vast and enormous that they polluted the entire region of Egypt on all sides. There then arrived a grievous and savage plague that day by day consumed all the household animals we call domesticated (*cicuri*) in Latin, sparing only the people. Behold, next boils with swollen pustules attacked both men and livestock. What can we say about the hail that, as Holy Scripture attests, was so great and massive that it violently struck and injured men and livestock as well as every crop in the fields and all the trees? Moreover, concerning the locusts, we know from the Holy Scriptures that, marvelous to say, so vast, enormous, and overwhelming a host of them arrived or flew into Egypt, that they seemed innumerable. In short, we hear that there were so many and such great hordes of locusts that they altogether devastated and devoured all the land of Egypt, together with any crops and fruit and shade trees that happened to remain undamaged by the previous hailstorm. What shall we say about the darkness that is known to have been so thick and dense throughout the entire region of Egypt that it could be touched

constat ut attrectari et palpari possent, unde per universum triduum quo obscuritas illa duravit nemo fratrem suum videre nec ex
81 loco in quo erat recedere valuit? Postremo, cum Deus obstinatam
pharaonis pertinaciam cerneret neque praedicta flagra ullatenus
profuisse intelligeret, omnia Aegyptiorum—et brutorum et hominum—primogenita delere atque interimere constituit; quod postmodum ita fecit ut nulla in toto Aegypto domus, neque parva
neque magna, reperiretur in qua mortuus humi prostratus non ia-
ceret. Haec igitur ultima primogenitorum interemptio tantae effi-
caciae tantarumque virium fuisse videtur ut multo plus sola ipsa
quam novem aliae omnes priores plagae ad exeundum operatur.
Pharao quippe rex, extrema necessitate coactus, tandem Hebraeos
exinde abire permisit.

82   Ex Aegypto itaque Hebraei in hunc modum abeuntes per loca
ex tempestate deserta tendebant. In hoc ergo per vastas solitudines
tam longo itinere commeatus quem de provincia tulerant usque
unius integri mensis spatium, omnibus ciborum generibus interea
consumptis, necessario victu satisfecit. At vero cum non multo
post per extremam quamdam rei frumentariae inopiam azimis
panibus in eodem itinere vesci cogerentur, ad perpetuam tantae rei
memoriam ab ea postea egressione hactenus Iudaei quotannis dies
festos celebrant et solemne quoddam octo dierum pascha, veteri
priscorum suorum more, in anniversaria azimorum commestione
venerantur. Unde ea festivitas ab effectu azimorum nomen non
immerito sortita est.

83   Interea pharao, poenitentia ductus quod Hebraeos a se abire
permiserat, ipsos iam paulo ante de provincia egressos cum exercitibus suis usque ad internicionem enixe persequebatur iamque
Hebraei Mari Rubro appropinquaverant quando magnos infestis-
simi regis exercitus a tergo respexerunt. Quod ubi Moyses, Hebraeorum ductor, prospexit, sua illa divina et consueta virga tantorum miraculorum operatrice mare ipsum e vestigio percussit, quod
in duas partes—mirabile dictu—ita seorsum divisit ut expeditum

and felt, so that during the three-day span that the darkness lasted no one could see his brother or move from the place where he was. At length, when God saw Pharaoh's stubborn obstinacy, and realized that the plagues had done no good, he decided to annihilate and destroy all firstborn offspring of the Egyptians, both man and beast; and he did so thereafter, so that in all of Egypt no house could be found, great or small, in which a corpse did not lie stretched out on the ground. This final destruction of the firstborn then seems to have had such a powerful effect that it alone contributed much more to the exodus than all nine previous plagues. For Pharaoh the king, compelled by extreme necessity, finally allowed the Hebrews to depart from Egypt. 81

The Hebrews therefore left Egypt in this fashion and proceeded through places that at that season were a desert.[162] During their long journey through the vast wilderness, the provisions that they had brought from Egypt for the space of an entire month sufficed for their necessary sustenance even after they had consumed all other kinds of food. But soon thereafter their desperate lack of grain during the journey compelled them to feed on unleavened bread. Hence, to commemorate this great event forever, since their exodus from Egypt to the present, the Jews each year celebrate feast days, and according to the ancient custom of their ancestors, they venerate the solemn Passover of eight days by the annual eating of unleavened bread. Thus the festival has aptly taken its name from this use of unleavened food. 82

Meanwhile, Pharaoh felt regret that he had let the Hebrews depart, and a little before they left his land, he strenuously pursued them with his armies to slaughter them. Just as the Hebrews were approaching the Red Sea, they looked back and beheld the hostile king's great armies behind them.[163] When Moses, the leader of the Hebrews, saw this, he at once struck the sea with his divine staff, a frequent worker of great miracles; and the sea—wondrous to say!—parted so that it offered a clear path on 83

iter per siccum solum Hebraeis dumtaxat transeuntibus praebue-
rit. Verum Aegyptii, qui a tergo paulo longius sectabantur, audax
et temerarium Hebraeorum facinus conspicati, velut de illorum
salute desperantes eos in manifestam quamdam et certam perniciem ruere arbitrabantur; sed ut propius accesserunt, eos ipsos ad
oppositum litus per iter siccum incolumes evasisse manifestissime
84 cognoverunt. Quocirca per eamdem ut ipsi viam persequendi gratia ingressi, omnes ad unum (ita ut ne nuntius quidem tantae cla-
dis superesset) submersi periere; undis enim utrumque celeriter
coeuntibus, profundum pelagus omnes excepit. Cum vero Moyses
totum Hebraeorum populum per mare incolumem transisse, Aegyptios autem inter transeundum omnino periisse conspiceret,
tanta laetitia tantaque hilaritate perfusus est ut statim in suavissimum hymnum illum Hebraeis carminibus lepide decantatum pro-
rumperet, cuius primi versus exstant: 'Cantemus Domino! Glo-
riose enim magnificatus; equum et ascensorem deiecit in mare' et
reliqua huiusmodi gaudii alacritatisque plenissima.

85   Cum ergo Hebraei Mare Rubrum incolumes — incredibile dictu
— transivissent, per vastas solitudines tendebant atque iter incep-
tum prosequebantur; ac multis in tam longo itinere miraculis
procedentibus[54] demum in Montem Sinai[55] pervenerunt, ubi aliquamdiu permanserunt. In hoc namque loco quadraginta dierum
inediam, mirabile dictu, tolleravit; in hoc denique loco fruens aspectu cum Deo facie — ut aiunt — ad faciem loquebatur. Quid
plura? Sexcenta alia sunt huius sanctissimi viri miracula quae et
antequam de Aegypto egrederetur et postquam egressus est per
manus suas divinitus provenerunt, ut Athanasius in libris de vita
et moribus suis multo latius et uberius explicavit, sed ne longiores
86 simus praetermittere maluimus. De monte tandem, sacrificiis Deo
rite peractis, cum turmis suis abivit atque omnia usque ad Iordanem fluvium in dicionem[56] suam magna cum gloria redegit. Nonnullas insuper urbes condidit. In terram tandem promissionis ad

dry ground to the Hebrews alone as they crossed. But when the Egyptians, following at some distance, saw the Hebrews' bold and daring feat, they thought that, despairing of their survival, they were plunging into clear and certain destruction. Yet when they came closer, they realized that they had escaped unharmed to the opposite shore over a dry path.[164] To pursue them, the Egyptians therefore, followed the same path as the Hebrews had, but drowned and perished to a man, so that no messenger survived to report so great a disaster: for the waters converged swiftly from each side, and the deep sea swallowed them all up. When Moses saw that all the Hebrew people had passed across the sea unharmed, and that the Egyptians had completely perished in their crossing, he was filled with such joy and cheer that he at once burst out singing that famous sweet hymn, charmingly intoned in Hebrew strains, which begins "Let us sing to the Lord! For He is gloriously exalted; the horse and the rider He cast into the sea" and the rest, filled with gladness and zeal.[165]

Now, when the Hebrews had crossed the Red Sea unharmed — incredible to relate! — and proceeded through vast deserts, they continued the march they had undertaken; and after many miracles occurred on this long journey, at last they reached Mount Sinai, where they dwelt for some time. In this place, Moses endured a fast of forty days — wondrous to say! — and in this place he had a vision and spoke with God face to face, as they say.[166] To be brief, by the hands of this most holy man countless different miracles occurred by divine power both before he left Egypt and after leaving it, as Athanasius more extensively and copiously recounts in his books on his life and character; but we have chosen to omit these to avoid prolixity.[167] Having made due sacrifices to God, Moses at length departed from the mountain with his troops, and to his great glory brought all the land as far as the Jordan river under his sway. He also founded several cities. Yet by God's prohibition, he was not able to reach the Promised Land to which he

84

85

86

quam Hebraeorum populum traducebat, Deo prohibente, perve-
nire non potuit. Ad extremum tantae modestiae in omni aetate sua
fuisse perhibetur ut cum diuturnam centum ac viginti annorum
vitam gloriosissime peregisset neque oculi caligarunt neque dentes
ulla ex parte conciderunt, qua quidem aetate mortuus ad caelos
87   evolavit. Hic enim fuit ille qui ab humani generis origine usque ad
tempora sua repetita divinas leges sacris litteris explicavit atque
quinque illos celebratos famososque libros Graeco 'Pentateuchi'
nomine nuncupatos mirabiliter divinitusque conscripsit, in quibus
profecto omnia sacrarum ac divinarum scripturarum fundamenta
optime simul atque pulcherrime iaciuntur.

Sed antequam ad eorum praeceptorum explanationem ve-
niamus, quae ad hoc nostrum propositum pertinere et spectare
videntur, non ab re visum est ut aliquae huius Hebraei populi—
cui soli lex data fuisse scribitur—ab omnipotenti Deo privilegia
breviter referamus, quibus ceteris omnibus totius terrarum orbis
88   gentibus longe praestitisse creduntur. Hic est enim populus ille cui
dumtaxat eloquia Dei in sancta eius lingua credita fuere. Hic est
populus ille qui solus prophetas habuit. Hic est, inquam, populus
ille pro quo—ut Aegyptiaco ergastulo, sacrificandi gratia, egrederetur—tanta et tam magna coram pharaone miracula facta sacra
veteris testamenti scriptura commemorat. Hic est populus ille qui
postquam ex Aegypto egressus est, dum per asperrimas eremos
(viae ignarus) tenderet, Deus (itineris sui ductor) per diem in columna nubis et per noctem in columna ignis, ne quando aberraret,
ante eum semper praecedebat. Hic est populus ille cui ut[57] incolumis transiret Mare Rubrum—per percussionem mosaycae virgae
mirabiliter divisum—iter tutum, solidum ac securum praebuit.
Hic est populus ille quem Deus coturnicibus et manna in terra ob
humanorum cibarioum penuriam demissis mirabiliter pavit. His
est populus ille qui aqua—ut dicitur—viva de petra divinitus
emanante cum iam siti periret mirum in modum satiatus est. Hic
est populus qui ad elevationem dumtaxat mosaycarum manuum

was leading the Hebrew people. At the very end, they say that he had shown such moderation in all of his life that his vision was clear and he had lost none of his teeth when he had most gloriously completed a long life of 120 years, at which age he died and ascended to heaven.[168] In his holy writings, this man set forth the divine laws recorded from the origin of the human race to his own time, and wondrously and divinely composed the famous and celebrated five books called in Greek the Pentateuch, which with superb beauty laid all the excellent and elegant foundations of sacred and divine scriptures. 87

But before proceeding to discuss God's commandments, which seem to pertain and belong to our purpose, it seems appropriate to recount briefly the privileges granted by almighty God to the Hebrew people, who (it is written) alone received His Law, by which they are believed to surpass all the other nations of the entire world. This is the only people to whom God entrusted His utterances in His holy language.[169] This is the only people who had prophets. This is the people for whom, according to the Holy Scripture of the Old Testament, such great miracles were performed before Pharaoh so that they might depart from their Egyptian prison farm to make sacrifice. This is the people that left Egypt and passed through harsh deserts, not knowing their way; but God, who guided their journey, always went before them lest they stray, appearing by day as a pillar of cloud and by night as a pillar of fire. This is the people to whom God offered a safe, solid, and secure path for crossing the Red Sea unharmed when it was miraculously divided by a blow of Moses' staff. This is the people whom God wondrously fed by sending partridges and manna to earth when they lacked human food. This is the people who, dying of thirst, were wondrously filled with living water (as we say) flowing from a stone by divine will. This is the people who, merely by 88

Amalechitas, acerrimos et infestissimos hostes suos ac potentissimas gentes, assidue vincebat. Hic est denique populus ille qui per tonitrua et fulgura, per nubes, per buccinas, per fumigationem sancti montis quo Deus in dationem legis descenderat divina mandata, duabus lapideis tabulis digito Dei scripta, recepit. De quibus ceteris huius quondam felicissimi populi miraculis victoriisque atque gloriosis nonnullorum aliorum excellentium Hebraeorum virorum gestis omnino penitus omissis nonnulla nunc — praesertim occasione oblata — brevissime in medium adducemus, quae ad praesens, ut diximus, propositum vel maxime pertinere videntur.

89   De mosaycis igitur legibus breviter tractaturi pauca idcirco recitabimus ut ad solida et aeterna et, ut ita dixerim, beata et non adumbrata, caduca et calamitosa Ihesu Christi, Domini et Salvatoris nostri, mandata tandem aliquando perveniamus. In veteri lege licet decem illa celebrata ac salubria de dilectione veri et omnipotentis Dei atque proximi caritate sine ulla titubatione contineantur, tria tamen et quidem singularia et praecipua deesse et deficere videntur, quae imperfectionem praedictae legis plane ⟨et⟩ aperte declarant. Primum est ut nulla earum legum observatoribus transgressoribusque pro convenientibus praemiis bona nullave pariter pro debitis poenis mala, nisi momentanea quaedam et caduca et vilia, promittantur, irrogentur, exhibeantur. Secundum est ut nonnulla solemnia sacrificia sua partim impura partim frivola partim sanguinolenta appareant. Tertium ut aliqua de certa et expressa quorundam comestibilium prohibitione mandata in mirum ⟨modum⟩ servilia et non libero homine digna videantur. De quibus quidem omnibus, ut paulo clarius et evidentius ostendantur, singillatim pauca enarrabimus, a praemiis observantium incipientes.

90   'Si omnia,' ut legislator quodam loco inquit, 'mandata mea servaveris,' Dei nomine loquens, 'faciet te Dominus Deus tuus excelsiorem cunctis gentibus quae versantur in terra venientque super te universae benedictiones istae: benedictus tu in civitate et benedictus in agro; benedictus fructus ventris tui et fructus terrae tuae

the raising of Moses' hands, strenuously conquered the Amalekites, a powerful race that was their savage and deadly enemy. This is the people, to conclude, who amid thunder, lightning, clouds, trumpets, and incense burned on the holy mountain, where God had descended to give His laws, received the divine commandments written by God's finger on stone tablets. Despite the opportunity offered, we shall omit other miracles of this most fortunate people and the victories and glorious feats of other excellent Hebrew men, and briefly cite only those topics that seem, as we said, most relevant to the present discussion.

Turning now briefly to the laws of Moses, we shall review a few   89
things in order finally to arrive at the commandments of our Lord and Savior Jesus Christ, which are solid, eternal, and (as it were) blessed, rather than shadowy, transitory, and disastrous. Although the Old Law certainly contains the ten famous and salutary commandments about the love of the true and almighty God and love of one's neighbor, there seem to be three singular and salient points that are missing, that clearly and openly demonstrate the imperfection of said Law. [I] First, concerning those who respect or break these laws, no goods as appropriate rewards or evils as condign punishments are promised, imposed, or set out, excepting some temporary, transient, and worthless ones. [II] Second, several of their solemn sacrifices seem unclean, silly, and bloody. [III] Third, some of their fixed and explicit commandments prohibiting various foods seem strangely servile and scarcely worthy of a free man. Beginning with the rewards of the faithful, we shall make some brief observations on all these points individually, so that they are more clearly and openly shown.

[I] As the lawgiver says in a certain passage, speaking in God's   90
name, "If you keep all my commandments, your Lord God will make you higher than all the other nations that dwell on the earth; and all these blessings will come upon you. You will be blessed in the city and blessed in the country. The fruit of your womb will be

fructusque iumentorum tuorum, greges armentorum tuorum et caulae ovium tuarum; benedicta horrea tua et benedictae reliquiae tuae; benedictus eris ingrediens et benedictus egrediens; dabit Dominus inimicos tuos qui consurgunt adversum te corruentes in conspecto tuo per unam viam venient contra te et per septem fugient a facie tua; emittet[58] Dominus benedictionem super cellaria tua et super omnia opera manuum tuarum benedicetque tibi in terra quam acceperis suscitabitque te Dominus sibi in populum ⟨sanctum⟩ sicut iuravit tibi.[59] Abundare te faciet Dominus omnibus bonis fructu terrae tuae; aperiet Dominus thesaurum suum, optimum caelum, ut pluviam tribuat terrae suae in tempore suo benedicetque cunctis operibus manuum tuarum et fenerabis gentibus multis et ipse a nullo fenus accipies. Constitue te Dominus in caput et non in caudam et eris semper supra et non subter.'

91   Haec sunt benedictiones quas cunctis suarum legum servatoribus se daturum plana et aperta voce repromittit. Simile quiddam in maledictionibus transgressorum his verbis ostenditur: 'Si mandata mea,' inquit Deus, 'transgressus fueris venient super te omnes maledictiones istae: maledictus eris in civitate, maledictus in agro, maledictum horreum tuum et maledictae reliquiae tuae; maledictus fructus ventris tui et fructus terrae, armenta boum tuorum et greges ovium tuarum; maledictus eris egrediens et maledictus ingrediens; mittet Dominus super te famem et esuriem et increpationem in omnia opera tua quae tu facies donec conterat et perdat te; adiunget tibi pestilentiam donec consumat te; percutiet te Dominus egestate, febre et frigore, ardore et aestu et aere corrupto ac robigine et persequatur donec pereas. Sit caelum quod supra te est aeneum et terra quam calcas aenea;[60] det Dominus imbrem, terrae tuae pulverem et de caelo descendat supra te cinis donec contera-

blessed, and the crops of your land, and the young of your live-stock, and the calves of your herds and the lambs of your flocks. Your barn will be blessed, and your surplus will be blessed. You will be blessed when you come in and blessed when you go out. The Lord will grant that the enemies who rise up against you, converging in your sight, will come at you from one direction but flee in seven from your face. The Lord will send a blessing on your storehouses and on all the works of your hands, and will bless you in the land He has given you. The Lord will raise you up as His holy people, as He swore to you. The Lord will grant you abun-dance in all goods by the fruit of your land. The Lord will open his storehouse, the excellent heavens, so as to send rain to His land in season and will bless all the works of your hands. And you will lend to many nations but borrow from none. The Lord will make you the head and not the tail, and you will always be at the top, and never at the bottom."[170]

These are the blessings that He promises in a plain and open 91 voice to all who keep his laws. Something similar is revealed in the curses on transgressors, in these words: "If you disobey my com-mandments," says the Lord, "all these curses will come upon you. You will be cursed in the city, cursed in the country, your barn will be cursed and cursed your surplus; cursed the fruit of your womb and the fruit of your land, the herds of your cattle, and the flocks of your sheep. You will be cursed when you go out and cursed when you come in. The Lord will send on you famine and hunger and rebuke on all the works that you do, until He crushes and destroys you. The Lord will send plague upon you until it con-sumes you. The Lord will strike you with poverty, fever, cold, heat, burning, with foul air and blight, and will pursue you until you perish. The heaven above you will be of bronze, and the earth that you tread will be of bronze. The Lord will turn the rain of your land into dust. And the ashes will descend upon you from heaven until you are crushed. The Lord will hand you over, collapsing

ris; tradat te Dominus corruentem ante hostes tuos et per unam
viam egrediaris contra eos et per septem fugias et dispergaris per
omnia regna terrae sitque cadaver tuum in escam cunctis volatili-
bus caeli et bestiis terrae et non sit qui abigat; percutiat te Dominus ulcere Aegypti et partem corporis per quam stercora egeruntur[61] scabie quoque et prurigine ita ut curari nequeas; percutiat te
Dominus amentia et caecitate ac furore mentis et palpes in meri-
die sicut palpare solet caecus in tenebris et non dirigas vias tuas
omnique tempore calumniam sustineas et opprimaris violentia nec
habeas qui liberet te. Uxorem accipias et alius dormiat cum ea;
domum aedifices et non habites in ea; plantes vineam et non vin-
demies eam; bos tuus immoletur coram te et non comedas ex eo;
asinus tuus rapiatur in conspectu tuo et non reddatur tibi; oves
tuae dentur inimicis tuis et non sit qui te adiuvet. Filii tui et filiae
tradantur alteri populo videntibus oculis tuis et deficientibus ad
conspectum eorum tota die et non sit fortitudo in manu tua. Fructus terrae tuae et omnes labores tuos comedat populus quem
ignoras et sis semper calumnias sustinens et oppressus cunctis
diebus et stupens ad terrorem eorum quae videbunt oculi tui; percutiet te Dominus ulcere pessimo in genibus et in suris sanarique
non possis a planta pede usque ad verticem tuum ducetque te
Dominus et regem tuum quem constitue⟨ri⟩s super te in gentem
quam ignoras tu et patres tui et servies ibi diis alienis ⟨e⟩ ligno et
lapidi et eris perditus in proverbium ac fabulam omnibus populis
ad quos te introduxerit Dominus. Sementem multam iac⟨i⟩es in
terram et modicum congregabis, quia locustae devorabunt omnia;
vineam plantabis et fodies et vinum non bibes nec colliges ex ea
quippiam, quoniam vastabitur vermibus; olivas habebis in omnibus terminis tuis et non ungeris oleo, quia defluent et deperibunt.

before your enemies. You will come at them from one direction, and flee in seven; you will be dispersed through all the kingdoms of the earth, and your corpse will be food for all the birds of the air and the beasts of the earth; and there will be no one to drive them away. The Lord will strike you with the boils of Egypt, and the part of your body where your excrement passes will be afflicted with scabies and with an itch that cannot be cured. The Lord will strike you with madness and blindness and mental frenzy, and you will grope at midday as a blind man in his darkness; and you will not direct your path, but at every hour suffer calamity and be oppressed by violence; nor will you have anyone to free you. You will take a wife, and another will sleep with her. You will build a house, and not live in it. You will plant a vineyard and not harvest it. Your ox will be slaughtered in your sight, but you will not eat of it. Your donkey will be stolen in your sight, and will not be returned. Your sheep will be given to your enemies, and no one will help you. Your sons and daughters will be given to another people, and your eyes will watch and fail at the sight of them the entire day, and your hand will have no strength. A people whom you know not will eat the fruits of your land and all your labors, and you will always bear slanders and be every day oppressed, and stunned by the terror of what your eyes see. The Lord will strike you in the knees and in the legs with a horrible sore, and you will be unable to healed from the sole of your foot to the top of your head. The Lord will lead you and the king you appointed over you to a nation unknown to you and your fathers, and there you will serve foreign gods made of wood and stone. You will be condemned to be a proverb and fable among all nations to whom the Lord leads you. You will sow much seed on the field, but will gather only a little, for the locusts will devour it all. You will plant vineyards and cultivate them, but you will not drink the wine nor gather anything from it, since worms will consume them. You will have olive trees in all your bounded lands, but you will not anoint

Filios generabis et filias et non frueris eis, quoniam ducentur in captivitatem. Omnes arbores tuas et fruges tuas robigo consumet. Advena qui tecum versatur in terra ascendet[62] super te eritque sublimior; tu autem descendes et eris inferior. Ipse fenerabit tibi et tu non feneraberis ei; ipse erit in caput et tu eris in caudam et erunt in te signa atque prodigia et in semine tuo usque in sempiternum. Servies inimico tuo quem immittet Deus tibi in fame et siti et nuditate et omnium penuria et imponet iugum super cervicem tuam donec te conterat. Adducet Dominus super te gentem de longinquo et de extremis terrae finibus in similitudinem aquilae volantis cum impetu, cuius linguam intelligere non possis: gentem procacissimam quae non deferat seni nec misereatur parvuli et devoret fetus[63] iumentorum tuorum et fruges terrae tuae donec intereas et non relinquat tibi triticum, ⟨vinum⟩ et oleum, armenta boum ⟨et⟩ greges ovium donec te disperdat et conterat in cunctis urbibus tuis et destruentur muri tui firmi atque sublimes in omni terra quam dabit tibi Dominus Deus tuus et comedes fructum uteri tui et carnes filiorum tuorum et filiarum tuarum.' Et paulo post, in agrum maledictionum et exsecrationum calce verba haec ponit: 'Super filii et filiae carnibus et illuvie secundinarum quae egrediuntur de medio feminum eius et super liberis qui eadem hora nati sunt. Comedent enim eos clam[64] propter rerum omnium penuriam in obsidione et vastitate qua opprimet te inimicus tuus intra portas tuas.'

92   Et ⟨cum⟩ cuncta ista benedictionum maledictionumque genera his verbis, ut a nobis recitata sunt, ex Hebraea in Latinam linguam a Hieronymo nostro egregie vereque conversis plane et aperte explicasset, ne ab aliquo forte ignorarentur, iussit Deus ut in propatulo in duobus montibus, editis locis, apponerentur, per quos totus populus in terram promissionis contendens transiturus erat.

yourself with oil because the olives fall and rot. You will beget sons
and daughters, but you will not enjoy them because they will be
led into slavery. All your trees and crops will be consumed by
blight. The alien living in your land will rise above you and be
higher, but you will sink and be lower. He will lend to you, but
you will not lend to him; and he will be the head, and you the tail.
And these things will be a sign and wonder to you and to your
seed forever. You will serve your enemy whom God sends to you
in hunger, thirst, nakedness, and want of all things; and He will
put a yoke on your neck until it crushes you. The Lord will bring
a nation against you from afar and from the furthest ends of the
earth, attacking like a flying eagle, whose language you will not
understand: a most brazen nation that respects not the old nor
pities the young. They will devour the young of your livestock and
the crops of your land until you perish. And they will not leave
you any grain, wine, or oil, nor the calves of your cattle and the
flocks of your sheep until you are destroyed and crushed in all
your cities. Your solid and towering walls will be destroyed in all
the land that the Lord God will give you, and you will eat the fruit
of your womb and the flesh of your sons and your daughters."[171]
Soon thereafter, at the end of these harsh curses and execrations,
he adds these words: "Besides, the sons and daughters will feed in
secret on the flesh and the filth of afterbirth that comes from between her thighs and additionally on the children who were born
in that hour; for they will eat them clandestinely because of the
dearth of all things in the midst of the siege and devastation with
which your enemy within your gates will oppress you."[172]

Now, when he had thus plainly and openly expounded all these 92
kinds of blessings and curses in these words, which we have recounted—which Jerome translated truly and outstandingly from
Hebrew into Latin—lest anyone be ignorant of them, God commanded them to be placed out in the open on the summits of two
mountains, where all the people would pass as they proceeded

Moyses enim in *Deuteronomio* verba haec posuit: 'En propono in conspectu vestro hodie benedictionem et maledictionem. Benedictionem si oboedieritis mandatis Domini Dei nostri quae ego praecipio vobis, maledictionem si non audieritis mandata Domini Dei nostri sed recesseritis de via quam ⟨ego⟩ nunc ostendo vobis et ambulaveritis post deos alienos quos ignoratis. Cum vero introduxerit te Dominus Deus tuus in terram ad quam pergis habitandam, pones benedictionem super Montem Garizim,⁶⁵ maledictionem super Montem Hebal, qui sunt trans Iordanem post viam quae vergit ad solis occubitum in terra Chananei, qui habitat in campestribus contra Galgalam,⁶⁶ quae est iuxta vallem tendentem et intrantem procul. Vos enim transibitis Iordanem ut possideatis terram quam Dominus Deus vester daturus est vobis et habeatis atque possideatis eam' et reliqua huiusmodi prosecutus est.

93   In omnibus igitur benedictionum maledictionumque praedictarum generibus nihil boni in quoddam legalis, ut ita dixerim, oboedientiae praemium nihilve mali in aliquam abominabilis praeva⟨rica⟩tionis⁶⁷ poenam nisi caducum, nisi momentaneum, nisi terrenum accuratis mosaycarum legum servatoribus transgressoribusque repromittebatur. Iudaei enim quamvis uni et soli ac omnipotenti Deo sacrificarent supplicarentque, sola tamen temporalia et visibilia bona ab illo exspectabant. Atque haec de primo divisionis nostrae membro hactenus dixisse sufficiat.

94   Nunc de sacrificiis, ut praediximus, pauciora attingamus. Tria sacrificiorum genera ceteris omnibus celebratiora in Veteri Testamento fuisse legimus. Primum ex mera quadam totius populi devotione procedebat et 'holocaustum' vocabatur. Secundum pro aliqua certi beneficii impetratione fiebat et hoc generali vocabulo 'sacrificium' vel 'oblatio' appellabatur. Tertium pro peccatorum re-

95   missione agebatur ac 'pacificum' dicebatur 'holocaustum.' Sacrificium de animalibus tantummodo celebrabatur atque quandoque de bovibus quandoque de ovibus quandoque de capris, interdum de agnis interdum de ovibus perficiebatur; atque si animal immo-

toward the Promised Land. In Deuteronomy, Moses speaks these words: "See, I am setting before your sight today a blessing and a curse: the blessing if you obey the commands of the Lord our God that I am giving you, the curse if you disobey the commands of the Lord our God but turn from the path that I am now showing you, and walk after foreign gods whom you know not. And when your Lord God has brought you into the land where you go to dwell, you will put the blessing on Mount Gerizim, and the curse on Mount Ebal. They are across the Jordan by the road that slopes toward sundown in the land of the Canaanites, who dwell in the plains opposite Gilgal, which lies next to the valley that runs and penetrates quite far inland. For you will cross the Jordan to possess the land that the Lord your God will give you to have and possess," and so forth, as he continues.[173]

In all the kinds of blessings and curses just cited, nothing good   93
was held out to punctilious observers of the Mosaic laws as a reward for legal obedience, so to speak, and to violators nothing evil was held out as a punishment for abominable transgression, except what is transitory, momentary, and earthly. For although the Jews sacrificed to and supplicated the one and only almighty God, they expected only temporal and visible goods from Him. Let these remarks suffice for the first section of our discussion.

[II] Now let us briefly touch upon sacrifices, as we promised.   94
In the Old Testament we read that three kinds of sacrifices were more celebrated than all the others. The first was born of the people's pure devotion and was called the "holocaust" (burnt offering). The second was performed to obtain a certain benefit, and was called by the general name of "sacrifice" or "offering." The third was performed for the remission of sins, and was called the "peace offering." Sacrifices were made only of animals — variously, oxen,   95
sheep, or goats; they were sometimes performed with lambs or sheep; and if the animal to be slaughtered was taken from the

landum de armento sumebatur, in hunc modum immolabatur.
Nam Moyses in tali immolatione 'Ponet,' inquit, 'sacerdos super
hostiae caput manus et acceptabilis erit immolabitque vitulum coram Domino et offerent filii Aaron sacerdotes sanguinem eius
fundentes per altaris circuitum quod est ante ostium tabernaculi
detractaque pelle hostiae. Artus in frust[r]a concident et subicient
in altari⟨s⟩ ignem strue lignorum ante composita.' Et paulo post
ait: 'Quod si de pecoribus oblatio est, de ovibus sive de capris holocaustum agnum immaculatum et absque macula offeret immolabitque ad latus altaris quod respicit ad aquilonem coram Domino.
Sanguinem vero eius fundent super altare filii Aaron per circuitum
dividentque membra et omnia quae adhaerent iecori et imponent
super ligna quibus subiciendus est ignis. Intestina vero et pedes
lavabunt aqua et oblata omnia adolebit sacerdos super altare in
holocaustum et odorem suavissimum Domino. Sin autem de avibus oblatio holocausti fuerit Domino de turturibus et pullis columbae offeret eam sacerdos ad altare et retorto ad collum capite ac
rupto[68] vulneris loco decurrere faciet sanguinem super crepidinem
altaris. Vesiculam vero gutturis et plumas proiciet prope altare ad
orientalem plagam in loco in quo cineres effundi solent confrin-
getque ascellas eius et non secabit nec ferro dividet eam et adolebit
super altare lignis igne subposito.'

96   Atque haec de holocaustis. Nunc ad sacrificia vel oblationes accedamus. Moyses 'cum obtulerit,' inquit, 'anima oblationem sacrificii Domino, si simila eius oblatio fuerit fundet super eam oleum et
ponet tus ac defere[n]t ⟨ad⟩ filios Aaron sacerdotes, quorum unus
tollet pugillum plenum similae et olei ac totum tus et ponet memoriale super altare in odorem suavissimum Domino. Quod autem reliquum fuerit de sacrificio erit Aaron et filiorum eius, sanctum sanctorum de oblationibus Domini.[69] Cum autem obtuleris
sacrificium coctum in clibano de simila, scilicet panes absque fermento conspersos oleo et lagana azyma oleo lita. Si oblatio tua

herd, it was slaughtered in this way. About this slaughter, Moses says: "The priest shall place his hands on the head of the victim, and it will be acceptable, and he shall slaughter the young calf before the Lord, and Aaron's sons the priests shall make an offering by sprinkling its blood all around the altar at the entrance to the tabernacle, having skinned the victim. They shall cut the limbs into pieces and place them on the altar fire built of wood."[174] And soon thereafter he says: "If the offering is from the flock, either the sheep or the goats, he shall offer as a holocaust a ram perfect and without defect, and shall sacrifice it in the presence of the Lord on the side of the altar that faces north. Aaron's sons shall sprinkle its blood round about on the altar, and shall divide its limbs and all the parts around the liver, and shall place them upon the wood that shall then be set afire. They shall wash the innards and feet with water, and the priest shall bear them all and burn them on the altar as a burnt offering and an aroma pleasing to God. If a burnt offering of birds is made to the Lord—of turtledoves or squab—the priest shall offer it on the altar, breaking its neck and letting the blood drain from the site of the wound upon the altar base. He shall cast the crop and feathers near the altar on the eastern side, where the ashes are usually dumped. He shall tear its wings off, but not cut it or divide it with iron, and shall burn it on the wood lit on the altar."[175]

So much for burnt offerings. Let us now turn to sacrifices or offerings. "When the soul makes an offering of sacrifice to the Lord," Moses says, "let his offering be of flour, and let him pour oil and incense on it; and take it to Aaron's sons the priests. One of them shall take a handful of the flour and the oil and the incense, and will place this as a memorial on the altar as an aroma pleasing to the Lord. The grain left over from the sacrifice will belong to Aaron and his sons, a most holy offering made to the Lord. If you bring an offering of flour baked in an oven, let it be cakes without yeast sprinkled with oil, and unleavened wafers brushed with oil. 96

fuerit de sartagine similae conspersae oleo et absque fermento, dividies eam minutatim et fundes super eam oleum. Sin autem de craticula sacrificium, aeque simila conspergetur oleo,[70] quam offerens Domino trades in manibus sacerdotis, qui cum obtulerit eam tollet memoriale de sacrificio et adolebit super altare in odorem suavitatis Domino. Quidquid autem reliquum est erit Aaron et filiorum eius, sanctum sanctorum Domino.'

97   Quid de sacrificiis dicemus? Nonne ea quae de ipsis pacificis scribuntur duobus praedictis similia videbuntur vel potius ⟨per⟩ similia[71] ac paene paucis commutatis eadem erunt? Huiusmodi namque sacrificia quae pro integra quadam perpetratorum peccatorum remissione celebrabantur varia ac diversa erant ceu varie partim per ignorantiam partim per malitiam peccabant. Haec enim prisci et sacri textus verba sunt: 'Quod si hostia pacificorum fuerit eius oblatio et de bobus voluerit offerre, marem sive feminam immaculatam offeret coram Domino ponetque manum super caput victimae suae, quae immolabitur in introitu tabernaculi fundentque filii Aaron sacerdotes sanguinem per altaris [per] circuitum et offerent de hostia pacificorum Domino adipem qui operit vitalia et quidquid pinguedinis est intrinsecus, duos renes cum adipe quo teguntur ilia et reticulum iecoris cum renunculis, adolebuntque ea super altare in holocaustum lignis igne subposito in oblationem suavissimi odoris Domino. Si vero de ovibus erit eius oblatio et pacificorum hostia[m] sive masculum sive feminam obtulerit immaculata erunt. Si agnum obtulerit coram Domino ponet manum super caput victimae suae, quae immolabitur in vestibulo tabernaculi testimonii fundentque filii Aaron sanguinem eius per circuitum altaris et offerent de pacificorum hostia sacrificio Domino adipem et caudam totam cum renibus et pinguedinem quae operit ventrem atque universa vitalia et utrumque renunculum cum adipe quae est iuxta ilia reticulumque iecoris cum renunculis et adolebit ea sacerdos super altare in pabulum ignis et in

If your offering is fried in a pan, let it be flour sprinkled with oil without yeast; crumble it and pour oil on it. If your sacrifice is prepared on a grill, let it too be flour sprinkled with oil; and you shall offer it to the Lord in the hands of the priest, who, when he offers it, shall take it as a memorial of sacrifice and burn it on the altar as an aroma pleasing to God. The rest of the offering will belong to Aaron and his sons, the holy of holies to the Lord."[176]

What shall we say about sacrifices? Isn't what is written about 97 peace offerings similar to, or rather, quite similar to and (with few changes) the same as the previous two sacrifices? Such sacrifices, celebrated for the full remission of sins committed, were diverse and various, just as they sinned variously, partly through ignorance, partly through wickedness. These are the words of the ancient and holy writ: "If someone's sacrifice is a peace offering, and he chooses to sacrifice from the herd, let him offer a male or female without defect before God. He shall lay his hand on the head of his victim, which shall be slaughtered at the entrance of the tabernacle. The priests, the sons of Aaron, shall sprinkle the blood all around the altar. From the peace sacrifice they shall offer to the Lord the fat that covers the innards and any fat that is within, the two kidneys with the fat covering the loins, and the caul of the liver with the kidneys. And they shall burn them on the altar as a burnt offering on top of the firewood as an offering of an aroma pleasing to the Lord. If his offering is taken from the flock and is a peace offering victim, whether he sacrifices a ram or ewe, it shall be without defect. If he offers a lamb before the Lord, he shall place his hand on the head of his victim, which shall be slaughtered in the vestibule of the tabernacle of testimony, and Aaron's sons shall sprinkle its blood all around the altar. From the peace-sacrifice victim they shall offer to the Lord the fat and the entire tail with the kidneys, and the fat covering the belly and all the innards, and both kidneys with the fat near the loins and the caul of the liver with the kidneys. And the priest shall burn them on the

oblationibus Domino. Si capra fuerit eius oblatio et obtulerit eam
Domino ponet manum suam super caput eius immolabitque eam
in circuitu tabernaculi testimonii et fundent filii Aaron sanguinem
eius per altaris circuitum tollentque ex ea in pastum ignis dominici
adipem qui operit ventrem et qui tegit universa vitalia et †ani-
mam[72] iecoris cum renunculis adolebitque ea super altare sacerdos in alimoniam ignis et ⟨oblationem⟩ suavissimi odoris. Omnis
adeps Domini erit iure perpetuo in generationibus et cunctis habi-
98   taculis vestris nec sanguinem nec adipem omnino comedetis.' Et
paulo post ait: 'Offeret pro peccato suo vitulum immaculatum Domino et adducet illum ad ostium tabernaculi testimonii coram
Domino ponetque manum super caput eius immolabitque eum
Domino. Hauriet quoque de sanguine vituli inferens illum in ta-
bernaculum testimonii cumque intinxerit digitum in sanguinem
asperget eum septies coram Domino ⟨contra⟩ velum sanctuarii
ponetque de eodem sanguine super cornua altaris,' et sexcenta
alia huiusmodi impedimentis involucrisque et confusionibus referta subiunxit, quae si per singula recenseremus profecto ingens
quoddam ac maximum exinde volumen conficeremus.

99   Tertium erat de certa quadam nonnullorum comestibilium
prohibitione; inter cetera namque quibus per mosaycam legem Iudaei vesci prohibebantur omnis sanguis omnisque adeps comme-
morabatur. Caro quoque suilla et aliorum immundorum, profano-
rum et pollutorum animalium tam terrestrium quam volatilium et
aquatilium carnes vetabantur. Sic enim praedictis *Pentateuchi* locis
scribitur: 'Haec sunt animalia quae comedere debetis: de cunctis
animantibus terrae omne quod habet divisam ungulam et ruminat
in pecoribus comedetis. Quidquid autem ruminat ⟨quidem⟩ et
habet ungulam sed non dividit eam, sicut camelus et cetera huiusmodi, non comedetis illud et inter immunda computabitis. Cyrogallus,[73] qui ruminat ungulamque non dividit, immundus est. Le-
pus quoque (nam et ipse ruminat sed ungulam non dividit) et sus,

altar as food for the fire, and as offerings to the Lord. If the offering is a she-goat and he will offer it to the Lord, he shall place his hand on its head and slaughter it in the circle of the tabernacle of testimony. Then Aaron's sons shall sprinkle its blood all around the altar; and will take from it as food for the Lord's fire the fat covering the belly and covering all the innards, and the caul of the liver with the kidneys. And the priest shall burn them on the altar as fuel for the fire and as an offering of a pleasing aroma. All the fat is the Lord's by a perpetual statute for your generations and all your dwellings, and you shall not eat any blood or fat."[177] Soon 98 thereafter he says: "He shall sacrifice to the Lord a calf without defect for his sin, and shall lead it to the entry of the tabernacle of testimony before the Lord. He shall place his hand on its head and slaughter it for the Lord. Then he shall take some of the calf's blood into the tabernacle of testimony; and dipping his finger into the blood, he shall sprinkle it seven times before the Lord in front of the curtain of the sanctuary, and place some of the blood on the horns of the altar."[178] And he adds countless other precepts filled with such obstacles, enigmas, and obfuscations; if we reviewed each one of them, we would compose an absolutely huge and enormous volume.[179]

[III] Our third point concerned the fixed prohibition of certain 99 foods. Among the other things that Mosaic Law forbade the Jews to eat all blood and fat were mentioned. Pork and the meat of other unclean, profane, and polluted animals—on land, in the air, or in the water—were forbidden. In passages of the Pentateuch, it is written: "These are the animals that you may eat. Of all the land beasts, you may eat any one that has a split hoof and chews the cud among domestic animals. But you shall not eat and shall count among the unclean any beast that chews the cud but has no split hoof, such as the camel and others like it. The rock badger, which chews the cud but does not have a split hoof, is unclean; also, the hare, that chews the cud but does not have a split hoof,

qui cum ungulam dividat non ruminat. Horum carnibus non ves-
cemini nec cadavera contingetis, quia immunda sunt vobis. Haec
autem sunt quae gignuntur in aquis et vesci licitum est: omne
quod habet pennulas ⟨et squamas⟩ tam in mari quam in flumini-
bus et stagnis comedetis. Quidquid autem pennulas et squamas
non habet eorum quae in aquis moventur et vivunt abominabile
vobis exsecrandumque erit. Carnes eorum non comedetis et morticina vitabitis. Cuncta quae non habent pennulas et squamas in
aquis polluta erunt. Haec sunt quae de avibus comedere non debetis et vitanda sunt vobis: aquilam et grypem[74] et alietum et milvum
ac vulturem iuxta genus suum, bubonem et mergulum et ibin,
cycnum et onocrotalum et porphirionem, erodionem et chara-
drion, upupam et vespertilionem. Omne de volucribus quod gradi-
tur super quattuor pedes abominabile erit vobis' ac reliqua huiusmodi multa prosequitur. Et in fine verba haec ponit: 'Qui tetigerit
morticina eorum immundus erit usque ad vesperum et super quod
ceciderit quidquid de morticinis[75] polluetur tam vas ligneum et
vestimentum quam pelles et cilicia; vas fictile in quo horum quidquam intro ceciderit polluetur et ideo frangendum est.'

100   At vero ut ab uno inter alia prohibito cetera huiusmodi qualia
sint bene cognoscere ac probe intelligere valeamus, ipsum de suillis
carnibus non comedendis prohibens praeceptum a diligentioribus
rerum naturalium indagatoribus contra naturam non immerito
datum esse censetur. Sues enim nihil aliud in se ipsis laudandum
atque appetendum praeter escam solam habere perhibentur, quibus quidem ne putrescerent animam ipsam datam fuisse celebrata
quaedam et oratorum et poetarum et historicorum et philosophorum sententia fuit, qua pecude, quia erat hominibus ad vescendum
apta, nihil genuit natura fecundius. Unde celebre illud Iuvenalis
poetae exstat, ubi de apris loquens 'animal,' inquit, 'propter convi-
via natum.'

101   Haec tria utpote ceteris principaliora et multa alia huiusmodi in
lege mosayca continebantur quae partim momentanea partim con-

and the pig, that has a split hoof but chews not the cud. You shall not eat of their flesh, nor touch their carcasses, for they are unclean for you. These are the creatures that are born in the water and which may be eaten: you may eat any that have fins and scales in the sea, in rivers, or in lakes. Any that live in the water without fins or scales are an abomination and curse to you. You shall not eat their flesh, and shall avoid them when dead. All aquatic creatures that lack fins and scales are unclean. These are the birds you should not eat and must avoid: the eagle, the griffin, the kite, any kind of vulture, the horned owl, the gull, the ibis, the swan, the pelican, the waterfowl, the heron, the stork, the hoopoe, and the bat. All flying things that walk on four legs will be an abomination to you,"[180] and he adds many other such things.[181] At the end he writes: "Whoever touches a dead animal shall be unclean until evening, and anything on which a dead thing falls is polluted, such as a wooden vessel or a garment of hide or fur. An earthen vessel into which it falls is polluted, and must therefore be broken."[182]

Let us grasp and clearly understand the nature of the rest of these prohibitions by selecting one of them. Diligent investigators of natural science rightly deem the commandment prohibiting the consumption of pork as contrary to nature. For the only laudable and desirable feature of pigs is their value as food. In the famed opinion of orators, poets, historians, and philosophers, pigs were given life so that they would not rot; and since it was well adapted for human consumption, nature made it the most prolific animal.[183] This is why the poet Juvenal, writing about boars, coined the famous phrase: "a beast born for a feast."[184] 100

Now, to everyone who carefully and diligently considers these three preeminent doctrines of Mosaic law, and many others like 101

fusa partim servilia cunctis hominibus singula quaeque diligenter
et accurate considerantibus videbuntur. Non enim immolationibus
ac sanguine brutorum multo colendus est Deus. Nam quae ex
trucidatione immolantium vel Deo vel immolatoribus ipsis voluptas esse potest? Sed mente pura, bono honestoque proposito
quod dignis ac devotis et religiosis cuiuscumque sacerdotis verbis
maxima cum devotione prolatis pie admodum declaratur. Huiusmodi namque debitum et conveniens sacrificium sola ac recta
benedictio est, quae quidem, ut dictum, religiosis et piis dumtaxat
verbis explicatur. Cum ergo haec omnia ita sint profecto neque in
confusione paganorum, quos aliis verbis plerumque gentiles appellamus, neque in caecitate et obstinatione Iudaeorum quaerenda est
religio sed apud eos solos qui Christiani nominantur. Hi enim—
virtutibus approbatis, vitiis vero versa vice penitus omninoque
reiectis—omnipotenti Deo non crebris vivorum hominum truci-
dationibus, non continuis gregum et armentorum immolationibus,
non spurco ac foedo brutorum sanguine sed piis dumtaxat verbis,
summa cum devotione ex integra et immaculata ac sincera sacer-
dotii mente prolatis, verisque cultibus omnipotenti Deo sacrificare
consueverunt.

102   Ceterum cuncta Veteris Testamenti praecepta ob duas dumtaxat causas laudabilia videntur. Primo quia ad verum omnipotentis Dei cultum humanas mentes dirigebant, cum ceterae omnes gentes ad idolatriam converterentur. Secundo quia adveniente
temporis plenitudine evangelicam quamdam legem fore portende-
bant,[76] quae clara, quae libera, quae salubria praecepta plane et
aperte contineret atque observatoribus insuper suis aeterna prae-
mia largiretur, praevaricatoribus vero—versa vice—perpetuas poe-
103   nas irrogaret. Unde illa Pauli apostoli verba exstant: 'Itaque lex
pedagogus noster fuit in Christum, ut ex fide iustificaremur.'
Qua propter post quingentos supra mille circiter annos (tot enim
temporum curricula inter umbratilem Veteris ⟨Testamenti⟩ legisla-
tionem ac salubrem Ihesu Salvatoris nostri nativitatem inter-

them, they must seem in part impermanent, in part confused, and in part servile. God should not be worshiped by the slaughter and copious blood of beasts. (What pleasure can God or even the sacrificers take in the slaughter of victims?) Rather, He should be worshiped by a pure mind and a good and noble intention, as is made clear by the dignified, devout, and pious words spoken with great devotion by any priest. The proper and suitable sacrifice is solely the just blessing that (as we said) is couched in pious and religious words.[185] But since this is so, religion is not to be sought either in the confusion of the pagans—whom we often call by different terminology the Gentiles—or in the blindness and stubbornness of the Jews, but rather only among those called Christians. Embracing virtues and, contrariwise, completely rejecting vices, the Christians customarily sacrifice to almighty God, not by the frequent slaughter of living human beings, nor by the continual sacrifice of flocks and herds, nor by the foul and filthy blood of beasts, but simply by their pious words, spoken with the greatest devotion by the pure, unstained, and sincere mind of the priesthood, and by the true forms of worship.

Yet all the commandments of the Old Testament seem laudable for at least two reasons. First, they guided the minds of men toward the true worship of almighty God, when all the other nations turned to idolatry. Second, as the fullness of time approached, they presaged that there would be an evangelical Law that would contain clear, free, and salutary commandments, and would besides grant eternal rewards to the observant, and impose eternal punishments on transgressors. This is why the apostle Paul used these words: "So the law was our guide to Christ, that we might be justified by faith."[186] Therefore after approximately 1,500 years (so many ages intervened between the foreshadowing legislation of the Old Testament and the salutary birth of our Savior

102

103

cesserunt) Christus, ut humanum genus primi parentis praevaricatione usque a conditione orbis tanto ante damnatum redimeret, ab
omnipotenti Deo — humana carne suscepta — missus est in mundum. Hanc occasionem, hanc temporis opportunitatem, quam
Graeci expressius 'euceriam' dicunt,[77] Paulus apostolus ad Galatas
scribens 'plenitudinem temporis' appellare non dubitavit.

104   Huiusmodi Dei et Domini nostri in homines beneficentia ulla
maior nec esse neque utilius consulere neque beneficentius provi-
dere neque denique gloriosius conducere conferreque potuit quam
cum ipsa praedicti Dei sapientia, id est unicus filius eius, cui sub-
stantialis et coeternus sibi totum hominem suscipere dignatus et
verbum caro factum habitavit in nobis. Atque trigesimo postea
aetatis suae anno evangelicam doctrinam manifestare et praedicare
coepit, quae quidem partim frequentibus quotidianisque miraculis
partim sanctimonia vitae suae partim salutaribus praeceptis ac salubribus mandatis tantam auctoritatem dignitatemque suscepit ut
cum crebris praedicationibus suis et evangelistarum et apostolorum testificationibus, tum etiam solemnibus eorundem sanc-
to⟨rum⟩ hominum scriptis, non modo veterem legem penitus et
omnino abolevisse sed etiam universam paene terrarum orbem
gloria et maiestate sua iam diu replevisse ac per hunc modum sola
regnasse, quin immo altera abolita imperasse videatur.

105   De quo quidem si quis forte admiraretur quonam modo haec
tanta ac tam admirabilia et paene incredibilia de certa quadam et
expressa veteris legis multis et magnis miraculis ab omnipotenti
Deo late et clare abolitione fieri potuerint, suspicatus omnis, profecto talis admiratio talisque suspitio omnino penitusque cessabit
quando quidem tres subsequentes libros nostros paulo diligentius
et accuratius perlegerit. In quorum primo de vita et moribus ac
miraculis Ihesu Christi Domini nostri manifestissime agitur. In
secundo de salubritate, utilitate ac necessitate doctrinae suae evidenter traditur, quae quidem disciplina nihil aliud quam discretio
morum et exemplar iustitiae fuit. In tertio de morte ac resurrec-

Jesus), Christ was sent by almighty God into the world to assume human flesh and to redeem the human race, condemned by the transgression of our first parent ever since the creation of the world. In his epistle to the Galatians, the apostle Paul did not hesitate to describe this occasion, this temporal suitability, which the Greeks more precisely call *eukairia*, as the "fullness of time."[187]

No benefit could have been greater, more usefully planned,   104
more generously provided, or more gloriously bestowed by our God and Lord upon human beings than when the wisdom of God, that is, His only Son, equal in substance and coeternal with the Father, deigned to take upon Himself full humanity, and as the Word made flesh, dwelt among us. After his thirtieth year, He began to declare and preach his evangelical teaching. In part by His frequent and daily miracles, in part by the holiness of His life, and in part by its salutary precepts and salubrious commandments, His teaching gained great authority and stature. Hence, by His repeated sermons, by the testimony of the evangelists and apostles, and by the pious writings of the same holy men, His teaching not only completely and utterly abolished the Old Law, but filled practically the entire world with its glory and majesty, and in this way held sole sway; indeed, having abolished the other Law, it took command.

Now, if anyone wonders how so many marvelous and nearly   105
incredible things could arise from the certain and clear abolition of the Old Law by many great miracles performed clearly and on a wide scale by God almighty, his every doubt, wonder, and mistrust will altogether cease if he will diligently and carefully read our next three books. In the first of these books, the life, character, and miracles of Jesus Christ our Lord are clearly set forth. In the second, we vividly relate the salubrity, utility, and necessity of His teaching, which is nothing other than the discernment of morals and an exemplar of righteousness. In the third, His death and

tione sua late ampleque tractatur, quemadmodum ex accurata quadam praedictorum librorum lectione clarissime apparebit.

106   Sed cum inter se varia Veteris et Novi Testamenti praecepta videantur et sint, ab uno Deo utraque tam diversa processisse quis-
quis dubitaret, vel quod maiora vel quod minora in veteri lege, in
Evangelio vero maiora mandarentur de eodem ambigens suspicaretur, parumper quaeso consideret unum et eumdem patrem familias, iustissimum quidem virum, aliud his quibus servitutem du-
riorem utile fore iudicaverit, aliud eis quos in filiorum gradum
adoptaverit imperare consuesse. Rursus paulisper animadvertat
eumdem medicum ad reparandam vel obtinendam humani corporis salutem alia per ministros suos imbecillioribus, alia per semet
107 ipsum valentioribus remedia ministrare solitum. Ut enim ars medicinae cum eadem maneat neque ullo pacto ipsa mutetur, mutat
tamen praecepta languentibus, quia mutabilis est nostra valitudo,
ita divina providentia, cum sit omnino incommutabilis, mutabili
tamen creaturae varie opitulatur et subvenit et pro diversitate mor-
borum aliis alia iubet aut vetat. In duo enim genera, quantum ad
hoc praesens propositum spectat, homines distributi videntur, in
quorum uno turba est impiorum (veteris scilicet exterioris ac terreni hominis) in altero vero multitudo piorum (interioris videlicet,
108 novi ac caelestis hominis) continetur. Sed ⟨ab⟩ Adam primo homine usque ad Iohannem Baptistam ecclesiastica historia terreni
hominis vitam moresque describit, cuius quidem historia[m] di-
vulgato Veteris Testamenti nomine quasi terrenum pollicentis regnum appellatur et dicitur; quae Tora nihil aliud est quam quaedam
mystica novi populi imago et aperta Novi Testamenti umbra sempiternum caelorum regnum absque aliqua dubitatione pollicentis,
cuius quidem populi vita e felicissimo Domini nostri adventu in
summa quadam et admirabili humilitate incipit et usque ad ultimum generalis iudicii diem extenditur, quando ipse Dominus et

resurrection are treated in considerable detail, as a careful reading of these books will make abundantly clear.

But since the commandments of the Old and New Testaments 106 both seem to be and are disparate, wouldn't anyone have doubts whether two things so diverse might have come from one God? Or since the Old Law's commandments are greater or smaller, but the Gospel's are greater on the same subject,[188] mightn't someone be perplexed and mistrustful? Yet let such a person please consider a little while how one and the same head of household, a most righteous man, would often give orders differently to those whom he judges to merit harsh servitude and those whom he has adopted as his children. Or let him observe how the same physician, seeking to restore or secure the health of the human body, often administers remedies to the weaker by his assistants, and to the healthier himself. Just as medical science remains the same and 107 cannot by any means be changed, but changes its prescriptions to the sick because our state health is changeable, so too divine providence, while remaining immutable, comes to the aid of mutable creatures in various ways, and in line with the variety of diseases enjoins or forbids different things for different individuals. For present purposes we see that people are divided into two classes: in one is comprised the host of the impious (i.e., the old, external, and earthly man); in the other the multitude of the pious (i.e., the new, internal, and heavenly man). Church history from 108 Adam, the first man, to John the Baptist describes the life and customs of earthly man, whose history which is commonly known as the Old Testament as if promising an earthly kingdom. The Torah is simply a mystic image of a new people and a clear foreshadowing of the New Testament, which beyond any doubt promises the eternal kingdom of heaven. And the life of its people begins with the blessed coming of our Lord in the utmost marvelous humility and extends to the final day of the universal judgment,

Salvator noster ad iudicandum vivos pariter et mortuos cum clari-
tate et maiestate sua iterum in mundum venturus est.

109   Sed antequam ad institutum dicendi ordinem deinceps prose-
quamur non alienum fore existimavimus si in extremo huius primi
libri calce, ad omnipotentem Deum et Ihesum Christum Dominum nostrum et spiritum sanctum tota ac sincera mente parumper
conversi, nonnullas tribus praedictis divinis personis de pretiosa
totius humani generis redemptione ac de amplissima et opulentis-
sima evangelicae legis donatione brevissime simul atque devotissime gratias agamus ac etiam breviusculas quasdam preces suppli-
cationesque effundamus, maxima cum devotione obsecrantes ut
gratiam suam nobis ita pie, ita suppliciter, ita devote postulantibus
concedere atque impartiri digne⟨tur⟩ quatenus nos divino illo fa-
vore auxilioque adiuti ea quae iam animo et mente congrua et or-
dinata serie digessimus litteris mandare ac extrinsecus perficere et
110 absolvere valeamus. Itaque gratias agimus tibi, Deus omnipotens,
quoniam mundum hominis causa creare voluisti atque ipsum,
paulo post creationem suam in peccati labem ex propria transgressione dilapsum, per unici filii tui incarnationem et salutiferam
mortem ab aeterna poena redemisti; ac in hunc modum postea
redemptum per sacrosanctam evangelicae legis traditionem non
solum a sanguinolentis et foedis gregum et armentorum immolationibus liberasti sed etiam piis quibusdam et puris libationibus
ita instituisti ut exinde aeterna caelorum regna manifeste nanciscе-
111 retur. Concede quaesumus ut ea quae pro catholica et orthodoxa
Christi Domini nostri fide adversus Iudaeos et gentes — sic enim
hoc nostrum quodcumque sit opus, iam bonis om⟨i⟩nibus incep-
tum, difficile sane atque arduum inscribi et intitulari volumus —
perficere et absolvere valeamus; in quo quidem tam laudabili, tam
pio ac tam devoto officio eumdem Deum et Dominum nostrum
Ihesum Christum una cum Spiritu Sancto, quando boni gratia id
agimus, ex sua quadam immensa et infinita pietate in Christianae

when our Lord and Savior will Himself come again into the world in splendor and majesty to judge both the living and the dead.

Yet before proceeding to the discourse we have proposed and 109 begun, we deemed it appropriate at the very end of this first book to turn briefly to almighty God and to Jesus Christ our Lord and to the Holy Spirit with all the purity of our heart. Let us briefly and devoutly give thanks to these three divine Persons for the precious redemption of the entire human race and for the generous and bountiful gift of the Law of the Gospel. Let us pour forth some brief prayers and supplications, beseeching Him with the greatest devotion to deign to grant and impart grace to us as we piously, humbly, and devoutly pray, so that aided by divine favor and assistance we may be able to commit to writing and successfully complete the subjects that our heart and mind have arranged in a coherent and orderly sequence. Thus we thank you, almighty 110 God, for you chose to create the world for the sake of man, and when soon after his creation he fell by his own transgression into the stain of sin, you redeemed him from eternal punishment through the incarnation and salvation-bringing death of your only Son. Having redeemed him in this way, through the sacrosanct tradition of the Law of the Gospel you not only freed him from the foul and bloody slaughtering of flocks and herds, but you also instructed him in pious and pure libations, so that he would clearly attain the eternal kingdom of heaven. Grant us, we pray, 111 that on behalf of the catholic and orthodox faith in Christ our Lord, we may be able to finish and complete our treatise *Against the Jews and the Gentiles* — for thus we have chosen to entitle and inscribe this work of ours, whatever it may be, now begun under good auspices, albeit very difficult and arduous.[189] In this laudable, pious, and devout duty, we believe, hope, and desire that, since we are doing this for a good purpose, God, our Lord Jesus Christ, and the Holy Spirit will rightly aid us out of their immense and infinite mercy for the preservation and expansion of the Christian

fidei conservationem atque amplificationem et propensissima quoque in bonorum zelatores benignitate non iniuria adiutores fore credimus, speramus et cupimus.

112 Se⟨d⟩ quoniam de praeparatione evangelica satis hactenus dixisse videmur et hunc primum librum iam in mediocrem quamdam magnitudinem pervenisse conspicimus, nunc ad secundum de mirabilibus, gloriosis simul atque salubribus praedicti Ihesu Christi gestis deinceps procedemus.

faith, and out of their eager beneficence toward promoters of the good.

Now that we seem to have said enough about the preparation of the Gospel, and see that this first book has already reached a moderate size, we shall proceed to the second book concerning the miraculous, glorious, and salutary acts of Jesus Christ. 112

LIBER SECUNDUS[1]

De vita et moribus ac miraculis Christi

1 Deus igitur humanum genus, quod totum ex una primi hominis praevaricatione corruerat, ob ineffabilem clementiam suam redimere cupiens Filium coaequalem sibi caelitus in terras dimittere constituerat, ut humanam carnem susciperet onerosamque corporeae molis sarcinam suscipiens per cuncta communis vitae impedimenta pro humana redemptione ad patibulum usque traduceret, quemadmodum in primo libro de praeparatione evangelica dixisse meminimus. Sed cum a primaeva hominis transgressione usque ad saluberrimam Salvatoris nativitatem plurima ac paene infinita temporum curricula intercesserint, prophetas interim divino quodam spiritu afflatos multa de hoc humani generis redemptore praedixisse manifestum est.

2 Post ducentos circiter supra quinque a creatione mundi annorum milia in ipsis falsorum deorum cultibus ubique pullulantibus iam opportunum destinandi tempus appropinquasse prospiciens Filium suum legavit ad homines. Siquidem Iudaei, quibus solis divina arcana atque, ut ait apostolus, 'eloquia Domini credita fuisse' constabat, relicto Deo vivo irretiti daemonum fraudibus aberraverant, nec per prophetas increpiti ad rectam vivendi viam reduci cupiebant. Quod ideo eum fecisse existimatur et creditur ut humanum genus ab impiis et vanis falsorum deorum cultibus ob hanc Filii sui legationem ad cognoscendum et colendum verum deum converteretur.

3 Quocirca virginem quamdam nomine Mariam, Ioachini cuiusdam et Annae filiam, humilitate vitae et sanctimonia morum ceteris omnibus longe praeferendam, e toto Hebraeorum genere delegit, e qua eius Filius carnem suscipiens divinitus nasceretur. Inde

BOOK TWO

The Life, Morals, and Miracles of Christ

After the entire human race had fallen by the sole transgression of 1
the first man, God in His ineffable clemency desired to save them
and decided to send down His Son, coequal with Himself, from
heaven to earth, so that He would assume human flesh. Then, as-
suming the weighty burden of corporeality, He would carry it even
unto the cross, seeking mankind's redemption by suffering all the
hardships of our common life, as we recall saying in the first book,
concerning the preparation for the Gospel. Now, between man's
primeval transgression and the most salutary birth of our Savior
there elapsed numerous, nearly infinite temporal cycles. Thus, it is
clear that in this interval prophets inspired by the divine spirit
foretold many things about the Redeemer of the human race.

After some 5,200 years from the creation of the world,[1] while 2
the cults of false gods were propagating everywhere, God saw that
the proper time had arrived for His appointment, and sent His
Son as an envoy to mankind. For the Jews, to whom alone divine
secrets and "the words of the Lord were entrusted" (as Paul says),[2]
had abandoned the living God and strayed, ensnared by fraudu-
lent demons; and even when rebuked by their prophets, they
would not return to the right way of living. It is thought and believed that God acted in this way so that by His Son's mission the
human race might turn from impious and vain cults of false gods
to the knowledge and worship of the true God.

On this account He chose from the entire Hebrew race a virgin 3
named Mary, the daughter of Joachim and Anna, who was preferred before all others for the humility of her life and holiness of
her character; from her God's Son would take on flesh in a divine

namque humani generis Salvator oriundus erat Abrahae quippe ⟨cui⟩ angelico oraculo—tamquam Dei interprete referente—promissum fuerat, ut in semine suo omnes gentes benedicerentur; ex cuius semine populus Israel, unde virgo Maria descendit, quae Christum peperit. Haec eadem promissio ad Isaac Abrahae filium, ad Iacob quoque eius nepotem facta ac repetita est, qui 'Israel' novo quodam cognomine appellabatur, quod angelo in mutuo congressu viriliter restitisset. Postquam enim cum angelo luctatus est, Israelis meruit nomen accipere.

4   Ab hoc igitur fortissimo viro universus ille Hebraeorum populus tamquam a stipite quodam et propagatus et nominatus est, quod nomen usque adeo invaluit ut huius populi deus appellaretur 'deus Israel,' non quod ipse ⟨non⟩ sit deus omnium gentium sed quia in isto peculiari et praecipuo populo virtutem promissorum suorum manifestius apparere voluit. Hic enim populus primo in Aegypto, velut certa quaedam apium examina ac formicarum agmina, mirabiliter mutiplicatur et ita pullulavit ut in miraculum usque procederet. Non plures enim quam septuaginta animae ducentis circiter annis, quo quidem tempore Aegyptiis servierunt, sexcenta virorum milia, absque mulieribus et parvulis, pepererunt; ac postea ab illa Aegyptiaca atque nimirum barbarica servitute per Moysen divine legislatorem [in] multis signis portentisque liberatus, debellatis insuper plurimis et variis gentibus, terram etiam repromissionis accepit, in qua reges suos de tribu Iuda exortos tam diu regnasse memoriae prodidere. Qui Iudas unus ex duodecim filiis Israel, nepotis Abrahae, fuit atque inde 'Iudaei' cognominati sunt, vel potius ab altero eiusdem nominis Iuda sic nuncupati fuisse dicuntur, propterea quod cum in deserta quadam Syriae parte eos consedisse conspiceret dux et princeps examinis eorum fuerit. Et hinc, abolito veteri Hebraeorum nomine, Iudaei appellati sunt et terra quam incoluere Iudaea.

5   Hi itaque multa, ipso Deo adiuvante, praeclara fecerunt, multa quoque adversa pro sceleribus suis eo flagellante perpessi sunt,

birth. For the savior of the human race was to descend from Abraham, to whom it had been promised by an angel, God's messenger, that all peoples would be blessed in his seed.[3] And from his seed sprang the people of Israel, from whom descended the virgin Mary, who bore Christ. This same promise was made and repeated to Abraham's son Isaac and to his grandson Jacob, who was called by the new name Israel because in an encounter with the angel he resisted manfully.[4] Having wrestled with the angel, he deserved to receive the name Israel.

Now from this stalwart man the entire people of the Hebrews 4
took their name and propagated as if from the trunk of a tree. This name gained so much strength that the God of this people was called the God of Israel, not because He was not the God of all nations, but because he chose to reveal the power of his promises most clearly among this peculiar and special people. This people first multiplied marvelously in Egypt, and proliferated to a miraculous degree, like swarms of bees or armies of ants. For in the course of some two hundred years when they served the Egyptians, no more than seventy souls produced six hundred thousand men, not counting women and children. And later, when the many signs and portents of their divine lawgiver Moses had freed them from utterly barbaric slavery in Egypt, they conquered many different nations and took possession of the Promised Land, in which the kings from the tribe of Judah reigned for so long a time, as their history records. Judah was one of the twelve sons of Abraham's grandson Israel, and the Jews took their name from him, or rather are said to have been named after a different, homonymous Judah, because when he saw that they had settled in a certain part of Syria, he became the leader and ruler of their colony. Hence, abandoning the ancient name of Hebrews, they were called Jews, and the land they inhabited Judea.[5]

With God's help, they accomplished many splendid things, but 5
also suffered many hardships when He scourged them for their

donec hoc sacrosanctum Mariae semen hominibus proveniret, cui promissum fuerat ut in eo omnes gentes benedicerentur. Has ergo divinas omnipotentis Dei promissiones tunc impletas esse conspicimus cum Iesus per virginem genitricem ex hoc nobilitato genere, velut supra manifestissime expressimus, propagatam in lucem editus humano generi apparuerit, quod Paulus apostolus ad Galatas scribens his verbis expressisse videtur: 'At ubi venit plenitudo temporis misit Deus filium suum natum ex muliere, factum sub lege, ut eos qui sub lege erant redimeret' et reliqua.

6   De hac tam pretiosa ac tam admirabili virgine Esaias propheta, quasi in principio sui voluminis, tanto ante vaticinatus in hunc certe modum praedixerat: 'Ecce virgo concipiet et pariet filium et vocabitur nomen eius Emmanuhel,' quod interpretatur 'nobiscum Deus.' Et paulo post: 'Egredietur,' inquit, 'virga de radice Iesse et flos de radice eius ascendet' et quae sequuntur. Haec est illa virga, vel virgo potius, de radice Iesse orta quae ex genere regali ac pontificali originem traxit. Huiusmodi igitur sanctissima virgo Iosepho cuidam viro, pauperi optimo ac castissimo et in laboriosa lignorum dolatione fabricationeque vitam suam—quamquam generosissimus esset—exercenti (nam a veteribus patriarchis et regibus genus suum traducebat), iam desponsata erat.

7   Hanc itaque tam sanctam et tam generosam virginem Deus e toto Hebraeorum genere, ut diximus, delectam de divina eius conceptione simul atque futuro partu suo per Gabrielem angelum, vel potius archangelum, decentius et convenientius quam per aliquem alium cuiuscumque alterius hierarchiae diligenter admonuit. Hoc enim nomen ex Hebraea in Latinam linguam conversum 'fortitudinem Dei' plane et aperte significat, atqui incarnationis et creationis opus omnipotentiae Dei et patriae potestati, licet trinitatis opera extrinsecus—ut theologi nostri testantur—indivisa esse videantur, accommodatius quam aliis divinis personis non immerito attribuatur. Quippe ab eisdem patriarchis et regibus propterea originem suam trahere videbatur, quod divina lege cavebatur ne

wicked acts, until the sacrosanct seed of Mary came to mankind, the seed in which God had promised all nations would be blessed. We see that these divine promises of almighty God were fulfilled when Jesus appeared to the human race, propagated and brought to light by a virgin mother from this noble line, as we have clearly stated. Writing to the Galatians, the apostle Paul appears to state this in these words, "But when the fullness of time had come, God sent His Son, born of a woman, made under the Law, to redeem those who were under the Law," etc.[6]

Toward the beginning of his book, the prophet Isaiah had long 6 before foretold this precious and wonderful virgin, predicting her in this way, "Behold a virgin shall conceive and bear a son, and his name will be called[7] Emmanuel," which means "God with us."[8] And soon thereafter, he says, "There shall come forth a rod out of the stem of Jesse, and a flower will grow from his root," etc.[9] She is the rod (*virga*) or rather virgin (*virgo*) who came from the root of Jesse, and traced her descent from a royal and priestly line. This most holy virgin had already been betrothed to one Joseph, a virtuous and chaste pauper who spent his life laboriously hewing and fashioning wood, even though he was noble and traced his descent from ancient patriarchs and kings.

God duly forewarned this holy and noble virgin—who was 7 chosen, as we said, from the entire race of the Hebrews—of her divine conception and coming childbirth; and He did so through the angel, or rather the archangel Gabriel, more suitably and aptly than through any other angel of any other order:[10] for translated from Hebrew into Latin, his name plainly and clearly means "God's strength."[11] Although the works of the Trinity seem indivisible, as our theologians attest, this work of incarnation and creation is more appropriately ascribed to God's omnipotence and paternal power than to the other divine persons, and rightly so. For she seemed to draw her origins from patriarchs and kings for the reason that divine law forbade any woman who was entitled to

ulla mulier ad quam patris hereditas pertineret, quemadmodum
Mariae contingebat, quoniam pater eius masculis carebat, viro
alienae tribus nuberet.

8   Si igitur Iosephum Mariae virum ab ipso David generis originem traduxisse cognovimus, ceu ex maiorum suorum cathalogo
—quos singillatim Mattheus et Lucas evangelistae magna cum
diligentia recensuerunt—palam et aperte deprehenditur, ob praedictam apud Hebraeos legem de mulieribus non alienis sed cogna-
tis et gentilibus nubendis, Mariam e davitica stirpe descendisse
manifestum est. Quocirca cum memoratus evangelista Hebraeus
ad Hebraeos hebraice, ut ab eis rogatus fuerat, evangelium conscri-
beret ac veteri inter Hebraeos consuetudine Mariae mentionem
in genealogia Salvatoris facere prohiberetur, quoniam cavebatur
ne generationum cathalogus per feminas texeretur, clanculum et
speciose admodum per virorum genealogias virginis originem—
servatis Hebraeorum moribus—deprehendi concupivit et voluit.
Quod quidem Lucas, eius vestigia—utpote primi Evangeliorum
scriptoris—postea imitatus, asserere et confirmare non dubitavit.

9   Paulus quoque apostolus Christum ex semine David secundum
carnem factum esse testatur. Unde Mariam de stirpe David aliquam consanguinitatem duxisse dubitare non possumus. Cuius
quidem semine, quoniam nec sacerdotale genus tacetur, insinuante
Luca quod cognata eius esset Elisabeth, quam dicit de filiabus
Aaron, firmiss⟨im⟩e tenendum est carnem Christi ex utroque genere propagatam et regum et sacerdotum, in quibus personis apud
populum Hebraeorum mystica unctio figurabatur, id est chrisma,
unde Christi nomen elucet, tanto etiam ante ista evidentissima
10   significatione praenuntiatum. Unguento namque perfundi regiae
ac sacerdotalis potestatis insigne apud Hebraeos erat, ut quomodo apud nos diadema et purpura solis imperatoribus dabatur
sic apud Hebraeos regnaturi sacerdotioque functuri perfundeban-
tur unguento, ex quo 'christi' appellabantur, hoc est uncti. Proinde
et Cyrum Persarum regem et Saul quoque 'christos' in sacris litteris

inherit from her father—which was the case with Mary, since her father had no sons—to marry a man from another tribe.

Now we know that Mary's husband Joseph traced his descent 8 from David, as is discovered clearly and openly from the catalog of his ancestors, which the evangelists Mark and Luke reviewed in careful detail.[12] So it is clear in view of the aforementioned Jewish law by which women must not wed outsiders, but kinsmen and clansmen, that Mary was descended from David's tribe. When the Jews asked the Jewish evangelist [Mark] to write his Gospel in Hebrew, he was forbidden to mention Mary in the Savior's genealogy, since ancient Jewish custom prohibited the citation of women in ancestral catalogs. Hence, while observing Jewish customs, he wished and chose, quite stealthily and gracefully, to let the reader infer the virgin's origins from the genealogies of men. Later Luke followed in the footsteps of Mark, the first writer of Gospels, and did not hesitate to assert and confirm this.

The apostle Paul also attests that Christ in the flesh was con- 9 ceived from the seed of David.[13] Hence, we cannot doubt that Mary derived a degree of kinship from the line of David. In this seed, the priestly race is also mentioned, since Luke implies that Mary's cousin was Elizabeth,[14] who he says descended from Aaron's daughters.[15] Hence we must firmly believe that Christ's flesh on both sides sprang from kings and priests; and among the Jews their persons were represented by a mystical anointing, or chrism, which lends splendor to Christ's name, heralded so much earlier in that manifest meaning. Among the Jews, being anointed with oil 10 was a badge of royal and priestly power: just as we give a diadem and purple robes only to emperors, so the Jews poured ointment on those who were to rule or serve as priests, who were hence called *christi*, or "anointed ones."[16] Thus, in the Holy Scriptures we read that both the Persian king Cyrus and Saul were called

legimus appellatos; et in eodem sanctarum scripturarum campo 'Nolite tangere christos meos' et cetera huiusmodi scriptum esse conspicimus.

11   Et ne in laudationem huius divinae virginis oratione nostra longius progrediamur, alienis ac paucis laudibus suis, ne nimii simus, contenti erimus, quemadmodum a Sedulio poeta elegantissime simul atque verissime dictum est, quod sacrosancta mater ecclesia publicis orationibus suis in hunc modum approbasse videtur: 'Salve sancta parens enixa puerpera regem' et quae sequuntur. Haec est enim illa virgo quae a prophetis quidem praenuntiata, a patriarchis figuris et aenigmatibus praesignata, ab evangelistis exhibita et monstrata, ab angelo demum venerabiliter atque officiosissime salutata fuisse narratur. Haec est, inquam, illa virgo quae absque peccato originali a nonnullis claris novellisque doctoribus pie admodum concepta existimatur et creditur. Haec est denique illa virgo quae post mortem suam una cum corpore—mirabile dictu—ab angelicis spiritibus assumpta ad caelos usque

12   transcendit. De hoc sanctissimo beatae virginis corpore antequam assumetur Dionysius Areopagita, in libro *De divinis nominibus* loquens, verba haec ponit: 'Namque et apud ipsos divino spiritu plenos pontifices nostros cum et nos, ut nosti, et plerique ex sanctis fratribus nostris ad contuendum corpus illud quod auctorem vitae Deumque coeperat convenissemus, aderat autem et frater Domini, Iacobus, et Petrus, supremum decus et antiquissimum theologorum columen. Deinde post contuitum placuit ut infinite potentem divinae infirmitatis bonitatem pontifices laudarent omnes quisque pro captu suo' et reliqua huiusmodi. Si quis vero haec

13   quae dicta sunt forte admirabilia atque incredibilia fuisse arbitraretur, omnem profecto illam admirationem suam una cum titubatione relinqueret quandocumque eam ipsam, cui admirabilia et incredibilia ista attributa cernuntur, veram omnipotentis Dei matrem exstitisse vel parumper consideraverit, quod quidem et

christi.[17] And in the same realm of holy writings we find phrases like "Do not touch my anointed," and similar expressions.[18]

Lest we discourse too long in praising the divine virgin, we shall 11 content ourselves with a few laudations by others, to avoid prolixity. For example, the poet Sedulius described what Holy Mother Church approves in her liturgies, writing with great elegance as well as great truthfulness in these words: "Hail, holy mother delivered of a king in childbirth," etc.[19] This is the virgin heralded by the prophets, presaged by the patriarchs in symbols and mysteries, expounded and revealed by the evangelists, and finally hailed with great veneration and deference by the angel. This is the virgin, I say, who was conceived without original sin, as theologians, both famous ones and more recent, piously hold and believe.[20] In sum, this is the virgin who, after her death, was taken up by angelic spirits together with her body—wondrous to say!—and ascended into heaven.[21] Speaking about the most holy body of the blessed 12 virgin before her assumption, Dionysius the Areopagite in his book *On the Divine Names* writes, "Now, as you know, together with our divinely inspired priests, several of our holy brothers and I had gathered to contemplate the body which had taken in God, the Author of life; and there were present James, the Lord's brother, and Peter, the highest glory and most ancient pillar of theologians. And after contemplating it, we decided that all the priests would praise the infinitely powerful goodness of the divine weakness, as each was capable," etc.[22] If anyone considers what we 13 have said to be wondrous and incredible, he will completely abandon his wonder and doubt if he even briefly considers that the woman credited with such wondrous and incredible things was the true mother of almighty God, something that we deem more

admirabilius et incredibilius ac ceteris omnibus dignitatibus suis
longe praeferendum esse censemus.

14   Deus itaque Mariam per hunc modum ideo admonuisse visus
est ne forte harum rerum ignara virgo ob tantum ac prorsus tam
incredibile miraculum subito obstupesceret, nisi divino prius oraculo admoneretur. Facile enim fieri poterat ut tanti ignara secreti
aliquid de se crudele decerneret et quantum honestatis amatrix
tantum infamiae et turpitudinis impatiens vel ad laqueum subito
vel ad gladium convolaret vel saltem animo ac mente consterna-
retur, atqui illum uterum ab omni perturbatione alienum fore
15   oportebat quem hominum creator ingressurus erat. Decebat quoque illam animam a cunctis alienarum cogitationum tumultibus
abhorrere quae tanti electa fuerat ministra mysterii. Angelus igitur,
virgine angelica prius salutatione impartita, filium quemdam post
divinam eius conceptionem, ut sibi iniunctum erat, opportuno
tempore parituram plane et aperte denuntiavit, qui quoniam humanum genus ex prisca hominis transgressione damnatum exinde
redimeret; idcirco proprio nomine Iesus appellaretur, quod latine
'Salvatorem' significat. Atque hoc ego sacrosanctum Dei nomen in
Hebraea potius quam vel in Graeca vel in Latina vel in alia quamvis lingua commemorari debuisse arbitror, quoniam speciosius ac
decentius in sacro quam in profano idiomate sanctum nomen
16   nuncupari oportebat. Lingua vero Hebraea sancta vulgo appellatur
vel quod Deus ea lingua—ut aiunt—primum hominem fuerit af-
fatus vel quod sacra legis et prophetarum eloquia illis litteris, utpote ceteris dignioribus, annotata fuisse cernantur. Unde etsi angelus hebraice—ut creditur—ad Mariam et Ioseph loqueretur,
verbo tamen Graeco vel Latino, si decentius fuisset, in Hebraeo
sermone commode et eleganter uti poterat. Ideo inquit nomen eius
non 'Soter' graece, non latine 'Salvator' sed 'Iesus' hebraice vocabitur, quod quidem angelum de caelo ab ipso Deo ad Iosephum de-
tulisse legimus.

wondrous and incredible than, and to be preferred to, all her other remarkable qualities.

Thus, God forewarned Mary in this way lest such a great   14 and incredible miracle suddenly stun the virgin, unaware of these things, unless she were warned by divine prophecy.[23] It could easily have happened that, ignorant of this great secret, Mary would have resolved to take cruel action against herself: enamored of her honor and unable to bear shameful disgrace, she might have had recourse to the noose or the sword, or at least have been confused in heart and mind, when in fact there should have been no disorder in her womb, which the Creator of mankind was soon to enter. Also, it was only fitting that the soul chosen as minister to   15 such a great mystery should be free from every disturbance of extraneous thoughts. So the angel, having first greeted the virgin with an angelic greeting, clearly and openly announced (as he was bidden) that at the right moment she would bear a Son after His divine conception. And since He would redeem the human race, condemned by man's ancient transgression, He would fittingly be called Jesus, a name that Latin translates as "Savior."[24] I thought it necessary to record God's sacrosanct name in Hebrew, rather than in Latin, Greek, or another language, since a holy name had to be expressed more gracefully and suitably in a holy language than in a profane one. The Hebrew language is commonly called holy either   16 because God addressed the first man in it (so they say), or because we see that the holy texts of the Law and the prophets were written in it, as more worthy than others. Thus, although we believe that the angel spoke to Mary and Joseph in Hebrew, he could easily and elegantly have used a Greek or Latin word, if it would have been more fitting, in his Hebrew speech. Therefore, he said, His name shall be called, not *Soter* in Greek or *Salvator* in Latin, but Jesus in Hebrew.[25] And this is how we read that the angel, sent from heaven by God, announced it to Joseph.[26]

17   Maria vero de his quae ab angelo audierat utpote impossibili-
bus, quod virum nullo umquam tempore cognoverat, vehementius
quam dici potest primitus admirata, ut postmodum de divinae
conceptionis forma certior facta est divinae voluntati nequaquam
repugnavit, siquidem nihil esse posse existimabat quod ab omnipotenti Deo vel facile fieri non posset. Haec enim et huiusmodi
'Ecce virgo concipiet et pariet filium' et quae sequuntur in propheta legerat, sed quemadmodum fieret legere non poterat quod
hominibus nondum revelatum angelicis scriptibus usque ad hanc
tam salubrem ac tam salutiferam annuntiationis diem servabatur,
18   quae quidem octavo kalendas aprilis exstiterat. Haec namque est
illa salutaris, felix ac beata et omnibus saeculis celebranda dies in
qua cuncti Christiani nominis cultores invicem gratulari, exsultare
et iubilare debent, quod ab angelis quotannis — hac ipsa humanae
salutis die — in caelis fieri non impie crediderim ut diem festum
celebrantes vicissim gratulentur, quoniam exinde initium humanae
redemptionis apparuit. Angelus autem, ubi ex humilibus respon-
sionis suae verbis — quae de se ancillam Domini, cum mater foret,
respondere non dubitavit — divinae voluntati consensisse ac per
hunc modum concepisse percepit, mox e conspectu eius evanuit.
19   De caelo namque Sanctus Dei Spiritus descendit sanctamque
virginem, cuius utero se insinuaret, elegit. Illa vero, divino spiritu
hausto repleta, concepit et sine ullo attractu viri repente virginalis
uterus intumuit. Atqui Maria ex hoc tam subito et tam repen-
tino angeli recessu sola in intimis domus suae penetralibus, ubi
huiusmodi annuntiationem devotissime susceperat, remotis arbitris secum animo revolvebat. Unde, cum inter cetera ab angelo de
Elisabeth cognata sua — Zachariae cuiusdam prophetae uxore —
admonita esset quod sexto iam mense in senectute sua, mirabile
dictu, sterilis concepisset, eam visere constituit. Proinde de Nazareth, quodam Galileae oppido, in montanam et editam Iudaeae

Now when Mary heard from the angel such impossibilities — 17
for she had never known a man[27] — at first she was astonished beyond words; but later, when she learned how the divine conception would take place, she in no way resisted the divine will,
knowing that almighty God could easily do anything.[28] She had
read in the prophet, "Behold, a virgin will conceive and bear a
son," and what follows.[29] But she could not read how this would
happen: for it had not yet been revealed to men in angelic writings, but was reserved for the salutary and saving day of the Annunciation, which was March 25.[30] This is the salutary, happy, and 18
blessed day destined to be celebrated throughout the centuries
when all the devotees of the Christian religion should exult, rejoice, and congratulate each other. I piously believe that the angels
in heaven do the same each year on this day of human salvation:
celebrating this holiday they congratulate each other because it
was the beginning of human redemption. As soon as the angel
perceived from the humble words of her reply — which, as a future
mother, the handmaid of the Lord did not hesitate to give about
herself — that she acceded to the divine will and in this way had
conceived, he soon vanished from her sight.

God's Holy Spirit descended from heaven, and chose to be im- 19
planted in the womb of this holy virgin. Filled with the divine
Spirit that she had absorbed, she conceived, and even without
contact with a man her virgin womb began to swell. After the
angel's sudden and immediate departure, Mary was now alone in
the inner chambers of her home, where she had devoutly received
the Annunciation, and pondered these things in her heart without
any witnesses. Among other things, Mary had learned from the
angel that her cousin Elizabeth, the wife of the prophet Zachariah,[31] formerly barren, had conceived in her old age — wondrous
to say! — and was in her sixth month; and so she decided to visit
her. Accordingly, she traveled from the town of Nazareth in Galilee to the lofty city in the mountains of Judea where Elizabeth

20   urbem, ubi illa degebat, visendi gratia perrexit. Itaque non a publico virginitatis pudor, non a studio asperitas montium, non ab
officio longitudo itineris retardavit, quae antea in intimis domus
suae penetralibus meditandi et orandi ac contemplandi causa ver-
sabatur. Ut autem domum suam ingressa salutem dedit, divinitus
factum est ut semestris infans ad salutantis Mariae verba — incredibile dictu — in materno utero exsultaret, quasi Deum in utero
virginis paulo ante conceptum veneraretur, et Elisabeth (divino
spiritu repleta) Mariam prae cunctis mulieribus beatam et bea-
tum fructum ventris sui hilarius exclamaret. Quo Maria audito,
in suavissimum illud hymnum 'Magnificat anima mea Dominum'
et reliqua divinae magnificentiae maiestatisque plenum confestim
prorupit, qui quotidie per quasquam terrarum orbis ecclesias ubique in plerisque canonicis solemnibusque horis a sacerdotibus de-
cantatur. Haec Mariae de Elisabeth cognata sua visitatio quotannis a militante ecclesia propria in visionis die celebratur atque
huiusmodi festivitas ab ipsa visitatione 'visitata' nuncupatur.

21   Cum intumescentem deinde uterum ubi post tres menses domum reversa est vir eius conspicaretur, de vitio virginis suspicari et
ita suspicari coepit ut eam dimittere cuperet. Dum haec igitur secum ipse cogitaret, ecce angelus in somnis apparuit cunctaque
quemadmodum gesta erant palam et aperte significavit ideoque
ne sponsam dimitteret ipsum etiam atque etiam admonivit. Non
multo post, imperante Augusto Caesare, quadragesimo secundo
imperii sui anno, iam tota Aegypto ex Antonii et Cleopatrae interitu in dicionem suam redacta ac paene toto orbe pacato, factum
est ut iuxta eius edictum universus mundus describeretur censere-
turque. Hoc propterea institutum erat ut cuncti homines in quadam tributi solutione Caesarem recognoscerent. Singuli igitur in
propria patria nomina sua profitebantur ac per hunc modum re-
22   censebantur. Haec prima census descriptio sub Cyrino[2] Syriae

lived, to pay her a visit. Mary had kept to the inner chambers of   20
her home in order to meditate, pray, and contemplate. But now
she was not deterred by virginal shame from public appearance,
nor by the harsh mountains from her zeal, nor by the long journey
from her duty. When she entered the house and greeted Elizabeth,
by divine prompting—incredible to relate!—the six-month-old
infant jumped up in its mother's womb at Mary's greeting, as if
worshiping God, conceived shortly before in the virgin's womb.
Then Elizabeth, filled with the divine spirit, joyfully exclaimed
that Mary was blessed above all women and that the fruit of her
womb was blessed.[32] When Mary heard this, at once she burst
forth in that sweet hymn "My soul does magnify the Lord," and
the rest of those words full of divine magnificence and majesty.[33]
Even now, priests daily sing this hymn in all the churches of the
world at various canonical and solemn hours. Mary's visitation of
her cousin Elizabeth is celebrated yearly by the militant church on
the day of the visit, and this festival is called the "Visitation," after
its original name.[34]

    Three months later, Mary returned home; and when her hus-   21
band saw the swelling of her womb, he began to suspect that the
virgin had been violated, and to suspect it so strongly that he
wished to send her away. While he pondered the situation, behold, an angel appeared to him in a dream, explicitly and openly
explaining how all these things had happened, and warning him
emphatically not to send his bride away.[35] Not long thereafter, in
the forty-second year of his reign, the emperor Caesar Augustus,
who had conquered all of Egypt after the death of Antony and
Cleopatra, and had brought peace to nearly the whole earth, issued an edict that the entire world should be registered in a census. Caesar took this measure so that all men would recognize him
by the payment of a certain tribute; and accordingly, individuals
declared their names in their homeland and were thus registered.
This first registration in a census took place under Cyrenus, the   22

praeside facta est. Quod sic esse Iosephus illustris Hebraeorum historicus commemorat. Ita enim decimo octavo *Antiquitatum* libro locutus est: 'Cyrinus vir unus ex consensu curiae Romanae per singulos magistratus ad gradum consulatus ascendens tandem ex imperio Caesaris ad Syriam venit, ut gentibus censum imponeret' et quae sequuntur. Huiusmodi igitur Caesaris edicto Iosephus et Maria parere cupientes in Bethlehem³ patriam suam profitendi gratia conscenderunt; in quo quidem itinere asinum simul atque bovem — alterum pro vectura virginis iam partu propinquae, alterum vero pro viatico, ne forte commeatus in via deficeret — secum eo usque conduxerunt ac tandem vicum intrarunt.

23   Sed cum iam cuncta illius vici diversoria, ob multitudinem illorum qui illuc profitendi gratia certatim concurrebant, referta essent, locum proprium ibidem reperire non potuerunt. Unde, necessitate quadam ingruente, tugurium quoddam satis ignobile satisque abiectum subire coacti sunt. Atque dum ibi una cum memoratis brutis suis morarentur, forte evenit ut Maria, appropinquante iam partu, in tam humili et tam abiecto loco inter bruta adeo stolida Filium Dei, sine aliquo corporis dolore vel potius cum magna voluptate, pareret. Integra enim et immaculata integrum et immaculatum filii sui corpus — mirabile dictu — in lucem edidit. Proinde, post eius adorationem, absque aliquo obstetricum ministerio, ceu nonnulli leves scriptores — haud impio errore ducti — memoriae prodidisse videntur, infantem in lucem editum propriis manibus ipsa suscepit pannisque involvit et reclinavit eum in praesaepio.

24   De hac ineffabili divini infantis nativitate iubilans sacrosancta Romana ecclesia ea ipse die cantare non cessat: 'Haec est dies quam fecit Dominus. Exsultemus et laetemur in ea.' De hoc itaque divino mysterio, quia prae magnitudine eius digne loqui non possimus, omnino tacere satius esse duximus quam pauca dixisse. Haec enim Domini nostri Salvatorisque nativitas usque adeo facultatem humani excedit eloquii ut merito ad utramque — divinam

governor of Syria. Josephus, the illustrious historian of the Jews, mentions the fact, writing in Book 18 of his *Jewish Antiquities*, "Cyrenus, one man who, with the senate's approval, had risen through various magistracies to the rank of consul, now went at Caesar's command to Syria to implement the census among the nations," etc.[36] Seeking to comply with the emperor's edict, Joseph and Mary went down to their native Bethlehem in order to be registered.[37] On their journey, they took with them a donkey and an ox—the first as a vehicle for the virgin, whose term was near, and the second as travel funds, in case their provisions ran out on the way—and at last they entered their village.

By now, all the inns of the village were filled by the multitude of 23 people who had eagerly hastened there to be registered, and they could find no proper lodging. Beset by necessity, they were forced to enter a very base and sordid hut. While they were staying there with their animals, it happened that Mary went into labor and, without any pain but rather with great pleasure, bore the Son of God among brute beasts in this humble and sordid place. Untouched and unstained, she brought forth—wondrous to say!— the untouched and unstained body of her son. Then, after adoring him, without the aid of a midwife—which some unreliable writers seem to have recorded, moved by a pious error[38]—she took up the newborn infant in her arms, wrapped him in swaddling clothes, and laid him in a manger.

Celebrating the ineffable nativity of the divine infant, the Holy 24 Roman Church never ceases to sing on its festival: "This is the day the Lord has made. Let us rejoice and be glad in it."[39] This divine mystery is of such magnitude that we cannot worthily discuss it, and so we have thought it better to remain silent rather than to say too little.[40] The nativity of our Lord and Savior so far exceeds the faculty of human eloquence that the words of the prophet

scilicet et humanam — naturam referatur quod per Esaiam[4] prophetam dictum est: 'Generationem eius quis enarrabit?' Nos itaque
divina illa omnino praetermissa de hac inferiore quae in terra facta
est quaeque testibus celebratur innumeris vix pauca dicere effarive
25 audemus. Haec namque nativitas omnem intelligentiam exsuperat
et cuncta naturalium natorum exempla transcendit. Nam antequam sponderetur virgo concepit; peperit antequam nuberet et
quod mirabilius est ac cuncta miracula excellit, et mater et virgo
cepit esse post partum. Virgo enim concepit, virgo peperit, virgo
post partum illibata permansit. De hoc eodem poeta sacrorum
carminum loquens sic inquit: 'Virgo Dei genitrix quem totus non
capit orbis / in tua se clausit viscera factus homo. / Vera fide geni-
tus purgavit crimina mundi / et tua virginitas inviolata manet.'
26 Natus est igitur caelestis puer in parvo quodam vico nomine Bethlehem (haec est enim illa Bethlehem idcirco 'sancta' a nostris non
immerito nuncupata quod mundi genuerit Salvatorem et generosis
quidem parentibus, ut supra diximus), natus primo humanae salutis anno, qui ab eius ortu salubritatis nomen accipiens in dies semper usque ad hunc quinquagesimum quartum supra millesimum
quandringentesimum maiori Christianorum populorum devotione
gloriosius perseverat; et natus est a creatione mundi centesimo
nonagesimo nono supra quinquies mille, ab Urbe vero condita
septingentesimo quinquagesimo secundo, olimpiade centesima no-
nagesima quarta.
27   In hoc sacrosancto divinae nativitatis loco non multo post am-
plum quoddam monasterium aedificatum esse constat, quod usque ad haec nostra tempora magna Christianorum populorum
celebritate perdurat. In eadem forte — ut fit — regione plerique pastores pascendi pecoris sui gratia versabantur. Quippe ob naturalem
quamdam terrae ariditatem arenarumque ubertatem in universa
paene regione illa nihil omnino frugum gignebatur ac propterea
cuncta plena pastoribus erant et variis pecudibus habundabant, ut
terrarum sterilitatem pecorum multitudine compensarent. Quod

Isaiah may justly be applied to its double nature, both divine and human, "Who shall declare his generation?"[41] So leaving aside the divine birth, we scarcely dare to say a little about the lesser birth that occurred on earth and is celebrated by countless witnesses. The Nativity surpasses all understanding and transcends all instances of natural births. For the virgin conceived before she was betrothed; she gave birth before she wed; and—what was is more marvelous and exceeds all miracles—she began to be both mother and virgin after childbirth. As a virgin she conceived, as a virgin she gave birth, and as a virgin she remained intact after childbirth. The poet of sacred poems writes about this in these words: "O Virgin Mother of God, He whom the whole world does not contain, enclosed Himself in your womb, being made man. Born in true faith, He cleansed the sins of the world, and your virginity remains inviolate."[42] Thus, the heavenly boy was born in a small village called Bethlehem. Our Latin writers justly call this Bethlehem "holy," because it gave birth to the Savior of the world, and one born of noble parents, as we said earlier. He was born in the first year of human salvation, a year that takes its name of salvation from His birth, and that each day—up to our year 1450— continues ever more gloriously in the increasing worship of Christian nations.[43] His birth took place in the year 5199 after the Creation of the world;[44] in the year 750 since the foundation of Rome; and in the 194th Olympiad.

25

26

Not much later, we learn, a large monastery was built on the most sacred site of the divine nativity, which survives even today amid great crowds of Christian peoples. In that same region, as is usual, several shepherds were attending to the feeding of their flocks. Given the natural dryness of the soil and the abundance of sands, nearly the entire region produced no crops, and for that reason there were shepherds everywhere and abundant flocks, so that the multitude of livestock offset the barrenness of the land.

27

sic esse et Amos Tecuites,[5] unus ex duodecim prophetis qui pastor exstiterat, ex oppido Tecuae[6] oriundus, plane et aperte declarat. Id profecto oppidum non plus quam sex circiter milibus passuum a commemorata Salvatoris nostri patria distabat. Huiusmodi igitur
28 pastores greges suos, partitis inter se vigiliis, custodiebant. Itaque innumera quaedam angelorum multitudo humani generis Salvatorem cum magna exsultatione ac iubilatione illis pastoribus natum denuntiaverunt. Clamabant enim: 'Gloria in altissimis Deo et in terra pax hominibus bonae voluntatis.' Hunc Hieronymus noster in quodam Hebraicarum quaestionum libro illum locum esse testatur in quo Iacob, post mortem atque humationem Rachel uxoris suae de Bethlehem egressus, tabernacula—pascendi gregis sui causa—fixerat; quem locum Hebraei 'trans turrem eder' hebraice, hoc est gregis videlicet congregationis et coetus, propterea vocaverunt, quasi ibidem futuros angelorum greges vaticinarentur, id quod iam tunc mysterio aliquot ante annorum milibus monstrabatur.
29 Pastores autem huiusmodi clamoribus magno primum pavore perterriti, ut paulo post ab ipsis angelicis nuntiis signa divinae voluntatis acceperunt, extemplo usque in Bethlehem perrexerunt, ut hunc Dei filium paulo ante natum etiam atque etiam intuerentur. Eo usque igitur accedentes, infantem in praesaepio iacentem—quemadmodum ab angelis nuper acceperant—cum parentibus invenerunt. Quocirca quicumque eos haec et cetera huiusmodi postea referentes audiebant vehementer admirabantur; omni siquidem admiratione plenissimum erat et super spem exspectationemque mortalium videbatur quod Deus humanam carnem suscepisset e caelisque, ut cum hominibus salutis suae causa conversaretur, in terras descendisset.
30 Atque haec omnia superius a nobis commemorata Sedulius poeta his verbis eleganter expressit:

Haec ventura senes postquam praedixere prophetae
angelus intactae cecinit properata Mariae

This is plainly and openly declared by Amos the Tekoite, the only shepherd among the twelve prophets and a native of Tekoa,[45] a town located just six miles from the birthplace of our Savior.[46] Such shepherds guarded their flocks, watching by turns at night. To these shepherds, then, an innumerable host of angels proclaimed the birth of the Savior of the human race with great exultation and jubilation.[47] They cried out, "Glory to God in the highest, and on earth peace to men of goodwill."[48] In his book *Jewish Questions*, our own Jerome cites the place where Jacob, after the death and burial of his wife Rachel, left Bethlehem and pitched a tent for feeding his flock.[49] In Hebrew, the Jews called this place "beyond the tower of Eder" — meaning the tower of the "flock, congregation, or assembly" — as if they were prophesying that there would be hosts of angels in that place, a fact that was revealed in a mystery some thousand years earlier.[50] The shepherds were at first frightened with great fear by these exclamations, but they soon accepted the signs of God's will from the angelic messengers, and at once they set forth for Bethlehem to gaze intently upon the newborn son of God. When they approached, they found the infant lying in a manger, as they had heard from the angels, with His parents. All those who afterward heard them relating these and other events were greatly astounded. For that God had assumed human flesh, and had descended from heaven to earth to dwell among men for their salvation, filled everyone with astonishment and exceeded the hopes and expectations of mortals.[51]

Everything we have related has been elegantly expressed by the poet Sedulius:

After the prophets of old had predicted these future events,
The angel sang of their approach to the Virgin Mary;

28

29

30

et dictum comitata fides uterumque puellae
sidereum mox implet onus rerumque creator
nascendi sub lege fuit; stupet innuba tensos
virgo sinus gaudetque suum paritura parentem.
Iamque novem lapsis decimi de limine mensis
fulgebat sacrata dies cum virgine feta
promissum complevit opus: 'verbum caro factum,'
in nobis habitare volens. Tunc maximus infans
intemerata sui conservans viscera templi
illaesum vacuavit iter pro virgine testis
partus adest, clausa ingrediens et clausa relinquens.
Quae nova lux mundo, quae toto gratia caelo!
Quis fuit ille nitor Mariae cum Christus ab alvo
processit splendore novo velut ipse decoro
sponsus ovans thalamo, forma speciosus amoena
prae natis hominum, cuius radiante figura
blandior in labiis diffusa est gratia pulchris.
O facilis pietas! Ne nos servile teneret
peccato damnante iugum servilia summus
membra tulit Dominus primique ab origine mundi
omnia qui propriis vestit nascentia donis
obsitus exiguis habuit velamina pannis.
Quemque procellosi non mobilis unda profundi
terrarum non omne solum speciosaque lati
non capit aula poli, puerili in corpore plenus
mansit et angusto Deus in praesaepe quievit.
Salve sancta parens, enixa puerpera regem,
qui caelum terramque tenet per saecula, cuius
numen aeterno complectens omnia gyro

And with her faith attending the word, a heavenly weight
Soon filled the maiden's womb, and the Creator of the world
Was subject to the law of birth. The unwed virgin marveled
At her distended lap and rejoiced to give birth to her Begetter.
And so after nine months fell, on the threshold of the tenth,
The sacred day shone forth when the pregnant virgin
Fulfilled that promised work, "the Word made flesh,"
That chooses to dwell among us. Then the great infant,
Leaving the innards of His temple intact,
Cleared his path unharmed as a witness to virginity.
His birth arrives, entering what was closed, and leaving it
   closed behind.
What new light for the world, what grace for all heaven!
What brilliance there was when from Mary's womb
Christ came forth in new splendor, just as from his glorious
Wedding chamber a joyful bridegroom,
Whose charming aspect makes him handsome
Beyond the children of men; and as His figure shone,
A milder grace was spread over His fair lips!
O generous mercy! Lest a slave's yoke hold us fast
Through our damning sin, the supreme Lord bore a servile
   body,
And He who since the Creation has clothed the nascent world
   in His gifts
Was wrapped in scanty rags that covered Him.
Though neither the stormy sea's tossing waves,
Nor all the earth's soil, nor yet broad heaven's fair palace
Could contain Him, He dwelt whole in a child's body,
And rested, our God, in a cramped manger.
Hail, holy mother, who in childbirth produced a king
Who eternally rules heaven and earth, whose divine power,
Embracing all in an eternal circle, abides,

imperium sine fine manet, quae ventre beato
gaudia matris habens cum virginitatis honore
nec primam similem visa est nec habere sequentem.
Sola sine exemplo placuisti femina Christo.
Tunc prius ignaris pastoribus ille creator
enituit quia pastor erat gregibusque refulsit
agnus et angelicus cecinit miracula coetus.

31   Parentes vero postea octavo nativitatis suae die iuxta legem infantem circumciderunt ac nomen eius Iesum vocaverunt, quod vocatum ab angelo fuerat priusquam nasceretur. Id nomen Hebraeo sermone—ut antea diximus—'Salvatorem' significat. Haec igitur duo praedicta (Emanuel et Iesus) nomina alterum a propheta alterum ab angelo mirabiliter profecto ac divinitus praenuntiata fuisse videmus, ut qui Emanuel (hoc est 'nobiscum Deus') antea futurus erat postea Iesus (id est 'Salvator') foret eo quod universum humanarum genus salvaturus esset. Praedictis duobus nominibus evangelista non immerito tertium adiecit; nam 'Christum' appellavit, non quia veteri Hebraeorum ritu in regem vel in sacerdotem ungeretur, sed quoniam Spiritus Sanctus id purificaverat quod de Maria virgine in corpus Salvatoris assumpserat. Quod autem olim per unctionem praestabat Deus illis qui in reges vel in sacerdotes ungebantur, hoc illi homini—expiatione addita—Spiri-

32   tum Sanctum praestitisse cognovimus. Plura enim unguentorum genera quondam in sacris litteris fuisse legimus; variis quippe unguentorum generibus sacerdotes, reges et prophetae ungebantur. Nam primo in *Exodo* chrisma sacerdotale conficitur, quo postea sacerdotes in *Levitico* 'uncti' referebantur. Erat et aliud unguentum quo in ungendis et Saul et David et Salomone ac ceteris eorum regibus utebantur. Chrisma insuper propheticum exstabat, quo et prophetae ungi videbantur. Sic enim Elias Helisaeum, ut sibi iniunctum fuerat, in prophetam unxisse scribitur. At vero super

An empire without end. By your blessed womb,
You know a mother's joys and a virgin's honor,
Having no woman as precedent or successor.
A woman without parallel, you alone pleased Christ.
Then the Creator first shone forth to unwitting shepherds,
Himself a shepherd, and gleamed before his flock as a lamb,
While an angelic host sang these miracles.[52]

On the eighth day after His birth, the parents had the child 31
circumcised according to the law, and called His name Jesus,
which the angel had called Him before He was born.[53] As we said
earlier, in Hebrew the name means "Savior." We see that the two
names Emmanuel and Jesus were miraculously and divinely heralded, the one by the prophet, the other by the angel: for the man
who was previously to be Emmanuel (that is, "God with us")
would later be Jesus (that is, "Savior"), because He would save the
entire human race.[54] To these two names, the evangelist justly
added a third, calling him "Christ," not because he was anointed as
king or priest by ancient Jewish rite, but because the Holy Spirit
had purified what was taken into the Savior's body from the virgin Mary.[55] We know that what God once granted by anointing
to those who were anointed kings and priests was granted by
the Holy Spirit to this man, together with atonement. Now we 32
read in the Holy Scriptures that there were several kinds of ointments: for in fact, priests, kings, and prophets were anointed with
different ointments. First, a priestly chrism is used in Exodus,[56]
by virtue of which later in Leviticus priests were referred to as
anointed.[57] There was another ointment used in anointing Saul,
David, Solomon, and their other kings. There was also a pro-
phetical chrism with which prophets, it seems, were anointed.
Thus it is written that Elijah anointed Elisha as prophet, as he
had been commanded to do.[58] Yet above all these kinds of oint-

omnia haec unguentorum genera spirituale quoddam unguentum
erat, quo quidem Salvatorem divinitus unctum fuisse intelligimus
et 'oleum exsultationis' appellabatur. Unde ad eum sic dicitur:
'Propterea unxit te Deus, Deus tuus, oleo exsultationis prae parti-
cipibus tuis.'

33   Prius vero quam haec agerentur, stella quaedam in caelis
aperta luce claruit, quam cum omnes mediis diebus praeter communem stellarum consuetudinem illucescentem conspicere⟨n⟩t
(erat quippe illustrior ceteris pulchriorque sideribus atque propterea facile in se intuentium oculos animosque converterat) ingenti
ac paene incredibili admiratione supra quam dici potest tenebantur
quod quidquid portenderet—aliquid enim magnum portendere
arbitrabantur—nequaquam intelligebant. Hanc stellam invisibilem quamdam divinamque virtutem Iohannes Chrysostomus in
specie tamen stellae, ut videretur, apparentem quodam loco scribens fuisse testatur. At reges quidam Orientis, qui sive ob sapientiae suae magnitudinem sive quod ex Magorum gente oriundi
essent 'Magi' appellabantur, hanc tam inusitatam et tam admirabilem stellam divinam Filii Dei nativitatem soli ex omnibus portendere cognoverunt, quoniam a Balaam—vetustissimo quodam
propheta—genus suum ab origine traducebant, a quo stellam
quamdam ex Iacob oriundam iamdiu prophetatum esse constabat.
Quam cum extra ceterarum stellarum ordinem conspexissent, eam
nimirum fore intelligebant unde Iudaeorum regis nativitas ex illa
veteri maioris sui prophetia tam manifeste ac tam aperte portende-
retur.

34   Hos Magos sive sapientes sive reges alii Chaldaeos alii Persas
exstitisse, alii a Balaam veteri propheta descendisse tradiderunt.
Hos, inquam, Magos veteres catholicae ecclesiae doctores sapientes
quosdam Chaldaeorumque philosophos, moderni autem et sapientes et reges fuisse existimarunt, quod in regionibus illis antiquitus sapientes dumtaxat regnare viderentur. Sed quicumque tandem

ments there was a sort of spiritual ointment, with which we understand that the Savior was divinely anointed, and it was called the "oil of gladness." Hence, He was told, "Therefore God, your God, has anointed you with the oil of gladness above your companions."[59]

Before this happened, a star shone forth brightly in the sky, which everyone could see shining at midday, unlike any common star: for being more splendid and beautiful than the other stars, it easily attracted the eyes and minds of all who beheld it. With immeasurable and nearly incredible amazement, they were ineffably transfixed because they could not grasp what it portended, for they deemed that it surely portended something great. Writing in one of his works, John Chrysostom asserts that this star was an invisible and divine force appearing so as to be seen in the form of a star.[60] Certain kings of the Orient called Magi—either because of their great learning, or because they came from the nation of the Magi—were the only ones anywhere who recognized that this most unusual and marvelous star portended the divine birth of God's son. They traced their race from the ancient prophet Balaam, who was known to have prophesied long ago that a star would descend from Jacob.[61] So when they beheld this extraordinary star, they grasped that it manifestly and openly portended the nativity of the king of the Jews according to the old prophecy of their ancestor.

Some have said that these Magi—whether wise men or kings—were Chaldeans, others that they were Persians; others said that they descended from the ancient prophet Balaam. Now, the ancient doctors of the Catholic Church thought that these Magi were certain wise men and philosophers of the Chaldeans, whereas the moderns think they were both wise men and kings, since in ancient times in these lands only wise men were seen to reign.

33

34

hii fuerunt, Orientales fuisse manifestum est, ut his verbis poeta ille testatur:

> Talia Bethleis dum signa geruntur in oris
> Eoi venere Magi saevumque tyrannum
> grandia sollicitis perturbant nuntia dictis.

Et alius poeta: 'Gens est,' inquit,

> ulterior surgenti conscia soli
> astrorum sollers ortus obitusque notare;
> huius primores nomen tenuere Magorum.
> Hinc lecti proceres Solymos per vaga viarum
> Deveniunt regemque adeunt

et quae sequuntur.

35   Ubi ergo dignissimi viri huiusmodi stellae signum viderunt quae per multum tempus ante apparuerat—si enim quando divinus puer natus est in Palaestina tunc illis stella apparuisset in Perside plurimum in itinere temporis contrivissent ac per hoc nequaquam illum adhuc in pannis involutum invenire potuissent, quemadmodum ad maiorem admirabilioris miraculi evidentiam adorari oportebat—extemplo cum regalibus apparatibus e patria moverunt ut stellam itineris sui ductricem sequerentur. At stella illa paulo eos dedita opera praecedebat, ne forte e recta via aberrarent, nisi eam antecedentem continue vidissent donec ad signum suum quotidie tendentes vergerent.

36   Ut igitur Magi in Iudaeam applicuerunt amplius stellam non prospiciebant, quod ideo contingebat ut certo quodam itineris sui duce amisso in regiam urbem Hierosolymam infantis percontandi gratia contendere cogerentur, quoniam vel regiam urbem opportunum regiae nativitatis locum esse opinabantur vel saltem ubi puer natus esset neminem Hierosolymitanum propemodum ignorare arbitrabantur. Hoc autem propterea fiebat ut tanti ac singularis

Whoever they were, they were clearly from the East, as the poet attests in these words,

> As these portents were borne in the regions of Bethlehem,
> The Magi arrived from the East, and their weighty reports
> Troubled the savage tyrant with disturbing news.[62]

And another poet writes,

> There is a distant race privy to the sun's rising,
> Skilled at recording the rising and setting of the stars,
> Whose ancestors had the name of Magi.
> Their chosen leaders arrive by wandering routes
> At Jerusalem and approach the king,[63]

and so forth.

So when these worthy men saw the sign of the star, which had   35
appeared in the distant past, they at once set forth from their
country in royal garments, following the star as the guide of their
journey. For if the star had appeared to them in Persia when the
divine child was born in Palestine, they would have spent a long
time traveling, and could not have found the child wrapped in
swaddling clothes, as they had to worship Him as a greater proof
of the marvelous miracle. And by design the star went a little
ahead of them, so that they would not stray from the right way, if
they did not continually see it go before, until heading toward
their sign each day, they reached the end of the journey.

Now, when the Magi arrived in Judea, they no longer saw the   36
star: for it happened that they had lost the reliable guide for their
journey and were forced to enter the royal city of Jerusalem to
make inquiries about the child. (Either they thought that the royal
city was a suitable place for a royal birth, or they believed that everyone in Jerusalem would know where the child had been born.)
Hence it was that the birth of this Child, who was both the great

tam Iudaeorum regis simul atque omnipotentis Dei Filii nativitas cunctis regiae urbis incolis ac civibus primum manifestaretur. Paulatim deinde fama—ut fit—in dies crebrescente ubique apud Iudaeos vulgaretur, ne forte ullam perfidiae suae excusationem postea habere possent.

37   At ubi huiusmodi Orientis reges Hierosolymam applicuerunt, magno quodam inveniendi infantis fervore perciti, ubinam rex Iudaeorum natus esset vulgo percontabantur. Postea vero quam Herodes, Antipatris Ascalonitae et matris Cypridis Arabicae filius, qui eo tempore pro Caesare Augusto Romanorum imperatore in Iudaea regnabat, Magos in Hierosolymam ut Iudaeorum regem nuperrime natum quaererent de longinquis Orientis partibus adventasse cognovit, cum complicibus suis illico ingenti dolore corripitur, quod per hanc regis Iudaeorum nativitatem regnum suum amissum iri verebatur, quoniam ipse peregrinus alienigenaque primum in Iudaea regnare videbatur. Iudaeorum enim regnum sub propriae gentis principibus—hoc est iudicibus primo, deinde regibus, postremo pontificibus—a Moyse usque ad imperium praedicti Augusti gubernatum fuisse apparebat. Ipse vero Herodes, sive Idumeus, ut Iosephus, sive Ascalonita, ut Africanus tradit, quicumque tandem fuerit, primus exterae gentis—ex senatus consulto Augusto imperante—Iudaeorum regnum susceperat.

38   Quocirca pontifices et scribas populi—qui ceteris sapientiores habebantur—in unum congregavit locumque ab eis regiae nativitatis sciscitatus, ubi illum in Bethlehem esse percepit Magos clanculum ad se accivit, ne populus ea quae a Magis vulgo dicebantur regem magnificare suspicaretur ac propterea regis dignitas contemneretur neve Iudaei protectorem et salvatorem suum et ad liberationem illius gentis ortum, ut sacra prophetarum eloquia testabantur, quemadmodum a sapientibus suis audiverat, si forte 39 (ut cupiebat) persequens caperet, e suis manibus eriperent. Ideoque eos—ut diximus—ad se accitos, tempus stellae quae apparuerat paulo accuratius percontabatur, ut certa quadam loci simul

and extraordinary King of the Jews and the Son of almighty God, was first made known to all the inhabitants and citizens of the royal city. As often happens, the rumor gradually grew each day and spread everywhere among the Jews, so that later they could find no excuse for their perfidy.

When the kings of the East had reached Jerusalem, they were   37
stirred by a great passion for finding the child, and asked everyone where the king of the Jews had been born. At that time, the Roman emperor Caesar Augustus had chosen Herod, the son of Antipater of Ascalon and Cypris of Arabia, to rule in Judea on his behalf. When he learned that the Magi had come from the distant Orient to find the newborn king of the Jews, he, together with his attendants, was at once seized by immeasurable distress: for he feared that the birth of a king of the Jews would cause him to lose his kingdom, since he was the first to reign in Judea as a foreigner and stranger.[64] We see that the kingdom of the Jews was governed by rulers of their own nation—first by judges, then by kings, and finally by high priests—from Moses to the empire of Augustus. Herod, who was either from Idumea (according to Josephus)[65] or Ascalon (according to Africanus)[66]—whoever he was in the end— was the first of a foreign race to take up the rule of the Jews by the senate's decree under Augustus.

As a result, Herod assembled the priests and scribes of the   38
people, who were considered wiser than the others, and asked them the site of this royal birth. Having learned that it was Bethlehem, he sent for the Magi in secret, lest the people suspect that the king was attaching importance to the public statements of the Magi, and therefore despise the king's dignity; or lest the Jews— should Herod pursue and capture Him, as he longed to do— snatch from his hands their protector and Savior and the one born for the liberation of that race, as the sacred words of the prophets attest, as he had heard from his own sages. Therefore, having sent   39
for the Magi, as we said, he carefully inquired about the time of

atque temporis regiae nativitatis cognitione habita opportuno postea tempore infantem regem facilius, ut cupiebat, interimere posset; quos cum aperte, sicut viderant, interroganti Herodi de nativitatis loco[7] respondissent in Bethlehem, inde admonitos abire permisit. Id enim oppidum regiae nativitatis locum cognoverunt. Repente inde egredientes, versus Bethlehem contenderunt, ubi infantem natum esse acceperunt.

40   Ut vero regia urbe egressi sunt, antecedentem stellam — mirabile dictu — subito respexerunt, quam cum vidissent dici non potest quanto et quam singulari gaudio propterea replerentur, quod certum itineris sui ductorem — quem iam amisisse putabant — tam insperato ac tam opportuno tempore recuperassent. Itaque manifestum huius stellae suae indicium usque consequebantur donec supra domum ubi natus erat puer fixa stabilisque restaret, quod nisi ab evangelista dictum esset quis crederet stellam tam modicae parvitatis esse posse quae mansione sua tam parvulum tugurium propalam indicaret, cum astrologorum omnium consensu quaeque stellarum minima maior tota terra feratur? Ideoque illi de invisibili Dei virtute Chrysosthomi sententiae libenter assentior, ut in exitu

41   Israhel de Aegypto per columnam nubis contigisse legimus. Magi igitur hanc stellae stationem conspicati, quasi tacitam quamdam eius locutionem animadvertentes, in eam domum intrarunt quae eius indicio portendi videbatur. Ibi infantem cum Maria, matre eius, invenerunt, quem ut viderunt statim adorandi gratia in terram prociderunt ac per hunc modum summa quadam devotione primum adorarunt. Ei deinde, utpote immortali Deo in mortali[8] carne regnanti, aurum, thus et mirram, sua quique pretiosa munera de longinquis Orientis partibus usque delata, libentissime simul atque devotissime obtulerunt.

42   Haec munerum sacramenta pulcherrime Iuvencus[9] presbyter Hispanus, qui hexametris versibus evangelia composuit, uno versiculo comprehendit:

the star that had appeared so that if he knew with certainty the time and place of the royal birth, he could more easily kill the child-king at the opportune time, as he desired. When Herod asked them about the time of the birth, they openly replied what they had seen, and about the place of the nativity they replied, "Bethlehem"—for they knew that this town would be the site of the royal birth—and he allowed them to go with a warning.[67] Setting forth at once, they made for Bethlehem, where they believed that the child had been born.

As they left the royal city—wondrous to say!—they suddenly   40 saw the guiding star again and, upon seeing it, were filled with great and singular joy that cannot be described: for at this unexpected and opportune time they recovered this reliable guide for their journey, which they thought they had lost.[68] They now followed the clear sign of this star until it stopped, fixed and unmoving, over the dwelling where the child had been born. If the evangelist had not said so,[69] who would believe that the star was so tiny that its stopping could clearly indicate such a small hut? For all astronomers agree that even the smallest of stars is larger than the whole earth. Hence, I gladly concur with the view of John Chrysostom's *On God's Invisible Power*,[70] for we read that it befell Israel to leave Egypt in the Exodus led by a pillar of cloud.[71] When the   41 Magi saw the star stopped, and noted this as a sort of silent statement, they entered the dwelling that the star seemed to portend. There they found the child with His mother Mary, and as soon as they had seen Him fell at once to the ground to worship Him, and in this way first worshiped Him with the greatest devotion. Then they gladly and devoutly offered Him gold, incense, and myrrh— each his own precious gifts of the distant East—as the immortal God reigning in mortal flesh.[72]

The Spanish presbyter Juvencus, who set the Gospels in hex-   42 ameters, described these sacramental gifts elegantly in a single verse:

Thus aurum murram regi hominique deoque
dona ferunt,

quod sacri doctores nostri exponentes Magos veram[10] (divinam
scilicet et humanam) naturam regalibus insignibus redimitam muneribus suis venerari voluisse testantur ac propterea thus Deo,
murram homini, aurum regi obtulisse creduntur. Quod noster
poeta Sedulius huiusmodi carminibus signasse traditur:

Aurea nascenti fuderunt munera regi,
thura dedere Deo, murram tribuere sepulchro.

Huiusmodi tam nova et tam inusitata divinae stellae apparitio a
sacrosanta Romana ecclesia singularibus et praecipuis solemnitati-
bus celebratur atque graece *epiphania* nuncupatur, quod latine 'ap-
paritionem' significat.

43   Magi ergo his omnibus mature ac solemniter gestis in patriam
suam, quod ab angelo esse⟨n⟩t admoniti ne ad Herodem redirent,
per aliam viam reverterunt. Quippe in mare descendentes usque in
Tharsis navigarunt. Quocirca, tametsi Herodes Magos per phan-
tasticam quamdam stellam deceptos esse primum arbitraretur, sese
nihilominus—vulgatis postea rebus quae in templo dictae fac-
taeque fuerunt—ab eis illusum cernens, quando aliter de ipsis ulcisci non posset, in Tharsenses impetum fecit eorumque naves in-
cendit, velut plurimis ante saeculis a David propheta his verbis
prophetatum esse videbatur: 'In spiritu vehementi conteres naves
Tharsis' et reliqua.

44   In hac ipsa Magorum de tam remotis ac tam longinquis regionibus peregrinatione duo prae ceteris mecum ipse etiam atque
etiam considerans satis admirari non possum. Unum, quaenam
ratio eos commoverit, quaenam etiam spes compulerit praemio-
rum ut ad ignotum regem per certa quaedam maris Herodisque
pericula adorandum contenderent, tam vastis praesertim terrarum

Incense, gold, and myrrh they bring
As gifts to the man, to God and king.[73]

When our holy doctors discuss the Magi, they affirm that they wished by their gifts to worship His true nature (divine and human) by adorning Him with royal insignia, and therefore are believed to have offered incense to God, myrrh to the human child, and gold to the king.[74] Our Latin poet Sedulius expressed this in these verses:

They poured forth golden gifts for the newborn king,
Gave incense to God, and dedicated myrrh to the sepulcher.[75]

The novel and unusual appearance of this divine star is celebrated by the Holy Roman Church with special and extraordinary solemnities, and in Greek it is called Epiphany, which in Latin translates as "appearance."

Having done all these things solemnly and in good time, the   43
Magi returned to their country by a different route, for the angel had warned them not to go back to Herod.[76] So they descended to the sea and sailed to Tarsus. Though Herod at first thought that the Magi had been deceived by an imaginary star, when news arrived of their words and deeds in the temple, he perceived that he had been tricked by them.[77] Unable to take revenge on them in any other way, he attacked the people of Tarsus and burned their ships, as several centuries earlier the prophet David had prophesied in these words: "With a violent wind you will break the ships of Tarsus," etc.[78]

In the long journey of the Magi from such remote and distant   44
lands, above all others I repeatedly reflect on two things by which I could not be more amazed. First, what reason moved them, or what hope of rewards drove them to set forth through certain perils of the sea and Herod to worship an unknown king, an infant separated from them by vast tracts of land who was a child

spatiis separatum infantem quoque et pauperem et apud barbaram
eorum gentem minime regnaturum. Alterum, quonam modo stella
illa usque adeo fulgeret ut solis radios praeter consuetam ceterorum siderum naturam proprio quodam praecipuoque fulgore
superaret; quonam modo etiam occultaretur omnino interdum
vero toto prorsus splendore radiaret; quonam insuper modo quan-
45 doque pergeret quandoque restaret. Nos autem haec omnia inter
cogitandum vehementer admirantes idcirco divinitus facta esse
existimamus et credimus, ut incredibilis Iudaeorum perfidia commemoratis duobus tantis tamque ingentibus miraculis tandem aliquando convinceretur. Illi enim audientes prophetas adventum
Christi verbis et scriptis suis saepenumero pollicentes parum at-
tente eorum verba pensabant. Unde Deus e longinquis regionibus
venire fecit et barbaros, ut illi Persico primum sermone discerent
46 quae prophetis nuntiantibus discere noluerunt. Nam si Christum
post tot tantorumque de illo testimonia prophetarum non susce-
pissent, sese aliquatenus de sua forsitan ignorantia excusare va-
luissent. Nunc vero, cum Magos unius apparitione stellae et inqui-
sisse Christum et inventum suppliciter adorasse conspexerint, quo
tandem impietatem suam obducere colore postea potuerint non
sane intelligimus. Quae cum Iudaeos (et nunc viventes et qui in
Iudaica perfidia hactenus obierunt) non credidisse videamus, satis
eorum ignaviam vel impudentiam potius admirari non possumus,
quandoquidem aliquid simile Cyro Persarum regi in sacris eorum
litteris vel invito—volente Deo—accidisse compererim, qui illius
principis mentem ita divinitus praeparavit ut Iudaeorum populum
47 iugo Babylonicae captivitatis absolveret. Haec certe talia fuisse intelligimus ut etiam lapideas mentes ad lumen Dei omnino at-
trahere potuissent. Quocirca Magos beatos ac felices, Iudaeos vero
versavice prorsus infelices et miseros appellare non dubitarim, quoniam illi ante conspectum crudelissimi regis constituti priusquam
in carne viderent ipsum palam praedicare et confiteri non eru-

and poor and never destined to rule over their barbarous people? Second, how did the star shine forth so brightly with its own special splendor that it surpassed the rays of sun beyond the usual nature of other stars; how was it by turns completely obscured or radiant with full splendor; and finally, how did it sometimes travel and sometimes stop? Reflecting on all this with great wonder, we 45 think and believe that it occurred by divine power, so that the incredible treachery of the Jews might finally be exposed by the two great and enormous miracles just mentioned. For although they often heard the prophets promise the coming of Christ in their words and writings, the Jews weighed their words inattentively. Hence, God summoned barbarians from distant lands so that the Jews would first learn in the Persian language what they refused learn from their prophets' predictions. For if they did not embrace 46 Christ after so many testimonies of such great prophets, they might in part have been able to excuse their own ignorance. But when they saw that by the appearance of a single star the Magi had sought Christ and, having found Him, had humbly worshiped Him, we cannot possibly grasp on what pretext they could later conceal their impiety. When we see that the Jews—both those now living and those who previously perished in their Jewish treachery—did not believe these things, we cannot sufficiently wonder at their sloth or rather their impudence, especially considering what I learned from their scriptures, that something similar befell the Persian king Cyrus, against his will but by the will of God, who by His divine power so prepared the ruler's mind that he released the Jewish people from the yoke of the Babylonian captivity.[79] We see that these events were truly such that they 47 could easily have drawn even hearts of stone to the light of God. Hence, I don't hesitate to pronounce the Magi blessed and happy, and the Jews contrariwise most unhappy and miserable. The former, standing in the presence of a very cruel king, did not blush openly to proclaim and confess Christ, even before they saw Him

buerunt, isti vero, postquam propriis cum oculis conspexerunt incarnationis mysterium, abscondere ac occulere, quinimmo propalam denegare atque inficiari totis animi et corporis viribus
contenderunt.

48   Diebus deinde quadraginta post nativitatem intercedentibus,
quod opportunum puerperis masculum parturientibus purificationis tempus divina lege statuebatur, parentes puerum in templum
attulerunt, ut cunctis legitimis ad unguem obtemperarent. Nam
mosaicis legibus cavebatur ut quaecumque mulier masculum par-
turiret post quadraginta dies natum in templum immortali Deo
offerendum advehere[n]t. Et si forte primogenitus foret, ut ab omnipotenti Domino cui offerebatur vel agno immaculato, si dives,
vel duabus turturibus aut totidem culumbarum pullis, si pauper

49   esset, redimi oportebat. Unde quamquam Maria hac purificationis
lege minime teneretur, quod Spiritu Sancto — ut diximus — mirabiliter concepisset peperissetque, ne tamen in aliquibus legem solvere videretur Iesum in templum offerendi gratia detulit obla-
tumque ab immortali Deo seu turturibus seu columbis, quoniam
pauperes erant, iuxta veterem ac legitimum primogenitorum morem ipsum, tamquam primogenitum, redemerunt atque ad perpetuam quamdam huius rei commemorationem haec ipsa 'purificationis dies' quotannis ab ecclesia militante solemniter, frequentibus
hinc inde candelarum ac cereorum luminibus, celebratur.

50   Interea, dum haec et huiusmodi a parentibus agerentur,[11] ecce
homo quidam senex ac iustus, cui Symeon Cleophae filius nomen
erat, in templum de industria venit, quoniam a Spiritu Sancto
admonitus fuerat, ut eo tunc opportuno tempore accederet si divinas pollicitationes sibi ipsi divinitus factas videre cuperet. Ei namque Spiritus Sanctus promiserat ut non antea moreretur quam Ie-

51   sum in carne existentem propriis oculis intueretur. In templum
igitur — quemadmodum diximus — ingressus, ut Iesum vidit in ulnis amplexibusque propterea ipsum suscipere non formidavit quod
se Spiritu Sancto plenum esse animadvertebat simul atque divina-

in the flesh. But the latter, having seen with their own eyes the mystery of the Incarnation, sought to hide and conceal it, or rather publicly to deny and repudiate it with all their mental and physical powers.

Then forty days passed after the birth — the period that sacred 48 law established as suitable for the purification of mothers who have given birth to a male child — and the parents took the boy to the temple to comply precisely with all the requirements of the Law. For Mosaic Law prescribed that any woman bearing a male child would after forty days bring the infant to the temple to be presented to immortal God.[80] If the child happened to be the firstborn, he would have to be redeemed from almighty God, to whom he was offered, if he were wealthy, by a lamb without defect, if poor, by two turtledoves or two young pigeons.[81] Now, 49 Mary was not bound by the law of purification, since (as we said) she conceived and gave birth miraculously by the Holy Spirit. But not wishing to seem to breach the law in any way, she brought Jesus to the temple for the presentation, and upon doing so redeemed Him from immortal God by turtledoves or pigeons, since they were poor, according to the ancient and lawful custom of the firstborn, since He was the firstborn. For the perpetual commemoration of this event, this Feast of the Purification is solemnly celebrated each year by the Church militant, illuminated by a multitude of wax and tallow candles.[82]

Meanwhile, as the parents were performing these rites, behold, 50 a righteous old man whose name was Simeon, son of Cleophas, purposely entered the temple, for he had been advised by the Holy Spirit to approach at that timely moment if he wished to see realized the promises made to him from heaven. The Holy Spirit had promised him that he would not die until he beheld Jesus in the flesh with his own eyes.[83] Entering the temple, as we said, he saw 51 Jesus and was not afraid to take Him in his arms and embrace Him, for he felt himself filled with the Holy Spirit as soon as he

rum pollicitationum recordabatur. Per hunc igitur modum Iesum complexus, satis dici non potest quanto et quam incredibili gaudio repleretur. Quippe ex illis tam suavibus ac tam divinis amplexibus usque adeo gavisus est ut beata vita hic in terris frui videretur, qua cum diutius frui non posset dissolvi cuperet, ut per mortem — quando aliter fieri nequiret — ad perpetuam beatitudinis visionem

52 perveniret. Sic enim ad eum conversus inquit: 'Nunc dimittis servum tuum, Domine, secundum verbum tuum in pace, quia viderunt oculi mei salutare tuum quod parasti ante faciem omnium populorum lumen ad revelationem gentium et gloriam plebis tuae Israhel.' Quibus quidem tam sanctis ac tam salutaribus verbis omnes militantis ecclesiae sacerdotes, iuxta veterem quamdam et optimam Christianorum consuetudinem, post opportunam eucharistiae assumptionem, uti consueverant. Id ipsum Paulus apostolus postea — ut arbitror — imitatus dissolvi et esse cum Christo cupie-

53 bat. In hoc ergo infantili ac divino rege Symeon, velut in quodam splendidissimo cunctarum rerum spectaculo aliqua mysteria contemplatus, nonnulla de pretiosa atque salubri sui ipsius Salvatoris morte ac salute gentium futura esse praedixit.

Vix huiusmodi Symeonis verbis de Iesu expletis, anus quaedam prophetissa, Samuelis cuiusdam filia, nomine Anna non fortuito sed Spiritu Sancto admonita in templum venit, castitate et sanctimonia morum ceteris aetatis suae mulieribus — Virginem semper excipio — praeferenda;

> nam fuit natu gravior, quam in flore iuventae
> destituit viduam mors immatura mariti.
> Casta sed in templo semper ⟨pro⟩ coniuge vita
> et cultus cessere Dei.

54 Haec ita morata et sancta mulier, ac si divino quodam spiritu ageretur, sese continere non potuit quin Iesum verum et certum omnipotentis Dei Filium palam omnibus confiteretur, ne ulla vel parum idonea testificatio ad hanc Salvatoris nostri nativitatem deesse

recalled the divine promises. When he embraced Jesus in this fashion, he was filled with ineffable joy. The sweet and divine embrace filled him with such joy that he seemed to enjoy the blessed life here on earth; and since he could not enjoy it long, he wished to depart so that in death—if in no other way—he would achieve the perpetual vision of blessedness.[84] Turning to Him, he said: 52 "Now you dismiss your servant, O Lord, according to your word in peace; for my eyes have seen your salvation, which you prepared before the face of all peoples, a light for the revelation of the Gentiles and the glory of your people Israel."[85] According to the ancient and excellent Christian practice, all the priests of the Church militant customarily use these sacred and salutary words after duly receiving the eucharist. Later, the apostle Paul imitated this, I believe, when he wished to depart and be with Christ.[86] In this infant and divine king, Simeon contemplated mysteries as if in a radiant vision of all things, and predicted that several things would come to pass concerning his Savior's precious and salutary death and the salvation of the nations.[87]

As soon as Simeon had ended his words about Jesus, an elderly prophetess named Anna, who was the daughter of a certain Samuel, entered the temple, not by chance but advised by the Holy Spirit.[88] In chastity and sanctity of character, she was superior to the other women of her day (I always except the Virgin):

> Now heavy with age, in the flower of youth she
> Had been left a widow by the untimely death of her husband.
> But she was always in the temple, where her chaste life
> And worship of God took the place of her spouse.[89]

As if inspired by a divine spirit, this virtuous and holy woman 54 could not help but acknowledge openly to all that Jesus was almighty God's true and certain Son, so that our Savior's birth would lack no witness, however humble. For the birth of God's

videretur. Haec enim Filii Dei nativitas non solum ab angelis et prophetis, a pastoribus et parentibus, a Magis et peregrantibus, sed etiam a senioribus et iustis testimonium accepit. Omnis quippe aetas et uterque sexus eventuumque miracula huius tantae ac tam admirabilis rei fidem non immerito astruxerunt. Virgo namque generat, sterilis parit, mutus loquitur. Siquidem Zacharias, Iohannis praecursoris pater, cum mutus esset repente in eius nativitate locutus est. Elisabeth prophetat, utero clausus exsultat, vidua denique confitetur.

55   Ob haec tanta ac tam praecipua de divino infante testimonia eius fama in dies mirabiliter crescebat et ita quidem crescebat, ut Herodes de regno suo vehementius formidare inciperet quam cum illum primum natum esse a Magis accepisset. Ipsis enim Iesum natum antea praedicantibus non penitus crediderat, quod eos inani quadam et umbratili stellae suae apparitione delusos esse putaverat. Proinde hunc infantem de quo tanta et tam mirabilia quotidie praedicabantur divinum prorsus esse ratus interimere constituit, ne forte sibi peregrino et alienigenae regi regnum suum

56   praeriperetur. Eiusmodi facinus extemplo perpetrare conatus esset (tanta regni sui formidine agitabatur) nisi forte Romae penes Caesarem Augustum, ubique imperantem, duorum filiorum suorum delatione accusaretur. Nam eo huius delationis gratia profectus nefarias impiae necis cogitationes usque ad reversionem suam distulerat, ut concupitum facinus opportuniori tempore facilius confici posset, ne forte si tunc interemisset de illa nimia et inhumana crudelitate simul cum aliis facinoribus accusaretur. Sed ab

57   ipsa accusatione absolutus, post aliquot deinde mensibus in Hierosolymam reversus eadem regni sui formidine agitabatur. Unde, veritus ne memoratus infans, si diutius viveret, regno suo molestus foret, quoquo modo ipsum necare et interficere statuit. Mox itaque per edictum satellitibus suis imperavit ut omnes lactantes pueri a binis vel — ut expressius dicitur — citra biennium nati secundum

Son was witnessed not only by angels and prophets, by shepherds and parents, by the Magi and pilgrims, but even by righteous elders. People of every age and both sexes, and the miracles of these events, all contributed to belief in this great and wondrous fact. A virgin conceives, a barren woman gives birth, and a mute man speaks.[90] For Zachariah, the father of John, Christ's precursor, had been mute,[91] but he suddenly spoke at His birth.[92] Elizabeth prophesies, an infant in the womb leaps up, and finally a widow acknowledges Him.[93]

These great and extraordinary witnesses of the divine infant 55 caused His fame to grow marvelously day by day; and it grew so large that Herod began to fear for his reign more intensely than when he first learned of his birth from the Magi. For when they had previously foretold the birth of Jesus, he had not completely believed them, thinking that they had been deluded by the false and indistinct apparition of their star. But now believing the infant divine, of whom such great marvels were related every day, he decided to kill Him lest He wrest his kingdom from him, a foreign and alien king. He would immediately have attempted to 56 commit this crime—for he was tormented by such fear for his kingdom—if two of his sons had not denounced him in Rome before the universal emperor Caesar Augustus. On account of this accusation, he departed for Rome and postponed his nefarious plan of impious murder until his return. In this way, his desired crime could be perpetrated more easily and more opportunely, since if he had killed the infant then, he would be charged with excessive and inhuman cruelty along with his other crimes.[94] But 57 once absolved of these charges, he returned to Jerusalem after a few months and was again tormented by fear for his kingdom. Afraid that, if the infant lived longer, he would be troublesome to his kingdom, he resolved to destroy and eliminate Him in any way possible. And soon he issued a decree ordering that his henchmen cruelly and wickedly slay all the nursing boys whom his agents and

tempus quod explorans a Magis exquisierat quicumque in Bethlehem et in finibus suis a quaesitoribus exploratoribusque inveniren-
tur crudeliter atque nefarie nimis perimerentur, si quomodo et ipsum Iesum una cum coaequaevis et cum coaetaneis suis extinguere
potuisset, quoniam ex Michaeae prophetae oraculis locum nativitatis suae apud Bethlehem oppidum designatum esse perceperat.

58   O beati parvuli, beati inquam parvuli! Nam dum vos saevus
hostis interimere credit ad aeternam vitam felicitatemque perduxit.
Quo tetro et inhumano facinore statim per regios satellites saevis-
sime simul atque scaelestissime perpetrato, Iesum in tanta puerorum turba reperire non potuerunt, quod Ioseph pater de hac tam
nefaria parvulorum nece angelica visione antea admonitus cum eo
simul et cum matre sua in Aegyptum confugerat; quod prorsus
admiratione dignum videretur, nisi ea quae apud Aegyptios veteribus patriarchis acciderant velut quaedam huiusmodi admirabi-
59   lium ac divinarum rerum figura praecessisent. Illi enim mortem
quam domestica fames comminabatur fugientes in Aegyptum descenderunt; hic similiter, ad eadem loca contendens, mortem fugit
quae ipsi — Palaestinae nato — a Palaestinis per insidias tendebatur.
Nos rursus haec duo admirantes et animo ac mente saepenumero
revolventes nonnullas illorum quae postea in eadem provincia se-
cutae sunt figuras merito existimamus et credimus. Nam non
multo post Salvatoris fugam videre licuit illam provinciam —
magorum quondam philosophorumque parentem ac cunctarum
huiusmodi artium repertricem, porrorum etiam caeparumque
cultricem — contemptis omnibus illis repudiatisque doctoribus
Christum ceteris omnibus huius mundi pompis et illecebris prae-
60   ferentem. Et ut secundum veterem cuiusdam sapientis sententiam
brevissime simul ac verissime dixerim, non ita variis — mirabile
dictu — astrorum choris caelum refulgebat ut Aegyptus[12] innumeris monachorum ac virginum distinguebatur habitaculis. Quae
quidem tanta et tam evidens rerum mutatio quonam modo aliis

spies could find in Bethlehem or within his borders, and who had been born in two years or (more exactly) within two years of the time he had discovered when questioning the Magi. The goal was in this way to eliminate Jesus together with his coevals and contemporaries, for he had learned from the predictions of the prophet Micah that the town of Bethlehem had been identified as the place of his birth.[95]

O blessed little ones, blessed little ones, I say! While a cruel enemy believed he killed you, he brought you to eternal life and happiness. The king's henchmen at once most savagely and wickedly perpetrated this monstrous and inhuman crime, but could not find Jesus in the great crowd of little boys. For his father Joseph had been warned in a dream by an angel about this wicked slaughter of the innocents, and had fled to Egypt with Him and His mother.[96] This would seem quite amazing if the stories of the ancient patriarchs in Egypt had not anticipated it as a sort of prefiguration of these wonderful and divine events. For the ancient Jews went down into Egypt to flee the death that their domestic famine threatened; and Joseph likewise traveled to the same place, fleeing the death which the Palestinians had treacherously set for him, a native of Palestine. When we wonder at these two events and often consider them in our hearts and minds, we rightly think and believe that there were several forebodings of what later happened in the same province. Not only after the Savior's flight was it evident that this province — once the mother of magicians and philosophers, and the discoverer of all such arts, as well as the cultivator of leeks and onions[97] — despised and renounced such teachers, preferring Christ to all the pomp and enticements of this world. And in order to speak both most briefly and truly, quoting a sage's ancient opinion, "the heavens did not shine with so many varied groups of stars — wondrous to say! — as Egypt was distinguished by its countless dwellings of monks and virgins."[98] I do not see how such a great and manifest change of affairs can or

58

59

60

quibusdam causis quam memoratae Salvatoris fugae attribui et convenire possit et debeat non sane intelligo.

61   Haec tanta et tam[13] inhumana Herodis regis in innocentes parvulos crudelitas simul cum nefario illo ac scelesto sacrilegio quod in Salvatorem perpetrare atque machinari constituerat ita omnipotenti Deo displicuisse visa est ut paulo post vitam miserabiliter finierit, cum hactenus nimia cunctarum rerum prosperitate potiretur. Quippe antequam moreretur, tribus ex multis eius filiis interemptis, pluribus simul morbis vehementissime angebatur. Lentus namque ignis non tantum in superficiem corporis quantum intrinsecus incendium operabatur. Cibi quoque inexplebilis quaedam aviditas hominem incendebat nec tamen satietas umquam inerat; siquidem rabidis incitata faucibus valebat ingluvies. Intestina interius ulceribus rabida putrescebant; saevissimis etiam coli doloribus cruciabatur. Humor liquidus ac lividus erga pedes tumidos oberrabat. Similis illi et circa pubem erat afflictio, sed et verenda ipsa putredine corrupta scatebant vermibus. Spiritus insuper incredibilis, erecta tentigo, quae fuerat satis obscena diritate foetoris, et anhelitus exspiratione creberrima contractus denique per cuncta membra susbsistens vim noxiam efficiebat, quae omnem tollerantiae cruciatibus contuderat firmitatem. His igitur et huiusmodi intollerandis cruciatibus assidue vexatus mortem sibi ipsi consciscere voluit idque ut faceret malum quoddam simul atque cultrum efflagitaverat, quo praecordia sua nimirum transfixisset, nisi a quodam eius nepote nomine Achiabo ibidem forte assistente prohiberetur. Quid plura? Tandem morbo—intercuti⟨bu⟩
62   s et scaturientibus toto corpore vermibus—miserabiliter et digne moritur. Has tantas ac tam ingentes et inusitatas poenas Herodi ipsi divinitus illatas ab his quibus divinandi peritia inerat ob nefandam saevi hominis impietatem ac multa crudeliter gesta decimo septimo libro *Antiquitatum* testante Iosepho dicebatur; quod equidem mea sententia de nefasta illa et inhumana innocentium parvulorum occisione non iniuria interpretari posse existimo.

ought to be ascribed to or coincide with any other cause but the flight of the Savior.

Together with the vile and wicked sacrilege that he had decided 61 to devise and perpetrate against the Savior, King Herod's great and inhuman cruelty toward the innocents was seen to offend almighty God so much that shortly thereafter he ended his life in misery, although he had previously attained extraordinary prosperity in everything. Before he died, three of his many sons had been killed, and at the same time he was terribly afflicted by several maladies. A slow fever caused an inflammation not so much of the surface of his body as within. An insatiable appetite for food consumed him, but with no sense of fullness, since his gluttony prevailed, incited by his ravenous gullet. His raging bowels rotted with ulcers, and he was tortured by fierce pains of the colon; while a watery and discolored moisture settled in his swollen feet. He suffered a similar affliction in the groin, and his private parts, decaying with rot, teemed with worms. There was also an incredible odor; an erection, which was particularly obscene because of its offensive stench; and his labored breathing, drawn tight by frequent exhalations, lodging throughout his body, created a noxious force which, by its spasms, destroyed any resistant tolerance.[99] Plagued continually and intolerably by these and similar pains, he wanted to commit suicide; and to this end, he called for an apple and a paring knife. With the latter, he would have opened his chest, but his grandson named Achiabus, who happened to be there, prevented him.[100] In short, he finally died a miserable and 62 condign death, with the subcutaneous worms bursting out of his body. Men skilled in divination said that these great and unusual punishments were inflicted on Herod by heaven on account of this savage man's heinous impiety and many cruel deeds, as Josephus attests in Book 17 of his *Jewish Antiquities*.[101] Personally, I believe we can rightly interpret this with reference to his abominable and inhuman slaughter of the innocents.[102]

63   Nihil enim eo inhumano facinore crudelius tetriusque factum umquam fuisse arbitror; nec Pharaonem excipi volo, quoniam ille in Aegypto tale quiddam, variis tamen temporibus, efficere conatus est quale iste in Palaestina simul atque eodem tempore perpetravit. Plurima enim innocentium parvulorum milia uno tempore necata[14] fuisse non dubitamus, cum omnes memoratae provinciae infantes eius edicto mactarentur. Unde quanti et tam magni eorum ploratus atque plangentium matrum plangores et ululatus fuerint, cum passim parvuli a propriis uberibus raperentur et ad crudelem necem a satellitibus traherentur, non[15] satis existimare

64   possumus, nedum nostra oratione explicare valeamus. Nam, ut ait poeta ille de hac inumana impii regis crudelitate loquens, quasi luctuosam quamdam tragoediam facturus:

> Puerilia mactat
> milia plangoremque dedit tot matribus unum.
> Haec laceros crines nudato vertice ru[m]pit,
> illa genas secuit, nudum ferit altera pugnis
> pectus et infelix mater (nec iam modo mater)
> orba super gelidum frustra premit ubera natum.

Haec ingens miserarum parentum lamentatio ab Hieremia propheta, multis ante saeculis, his verbis praedicta invenitur: 'Vox in Rama audita est, ploratus et ululatus multus' et quae sequuntur.

> Quis tibi tunc lanio cernenti talia sensus?
> Quosve dabas fremitus, cum vulnera fervere late
> prospiceres arce ex summa vastumque videres
> misceri ante oculos tantis plangoribus aequor?

I think that no more cruel or abominable deed was ever com- 63
mitted than this inhuman crime; and I do not even except the
Pharaoh, who at various times attempted to do in Egypt what
Herod perpetrated in Palestine at one and the same time. We cannot doubt that thousands of innocent children were slain at the
same time, since all the infants of Herod's province were slaughtered by his edict. Hence we can hardly imagine, let alone for me
to be able to describe in words, what great and loud lamentations,
what laments and shrieks of wailing mothers were heard when
children everywhere were torn from their breasts and dragged to
their cruel death by Herod's henchmen. The poet Sedulius de- 64
scribes this inhuman cruelty of an impious king as if composing a
tragedy:

He slaughtered infants
By the thousands, afflicting countless mothers with a sole
lament.
One tore the mangled hairs torn from her bared head,
One tore at her cheeks, another struck her naked breast
With her fists, and a wretched mother (no longer a mother)
In vain pressed bereaved breasts against her frigid child.[103]

This vast lamentation of wretched mothers we find foretold many
centuries earlier by the prophet Jeremiah with these words: "A
voice was heard in Ramah of mourning and great weeping," and
following.[104]

What feelings, you butcher, did this sight inspire in you?
What groans did you utter, when the wounds, seething far and
wide,
You beheld from your high citadel, and saw this vast sea
embroiled
Before your eyes with countless lamentations?

Extinctisque tantum quamvis infantibus absens
praesens Christus erat, qui sancta pericula semper
suscipit et poenas alieno in corpore sentiet.

65   Herode igitur per hunc modum—ut merebatur—defuncto, Ioseph de eius morte ab angelo in somniis admonebatur atque propterea ut ex Aegypto in terram Israhel reverteretur certior reddeba-
tur. Sed ut Archelaum pro Herode patre suo in Iudaea regnare
percepit, in partes Galilaeae sese contulit atque in quadam eius
provinciae urbe—quae Nazareth dicebatur—aliquamdiu habitavit, ubi alius Herodes, defuncti regis filius qui et ipse Herode
cognomento Antipas appellabatur, tamquam tetrarcha quidam
66 regnabat. Pater quippe Herodes—praedictorum duorum filiorum
suorum, Philippi scilicet et Herodis, accusatione supra quam dici
potest offensus—Archelaum tertium filium sibi, ceteris duobus
eius accusatoribus praetermissis, successorem dumtaxat ac imperii
sui heredem testamento his pactis et condicionibus instituit, ut
insigna regni et regum diadema ab imperatore Romano, recognos-
cendi gratia, reciperet. Quare, ut insignia regni sicut institutum
erat a Caesare reportaret, Romam contendit. Illuc et duo fratres
eius a patre in testamento—ut diximus—praetermissi ad imperatorem confugerant, ne sua paterni regni portione ab Archelao
fratre defraudarentur; quibus omnibus Caesar diligenter auditis
paternum regnum ita partitus est, ut eius medietatem Archelao,
reliquam vero duobus fratribus suis aequis portionibus partiretur,
quoniam ille a patre heres testamento, ceteris omnibus omissis,
institutus fuerat. Unde in hac Caesaris partitione Archelao Iudaea,
67 Herodi Galilaea, Philippo Iturea provincia contigerat. Audiens
ergo Ioseph quod Archelaus, qui paterna acta prosequebatur, pro
Herode patre suo in Iudaea regnaret, in eas partes sese conferre
timuit atque in provinciam Galilaeae secessit, ubi etsi Herodes filius regnaret paterno tamen nomini, ob eam quam supra diximus
invidiam, ita infensus erat ut patris acta libentius rescidisset quam

Though far absent from these murdered infants,
Yet Christ was present, who always takes on holy perils,
And feels the punishments inflicted on another's body.[105]

When Herod, then, had died in this way, as he deserved, Jo- 65
seph learned of his death from an angel in a dream, and was
thereby assured that he could return to Israel from Egypt.[106] But
when he heard that Archelaus ruled in Judea in his father Herod's
stead, he went to Galilee and lived for a while in a city of that
province called Nazareth, where a different Herod (a son of the
dead king, and like him called Antipas) ruled as tetrarch.[107] Herod 66
senior had been so greatly offended by the accusation of his two
sons, Philip and Herod, that he had passed over his two accusers
and appointed his third son Archelaus as his successor and the
heir to his kingdom on these terms and conditions: that he would
receive the royal insignia and the royal diadem from the Roman
emperor as a sign of official recognition. Therefore, in order to
bring back the royal insignia from Caesar, as had been ordained,
he went to Rome, where his two brothers, excluded from their father's will, as we said, had appealed to the emperor so as not to be
cheated of their share of their father's kingdom by their brother
Archelaus. After Caesar had carefully heard the case, he divided
their father's kingdom as follows: half went to Archelaus, since he
had been made heir by his father's will, to the exclusion of the others; but the rest was divided equally between his two brothers.
Thus, under Caesar's division, Judea passed to Archelaus, Galilee
to Herod junior, and Iturea to Philip.[108] When Joseph heard that 67
Archelaus reigned in Judea, succeeding his father and continuing
his policies, he was afraid to return there and withdrew to Galilee.[109] For although Herod junior reigned there, the spite that we
have described made him so hostile that he would more gladly
have abolished his father's policies than imitate his actions in any

eius vestigia aliquatenus imitaretur; atque in Nazareth quadam eius provinciae urbe — ut dictum est — securius habitavit donec puer duodecim aetatis annos natus esset.

68   Ea enim quae exinde usque ad duodecimum aetatis suae annum intercesserant ab aliquo idoneo auctore nequaquam scripta sunt. Nonnulla vero in eo libro legimus qui *De infantia Salvatoris* inscribitur, sed illis tamquam frivolis et inanibus praetermissis institutum dicendi ordinem prosequemur. Non enim ab evangelista Mattheo seorsum — ut a quibusdam creditur — hebraice scripta fuerunt neque etiam ab Hieronymo postea in Latinum conversa idcirco fuisse existimamus et credimus, quod omnia quaecumque in eo libro continentur apocrypha habeantur et sint. Unde adduci non possum ut credam a Hieronymo illa ex Hebraea lingua in Latinam fuisse conversa, qui cuncta apocrypha ceteris quibuscumque scriptoribus acerbius et gravius insectatus est.

69   Duodecimo ergo aetatis suae anno parentes eius, ut in cunctis Dei mandatis legem servarent, Hierosolymam proficiscebantur. In lege enim cavebatur ut omnes homines quotannis solemni paschatis die in Ierusalem convenirent, quod ad continuam quamdam Aegyptii transitus commemorationem instituebatur. Nam ingens lues in admirabili illa et pervulgata primogenitorum pestifera calamitate ad perdendos Aegyptios divinitus immissa quaecumque Hebraeorum habitacula forte barbaricis domibus immixta ac finitima et contigua — incredibile dictu — praeteribat. Unde hebraice 'pesa' dicebatur, quod latine 'transitus' significat, quamquam Graeci nosque etiam — seu corrupte, ut in plerisque aliis, seu potius euphoniae causa — pro 'pesa' 'pascha' appellare consueverimus. Proinde omnibus — ut decebat — antea perfectis, viri a mulieribus seorsum iuxta legem revertebantur. Nam in ipsa profectione reversioneque virorum catervae a mulieribus separatae incedebant, ut cunctis solemnibus tantae celebritatis diebus integra vicissim castitate uterentur. Pueri vero utrobique, et inter mulieres et inter viros, convenire poterant.

way. And so, as we said, Joseph lived safely in Nazareth, a town of that province, until the boy was twelve years old.

No reliable writer has recorded the events of Jesus' life from that point until he was twelve.[110] In the book entitled *On the Savior's Infancy*, we read some things that are so silly and vain that we omit them and follow the proposed order of our account. We neither think nor believe, as some do, that this life was written separately in Hebrew by the evangelist Matthew and then translated into Latin by Jerome, since everything contained in this book is held to be and is in fact spurious. Hence I cannot be led to believe that Jerome translated it from Hebrew into Latin, for he sharply and authoritatively denounced all spurious works by any writers whatsoever.[111]

Now in His twelfth year, His parents set out for Jerusalem in order to observe the Law in all of God's commandments.[112] For the Law prescribed that each year everyone should gather in Jerusalem for the solemn feast of Passover, which had been instituted in the perpetual memory of the passing-over in Egypt.[113] During the wondrous and widespread deadly visitation of the firstborn, sent from heaven to destroy the Egyptians, the vast pestilence passed by the dwellings of the Hebrews, even though — wondrous to say! — they were mixed in with the nearby and adjoining barbarian houses. In Hebrew this was called *pesach*, which in Latin means "passing over," but both the Greeks and the Latins are used to calling it *pascha* instead of *pesach*, whether by corruption (as in many other words) or rather for the sake of euphony. Then after having duly completed all the rites, as was fitting, the men returned apart from the women, according to the Law. For both on the journey there and the return, the crowds of men walked separately from the women, so that they would mutually observe complete chastity during all the solemn days of this great feast. But children could gather in either group, among the women and among the men.

68

69

70 Itaque parentes eius in Galilaeam separatim — ut diximus — revertentes puerum inscii in Hierosolyma dimiserunt, siquidem Ioseph inter viros minime conspicatus ipsum in caterva mulierum esse arbitrabatur, quod et Mariae itidem contingebat, ut in virili comitatu cum patre convenisse existimaret quem in congregatione mulierum minime repererat. Qui, cum in rever⟨t⟩endo iter diei iam processisset, uterque ingenti quodam pueri absentis desiderio

71 anxius in congregatione sua quaeritabat. Dum vero eum tota die utrobique quaeritantes reperire non possent, postridie Hierosolymam reverterunt; ubi paulo accuratius explorantes quarto tandem die inter doctores Hebraeos in templo divinitus disputantem repererunt. De quo illi divinae legis magistri et professores vehementer admirabantur, quonam modo ea ab humano puero fieri possent incredibiliter obstupescentes. Nam, ut inquit Hieronymus, 'Duodecim annos Salvator impleverat et in templo sedens ac de quaestionibus legis Hebraeorum magistros interrogans magis docet dum prudenter interrogat.' Unde multum obstupescentes satis admirari

72 non poterant. Ut igitur eum parentes repererunt magno propterea gaudio tenebantur; Maria vero silente, Ioseph puerum cur ita parentes fecisset percontari non dubitabat. At illi eius responsum non intellexerunt quando se in his quae sui Patris erant prius esse oportere respondit. Peracta itaque cum Hebraeis doctoribus disputatione in Nazareth Galilaeae oppidum simul cum parentibus remeavit atque [in] cunctis eorum mandatis parere voluit.

73 Ab hac puerili Salvatoris aetate usque ad trigesimum aetatis annum nihil paene de gestis eius ab aliquo idoneo auctore scriptum reperitur. Sed si qua sunt, frivola quaedam et apocrypha habentur atque a catholica ecclesia repudiata et pro nugis ac deliramentis habita minime inveniuntur. Ideoque illis omnibus (si qua fuerunt, occulta enim et in eremis agitata interea fuisse aiunt, vel potius, si palam gesta, oblivioni dimissa esse constat) de indus-

74 tria praetermissis, anno quintodecimo imperii Tiberii Caesaris, procurante Pontio Pilato Iudaeam, tetrarcha autem Galilaeae

Now, when Jesus' parents returned to Galilee separately, as we   70
noted, they unintentionally left their son in Jerusalem. Not seeing
the boy among the men, Joseph thought that He was in the crowd
of women; and the same happened to Mary, who deemed that He
must have joined his father among the men, since she had found
Him nowhere in the women's congregation.[114] After they had spent
a day on the return trip, they were both anxious with great longing
for the missing boy and searched for Him in their congregations.
Having searched all day in both groups without finding Him, they   71
returned the next day to Jerusalem. After a more careful search, on
the fourth day they found Him among the Jewish teachers in the
temple disputing as if divinely inspired.[115] The masters and profes-
sors of divine Law were astonished and amazed beyond belief that
this human boy could speak in this way. For as Jerome writes,
"The Savior had completed twelve years; and seated in the temple
asking the Jewish masters about questions of the Law, he taught
them by His wise questions."[116] Completely astounded, they could
not sufficiently wonder at Him. Having found Him, the parents   72
were filled with great joy; Mary was silent, but Joseph did not
hesitate to ask the boy why he had treated his parents so.[117] They
did not understand His reply when He said that He had first to
be about His Father's business.[118] Now that the debate with the
Jewish teachers was over, He returned with his parents to Nazareth in Galilee, willingly obeying all their commands.[119]

From the Savior's boyhood to his thirtieth year, we find practi-   73
cally nothing about His deeds written by any reliable writer. What
writings we have are deemed silly and spurious, are repudiated by
the Catholic Church, and are considered frivolous delusions of
little value.[120] As a result, we have intentionally passed over all of
them: if there were any, it is agreed that they were secret and oc-
casionally circulated in the deserts, or if they were made public,
they were consigned to oblivion. In the fifteenth year of the reign   74
of Tiberius Caesar, Pontius Pilate was procurator of Judea. Herod

Herode, commemorati[s] Herodis regis filio, Philippo vero fratre eius tetrarcha Itureae et Trachoniditis regionis, et Lysania Abilinae tetrarcha, sub pontificibus Anna et Caiapha, quemadmodum Lucas evangelista Iosephusque testantur, Iohannes quidam Zachariae filius, divino spiritu ab utero matris plenus, in Iudaeae provinciae eremis magna vitae austeritate diutius habitaverat. Verum opportuno postea tempore in eremis commoratus, ad turbas et coetus hominum ibidem congregatos de Christo, humani generis salvatore, mirum in modum enarrare et praedicare coepit.

75   Hic est enim ille Iohannes qui nondum in lucem editus materno utero ad Iesum, in Mariae ventre delatum, mirabile dictu congratulandi atque adorandi gratia exsultavit. Hic est, inquam, ille Iohannes qui dum in antris solus, remotis arbitris, morabatur ob sanctimoniam vitae pilis camelorum induebatur et zona non lanea, ut apud Iudaeos moris erat, sed pellicea utebatur ac silvestria mella locustaque edebat, ut Iuvencus pulchre his versibus signavit:

> Texta camelorum fuerant velamina setis
> et zonae pellis medium cinxere prophetam.
> Edere locustas solitus ruralibus arvis
> et tenuem victum praebent silvestria mella.

Et dum cum hominibus conversabatur suasionibus suis baptisma pro salute humani generis in medium adducebat utque ab hominibus susciperetur palam et aperte admonebat. Hic est denique ille Iohannes quem Herodes tetrarcha praedictus, ei pluribus causis infensus, crudeliter nimis impieque interemerat, ne forte homines doctrinae suae persuasionibus allicerentur ac per hunc modum tandem ipse ab eius regno distraheretur.

76   Hanc tam iniquam ac tam impiam innocentissimi hominis, quinimmo sanctissimi viri, necem divinam ultionem a doctis ac sapientibus viris secutam fuisse credebatur. Nam magnos exercitus

the son of the famous Herod was tetrarch of Galilee; his brother Philip was tetrarch of the regions of Iturea and Trachonitis; and Lysanias the tetrarch of Abilene. Now, under the priests Annas and Caiaphas, as Luke the evangelist and Josephus attest,[121] John the son of Zachariah, who had been filled with divine spirit from his mother's womb, had long dwelt in the deserts of Judea in a life of great austerity.[122] But after he had stayed his due time in the deserts, he began in wondrous ways to preach and expound to crowds of men gathered together about Christ, the Savior of the human race.

This is the famous John, who, not yet born, while still in   75
his mother's womb—wondrous to say!—leaped up congratulating and worshiping Jesus, borne in Mary's womb.[123] This is, I repeat, the famous John who lived alone in caves with no neighbors and dressed in camel hides as a sign of holiness; and he wore a belt— not of wool, as was the Jewish custom—but of leather, and ate wild honey and locusts.[124] Juvencus nicely described this in these verses:

> His garments were sewn from camel hairs,
> And belts of leather girded the prophet's waist.
> He was used to eating locusts in country fields,
> And wild honey offered scant nourishment.[125]

When he spoke with men, in his sermons he introduced baptism for the salvation of humankind, and openly and plainly urged people to receive it. This finally is the famous John who was very cruelly and impiously put to death by Herod the tetrarch, who hated him for various reasons, fearing that people would be attracted by his persuasive teaching, and as a result would expel Herod from his kingdom.[126]

This most unjust and most impious death of an innocent per-   76
son—rather, of a most holy man—led, in the opinion of learned and wise men, to divine retribution. For they believed that in the

suos bello quod inter Aretham cognomine Petreium, Arabiae regem, ipsumque gestum postea fuerat, ut Iosephus tradit, deletos esse putabant. Quippe Herodiadem, Philippi Herodis fratris uxorem, Aristoboli filiam, exstitisse scribit, quam cum Herodes e cubiculo atque ex toro viri fratris sui abstraxisset ac legitima uxore, praedicti Arethae filia dimissa, sibi incestuosis nuptiis copulasset, ex hoc immani flagitio Iohannem Baptistam, cuius vehementes obiurgationes aequo animo tollerare non poterat, ab eo interfectum et inter illum quoque et Aretham ingens bellum exortum. Exinde insuper Herodem, cum praedictorum exercituum suorum internicione, regno expulsum fuisse testatur.

77   Hic igitur Iohannes, in hac ipsa de Salvatore suo praedicatione, tantas ac tam excellentes eius virtutes esse praedixit ut sese indignum qui eius calceamenta et portaret et solveret palam et aperte confitetur, quamvis ab utero matris sanctificatus esset. Paulo post huiusmodi sanctissimi hominis praedicationem et finitimorum populorum in Iordane fluvio ablutionem (nam batpizandi gratia eo usque assidue adventabat) Iesus, iam trigesimo fere aetatis suae anno, ad ipsum prope eumdem Iordanis fluvium contendit ut ab eo baptizaretur, non ut peccata sua — quae utique non habebat — sed ut carnis maculas quas gerebat hoc spirituali lavacro aboleret, ut quemadmodum Iudaeos suscepta circumcisione sic etiam gentes baptismo (id est purifici roris perfusione) salvaret.

78   Animadvertite, quaeso, animadvertite, inquam, quicumque haec nostra in manus legendi gratia sumpserit, qualia et quanta ac quam mirabilia simul et veneranda harum duarum divinarum personarum spectacula tunc hominibus illis ibidem assistentibus esse ac videri debuerint! Alterum enim videbant Iohannem post triginta annorum spatia ab eremi vastitate venientem, filium certe pontificis, nullis prorsus ex rebus ad victum necessariis indigentem, mirabilem profecto omnibus modis et per cuncta venerandum. Alterum quoque Filium omnipotentis Dei meram

war later waged between the Arabian king Aretas, surnamed Petreius, and Herod, the latter's great armies were annihilated, as Josephus relates.[127] He writes that Herodias was the daughter of Aristobulus and the wife of Herod's brother Philip, and that Herod — having repudiated his legitimate wife, the daughter of Aretas — stole her from the bed and chamber of his brother and slept with her in an incestuous marriage. For this heinous crime John the Baptist rebuked him so intolerably that Herod had him killed; and from it arose the vast war between Herod and Aretas.[128] And Josephus attests that this was the reason that Herod was driven from his kingdom, and that his armies were slaughtered.

In preaching about the Savior, John announced such great and 77 excellent virtues in him that he openly and plainly confessed that he was unworthy to carry or untie his sandals,[129] even though he himself had been sanctified from his mother's womb.[130] Soon after this holy man had preached and cleansed the local people in the Jordan river (for he arrived there for the sake of baptizing),[131] Jesus, who was now around thirty years old, came to him at the Jordan river to be baptized.[132] By this spiritual cleansing, he sought to wash away, not His sins — He had none — but the stains of the flesh that He bore, so that, as Jews were saved by accepting circumcision, He might save the Gentiles by baptism, that is, the sprinkling of purifying liquid.

Observe, please; observe, whoever takes this work of mine in 78 hand to read it, how great and how wondrous and how venerable the spectacle of these two divine persons must have been and appeared to those present! They beheld, on the one hand, John, who came from the wastes of the desert after thirty years, the son of a priest, who lacked none of the necessities of life, now wondrous in every respect and venerable in every way.[133] On the other hand, they gazed upon the Son of almighty God, imbued with pure di-

divinitatem redolentem intuebantur, speciosissimum cunctarum admirabilium rerum spectaculum et prorsus omni admiratione dignissimum.

79   Hunc ergo ubi Iohannes ad se venientem vidit, 'Ecce,' inquit, 'agnus Dei, ecce qui tollit peccata mundi,' eumque baptizare recusabat, quoniam se potius ab illo baptizari decere atque oportere censebat. Ipsum tamen in eodem baptizandi proposito persistentem coram pluribus Iudaeorum turbis, summa omnium devotione, devotissime baptizavit. Ab hoc ipso baptizandi officio 'Baptistae' postea cognomen accepit. Quo facto statim et ipse a Iesu baptizatus est. Universi autem Iudaeorum populi haec divina potius quam humana tantorum ac tam sanctorum inter se virorum baptismata maxima quadam devotione conspicati et ipsi certatim
80 non immerito baptizabantur. Nec mirum; in Iohanne enim Eliam cernebant atque in illius beati hominis recordationem per innumeras istius sanctissimi viri virtutes remeabant; in uno multo etiam maiore admiratione capiebantur, siquidem ille in urbibus saepenumero atque in urbanis domibus pascebatur, hic vero ab ipsis cunabulis in eremo semper habitabat. Nam praecursorem illius qui omnia vetera solvebat aliquo privilegio ceteros omnes antiquos
81 prophetas superare oportebat. Angelum insuper quemdam multis virtutibus praefulgentem plurimaque vultus gratia coruscantem post multa temporum curricula apud eos surrexisse et apparuisse intelligebant; novum praeterea praedicationis suae ritum longeque a ceteris veterum prophetarum generibus distantem ac diversum venerabantur. Nihil quippe usitatum atque solitum nuntiabat: nulla proelia, nulla certamina, nulla bella, nullas de acerrimis hostibus victorias, non morbos, non fames, non expugnationes Babylonicas ac Persicas, non urbium captivitates, non oppidorum desolationes ex divino eius ore audiebant, nec etiam eorum quidquam quae prius audire consueverant sed caelum dumtaxat et illud quod ibi promittebatur: regnum iustis futurum praedicabat, iniustis autem Gehennae supplicium et aeterna variarum poenarum tor-

vinity. This was a most beautiful spectacle of all things admirable, and indeed worthy of all admiration.

Now, when John saw Jesus approaching, he said "Behold the 79 Lamb of God, behold the one who takes away the sins of the world,"[134] and refused to baptize Him, for he thought it more fitting and right that Jesus should baptize him.[135] But when Jesus insisted on being baptized, he baptized Him most devoutly, and with the greatest devotion of all, before a large gathering of Jews. (From this service of baptism, he afterward acquired the sobriquet the Baptist.) After this rite, he was at once baptized by Jesus.[136] Upon seeing the mutual baptisms, more divine than human, of such great and holy men performed with utmost devotion, all the Jewish people themselves vied to be baptized, and rightly so.[137] Small wonder, for in John they saw Elijah, and that holy man's 80 countless virtues called them back to the memory of that blessed man. In one respect they were struck with even greater wonder, since Elijah was often fed in cities and in urban dwellings, whereas from birth John always lived in the desert. For by a special privilege the precursor of the man who would annul the old ways had to surpass all the other ancient prophets.[138] Moreover, they under- 81 stood that an angel resplendent with many virtues and radiant with grace in his visage had risen and appeared among them after many cycles of ages; and they revered his new rite of preaching, which was distant and different from the other kinds of the ancient prophets. For he announced nothing usual or customary: from his divine lips they heard nothing about battles, struggles, wars, victories over fierce enemies, plagues, famines, conquests of Babylon or Persia, enslavements of cities, or destructions of towns. They heard nothing that they had often heard before, but only about heaven and what was promised there: he preached a future kingdom for the righteous, and he threatened the wicked with the punishment of Gehenna and the eternal torments of various

menta post mortem minabatur. In Christo autem, ut paucis expediam, pulchra cunctarum rerum spectacula—et uno quidem aspectu—contemplari poterant.

82   In hoc sacrosancto Salvatoris nostri baptismate unum quiddam, ceteris paene omnibus mirabilius, contigisse legimus, quod tacite praeterire non possumus. Ubi enim amnem ingressus aquas attigisse visus est, non modo fluvius ipse—mirabile dictu—cursum reflexit in undas sed mare quoque aufugit, ceu pluribus ante saeculis a propheta quodam praedictum ac praenuntiatum esse constabat. Quod his versibus poeta noster eleganter expressit: 'Senserunt elementa Deum: mare fugit et ipse / Iordanis refluens cursum convertit in undas. / Namque propheta canens "Quidnam est, mare, quod fugis," inquit, / "et tu, Iordanis, retro quid subtrahis amnem?"' Nec mirum quippe in hoc ipso flumine haec talia praedicta, alias facta fuisse miracula Sancta Scriptura commemorat. Inter cetera enim aquas tum Iosue tum quoque Eliae temporibus partim instar montis intumescentes stetisse partim etiam hinc inde divisas exstitisse legimus.

83   Hisce tam pretiosis et tam salutaribus baptismatibus—ut diximus—absolutis, Spiritus Sanctus e caelis corporali specie, instar candidissimae columbae, extemplo descendit atque ut Salvator de aqua exivit supra eius caput astitit et subito huiusmodi vox 'Hic est Filius meus dilectus' et reliqua caelitus audita est. Quae vox apud David hoc modo praedicta invenitur: 'Et descendit super eum Spiritus Dei formatus in specie columbae candidae.' Qui quidem ob duas dumtaxat causas in tali specie venisse creditur: una quoniam hoc animal ceteris mundius ac mansuetius cerneretur, altera

84   quod nos veteris diluvii admonere videretur. Nam cum aliquando universum terrarum orbem naufragium commune mersisset et omne prorsus hominum genus illico submergendum periclitaretur interitu, manifesta illius animalis apparitio finem illius tempestatis ostendit. Ut enim per illud animal delato oleae ramo liberatio viventium hominum a fluctibus et undis intimabatur, ita per hoc

punishments after death.[139] But, to be brief, in Christ—and at a single glance—they could contemplate the beautiful vision of all things.

We read that there was one thing in the holy baptism of our 82 Savior that was more wondrous than all the others, and that we cannot pass over in silence. When they saw Jesus enter the river and touch its waters, not only did the river reverse its course (wondrous to say!), but the sea also receded, just as a prophet had foretold and predicted several centuries earlier.[140] Our poet expressed this elegantly in these verses: "The elements felt God's presence: the sea fled, and the Jordan flowing backward turned against its waves. For the song of the prophet says: 'Why, O sea, do you flee, and you, Jordan, why do you pull your river backward?'"[141] No wonder, since the Holy Scripture records that miracles predicted at this river were performed elsewhere. Among other things, in the times of Joshua and Elijah we read that the waters swelled up to the height of a mountain and parted.[142]

When these very precious and salutary baptisms had been com- 83 pleted, as we said, at once the Holy Spirit descended from heaven in the bodily form of a pure white dove; and as the Savior emerged from the water, it hovered above His head,[143] and suddenly the words were heard from heaven: "This is my beloved son," etc.[144] We find this saying foretold in David's psalms as follows:[145] "And the Spirit of God descended on him taking the form of a white dove."[146] We believe that the dove took this form for two reasons: first, because this animal is perceived as cleaner and tamer than others; and second, because it seems to remind us of the ancient flood. For when the universal disaster had once overwhelmed the 84 entire earth, and all the human race was in imminent danger of extinction by drowning, the manifest appearance of this bird portended the end of the calamity. As by the olive branch it bore the hint was given that the people would be delivered alive from the currents and waves,[147] so the clear and articulate words of the dove

idem salus humani generis mundo apparuisse expressa et articu-
lata vocis locutione significabatur. Atque huiusmodi candidae columbae apparitio his carminibus praeclare canitur:

> Ergo ubi fluminei post mystica dona lavacri
> egrediens siccas Dominus calcatur arenas.
> Confestim patuere poli sanctusque columbae
> spiritus in specie vestivit Christum honore.

85   Haec ipsa manifesta caelorum adapertio et eiusdem Sancti Spiritus in columbae specie apparitio ac divinae denique vocis exau-
dita locutio ad claram dumtaxat Filii Dei demonstrationem per-
tinebant. Per hunc ergo modum Iesus baptizatus, macerandae
carnis gratia exhortante eodem Spiritu, de Iordane in desertum
locum abire constituit. Haec eremus inter Hierusalem et Hieri-
co⟨n⟩ constituta diversis latronibus abundabat; ubi quadraginta
dies solus cum bestiis tantummodo, sine aliqua cibi et potus de-
gustatione, commoratus est, ut cibus primi hominis, quem per divini mandati praevaricatione⟨m⟩ tam amare gustaverat, hoc suo
salubri salutiferoque ieiunio solveretur.

86   Quod itidem de Moyse et Elia—duobus maximis prophetis
sanctissimisque hominibus—legimus, ut continuam quamdam totidem dierum inediam tollerarent; nec plus illis ieiunare voluit, ne
incredibilis carnis putaretur assumptio. Et quod mirabilius videri
debet, Iesum Deum simul et hominem—non esurientibus illis
puris hominibus in eodem temporis intervallo—sacris litteris esu-
riisse tradunt. Hanc mysticam Salvatoris esuriem quoddam humanae salutis ardens desiderium beatus Ambrosius significare testatur, ne forte puri homines maiorem potestatem quam Deus in
87   carne habuisse viderentur. Haec ergo dominica fames diabolo
temptandi sui occasionem praebuit. Deum enim in homine esse
suspicabatur; cum enim audisset venientem de caelo vocem atque
dicentem 'Hic est filius meus dilectus,' audisset etiam Iohannem
testimonium illi tam insigne perhibentem ac deinde ipsum esu-

signified that the salvation of the human race had been revealed to the world. This appearance of the white dove is excellently sung in these verses:

> Thus, after the mystical gifts of the bath in the river,
> The Lord emerges to tread the dry sand.
> At once the heavens were opened, and the Holy Spirit
> In the form of a dove clad Christ with honor.[148]

This manifest opening of the heavens, this appearance of the 85
Holy Spirit in the form of dove, and this utterance of God's voice
made audible served as clear proof of the Son of God. Having
been baptized in this way, Jesus was urged by the Holy Spirit to
mortify the flesh, and so decided to leave the Jordan for a place in
the wilderness.[149] Situated between Jerusalem and Jericho, this
desert teemed with various bandits; and here he spent forty days
alone among beasts, without tasting any food or water, so that by
this salubrious and salutary fast He would atone for the food of
Adam, the first man, which had tasted so bitter because he violated God's commandment.

We read that Moses and Elijah, the two greatest prophets and 86
holiest men, likewise endured a continuous fast of forty days;[150]
and Jesus was unwilling to fast longer than they, lest his assumption of the flesh might seem incredible. What is more miraculous,
the Holy Scriptures relate that Jesus, who was both God and man,
hungered, even though men of purity in those day were not hungry.[151] Saint Ambrose attests that the Savior's mystical hunger
signifies His burning desire for human salvation, lest men of purity seem to have had greater power than God in the flesh.[152] The 87
Lord's fasting offered the devil a chance to tempt Him. For the
devil suspected that God was in the man: he had heard the voice
from heaven saying "This is my beloved son";[153] he had also heard
John offering distinguished testimony for Him, and now saw Him

rientem videret, magna prorsus ambiguitate tenebatur. Nam neque hominem illum purum esse credebat ob ea quae de illo vox divina protulerat neque rursus Filium Dei esse existimabat quem esurientem cernebat. Itaque maxima rerum confusus angustia, cum ipsum esurientem animadvertit mox ad temptandum accessit, ut per temptationem saltem haec eius ambiguitas illucesceret.

88   Accedens itaque temptator voces emittit ancipites et ait ei: 'Si filius Dei es, dic ut isti lapides panes fiant, ne quando fame marcescas et corruas.' At ille respondens 'Non in solo,' inquit, 'pane vivit homo, sed in omni verbo quod procedit de ore Dei.' Tunc assumpsit eum diabolus in sanctam civitatem Hierusalem, quippe ob templum Dei et sancta sanctorum ac divinum cultum ceteris gentibus ad idolatriam conversis 'sancta civitas' dicebatur, et statuit eum supra pinnaculum templi, ubi excelsa doctorum ac magistrorum sedes erat, et dixit ei: 'Si filius Dei es, mitte te deorsum. Scriptum est enim quod angelis suis mandavit de te et in manibus tollent te, ne quando offendas ad lapidem pedem tuum.' Ait ei Iesus: 'Iterum scriptum est: "Non temptabis Dominum Deum

89   tuum."' Iterum assumpsit eum diabolus in montem excelsum valde et ostendit ei omnia regna mundi et gloriam eorum et dixit: 'Haec omnia tibi dabo si cadens adoraveris me.' Tunc dixit ei Iesus 'Vade Satanas,' non 'retro,' ut Petro Domini voluntati resistenti dictum est, quod significat 'sequere me,' sed 'Vade,' inquit, 'Satanas in ignem aeternum reversurus. Scribitur enim "Dominum Deum tuum adorabis et illi soli servies."' Tunc reliquit eum diabolus et ecce angeli accesserunt et ministrabant ei. Cum itaque gulam et avaritiam ac denique *cenodoxiam,* hoc est inanem gloriam, validiora humanae temptationis genera frustra expertus esset incassumque temptasset, victus demum superatusque evanuit. Angeli vero post

hungry, and so was seized with a great doubt. He didn't believe
that He was a pure man because of the divine words concerning
Him, nor did he believe Him to be the Son of God because he
saw Him hungry. Hence confused by this great dilemma, seeing
Him hungry, he approached to tempt Him so that by the temptation the doubtful point would be clarified.

So the tempter approached speaking ambiguous words and say-   88
ing to Him: "If you are the Son of God, tell these stones to become bread so that you may not be weakened by hunger and col-
lapse."[154] But He replied: "Man does not live by bread alone, but
by every word that comes from the mouth of God."[155] Then the
devil took Him up to the holy city of Jerusalem, which was so
called on account of God's Temple, the Holy of Holies, and its
divine worship when other nations had turned to idolatry. He
placed Him on the summit of the Temple,[156] which was the lofty
home of doctors and teachers, and said to Him: "If you are the
Son of God, cast yourself down. For it is written that He commanded His angels about you, and they will bear you up in their
arms, so that you do not strike your foot against a rock."[157] Jesus
said to him: "Again it is written: 'You shall not tempt the Lord
your God.'"[158] Again, the devil took Him up to a very high moun-   89
tain and showed Him all the kingdoms of the world and their
glory and said:[159] "I shall give you all of this if you fall down and
worship me."[160] Then Jesus said to him: "Go, Satan." (He did not
say "Go back," as was said to Peter when he resisted the will of the
Lord, and which meant "Follow me.")[161] Instead, He said, "Go,
Satan, and return to the eternal fire. For it is written: 'You shall
worship the Lord your God and serve Him alone.'"[162] Then the
devil left Him, and lo! the angels approached and ministered to
Him.[163] When the devil had vainly tried gluttony and avarice and
cenodoxia, or empty glory—which are the most powerful forms of
human temptation—at last conquered and vanquished, he disap-

hunc tam repentinum diaboli recessum subito assistentes ei opportuno tempore famulabantur.

90   Hanc diabolicam temptationem poeta noster pulchre eleganterque huiusmodi carminibus signavit:

> Inde quater denis iam noctibus atque diebus
> ieiunium dapibus Sacro Spiramine plenum
> insidiis temptator adit doctusque per artem
> fallaces offerre dapes: 'Si filius,' inquit,
> 'cerneris esse Dei, dic ut lapis iste repente
> in panis vertatur opem.' Miracula tamquam
> haec eadem non semper agat qui saxea terrae
> viscera frugiferis animans fecundat aristis
> et panis de caute creat! Hac ergo repulsus
> voce prius 'Hominem non solo vivere pane
> sed cuncto sermone Dei.' Labefactus et amens,
> altera vipereis instaurans arma venenis
> cum Domino montana petit cunctasque per orbem
> regnorum monstravit opes, 'Haec omnia,' dicens,
> 'me tribuente feres si me prostratus adores.'
> Quantum perversus tantum perversa locutus!
> Scilicet ut fragilis regni affectaret honores
> qui populis aeterna parat monstrumque nefandum
> pronus adoraret cuius super aethera sedens
> terra pedum locus est quem nullus cernit et omnis
> laudat in excelsis submissa voce potestas.
> Christus ad haec 'Tantum Dominum scriptura Deumque
> iussit adorari et soli famularier uni.'
> His quoque deficiens et gressibus audet iniquus
> ter sese attollens animo praestare superbo
> terque volutus humo fragili confidere bello.
> Tunc assumpsit eum sanctam sceleratus in urbem

peared. But after the devil's sudden departure, the angels instantly
appeared and opportunely ministered to Him.

Our poet nicely and elegantly described this temptation by the   90
devil in these verses:

Then for forty days and nights, as He abstains from food
But is filled with the Holy Spirit, the Tempter approaches
With guile and, skilled in artfully offering deceitful food,
Says "If you are the son of God, tell this rock to turn itself
At once into bread." As if He does not always perform
These very miracles Who enriches the stony bowels
Of the earth with grain, and creates loaves from the crag!
But with these words He first rebuffed him:
"Man does not live by bread alone, but by every one of
God's sayings." Weakened but furious, the devil
The Devil renews the battle with viperous venoms,
And with the Lord climbs the mountains and shows Him
All the wealth of kingdoms throughout the world,
Saying, "All this you shall have from me if you fall down
And worship me." His speech is as perverse as his own self!
As if the Lord should strive for the honors of fragile kingship
When He prepares eternal rewards for the people,
And prostrate should worship this unspeakable monster
When He sits above the heavens with the earth as his
    footstool,
And though none sees Him, all the powers laud Him on high
In humble words. To this Christ says, "The Scriptures bid us
Worship only the Lord God, and serve Him alone."
Defeated at this encounter too, the Unjust One
Dares rise up thrice with a proud spirit, and thrice treading
The ground, he pins his hopes on his flimsy warfare.
Then the Wicked One took Him up to the holy city,

et statuens alti supra fastigia templi
'Si natum genitori Deo tu te asseris,' inquit,
'impiger e summo demissus labere tecto.
Nam scriptura docet de te mandasse Tonantem.
Angelicis subvectus eas ut tutior ulnis
ad lapidem ne forte pedem collidere possis.'
O quam caeca gerit nigro sub pectore corda
mens tenebris obscura suis! Hunc ardua templi
culmina erectae quamvis fastigia pinnae
credidit in praeceps horrescere maxima summi
curavit qui membra poli caelosque per omnes
vectus in extremae descendit humillima terrae
inferiora petens sed non excelsa relinquens.
Dixerat et validi confessus cuspide verbi
quod temptare suum Dominum Deumque nequiret
victoris ora fugit gemens. Tunc hoste repulso
caelicolae assistunt proceres coetusque micantes
angeli Christo famulantur rite ministri.

91   Non multo post, dum Iesus in Galilaeam proficisceretur, factum est ut Andreas et Iohannes, duo praestantes memorati Baptistae discipuli, propter efficacem quamdam et assiduam doctoris sui
de Iesu Christo praedicationem ad ipsum converterentur ac veteri
illo eorum praeceptore penitus praetermisso hunc novum sequerentur. Huius divini potius quam humani ac novelli et inusitati
magistri incredibilem quamdam suavitatem ubi Andrea degustavit,
Simonem quemdam fratrem suum—qui postea Petrus a Iesu idcirco cognominatus est, ut ab altero eiusdem nominis homine
Chananaeo distingueretur, in parvo Galilaeae vico nato,[16] ubi Dominus aquas convertit in vinum—paulo accuratius quesivit inven-
tumque ut converteretur ad Iesum deduxit.

And placed Him upon the pinnacle of the great temple,
Saying, "If you claim to be the son of God the Father,
Then boldly jump and fall from this high roof.
For the Scriptures teach that the Thunderer
Gave a command concerning you, that the angels
Should bear you safely in their arm, lest by chance
You strike your foot against a rock." How blind
The heart within this black breast that this mind bears,
Darkened by its own shadows! It believed that Christ
Would fear plunging from the steep temple heights,
And the summits of the raised parapet — He who built the
    great
Structures of lofty heaven, descended through all the heavens,
And sought earth's inferior regions below
Without abandoning the highest. The demon spoke,
Confessing at the sting of his powerful words
That he could not tempt his Lord and God.
Groaning he fled the sight of the Victor. The enemy repulsed,
The heavenly princes and the sparkling hosts arrive,
And serve Christ like a ministering angel.[164]

Not much later, as Jesus was on his way to Galilee, it happened 91
that Andrew and John, two worthy disciples of the Baptist, were
converted by their teacher's persuasive and persistent sermons
about Jesus Christ; and completely abandoning their former in-
structor, followed this new one.[165] After Andrew had tasted the
incredible sweetness of this new and unusual teacher, more divine
than human, he diligently sought out his brother Simon, and having found him, led him to Jesus to be converted. (This Simon later
received from Jesus the second name Peter to distinguish him from
the Canaanite of the same name who was born in the small village
in Galilee where the Lord turned water into wine.)[166]

92   Ei postridie in Galilaeam exeunti Philippus quidam in itinere occurrit, qui a praedictis Andrea et Petro—quod omnes a Bethsaida oriundi erant—mirabilia quaedam de Christo audivera[n]t. Ideoque cum ab eo vocaretur facilius conversus ipsum prosequebatur; sed et ipse gustata divinae conversationis dulcedine, Nathanahelem quemdam fratrem suum—virum in omni prophetarum et legis doctrina peritissimum—de certo quodam et expresso Messiae adventu erudivit et docuit. Unde ut Iesus ad sese visendi gratia venientem prospexit, ad ipsum conversus 'Ecce,' inquit, 'vere Israhelita in quo dolus non est.' Qua de re ab eo unde se nosceret interrogatus, priusquam a Philippo fratre vocaretur, dum forte sub ficu esset, se eum cognovisse respondit. Proinde vehementer admiratus quod ab eo longius distante cognosci potuerit, cum nullo umquam tempore ab illo visus esset, ipsum verum Dei Filium ac

93 regem Israhel esse plane et aperte confessus est. Hunc tamen tam probum et tam eruditum virum in numero apostolorum ideo collocare noluit, quoniam primos fideles ac primitivae ecclesiae fundatores principesque et auctores rudes atque simplices homines propterea instituere voluit, ne prima hominum conversio humanae sed divinae potius sapientiae ascriberetur, quamquam Iesus commemoratos discipulos tunc non ita firmiter sibi adhaerentes habebat quin ad propria et familiaria negotia interdum remearent. Verum ob nonnulla ingentia miracula in oculis eorum gesta et celebrata paulo post ita coepit ut, ceteris omnibus omissis, ipsum solum tamquam unicum et verum magistrum sequerentur.

94   Ut igitur in Galilaeam venit, in Nazareth—parvo quodam eius provinciae vico, ubi nutritus fuerat—aliquamdiu habitavit. Ibi synagogam ingressus legit dixitque multa, quorum causa ipsum de muro praecipitare voluerunt. Unde in Capharnaum, maritimam Galilaeae provinciae urbem, descendit. Dum deinde nuptiae nescio quae in Cana, parvo quodam Galilaeae oppido, forte celebrarentur et Iesus et mater eius in Galilaeam proficiscerentur atque nuptiale ad convivium invitarentur, una cum commemoratis discipulis

The next day, as Jesus set forth for Galilee, on the way he met a   92
certain Philip, who had heard marvelous stories concerning Christ
from Andrew and Peter: for they all came from Bethsaida.[167]
Hence, when Jesus called him, he was easily converted and followed Him. Having tasted the sweetness of His divine conversation, Philip taught and instructed his brother Nathanael, a great
scholar of all the teaching of the Law and the prophets, about the
certain and manifest advent of the Messiah.[168] So when Jesus saw
him coming to meet Him, he turned to him and said: "Here is
truly an Israelite in whom there is no guile."[169] When Nathanael
asked Jesus how He knew him, He replied that before Philip had
called him, He knew him while he sat under a fig tree.[170] So
amazed that Jesus could know him from afar, having never seen
him before, Nathanael plainly and openly acknowledged Him as
God's true Son and the King of Israel.[171] Jesus chose not to in-   93
clude this very upright and learned man in the number of his
apostles; for he wished to appoint rude and simple men as the first
faithful and the founders and leaders of the primitive church, so
that the first conversions would be ascribed to divine wisdom
rather than human. Now, these chosen disciples were then not always so firmly loyal to Jesus that they did not sometimes return to
their own household business. But by virtue of several great miracles accomplished and performed in their sight, soon thereafter
they began to abandon everything else to follow Jesus alone as
their sole true master.

When He arrived in Galilee, he dwelt for some time in Naza-   94
reth, the small village of the district where He had been raised.[172]
There he entered the synagogue, where he read the Scriptures and
said many things that moved the priests to try to cast him headlong from the city wall.[173] So he went down to Capharnaum, a
coastal city of Galilee.[174] Later, when a wedding was being celebrated in Cana,[175] a small town in Galilee, Jesus and His mother
went there and were invited to the nuptial banquet, where they

95 interfuerunt. Has tam faustas ac tam felices nuptias quae divinos
convivas habere meruerunt Iohannis postea evangelistae nonnulli
fuisse propterea putaverunt quod Maria, diurnis nocturnisque orationibus in intimis domus suae penetralibus vacare solita, raro nisi
quadam vel implendae legis vel conservandae agnationis suae vel
quavis alia necessitate urgente in publicum prodibat. Nam et adi-
mplendae legis gratia in Bethlehem ut profiteretur et Hierosolymam in solemni paschatis die eam venisse legimus, cum prius
Elisabeth cognatam suam iam partui propinquam ministrandi
causa invisisset. Quod et Hieronymus de Iohanne in evangelii sui
prologo his verbis plane et aperte sensisse videtur: 'Iohannes,' inquit, 'a Deo electus est quem de nuptiis nubere volentem ad se
vocavit.'

96   Dum igitur solemnes earum nuptiarum convivae epularentur
potarentque, Maria—de sponsi honore, ut par erat, sollicita—vinum mensis actutum defuturum suspicabatur. Ideoque ad filium
conversa hunc vini defectum fore admonebat nisi quamprimum
provideretur. At ille nihil ad se ipsos pertinere respondit, velut
si ad evidentius tantae rei miraculum—ut postea evenit—totum
97 prius defecisse praestolaretur. Convivis postmodum frequentius—
ut fit—potantibus, vinum penitus defecisse omnibus innotuit.
Unde Iesus nuptialibus ministris subito imperavit ut aqua omnes
assistentes hydrias complerent; idque cum ministri divino man-
dato obtemperantes actutum fecissent (sex hydrias lapideas iuxta
veterem seniorum suorum traditionem, pro crebra et usitata ceterorum vasculorum ablutione, in propatulo astabant) usque ad
summum referserunt. Ex illis deinde aquariis vasis, obtemperandi
gratia, hauserunt haustumque archit⟨r⟩iclino principali nuptiarum
praefecto quam primum attulerunt; qui quidem, ubi ex aqua vinum factum fuisse gustavit, unde id provenisset ignorans satis admirari non poterat. Ministri autem qui hauserant non ignorabant.
Itaque huiusmodi tam admirabile et potius divinum et caeleste
quam humanum et terrestre vinum, frequentibus poculis affatim

were joined by the disciples.[176] Some have thought that this fortu- 95
nate and felicitous wedding, worthy of its divine guests, was that
of John who became the Evangelist: for Mary, who usually attended night and day to her prayers in the inner chambers of her
house, rarely appeared in public except to comply with the Law, to
aid her relatives, or out of some other urgent necessity. Thus, we
have read how she went to Bethlehem to comply with the Law,
and came to Jerusalem on the high feast of Passover, and how
earlier she had visited her cousin Elizabeth to aid her as she
neared childbirth. This is what Jerome seems to have expressed
plainly and openly concerning John in his preface to the latter's
Gospel: "John was chosen by God to be called to Himself from
the wedding when he wanted to wed."[177]

While the noble guests of the wedding ate and drank, Mary, 96
rightly worried about the groom's reputation, suspected that the
wine being served would soon run out. Turning to her son, she
warned Him that the wine would run out unless He acted at once.
But He replied that it was no concern of theirs, as if He was waiting for all of it to run out — as later happened — to make the miracle of this great feat even clearer. As the guests drank more freely, 97
as happens, everyone noticed that the wine had completely run
out. So Jesus at once bade the wedding servers to fill all the available jugs with water. The servants at once obeyed the divine commandment and filled them to the brim. (By the ancient tradition
of their elders, there were six stone jugs outside the house for the
frequent cleansing of other vessels according to custom.) They
drew from the water jugs to mix the drinks, and carried the draft
to the table of the chief steward as quickly as possible. He tasted
the wine made from water and, not knowing whence it came,
could not have been more amazed. But the servants who had
drawn it knew. This wonderful wine, more divine and heavenly
than human and earthly, was served in quite generous portions

per mensas appositum, a cunctis convivis — uno omnium con-
98 sensu — ceteris iam habitis longe suavius censebatur. De quo quidem sponsus, supra quam dici potest admiratus, architriclinum
ideo coram omnibus obiurgabat, quod vinum tam suave ceteris
omnibus multo nobilius contra consuetum degendi ac convivendi
morem usque ad extremum reservasset, quando extincta siti vina
non ita suavia et dulcia compotantibus in nuptialibus conviviis videri solent. Hoc ingens miraculum poeta noster exprimere volens
'Mirabile!' inquit,

> fusas
> in vinum convertit aquas: amittere gaudent
> pallorem latices, mutavit laeta saporem
> unda suum largita merum mensasque per omnes
> dulcia non nato praebuerunt pocula musto.

99 Ob hoc ergo tantum ac tam manifestum miraculum nonnulli
ex commemoratis eius discipulis, ceteris omnibus omissis, ipsum
sequebantur, in quibus et Iohannes praedictarum nuptiarum
sponsus, antequam cum nova nupta conveniret, Christum matri-
monio non iniuria praetulit.

100   Ceteri vero post magnam quamdam multorum piscium capturam, relictis et ipsi omnibus, secuti sunt. Cum enim ipse non
multo post forte secus stagnum Gennesareth staret, quod aliis
nominibus Mare Tiberiadis ac Mare Galilaeae variis de causibus
appellabatur, duas naves propinquas et otiosas vidit; nam piscatores descenderant ac retia lavabant. Ascendens autem in unam
navium quae erat Simonis, rogavit ut a terra paululum recederet;
101 quo facto, de navicula turbas iam propinquas edocebat. Sed ut
cessavit loqui, ad Simonem conversus, 'Duc,' inquit, 'in altum et
laxate retia in capturam.' At Simon tota nocte frustra sese labo-
rasse ac nil cepisse respondit. 'In verbo autem tuo,' ait, 'praeceptor
retia laxabo.' Cum hoc igitur iuxta mandatum Domini fecissent,
magnam piscium multitudinem ibidem conclusam usque adeo

throughout the meal, and was judged unanimously by all the
guests as sweeter by far than the ones already consumed. Amazed   98
more than words can tell, the groom rebuked the chief steward in
front of everyone for having kept this wine, sweet and nobler than
the others, for the last, contrary to the usual custom of entertain-
ing and dining: for once their thirst has been slaked, the drinkers
at a wedding seldom find wines as soft or as sweet.[178] Our poet
sought to describe this extraordinary miracle by saying:

> Wondrous!
> He turns the poured water into wine; and the liquids rejoice
> To lose their pale color; the happy waters change their flavor,
> Lavishing unmixed wine upon all the tables,
> Sweet cups not born of unfermented grapes.[179]

By virtue of this great and manifest miracle several of the disciples   99
abandoned everything else and followed Jesus. Among them was
John, the groom of the wedding just mentioned, who, before
sleeping with his bride, rightly preferred Christ to marriage.[180]

And after a great catch of fish, others, too, abandoned every-   100
thing and followed Him. For shortly thereafter, as He stood by
the lake of Genesareth — which for different reasons was also
called the Sea of Tiberias or Sea of Galilee —, He saw two ships
nearby but empty, for the fishermen had gone ashore and were
cleaning their nets.[181] Boarding one of the boats, which was Simon's, He asked to draw back a little from the land; and when this
was done, from the ship He taught the crowds that had gathered.
When He had finished speaking, He turned to Simon and said,   101
"Sail into the deep and let down your nets for the catch."[182] But
Simon replied that he had worked all night in vain and had caught
nothing. "But at your word, teacher," he said, "I will let down my
nets."[183] Then, when they had acted according to the Lord's commandment, they caught such a great multitude of fish that their

102 ceperunt ut prae multitudine retia rumperentur. Unde sociis in alia navi existentibus innuerunt ut adiuvandi gratia confestim ad se venirent; qui subito venientes ambas naviculas captis piscibus ita impleverunt referseruntque ut paene, prae magnitudine ponderis, mergerentur. Quod cum Petrus vidisset e vestigio ad genua eius provolutus 'Exi,' inquit, 'a me Domine, quia peccator sum.' Mentis enim stupor et — ut graece dicitur — *exstasis* in tanta piscium cap-
103 tura eum et omnes alios assistentes circumdederat. Hanc tantam ac tam repentinam piscium capturam poeta noster exprimens, 'Tantum,' inquit,

> apertos
> implevit captura sinus ut praeda redundans
> turbaret geminas cumulato pisce carinas.

104 Sed quo ordine vocati sunt omnes apostoli duodecim in evangelistarum codicibus non apparet, quando quidem non tantum ordo vocationis sed nec ipsa vocatio commemorata est omnium, sed tantummodo Philippi, Petri et Andreae et filiorum Zebedaei et
105 Matthei publicani, qui etiam Levi vocabatur. Admirabilem prae ceteris huius apostoli vocationem tacitus praeterire non possum. Nam dum Iesus per vias forte transiret Mattheum in teloneo[17] sedentem atque argentariam artem exercentem vidit et ait illi: 'Sequere me.' Ille vero dicto citius dominico imperio paruit eumque
106 secutus in domo sua magno convivio recepit. Singillatim vero ab eo nomen et primus et solus Petrus accepit, quem ex consona quadam Chaldaeae et Hebraeae linguae commixtione 'Bar-iona,' hoc est 'columbae filium,' ob probitatem vitae morumque simplicitatem nuncupavit. Nam filios Zebedaei non singillatim sed simul ambos non 'Boanerges'[18] — ut, testante Hieronymo, plerique putaverunt — sed emendatius 'Ben-erehem,' id est 'filios tonitrui' he-
107 braice appellavit. In hoc sane loco animadvertendum occurrit quod scriptura evangelica et apostolica non solum illos duodecim appellat discipulos suos sed omnes etiam qui in ipsum credentes ma-

nets broke from the weight. Then they signaled to their comrades   102
who were in the other boat to come at once to their aid; and arriving quickly, they filled and stuffed both boats with so many fish
that they almost sank under the weight. When Peter saw this, he
instantly fell to His knees and said: "Depart from me, Lord, for I
am a sinner."[184] For this great catch of fish had stupefied him, and
what the Greeks call "ecstasy" had overcome him and all others
who were present. Our poet describes this great and sudden catch   103
of fish as follows:

> So much did the catch fill the open holds
> That the abundant capture upset both boats
> With its heaps of fish.[185]

In the books of the evangelists it is not clear in what order all   104
twelve disciples were called. For not only the order of calling but
even the calling itself is not mentioned for them all except for
Philip, Peter, Andrew, the sons of Zebedee, and Matthew the
publican, who was also called Levi. I cannot pass over in silence   105
the calling of this last apostle, which was more remarkable than
that of the others. As Jesus happened to be on His way, He saw
Matthew sitting in the custom house changing money, and said to
him, "Follow me."[186] He instantly obeyed the Lord's command,
followed Him, and received Him in his house at a great banquet.
Peter was the first and only disciple to receive his name individu-   106
ally from Jesus,[187] who called him Bar-Jona, or "son of a dove,"[188]
by a harmonious blend of Chaldean and Hebrew, on account of
his upright life and pure character. For the sons of Zebedee he
did not name individually, but both together, calling them not
Boanerges—as many have thought, according to Jerome[189]—but
more correctly Ben-eherem, which means "sons of thunder" in
Hebrew.[190] At this point we should note that the evangelical and   107
apostolic scriptures call His disciples not only these twelve, but all
who believed in Him and were trained by His teaching for the

gisterio eius ad regnum caelorum erudiebantur, ex quorum multitudine hos duodecim Petrum, Andream, Iacobum Zebedaei, Iohannem fratrem eius, Philippum, Bartholomeum, Thomam, Mattheum, ⟨Iacobum⟩ Alphei, Thaddeum, Simonem Cananeum, Iudam Scariothis, qui postea tradidit eum, tantummodo elegit, quos et 'apostolos' nominavit.

108   Sed illud tam evidens tamque incredibile de aquae in vino conversione miraculum primum omnium ab eo factum fuisse constat. Perfecto itaque hoc vinario — ut ita dixerim — miraculo, Iesus simul et mater ac discipuli cognatique eius in Capharnaum, civitatem quamdam quae provinciae Galilaeae metropolis erat, post mortem Ioseph rursus propterea descenderunt, ut in principali eius provinciae urbe, ubi tunc suarum artium studia florebant, una

109   cum signis et miraculis sacra evangelii doctrina vulgaretur. Ibi non multis diebus commoratus, Hierosolymam postea, celebrandi paschatis gratia, perrexit. Dum ergo Iesus in templum sacrae urbis ambularet, boum, ovium, columbarum ac turturum et ceterorum omnium huiusmodi animalium, quae ad immolandum sacrificiis idonea putabantur, venditores emptoresque conspexit. Unde admodum indignatus quod in sacro templo, velut in profano quodam et celebrato cunctarum rerum venalium emporio decantatisque nundinis, mercaturarum negotiationes exercerentur, illico eorum cuncta simul cum assistentibus nu⟨m⟩mulariorum mensis pervertit eosque omnes — flagello de funiculis effecto — inde protinus huiusmodi terribilibus maiestatis suae verbis minabundus eiecit. Sic enim scriptum esse inquit: '"Domus mea domus orationis vocabitur." Vos autem mercimoniis vestris speluncam latronum effecistis.'

110   Pro pleniori vero harum rerum cognitione mutiplices Iudaeorum populos de cunctis paene regionibus ad templum Dei Hierosolymam confluere consuesse — quemadmodum legimus — ita omnibus huius nostri operis lectoribus plane et aperte significamus, ut legis divinae mandatis obtemperantes hostias immolarent. Quae quidem cum taurorum, arietum, hircorum pro divitibus, tum

kingdom of heaven.[191] But from this great multitude He only chose these twelve, whom He called apostles: Peter, Andrew, James the son of Zebedee and John his brother, Philip, Bartholomew, Thomas, Matthew, ⟨James⟩ the son of Alpheus, Thaddeus, Simon the Canaanite, and Judas Iscariot, who later betrayed him.[192]

Now it is agreed that this manifest and incredible miracle of   108
turning water into wine was the first of all the miracles that He performed. Having completed this vinous miracle, so to speak, Jesus went down to Capharnaum—a capital city in the province of Galilee—with His mother, His disciples, and His relatives.[193] For after the death of Joseph, they wished to spread the holy teaching of the Gospel by signs and miracles in the principal city of the province, where the study of the arts then flourished. After several   109
days spent there, He then went on to Jerusalem to celebrate Passover.[194] Now, as He walked in the temple of the holy city, He beheld people buying and selling cattle, sheep, doves, turtledoves, and all the animals considered suitable for sacrifice. He was highly indignant that they plied their trade in the holy temple as if it were a crowded secular market of sundry goods on offer during a fair. Suddenly, He overturned their booths, together with the nearby tables of the moneychangers; and making a whip of ropes, He drove them out, threatening them with the terrifying words of His majesty.[195] He said that it is written, "'My house shall be called a house of prayer.' But with your wares you have made it into a den of thieves."[196]

Now, to enhance understanding of these matters, we clearly and   110
explicitly inform the readers of this work that, as we read, various Jewish peoples habitually gathered from nearly every region at God's temple in Jerusalem in order to sacrifice victims according to the commandments of Divine Law. There were so many great sacrifices, especially on feast days, that they seem nearly miraculous:

quoque columbarum ac turturum pro pauperibus — festis maxime diebus — tot et tantae erant ut paene mirabiles viderentur. Cum autem contingeret ut qui de longinquis regionibus venerant victimas non haberent, sacerdotes omnia animalia quibus ad sacrificia opus erat ut venderentur constituebant, et ne forte in opibus et pecunia egentibus victimae aliquatenus deficerent num⟨m⟩ularios in templo, una cum memoratis hostiarum venditoribus, suis quoque locis collocabant, ut pecuniam sub cautione in opibus ⟨egentibus⟩ et potentibus mutuarent.

111   De hac tam repentina ac tam praepotenti evectione Iudaei supra quam dici potest vehementer admirabantur quaerebantque unde tantam sibi potestatem arrogaret ut quoscumque libuisset de templo eiceret. Sed quoniam multa ab eo miracula facta fuisse constabat, idcirco plurimi in eum crediderunt, quorum princeps Nicodemus quidam fuit, qui legem et prophetas prae ceteris illius temporibus hominibus probe ac integre interpretari et intelligere videbatur.

112   Ipse deinde et discipuli eius in Iudaeam provinciam venerunt ibique cum eis aliquantulum commoratus omnes qui ad se accidebant assidue per discipulos baptizabat. Id etiam Iohannes in Aenon iuxta Salim, ubi aquae plurimum affluebant, frequenter faciebat; nondum enim in vinculis erat. Postea vero quam Iesus Pharisaeos audisse cognovit quod plures a se quam ab Iohanne discipuli baptizarentur et fierent quamquam ipse non baptizaret sed discipuli eius, relicta Iudaea iterum in Galilaeam contendere statuit.

113   Transiens igitur per Samariam in Sychar, quamdam eius provinciae urbem, pervenit. In agro autem quodam ei urbi finitimo vetustus quidam celebratusque fons pullulabat, qui quidem Iacob veteris patriarchae fuerat et iuxta praedium situs erat quod ipse iam pridem Ioseph filio suo dederat; ubi Iesus ex longo itinere fatigatus supra puteum solus, quiescendi gratia, sedebat. Discipulos
114   quippe, ut cibos emerent, in urbem transmiserat. Forte eo tempore

for the rich offered bulls, rams, and goats; and the poor, doves and turtledoves. Since it happened that people who came from distant regions had no victims, the priests decided that all the animals needed for sacrifice should be offered for sale; and so that those with little wealth or money were not denied such victims, they assigned moneychangers to certain parts of the temple — together with the animal vendors — so that for a bond they could lend money to indigent and affluent alike.

Seeing this sudden and violent expulsion, the Jews were amazed beyond words and asked by what right He claimed the power to expel anyone He pleased from the temple.[197] But since they knew that He had performed many miracles, numerous people believed in Him. Foremost among these was a certain Nicodemus, a man who properly and without bias interpreted and understood the Law and the prophets better than any others in his time.[198] 111

After this, Jesus and His disciples went into the province of Judea, and he spent some time there with them and by means of His disciples diligently baptized all those who came to Him.[199] John, too, was often baptizing at Aenon near Salim, where water was abundant, for he had not yet been thrown into prison.[200] After Jesus had learned that the Pharisees had heard He was baptizing more disciples than John — although it was not Jesus himself but His disciples who baptized — He decided to leave Judea and go back to Galilee again.[201] 112

Passing through Samaria, He came to Sichar, a town of that province.[202] In a field near the town there was an ancient and famous spring which had belonged to Jacob, the ancient patriarch, and was near the estate that he had given to his son Joseph. Tired from the long journey, Jesus sat down to rest alone on the well,[203] for He had sent His disciples into the town to buy food.[204] Now, 113

114

mulier quaedam Samaritana, hauriendae aquae causa, ad puteum veniebat. Ad eam Iesus conversus aquae potum postulabat. At illa quod Iudaeus a se quidquam peteret vehementer admirata (quoniam Iudaei Samaritanis propterea non coutebantur quod circumcisionem et Pentateuchum tantummodo recipiebant, a ceteris vero omnibus abhorrebant; ii antequam a rege Assyriorum caperentur et in terra Israhel dimitterentur gentiles erant, sed post captivatem ad Iudaismum conversi sunt) ei aperta fronte respondere non dubitavit: 'Quonam modo,' inquit, 'o Iudaee' (Iudaeum enim ex legitimo et vario diversoque a ceteris gentibus vestimentorum habitu esse cognoscebat) 'a me aquae potum postulare ausus es'? Sed Iesus, mulieris admirationem cernens, omnia sibi enarrare coepit quaecumque ipsa in vita sua ullo umquam tempore egregia fecisset. Quocirca vehementius obstupescens, statim — hydria sua relicta — in urbem currebat, ut Samaritanis civibus Messiam a lege et prophetis plurimis ante saeculis tantopere decantatum, quemadmodum ipsa[19] arbitrabatur, iam mundo apparuisse atque adventasse nuntiaret. Ut vero urbem ingressa est, alta voce clamabat: 'Venite, cives et incolae, venite, inquam, et videte hominem qui omnia mihi paulo ante recitavit quaecumque in vita mea fecissem.' Proinde catervae hominum huiusmodi fama per universam civitatem invalescente, videndi gratia certatim concurrebant, ex quibus multi in eum crediderunt. Nam ob assiduas Samaritanorum preces biduum apud eos com[me]moratus nonnulla miracula faciebat; quapropter magnas hominum turbas ad se convertebat.

116   Post biduum abiens, demum in Galilaeam — ut diximus — perrexit. Ibi Galilaei magno eum honore propterea susceperunt quod omnium mirabilium recordabantur quae in Hierosolymis, solemni paschatis celebratione, ab eo facta fuisse conspexerant. Proinde in Cana — quod Galilaeae oppidum fuisse praediximus — iterato venit, ubi aquam in vinum mirabiliter antea converterat. Forte cuiusdam reguli filius in quodam commemorato eius provinciae oppido nomine Capharnaum graviter aegrotabat; de quo regulus

115

it happened at that time that a Samaritan woman came to the well
to draw water,[205] and Jesus turned to her and asked for a drink of
water. She was greatly surprised to be asked by a Jew, for the Jews
did not associate with the Samaritans,[206] since they recognized
only circumcision and the Torah but rejected everything else. (Before they were captured by the Assyrian king and settled in the
land of Israel, they had been Gentiles, but after their captivity
they were converted to Judaism.) But she did not hesitate to address him openly: "How do you, Jew, dare to ask me for a drink of
water?"[207] (She could tell that he was a Jew from the clothing
prescribed by the Law, which was different from that of other nations.) Perceiving the woman's surprise, Jesus began to relate all
the important things that she had done at any time in her life.[208]
Greatly astonished, she immediately left her water jug and ran to   115
the city to tell the Samaritan townsmen that the Messiah, so heralded by the Law and the prophets many centuries ago, as she
thought, had now come and appeared to the world. When she
entered the city, she cried out in a loud voice: "Come, citizens and
residents, come, I say, and see the man who just now recounted all
the events of my life."[209] When the rumor spread throughout the
entire city, crowds of people zealously gathered in order to see
Him; and many of them believed in Him.[210] For two days, Jesus
stayed among them in response to their continual prayers, and
performed a number of miracles, by which He converted great
masses of people.[211]

Two days later He left, and finally reached Galilee, as we said.   116
There the people of Galilee received Him with great honor, for
they remembered all the miracles that they had seen performed in
Jerusalem at the solemn celebration of Passover.[212] He came again
to Cana — which we previously said was a town in Galilee — where
He had miraculously turned water into wine.[213] It happened that
the son of a centurion in the previously mentioned town of this
region called Capharnaum was seriously ill; and the centurion in

vehementer sollicitus Iesum quotidie miracula facientem quaeritabat. Cum ergo ipsum de Iudaea in Galilaeam descendentem audisset, ad eum anxius veniebat et pro aegroto filio multum admodum flebilis et supplex obsecrabat. Iesus vero ingentem eius fidem conspicatus, etsi eos usque adeo durae cervicis iampridem exprobasset, ut numquam crederent nisi aperta miraculorum signa antea viderent, filium tamen eius postea vivere respondit.

> Non dixit 'victurus erit' sed 'iam quia vivit'
> more Dei, qui ⟨cuncta⟩ prius quam nata videndo
> praeteritum cernit quidquid vult esse futurum.

Quod regulus verum esse procul dubio existimans, magno cum gaudio domum suam revertebatur. Ei autem domum cum gaudio — ut diximus — revertenti nonnulli servi sui in itinere gratulabundi occurrerunt ac filium convalescere alacriter nuntiarunt. Verum cum proprium et opportunum sanitatis suae tempus a servis nuntiantibus paulo exquisitius percontaretur, filium ea proprie hora convaluisse cognovit qua Iesus ipsum vivere responderat. Itaque ubi regulus hoc de filio suo tantum et tam evidens miraculum palam et aperte conspexit, repente una cum universa eius domo in Iesum credidit.

117   Ob haec ergo et cetera huiusmodi ingentia eius miracula turbae multae de pluribus terrarum locis ipsum quocumque ibat passim sequebantur quoscumque infirmos et variis languoribus affectos ac demoniacos ad ipsum afferebant et subito curabat eos. Namque

> salutiferis incedens gressibus urbes,
> oppida, rura, villas, vicos, castella peragrans
> omnia depulsis sanabat corpora morbis.

Quod idcirco faciebat ut doctrinam suam, quam traditurus erat, tantis ac tam ingentibus miraculis praeparatam et tamquam solidis verisque fundamentis — ut ita dixerim — conditam ac fundatam

his great worry went in search of Jesus who was daily performing miracles.[214] When he heard that Jesus was coming down from Judea to Galilee, he anxiously approached Him, and beseeched Him, weeping and supplicating, to heal his sick son. Although Jesus had already rebuked them for stubbornness, and for not believing until they had witnessed miracles,[215] when He beheld his extraordinary faith, He replied that his son would live.[216]

> He did not say, "He shall live," but "now, since he lives,"
> Like God, who, seeing all things before they are born,
> Discerns as past whatever He wills to happen.[217]

The centurion believed this was true beyond a doubt and returned home with great joy. As he joyously returned home, as we said, some of his servants met him en route with congratulations and announced that his son was quickly recovering.[218] After carefully questioning his servants about the exact and propitious hour of his son's recovery, he realized that his son had recovered at the precise moment when Jesus had replied that his son lived.[219] Having plainly and openly witnessed this great and manifest miracle concerning his son, the centurion at once believed in Christ and all his household.[220]

By virtue of these and other extraordinary miracles of His, vast crowds of people from many lands followed Him wherever He went, and brought to Him those who were infirm and suffering from various illnesses and demons, and at once He cured them. For

> entering cities with salubrious steps, and passing through
> Towns, fields, country houses, hamlets, and fortresses,
> He drove off disease and healed all bodies.[221]

He did this so that the teaching that He was going to offer would be prepared by such great and extraordinary miracles, and thus based and founded on such solid and true foundations, as it were,

117

summa quadam veneratione dignam efficeret; sicut etiam post eiusdem traditionem doctrinae facere constituit, ut eam ipsam nonnullis etiam mirabilibus signis evidentius confirmaret.

118   Et paulo post in montem cum discipulis ascendit, ubi cum eis
mirabilia quaedam et vix credibilia locutus in planiorem et capa-
ciorem quemdam montis locum paululum descendit. Ibi, quasi in
campestri quadam regione sedens, coram discipulis et turbis sermonem illum salutarem habuit, in quo inter cetera de pluribus illis
celebratis beatitudinum speciebus aperte disseruit. Cum autem,
completo sermone, de monte descendisset, ecce leprosus quidam
coram turbis sequentibus accedebat ut mundaretur, et genibus
provolutus[20] adorabat eum ac dicebat: 'Si vis, Domine, potes
me mundare.' Et extendens Iesus manum—mirabile dictu—non
modo eum tactu ipso lepra non infecit sed totum leprosi corpus
119   dicto citius confestim mundavit. De quo quidem nemo eum quasi
contra legem fecisset accusare ausus est, sed omnes potius quotquot erant mundationis celeritate conspecta in stuporem attraxit,
ut pulchre his verbis exprimitur:

> Ecce autem mediae clamans ex agmine turbae
> leprosus poscebat opem variosque per artus
> plus candore miser: 'Si vis, Domine,' inquit, 'ab istis
> ⟨me⟩ maculis mundare potes.' 'Volo' Christus ut inquit
> confestim redit una cutis proprio⟨que⟩ decore
> laeta peregrinam muta[ve]runt membra figuram
> inque suo magis est vix agnitus ille decore.

Et ut sanavit, ne legem solvere videretur, 'Ostende' inquit 'te sacer-
doti et offer munus quod praecepit Moyses.' Erat quippe lex vetus
ne leprosus de mundatione sua ipse decerneret sed ut conspectu se
sacerdotis offerret et probationem suam oculis eius exponeret atque per hunc modum ex eius sententia in mundorum numerum

so as to be worthy of supreme veneration; just as He resolved to do after he had transmitted his teaching: to confirm it more clearly by miraculous signs.

Shortly thereafter He went up onto a mountain with his disci- 118 ples; and having said some wondrous and nearly incredible things, He came down a little to a more level and spacious part of the mountain. There, as if seated in a country field, before his disciples and the crowds, He preached his renowned sermon of salvation, in which among other things he expounded clearly the several famous kinds of beatitudes.[222] When the sermon was over, He descended from the mountain, when, in front of the crowds that followed Him, behold, a leper approached Him to be cleansed, and falling to his knees he worshipped Him and said: "If you will, Lord, you can make me clean."[223] And Jesus stretched out his hand, and — wondrous to say! — not only was He not infected with leprosy on contact, but He instantly cleansed the leper's entire body all at once. In this matter no one dared accuse Him of violating the 119 Law; instead, everyone present was astonished to behold this rapid cleansing, as is nicely expressed in our poet's words:

Behold, a leper crying from the middle of a packed crowd
Begged for help. More pitiful for the pallor spread over
His mottled limbs, he said: "If you will, Lord, you can
Cleanse me of these stains." When Christ said, "I will,"
At once his skin became uniform, and his joyful limbs
Exchanged their strange appearance for their proper beauty,
And he was scarcely recognizable in his true color.[224]

Now, when Christ had healed him, He said "Show yourself to the priest and offer the gift that Moses prescribed," lest He seem to break the Law.[225] For there was an ancient law that a leper could not himself decide to be cleansed, but should present himself for a priest's inspection and allow him to test him with his eyes. In this way, the priest could decide to return him to the number of the

rediret; nisi enim sacerdos leprosum mundatum fuisse asseruisset, adhuc cum immundis erat extra castra mansurus.

120   Non multo post Capharnaum ingressus centurionem quemdam pro fideli et pretioso servo suo paralytico devotissime obsecrantem his humillimis verbis exaudivit: 'Ego veniam et curabo eum.' Ad quod, cum centurio dominica accessione sese indignum esse respondisset ac satis superque satis sibi ad servi sui valitudinem esse dixisset si tantummodo verbo voluntatem suam expressisset, admirans Iesus se tantam fidem in universo Israhelitico populo non invenisse iis qui sequebantur aperte testatus est ac protinus, quemadmodum centurio postulaverat, sanavit illum.

121   Paulo post synagogam ingressus ibidem assistentes mirabiliter edocebat. Forte eo tempore in synagoga quidam erat qui spiritu immundo vexabatur. Hic ut Iesum vidit exclamans 'Quid nobis et tibi,' inquit, 'Iesu Nazarene? Venisti ante tempus perdere nos'? Et comminatus est ei Iesus dicens: 'Obmutesce et exi ab homine.' Huic ergo divinae voci repente malignus spiritus obtemperans ab homine exivit, ita ut furioso exitu ipsum discerperet. Unde omnes admirabantur et rumores per universam provinciam procedebant.

122   Et protinus de synagoga egredientes in domum Simonis et Andreae cum Iacobo et Iohanne venerunt. Tunc forte socrus Petri febricitabat; quam cum ipse a commemoratis discipulis febricitantem accepisset statim ad eam accessit et apprehensa manu eius continuo a febre adeo dimissa est ut praeter naturae legem ac contra consuetam medicorum curationem illico ministraret, quemadmodum his carminibus palam et aperte insinuatur:

Forte Petri validae torrebat lampadis aestu
febris anhela socrum dubioque in funere pendens

clean; for unless a priest had declared the leper clean, he had to remain outside the walls with the unclean.[226]

Shortly thereafter He entered Capharnaum, where hearing a 120 centurion piously beseech Him on behalf of a faithful and valuable servant of his who was crippled, He humbly said, "I shall come and cure him."[227] The centurion replied that he was unworthy to receive the Lord, but said that it would be quite sufficient for him and his servant's health if only He expressed His will in a word. Jesus was astonished, for He had not found such great faith in all the people of Israel, and said so openly to His followers. So at once He healed the cripple as the centurion had asked.

Soon thereafter He entered the synagogue in the same place 121 and taught his listeners miraculous lessons. It happened that at this time there was present in the synagogue a man tormented by an unclean spirit.[228] When he saw Jesus, he cried out: "What have you to do with us, Jesus of Nazareth? Have you come to destroy us before the time?"[229] Jesus threatened the spirit, saying "Be silent and come out of the man."[230] Obeying these divine words, the evil spirit at once came out of the man, and in his raging exit he tore at him. Everyone was amazed, and word of this spread throughout the region.

Leaving the synagogue straightaway, they came to the house of 122 Simon and Andrew with James and John.[231] It happened that Peter's mother-in-law had a fever; when Jesus learned from his disciples that she was in a fever, He went to her at once and took her hand; the fever immediately departed, such that His care surpassed the law of nature and the customary treatment of doctors. This is implied plainly and explicitly in these verses:

> It happened that a breath of fever was burning Peter's mother-in-law
> With the heat of a mighty torch, poised between life and death,

saucia sub gelidis ardebat vita periclis
incensusque calor frigus letale coquebat.
At postquam fessos Domini manus attigit artus
igneus ardor abit totisque extincta medullis
fonte latentis aquae cecidit violentia flammae.

123 Vespere autem facto, cum sol occubuisset, rursus afferebant ad
eum omnes male habentes et daemoniacos cunctosque curabat qui
variis languoribus tenebantur et daemonia eicieba[n]t. Post haec
turbis imperavit ut trans fretum irent; quo facto ipse una cum
discipulis in naviculam ascendit. Dum forte navigaretur Iesus dor-
mire coepit et subito, quasi de industria fieret, ingens tempes-
tas oritur. Proinde discipuli extimescentes et pavore percussi dor-
mientem Iesum excitaverunt, qui ut surrexit, redargutis primo de
incredulitate et pavore discipulis, mox ut cessarent ventis et mari
imperavit; et continuo facta est tranquillitas, ita magna ut turbae
de tanta hominis potestate—cui venti et maria parebant—satis
admirari non possent. Quod poeta his versibus expressit:

Ergo ubi pulsa quies cunctis clamantibus una
voce simul 'Miserere, citus! Miserere, perimus!
Auxilio succurre pio!' nil vota moratus
exurgens Dominus validis mitescere ventis
imperat et dicto citius tumida aequora placat.

124 Per hunc igitur modum tempestate sedata, in regionem Gerase-
norum transfretavit, quae urbs est Arabiae trans Iordanem, non
longe sita a stagno Tiberiadis, in quod porci—ut paulo post dice-
tur—praecipitati sunt. Ibi duo a daemonibus crudeliter vexati occurrerunt; ita enim de monumentis saevi exibant ut neminem per
viam illam transire permitterent. Hi ut Iesum viderent clamare
coeperunt: 'Quid tibi et nobis, Iesu fili Dei? Cur venisti huc ante
tempus torquere nos'? Et rogabant ut si eos inde eiceret in

Her stricken life was burning amid frigid dangers,
And the kindled heat was cooking the chill of death.
But after the Lord's hand had touched her weary limbs,
The fiery heat departed, and throughout her inward parts
The violent flame was quenched by a font of hidden water.[232]

When evening came and the sun had set, they again brought to   123
Him all who were ill or possessed, and He healed all those who
suffered various infirmities, and He cast out demons.[233] Then He
commanded the crowds to go across the sea;[234] thereupon, together with His disciples, He boarded a boat. While they were
sailing, Jesus fell asleep; and suddenly, as if by plan, a prodigious
storm arose.[235] Alarmed and fear-stricken, the disciples awoke Jesus; when He arose, He first reproached them for their lack of
faith and their fear, and then commanded the stormy sea to sub-
side. At once, there was calm, so great that the crowds could not
sufficiently wonder at the great power of this man, whom the
winds and seas obeyed.[236] Our poet expressed this in these verses:

> Now, when his sleep was broken by all of them crying out
>   together
> With one voice, "Have mercy quickly! Have mercy, we perish!
> Aid us with your faithful help!" Without delay,
> The Lord rose up and commanded the strong winds to abate,
> Instantly calming the surging billows.[237]

After the storm had been thus allayed, He crossed the sea to   124
the country of the Gerasenes,[238] a city across the Jordan in Arabia,
not far from Lake Tiberias, into which — as we shall see — the herd
of swine plunged. There He was met by two men cruelly afflicted
by demons, who emerged so savagely from the tombs that they let
no one pass. When the demons saw Jesus, they began to cry:
"What have you to do with us, Jesus, Son of God? Why have you
come here to torment us before the time?"[239] And they asked

quemdam duorum milium porcorum gregem non longe pascentem
125 transmitteret. Namque

> Domini praecepta tremens exire iubentis,
> spiritus infelix hominem non audet adire,
> effigiem repetens quam Christum cernit habere.
> Sed pecus, immunda gaudens lue, semper amicum
> sordibus atque olido consuetum vivere caeno
> pro meritis petiere suis tristesque phalanges
> porcinum tenuere gregem: niger, hispidus, horrens
> talem quippe domum dignus fuit hospes habere.

Et ait illis: 'Abite.' At illi exeuntes abierunt in porcos, qui magno
quodam impetu — ceu non naturalibus sed diabolicis stimulis agi-
tati — praecipites in mare superius memoratum proruperunt[21]
obrutique aquis obierunt. Pastores autem, magno pavore perterriti,
repente fugerunt in urbemque certatim abeuntes quemadmodum
stupenda res sese habuerat palam omnibus nuntiabant, quo audito
universa civitas ad Iesum venit.

126   Et paulo post octo dierum intervalla, dum de regione Gerase-
norum in Capharnaum reverteretur et in domo quadam forte mo-
raretur, paralyticum quemdam ad eum afferebant; quem cum ad
ipsum prae turba hinc inde opprimente afferre non possent, tectum illius domus nudaverunt, ut inde quando aliter fieri non posset paralyticum submitterent. Per tectum igitur tegulis patefactum
grabatum, in quo iacens paralyticus ferebatur, diligenter et accurate submiserunt. Videns autem Iesus fidem illorum dixit paralytico: 'Confide, fili: remittuntur tibi peccata tua.' Quod nonnulli
scribae permoleste tulerunt, in hac ipsa peccatorum paralytici di-
127   missione Iesum intra sese blasphemare dicentes. At Iesus, cum
cogitationes ipsorum animadvertisset, 'Quid cogitatis,' inquit, 'mala
in cordibus vestris? Quid est facilius dicere? "Dimittuntur tibi
peccata" aut dicere "Surge et ambula"? Ut autem sciatis quia filius

Him, if He cast them out, to send them into a herd of two thousand swine that was feeding nearby. For   125

> quaking at the Lord's words bidding him come out,
> The unhappy spirit dared not approach a man,
> Regaining the human likeness that he saw Christ bear.
> But, as they deserved, the grim bands attacked the swine,
> Delighting in filthy pollution, always a friend to dirt,
> Used to living in squalor and stinking mud,
> And occupied the herd of pigs: black, shaggy, and bristling,
> The guest was worthy to have such a house.[240]

And He said to them: "Depart."[241] They came out and entered into the swine which with great impetus—as if driven by diabolical goads, rather than natural ones—plunged headlong into the sea and drowned as the waters covered them. The swineherds were stricken with great fear and, as if racing each other, at once fled into the city, where they publicly reported to all how this amazing event had occurred; and hearing this, the entire city came to Jesus.[242]

After a short period of eight days, while Jesus was returning   126 from the country of the Gerasenes to Capharnaum, He happened to stay in a house, where they tried to bring a cripple to Him.[243] But because the crowd was pushing on all sides, they could not bring him to Him, so they stripped the roof of the house so that they could lower the cripple from there, since no other way was possible. And through a hole opened in the roof tiles, they carefully and cautiously lowered the pallet on which the cripple lay. Seeing their faith, Jesus said to the cripple: "Take heart, my son; your sins are forgiven."[244] Some scribes were greatly vexed by this, saying among themselves that Jesus blasphemed in forgiving the cripple's sins. But Jesus perceived their thoughts and said "Why do   127 you think evil thoughts in your hearts? Which is easier to say: 'Your sins are forgiven' or 'Arise and walk'? But so that you may

hominis habet potestatem dimittendi peccata in terra,' tunc ait paralytico: 'Surge, tolle lectum tuum et vade in domum tuam.' Et surrexit et abiit in domum suam. Videntes autem turbae timuerunt et glorificaverunt Deum qui tantam hominibus potestatem dederat.

128   Quidam deinde archisynagogus nomine Iairus, cuius filia vel modo defuncta vel quasi in mortis articulo constituta prope mortua erat, obsecrandi gratia ad eum accedebat rogabatque ut filiam eius vel sanaret vel a morte potius suscitaret. Quod cum Iesus accepisset, subito cum discipulis eum tendentem domum sequebatur. Euntibus vero illis mulier quaedam, de Caesarea Philippi oriunda, quae fluxum sanguinis duodecim annis patiebatur et omnia sua in medicos frustra erogaverat, magnopere confidebat ut si quid suum tangeret veteri eius aegritudine liberaretur. Unde retrorsum illis in itinere proficiscentibus (nam iuxta legem urbibus excludebatur) ut sibi prae turba licuit vestimenti sui fimbriam tetigit et confestim sanata est:

> Quae magnas tenuarat opes ut sanior esset
> exhaustaque domo nec proficiente medela
> perdiderat proprium pariter cum sanguine censum.

129   Atque ad perpetuam huius ingentis miraculi memoriam pro foribus domus suae basim quamdam in loco editiore collocaverant, in qua mulieris ipsius velut genibus provolutae palmasque tendentis imago aere videbatur expressa. Astabat autem e regione altera aerea statua fusa habitu viri stola compte circumdati, qui dexteram mulieri porrigebat; ad pedes vero huius statuae herba quadam specie nascebatur quae orta, in dies crescens, usque ad statuae illius fimbriam sive stolae illius aerei indumenti sese extendebat. Et cum ita crescens fimbriam tetigisset, tantas vires ad propellendos morbos ac languores acquirebat ut omnes corporis aegritudines vel solo vel exiguo tactu—incredibile dictu—propelleret; et tamen, antequam fimbriam illam crescendo attigisset, nihil eiusmodi vi-

know that the Son of Man has the power of forgiving sins on earth," He then said to the cripple, "Arise, take up your bed, and go home."[245] And the cripple arose and went to his home. Seeing this, the crowds were awed and glorified God for giving such great power to men.[246]

Then a leader of the synagogue named Jairus, whose daughter was recently deceased or in the grip of death, came to beseech Jesus, asking Him to heal his daughter or rather to raise her from the dead.[247] When Jesus had heard this, with His disciples He immediately followed the man to his home. As they walked, a woman from Caesarea Philippi,[248] who had suffered bleeding for twelve years and had spent all her money in vain on doctors, had great confidence that she would be freed of her former disease if she could touch some part of Jesus.[249] So she followed behind them as they set out on their journey (for under the Law she was excluded from cities); and when the crowd permitted, she touched the hem of his robe, and was immediately healed. 128

She had wasted her great wealth in order to be healed,
Ruining her home on a cure that failed,
Losing her estate along with her blood.[250]

In perpetual commemoration of this extraordinary miracle, they placed a pedestal on high ground in front of the door of her house, on which was carved in bronze an image of the woman prostrating herself at Jesus' knees and lifting up her hands. Nearby there also stood a statue cast in bronze from another region of a man neatly wrapped in a long robe and offering his right hand to the woman. At the foot of this statue emerged a plant that, having sprouted and grown every day, reached the hem of the statue, or of the bronze garment of the long robe. Having grown to touch the hem, it acquired such power to repel diseases and illnesses that even a single or slight touch of it could—wondrous to say!—expel all bodily afflictions; yet before it had grown to touch the hem, it had 129

rium habebat. Hanc statuam ad similitudinem vultus Iesu Christi formatam fuisse dicebant atque usque ad tempora Eusebii Caesariensis ⟨exstitit⟩.²² Eusebius ipse post trecentos circiter annos exstitisse testatur, quemadmodum propriis oculis sese et vidisse et inspexisse confirmat.

130   Pergens deinde in domum principis, ut
    ventum erat ad maesti lugentia culmina tecti
    deflentemque domum, moriens ubi virgo iacebat
    extremum sortita diem trepidusque tumultus
    omnia lamentis ululans implebat amaris
    funerosque modos cantu lacrimante gemebant,

ubi vidit tibicines et turbam de more funerum tumultuantem; veteri enim ritu tibicines mercede conducti ad excitandos luctus in funeribus adhibebantur. Atque ut recederent — quasi dormiret, non esset mortua puella — palam admonebat.

    'Ponite sollicita conceptos mente dolores.
    Hic sopor est,' Salvator ait, 'nec funus adesse
    credite nec somno positam lugete puellam.'

De quo vehementer eum propterea deridebant, quoniam puel-
131 lam ipsam obiisse plane et aperte cognoscebant. Iesus vero postea quam omnes iuxta eius imperium exiverant — non enim aperta tanti miraculi visione digni videbantur qui mirifica opera aspernabantur — e vestigio ingressus tenuit manum eius, hebraice dicens 'Iaalda cumi' non 'Tabita cumi,' ceu in evangelio corrupte ac mendose legitur, hoc est 'Puella surge,' et surrexit puella quasi ex somno expergisceretur. Namque

    gelida constrictum morte cadaver
    spiritus igne fovet verboque immobile corpus
    suscitat atque semel genitam bis vivere praestat.

no such power. It was said that this statue was formed in the likeness of Jesus Christ's visage and survived until the age of Eusebius of Caesarea. Eusebius himself attests that it survived some three hundred years later, and affirms that he saw and inspected it with his own eyes.[251]

Jesus now entered the house of the synagogue leader:[252]   130
When He arrived at the mournful roof of the sad dwelling
And weeping home, where the virgin lay dying,
Having reached her fatal day, the trembling tumult
Filled everything with howls and bitter laments,
Groaning funeral dirges in tearful chant.[253]

When He saw the flute players and the crowd in tumult as is customary at funerals (for by ancient custom flute players were hired for pay to heighten the mourning at funerals), He openly urged them to depart, since the girl was only asleep and not dead.[254]

"Dismiss the grief from your worried minds.
She slumbers," the Savior said. "Think it not
A funeral, and mourn not a girl who lies in sleep."[255]

At this, they sorely mocked Him, since they plainly and openly knew that the girl had died. Now, after everyone had left at His   131
command—for those who despised marvelous works seemed unworthy of witnessing such a miracle[256]—Jesus entered at once and, holding the girl's hand, said in Hebrew "Iaalda cumi," that is, "Arise, girl."[257] And the girl arose as if awaking from sleep. (He did not say "Tabita cumi," as it says in the Gospel's corrupt and erroneous reading.)[258] For

this corpse in the grip of frigid death
His spirit warms with fire, and He revives her rigid body
With a word: though she was born but once, He grants her a
    second life.

215

Obstipuere animis inopinaque vota parentes
aspiciunt versisque modis per gaudia plangunt.

Atque ad probandam huius incredibilis rei veritatem, ne aliquo
modo dubitari posset, cibos in medium apponi ut comederet
edixisse scribitur. Et exit fama in universam terram illam.

132   Tunc duo caeci Iesum inde transeuntem sequebantur, his verbis
clamitantes: 'Miserere nostri, fili David'! Sed cum in hac miserabili
oratione usque in domum perseverassent, ab eo interrogati sunt an
crederent quod ipse sibi visum restituere posset; qui actutum ab
illo fieri posse aperte responderunt, per tactionem dumtaxat ocu-
lorum amissam visionem recuperarunt. Namque

caeca praecantum
lumina diffuso ceu torpens ignis olivo
sub Domini micuere manu tactuque sereno
instaurata suis radiarunt ora lucernis.

Caeci vero, ubi amissum visum recuperarunt, e domo ipsa e vestigio egrediebantur tantique beneficii minime ingrati sese continere
non poterant quin magnitudinem miraculi praeter mandatum Domini per totam terram illam consonis hinc inde vocibus efferrent.

133   Statim autem post hanc caecorum egressionem hominem mutum et a daemonio vexatum ei obtulerunt; qui quidem mutus—
eiecto daemonio, mirabile dictu—locutus est. Etenim hunc 'sacro
ordine' curavit Deus,

versis in contraria causis,
daemonio vacuans, auditu et voce reformans.

134   Dum deinde Iesus una cum discipulis ac magna hominum multitudine in urbe⟨m⟩ nomine Naim tendens proficisceretur, factum
est ut adolescentis cuiusdam funus prope civitatis portam, solem-

> Her parents are amazed to see their unhoped-for prayers
> Answered, and weep for joy in different tones.[259]

As proof of the truth of this incredible feat, so that it could not be doubted in any way, it is written that he bade them set out food for her to eat.[260] And the fame of this spread throughout that land.[261]

As Jesus went on from there, two blind men followed him, cry-   132
ing out in these words: "Have mercy on us, Son of David!"[262] They continued their pitiful prayer as He entered a house, and He asked them if they believed that He could restore their sight. At once they clearly replied that He could. At his mere touch, they recovered the lost vision of their eyes. For

> the blind eyes of supplicants,
> Like a smoldering fire on which oil is poured,
> Flashed at the Lord's hand, and at his soothing touch
> Their renewed faces shone with their own lamps.[263]

When the blind men had recovered their lost sight, they immediately left the house; and in their gratitude for this great blessing, against the Lord's commandment, they could not help proclaiming this great miracle in unison throughout the land.

Immediately after this departure of the blind men, they brought   133
to him a deaf mute afflicted by a demon; when the demon was cast out—wondrous to say!—the mute man spoke.[264] For God healed him

> by divine order, reversing his condition,
> Cleansing him of the demon, and restoring his hearing and
>   voice.[265]

Then, as Jesus traveled to the city called Naim with his disciples   134
and a large multitude of people, it happened that the funeral of a young man was passing near the city gate, and the procession was

ni⟨ter⟩²³ pompam sequentibus civium turbis simul cum matre
vidua, efferretur; quam cum Iesus ideo vehementer flentem con-
spexisset, quod unicus ei fuerat ac propterea liberis carebat, misericordia motus 'Noli,' inquit, 'flere.'

> Nec remorata diu pietas, inimica doloris,
> auxilium vitale dedit tactoque feretro
> 'Surge,' ait, 'o iuvenis' parensque in tempore dicto
> mortuus assurgit[que] residensque loquensque revixit
> atque comes genitricis abit.

Non enim aliter illi divinae voci paruit qui mortuus erat quam si
vivus audisset confestimque surgens matrem cum pompa domum
revertentem sequebatur.

135   Post haec, convocatis duodecim discipulis, dedit illis potestatem
spirituum immundorum, ut omnem languorem cunctasque hominum aegritudines curarent. Sic enim inquit: 'Euntes autem praedicare et dicite quod iam appropinquavit regnum caelorum. Infirmos
curate, mortuos suscitate, leprosos mundate, daemones eicite. Gratis accepistis, gratis date' et reliqua huiusmodi. Interea Iohannes
Baptista ab Herode tetrarcha in carcerem missus in vinculis tenebatur, qui cum haec et huiusmodi stupenda Christi miracula
superius commemorata fama undique increbrescente audiret duos
ex discipulis suis ad eum legatos misit, qui ipsum an esset Messias
percontarentur; non quia ipse dubitaret, sed ut per hanc legationem aliis innotesceret quod ipse non ignorabat. His Iohannis ora-
toribus Iesus auditis, in hunc modum respondit: 'Ite,' inquit, 'renuntiate Iohanni quae auditis et quae vidistis: caeci vident, claudi
ambulant, leprosi mundantur, surdi audiunt, mortui resurgunt' et
quae sequuntur.

136   Cum per sata deinde in synagogam Iudaeorum transire⟨t⟩, forte
ibi quemdam aridam manum habentem invenit et sanavit eum, et
ita sanavit ut confestim manum extenderet. Nam

solemnly followed by crowds of townspeople and by the bereaved mother.[266] When Jesus beheld the mother weeping uncontrollably, because he had been her only son and therefore she was childless, He was moved by pity and said, "Do not weep."[267]

> Without delay, piety, the enemy of grief,
> Gave vital help and, having touched the bier,
> He said, "Rise, boy." And obeying the word at once
> The dead boy rose; and sitting, and speaking, lived again,
> Departing as his mother's companion.[268]

For the dead boy obeyed that divine voice as if he had been alive to hear it, and at once arose and followed his mother as she returned home with the procession.

After this, He gathered the twelve disciples and gave them power over unclean spirits, so that they could heal every human illness and disease.[269] He said: "Go and preach and say that the kingdom of heaven is near. Heal the sick, raise the dead, cleanse the lepers, cast out demons. You received without payment; give without payment," etc.[270] Meanwhile, John the Baptist was being held in prison by Herod the tetrarch; and when he heard of these and similar amazing miracles of Christ, previously mentioned by us, whose fame was growing everywhere, he sent two of his disciples as envoys to ask Him if He was the Messiah[271] — not because he doubted, but so that by this legation others would learn what he already knew. When Jesus had listened to these envoys, he replied thus: "Go, tell John what you hear and what you have seen: the blind see, the lame walk, the lepers are cleansed, the deaf hear, the dead are raised," etc.[272]

Then, after He had passed through the grain fields[273] and entered a synagogue of the Jews, he chanced to find there a man with a withered hand and healed him, and healed him in such a way that he at once stretched forth his hand.[274] For

135

136

imperio⟨que⟩ medens gelidam recalescere palmam
percipit[24] et reduci divino more saluti.

Paulo post caecum quemdam simul ac mutum qui a daemone vehementer vexabatur adeo curavit ut subito loqueretur et videret.
Namque

> Dominus mundi, lux nostra ⟨et⟩ sermo parentis,
> sordibus exclusis oculos atque ora novavit.

Quocirca omnes turbae etiam atque etiam obstupescebant ac dicebant: 'Numquid hic est filius David'? Praeter haec multa ingentia
eius miracula plurima insuper in parabolis[25] edocebat. Quo facto,
mox in patriam suam venit, ubi synagogam ingressus librum Es-
aiae prophetae coram astantibus perlegit, quem ei legendum obtu-
lerant.

137   Ceterum Iohannes, paulo post haec ipsa discipulorum suorum
relata responsa, ab Herode rege capite truncatus ex hac vita in caelum evolavit. Herodes vero de Iesu Christo nova quaedam ac quotidie mirabilia, increbrescentibus hinc inde rumoribus, audiebat.
Proinde qui tantorum operum effector esse posset vehementer admirabatur atque an esset Iohannes Baptista secum ipse cogitans
titubabat, qui ab ipso paulo ante decollatus a mortuis resurrexisset.

138   Atque ibi in patria sua paululum commoratus, quoniam propter
incredulitatem eorum perpauca illic miracula fecit, Hierosolymam
tertio contendit. Ibi certum quoddam aquarum stagnum ex iugi-
bus pluviis collectum erat, in quo immolandae hostiae primitus
lavabantur. In sacerdotalibus deinde vasis sic ablutae a cunctis omnino sordibus mundabantur. Huiusmodi aquarum stagnum quinque speciosas porticus[26] suis intervallis distinctas habebat, ut plurimis simul locis hostiarum latores ad lavacrum lavandi gratia
descenderent. Hic est ille celebris salubrisque locus qui vulgato
verbo 'piscina' dicebatur atque graece propterea *probatica* appellabatur, quod 'ovis' Graeca lingua *probaton* nuncuparetur, quoniam ut

by His command healing the gelid hand,
He saw it warm again, returned miraculously to health.[275]

Shortly thereafter, he healed a blind and mute man who was violently afflicted by a demon, so that he suddenly spoke and saw.[276]

The Lord of the world, our Light and Word of the Father,
Removed his squalor, and renewed his eyes and his sight.[277]

As a result, all the crowds were constantly dumbfounded, and said: "Can this be the Son of David?"[278] Besides these many extraordinary miracles, He taught many lessons in parables.[279] Having done this, He soon came to His homeland, where He entered the synagogue and read to the worshipers the book of the prophet Isaiah, which they had brought to Him to read.[280]

Now, soon after his disciples had reported Jesus' reply, John was 137 beheaded by king Herod and left this life to ascend into heaven. But Herod was hearing new marvels every day about Jesus Christ, as the rumors gathered strength from all quarters. He was exceedingly astonished that anyone could perform such great works and was inwardly perplexed whether this was John the Baptist, who, having just been beheaded at his command, had risen from the dead.[281]

After a brief stay in His homeland, where He performed few 138 miracles because they did not believe in Him, Jesus went to Jerusalem for the third time. There was a certain pool of water, collected from the constant rainfall, in which victims destined for sacrifice were first washed. Then they were cleansed of all dirt by being doused with water from the priests' vessels. This pool of water had five beautiful arcades set at intervals so that the sacrificers could approach it by several routes in order to wash their victims. This celebrated and salutary site in the Vulgate was named the pond (*piscina*), and in the Greek was called "probatic," from the Greek word for sheep, *probaton*, because they generally sacrificed

139 plurimum oves pro hostiis immolari consueverant. Haec probatica
piscina ad immolandarum — ut diximus — hostiarum immolatio-
nem antiquitus instituta ab initio fuerat. Appropinquante autem
post multa temporum curricula praetioso Salvatoris adventu, quotannis certa quadam die eius piscinae aquae ab angelo aperte[27]
movebantur iisque motis tanta salutis virtus divinitus infundeba-
tur ut qui primus ex languidis, quorum catervae in praedictis piscinae porticibus propterea iacebant, in aquam sic ab angelo motam
descendisset a quacumque detineretur aegritudine continuo libe-
rabatur. Quod idcirco evenisse non immerito creditur, quoniam
quaemadmodum per aquae ablutionem in sacro baptismate salus
humano generi parabatur, ita sanitas per aquae commotionem
languidis corporibus acquireretur.

140   Inter multos itaque variis languoribus oppressos forte unus erat
qui triginta octo annos perpetua quadam aegritudine laborabat atque ibidem angelicam aquae commotionem frustra hactenus exs-
pectaverat, quoniam quandocumque aqua ab angelo movebatur
alius aegrotus semper eo celerius surgebat ipsumque ingressus
praecedebat; ac per hunc modum tam diu ibi frustra permanserat.
Dum igitur Iesus forte per speciosas piscinae porticus pertransiret,
hunc tam diuturnum languidum respexit diuturnaeque et inveteratae aegritudinis suae miseratus an convalescere cuperet percon-
141 tabatur. Ille vero neminem se habere respondebat qui sese ad primam aquae commotionem in piscinam deferret, quod ipse per se
minime efficere poterat. Iesus autem his paucis verbis huic lan-
guido 'Tolle,' inquit, 'grabatum tuum et ambula.' Huiusmodi pauca
Salvatoris nostri verba usque adeo efficacia fuisse constat ut mox
pristinas sanitatis suae vires recuperaret insurgeretque; grabatum
enim parvulum, iuxta divinum Salvatoris edictum, tollens defere-
bat, de quo a Iudaeis vehementer redarguebatur, quoniam sabbato
142 grabatum apportaret. Languidus vero, quasi sese excusaret crimen,
in Salvatorem per hunc modum conferebat: 'Qui,' enim inquit, 'me
salvavit, ille mihi ut ita operarem iniunxit.' Sed Iudaei ipsum ulte-

sheep as the victims.[282] As we said, the original probatic pond was   139
established of old for the slaughter of victims. But after many cycles of ages, as the Savior's precious Advent drew near, on a certain
day each year the waters of that pond were visibly moved by an
angel. Such power of healing was infused in the stirred waters
that, of the patients lying in large numbers for that purpose in the
pool's arcade, the first who went down into the water thus moved
by the angel was instantly freed from whatever disease afflicted
him.[283] It is rightly thought that this happened because, just as
the salvation of the human race was being prepared through the
cleansing water of holy baptism, so the bodies of the infirm would
regain their health by the water's motion.

Among the many people suffering from different diseases, there   140
happened to be one who had continually suffered from disease for
thirty-eight years, but so far he had waited in the same place in
vain for the angel's stirring of the water: for whenever the angel
stirred the water, another sick person rose more quickly and entered the water before him; and thus he had waited there for so
long in vain. Now, when Jesus chanced to pass through the pool's
beautiful arcades, He beheld the long-term patient; and pitying his
chronic and longstanding disease, asked him if he wanted to be
healed. The sick man replied that he had no one to carry him   141
down to the pool at the first stirring of the water, for he could not
do this by himself. Jesus spoke a few words to the sick man: "Take
up your bed, and walk."[284] These few words of our Savior had
such evident power that the man soon recovered the strength of
his former health and arose. Obeying the Savior's divine injunction, he lifted up his small bed and carried it away; but the Jews
severely rebuked him for carrying his bed on the Sabbath.[285] As if   142
apologizing for a crime, the sick man ascribed everything to the
Savior, saying thus: "The man who saved me bade me to act in
this way."[286] The Jews pressed him further and asked who had vio-

rius quis sabbati violator esset interrogabant, at is nesciebat. Dum
vero paulo[28] post in templo ei ipsi obviam fieret, hominem ne
amplius peccaret diligenter admonuit, ne forte sibi deterius contingeret. Unde certior de eius Salvatore factus Iesum fuisse respondebat. Quocirca Iudaei ipsum velut suae legis direptorem et
contemptorem enixe persequebantur.

143   Unde illinc abiens, quod Iohannem ab Herode decollatum
fuisse audierat, in locum desertum seorsum secessit; quod cum
turbae audissent, eum prosecutae sunt. Quare paulo post miseratus in medium venit languidosque eorum curavit. Vespere autem
facto, discipulis de dimissione turbae admonebatur, quod desertus
erat locus et hora iam praeterierat. At Iesus turbis necessitatem
abeundi nequaquam ostendit, quoniam ibi erant quae manducare possent, ut paulo post manifestissime demonstravit. Discipulis vero se non nisi quinque panes et duos pisces habere respondentibus ut ad se referrent imperavit; quo facto et turba super
faenum — faenum forte astabat — discumbere iussa panes et pisces
accepit et suscipiens in caelum benedixit et fregit et dedit discipulis suis. Discipuli autem turbis tradiderunt et manducaverunt omnes et non modo saturati sunt quinque milia virorum absque mulieribus et parvulis sed etiam ex reliquiis fragmentorum quae
144   supererant duodecim cofinos impleverunt. Et ut vehementius ad-
miraremur, non parva puerorum ac mulierum multitudo erat, quae
nullo numero claudebatur, ut his verbis poeta noster expressit:

Maxima parvorum legio vel maxima matrum.
Quoque magis stupeas, cofinos ablata replerunt
fragmina bis senos populisque vorantibus aucta
quae redit a cunctis non est data copia mensis.

145   Iussit deinde ut in navicula versus Capharnaum transfretantes
eum praecederent quoad turbas dimitteret. Dimissa vero turba
orandi gratia solus in montem ascendit ibique usque ad quartam

lated the Sabbath, but he did not know. Soon thereafter, when Jesus met him in the temple, He solemnly warned the man to sin no more, lest worse befall him.[287] Hence knowing his Savior, the sick man now replied that it had been Jesus. As a result, the Jews earnestly persecuted Him for having breached and despised their Law.

Leaving this place, because Jesus heard that Herod had be- 143 headed John the Baptist, He withdrew to a deserted place; but the crowds heard of this and followed Him.[288] So soon thereafter, in His mercy He came forth and healed their sick. When evening came, His disciples urged him to dismiss the crowd, since the place was deserted and the hour was now late. But Jesus made clear that there was no need for the crowd to depart, since there was food there for them to eat, as he soon showed most clearly. When the disciples replied that they had only five loaves and two fish, He bade them bring these to Him. Thereupon, the crowd was told to recline on the hay that was there; and He took the loaves and fish, and raising them to heaven, blessed them and broke them and gave them to His disciples. His disciples gave the food to the crowds, who all ate; and not only were five thousand men filled, besides the women and children, but the remnants of the meal filled twelve baskets. To our greater amazement, there 144 were present a multitude of children and women of boundless number, as our poet wrote in these verses:

A countless group of children, and countless mothers.
And what is more amazing, the remains filled
Twelve baskets, and grew as the people ate,
And the abundance left from all their tables ceased not.[289]

He then bade His disciples to precede him by crossing in a boat 145 to Capharnaum while he dismissed the crowds.[290] Having dismissed the crowds, He climbed a mountain alone in order to pray, and completely alone, He stayed there until the fourth watch of

noctis vigiliam, remotis arbitris, permansit. Navicula autem in medio mari procellosis fluctibus iactabatur, quoniam venti sibi invicem adversabantur. Quarta ergo noctis vigilia Iesus supra mare ambulans ad eos periclitantes pervenerat. Unde si stationes et vigiliae militares in terna horarum spatia antiquitus dividebantur, ut apud historicos legisse meminimus, et Dominum quarta noctis vigilia ad eos periclitantes venisse scimus, ipsos tota prope nocte 146 periclitatos fuisse manifestum est. At illi velut phantasmate[29] quodam subita eius visione perterriti clamare coeperunt. Iesus autem clamantibus eis opitulari cupiens, 'Confidite,' inquit, 'et nolite timere, quoniam ego sum'; cui Petrus respondens: 'Domine,' inquit, 'si tu es, iube ut ego super aquas ad te veniam.' Sed cum Iesus sibi iuxta postulata adventum permisisset, descendebat de navicula et super aquas ambulabat ut ad Iesum perveniret. Ventum vero vehementer expertus timebat, quoniam mergi incipiebat, et dicens clamabat: 'Domine pereuntem salva.' Et continuo Iesus extendens manum suam apprehendit eum et de modica fide obiurgavit.

147   Cui portus fuit illa manus pelagique viator
libere per vitreos movit vestigia campos.

At ubi in naviculam ascenderunt, confestim ventus evanuit. Qui autem in navicula erant

miratur stupefacta cohors sub calle pedestri
navigeras patuisse vias;

unde conversi ad eum admirabundi adorabant dicebantque: 'Vere[30] filius Dei es'!

148   Transfretantibus postmodum in terram Gennesareth, quae Capharnaum finitima erat, ab incolis cognitus est. Unde subito collectam quorumcumque aegrotorum manum, ad eum attulerunt, qui omnes prope ipsum constituti summopere rogabant ut vel saltem fimbriam vestimenti tangerent. Et omnes quicumque te-

the night. Meanwhile, the boat was tossed in the middle of the sea by stormy waves as different winds collided. So at the fourth watch of the night, Jesus walked on the sea and came to His disciples in danger. Now, if the military stations and watches were divided of old in three-hour periods, as we recall reading in the historians, and we know that the Lord came to those in danger at the fourth watch of the night, then it is obvious that they were in danger all night.[291] At the sudden appearance of Jesus, like a ghost,   146 the disciples were terrified and began to cry out.[292] But Jesus, wishing to aid them amid their cries said, "Take courage, and don't be afraid, for it is I." Peter replied to Him, "Lord, if it is you, bid me come to you over the waters."[293] Jesus granted his request to come to Him, and Peter came down from the boat and was walking on the water to go to Jesus. But feeling the wind blowing violently, he grew frightened, since he began to sink, and he cried out saying, "Lord, save me, for I perish."[294] And immediately Jesus stretched forth His hand and caught him, rebuking him for his little faith.[295]

> That hand was a port, and the wayfarer of the sea   147
> Freely moved his steps over the crystalline fields.[296]

As soon as they had boarded, the wind fell. But those who were in the boat,[297]

> the astonished crowd, marveled that the seaways
> Stretched beneath a footpath.[298]

Turning to Jesus with wonder, they worshiped Him, and said, "Truly you are the Son of God!"[299]

Later, after they had crossed to the land of Gennasaret, which   148 borders on Capharnaum, the local people recognized Jesus.[300] At once they gathered and brought to Him a group of sick people, who stood near Him and urgently begged to touch at least the hem of His garment. And all those who touched it — wondrous to

tigerunt—mirabile dictu—a suis lang⟨u⟩oribus repente conva-
luerunt, ut optime poeta noster 'Gennesar,' inquit,

> soli Domino veniente coloni
> infirmos traxere suos, ut fimbria ⟨saltem⟩
> vix attracta Dei morbis medere⟨n⟩tur acerbis.
> Et quotquot tetigere iugem sensere salutem.
> Quam pretiosa fuit quae numquam vendita vestis
> ipsa omnes modici redimebat munere fili!

149   In hoc loco ad eum scribae et Pharisaei ex Hierosolymis accesserunt, ut de communi discipulorum suorum cum illotis[31] manibus comestione redarguerent. Et egressus inde secessit in partes
Tyri et Sidonis; et ecce quaedam mulier Chananaea in finibus illis
egressa in hunc modum clamabat: 'Miserere mei, Domine, fili David, quoniam filia mea a daemonio male vehementerque vexa-
tur.' Huiusmodi mulieris clamoribus quamquam Iesus non responderet, ipsa tamen clamare non desistebat. Proinde discipuli
rogabant ut mulierem dimitteret, quod post eos nimium clamaret.
At Iesus respondens ait: 'Non sum missus nisi ad oves quae ex
150   domo Israhel perierunt.' Illa vero nihilominus accedens adorabat et
dicebat: 'Adiuva me, Domine.' Qui iterum respondens 'Non est,'
inquit, 'bonum sumere panes filiorum et mittere canibus.' At illa
dixit: 'Etiam, Domine; nam et catelli de micis edunt quae de mensis dominorum suorum cadere consueverunt.' Unde Iesus magnitudinem muliebris fidei conspicatus 'Magna,' inquit, 'mulier est
fides tua. Fiat tibi sicut vis,' et sanata est filia eius ex illa hora,
quemadmodum a poeta nostro his egregiis carminibus signatum
est:

> Hinc Tyrias partes Sidoniaque arva petentem
> anxia pro natae vitio, quam spiritus atrox
> vexabat stimulis, mulier Chananaea rogabat,
> se canibus confessa parem, qui more sagaci

say!—suddenly recovered from their illnesses, as our poet elegantly writes:

> When the Lord came to Gennesar, the inhabitants of the land
> Brought their sick that, scarcely touching but the hem of God,
> They might be cured of their bitter diseases.
> And all who touched Him enjoyed enduring health.
> How precious was this garment which, never sold,
> Redeemed all by the gift of its humble thread![301]

In this place, the scribes and Pharisees came to Him from Jerusalem to reproach Him for eating in common with His disciples with unwashed hands.[302] Leaving that place, Jesus withdrew to the region of Tyre and Sidon. And behold, a Canaanite woman living in that territory came forward and cried out: "Have mercy on me, Lord, Son of David, for my daughter is grievously vexed by a demon."[303] Although Jesus did not answer the woman's cries,[304] she continued to cry out. Then the disciples asked Him to send the woman away because she kept crying out after them.[305] Jesus replied, saying, "I am sent only to the sheep of the house of Israel that were lost."[306] But she nonetheless drew near and worshiped, saying: "Help me, Lord."[307] Again He replied: "It is not good to take children's bread and cast it to the dogs."[308] But she said, "Yes, Lord, but even puppies eat the crumbs that fall from their masters' tables."[309] Perceiving the magnitude of the woman's faith, Jesus said, "Great is your faith, woman. May your wish be granted."[310] And her daughter was cured in that very hour.[311] Our poet described this in elegant verses:

> As he reached the region of Tyre and the Sidonian fields,
> A woman of Canaan, distressed by her daughter's disease
> (She was tormented by the goads of a savage demon),
> Beseeched Him, comparing herself to dogs who cleverly

149

150

semper adoratae recubant ad limina mensae
assueti refluas dominorum la⟨m⟩bere micas.
Vox humilis sed celsa fides, quae sospite nata
de cane fecit ovem gentisque in sentibus ortam
compulit Hebraei de gramine vescier agri.

151   Et cum inde per Sidonem versus mare Galilaeae transiret hominem surdum et mutum adducebant deprecabanturque ut manus
curandi gratia imponeret. Unde seorsum a turba hominem apprehendit digitosque suos in auriculas eius immisit et expuens tetigit
linguam suam atque in caelum suspiciens *Effeta* hebraice dicebat,
quod latine 'adaperire' significat. Et statim adapertae sunt aures
eius et solutum est vinculum linguae eius et loquebatur recte.
Namque

> voci patefecit iter nexuque soluto
> muta diu tacitas effudit lingua loquelas

et praecepit ne cui hoc tantum et tam evidens miraculum enarra-
ret. Quanto autem plus ipse de se sermones fieri prohibebat tanto
magis illi singulares eius virtutes praedicabant et de eo vehementius admirabantur, et inter cetera laudabant et dicebant: 'Bene omnia fecit; nam surdos fecit audire et mutos loqui.'

152   Post paucos dies ascendit in montem ibique ad eum, dum sederet, turbae multae habentes secum magnam quamdam plurium
claudorum, caecorum, debilium et aliorum languidorum multitudinem accesserunt eosque a diversis suis ⟨morbis⟩[32] — coram pro-
iectos et constitutos — ita curavit ut turbae mirarentur, quoniam
mutos loquentes, claudos ambulantes, caecos videntes conspicie-
bant ⟨et magnificabant⟩ Deum Israhel, ut eleganter poeta his versibus expressit:

> Alta dehinc subiens montis iuga plebe sequente
> milia caecorum, claudorum milia passim

Lie down near the edge of their beloved table
And often lap up the crumbs of their masters.
A humble word but lofty faith, which saved the daughter
And made a dog into a sheep, and caused a woman born amid
   the brambles
Of the Gentiles to feed on the grass of a Hebrew field.[312]

When Jesus had crossed Sidon in the direction of the Sea of   151
Galilee, they brought to Him a deaf mute, and begged Him to lay
His hands on him to cure him.[313] He took the man away from the
crowd, put His fingers in his ears, spat, touched his tongue, and
looking up to heaven said in Hebrew *Effetha*, which in Latin means
"open."[314] And straightway his ears were opened, and the bond of
his tongue was loosened, and he began to speak plainly.[315] For

> he opened the way for his voice, and the bond released,
> And the mute tongue poured forth long silenced speech.[316]

Jesus instructed them not to relate this great and evident miracle
to anyone.[317] But the more He forbade talk about Himself, the
more they proclaimed His singular virtues, and greatly marveled at
Him. Among other things, they praised Him and said: "He has
done everything well, for he has made the deaf hear and the mute
speak."[318]

After a few days He went up into a mountain, and while He sat   152
many crowds approached with a great multitude of the lame, the
blind, the infirm, and people sick with other illnesses; and as they
lay and were placed before Him, He cured them of their various
diseases, so that the crowds marveled: for they saw the mute
speak, the lame walk, and the blind see, and they glorified the God
of Israel.[319] As our poet wrote elegantly in these verses:

> Then climbing the high ridge of the mountain with the people
> Behind Him, a thousand blind men, and a thousand lame
>   ones,

leprosos⟨que⟩ simul populos surdasque catervas
invalidasque manus et quidquid debile vulgi
venerat, in priscum componit motibus usum
et revocata suis attemperat organa nervis.

153   Paulo post, convocatis Iesus discipulis suis, 'Misereor,' inquit,
'turbae quoniam iam triduo mecum commorati perseverant nec
habent quod manducent et dimittere eos ieiunos nolo, ne forte in
via deficerent.' Cui discipuli responderunt: 'Unde, ergo, in hac
eremo tot panes habere poterimus ut tantam et tam magnam turbam saturemus?' Percontatus igitur Iesus panum numerum, ut
audivit septem et paucos pisciculos pracecepit turbis ut super terram discumberent; quo facto, panes et pisciculos accepit et gratias
agens fregit et discipulis suis dedit, qui populo distribuerent, ita ut
omnes quotquot erant affatim saturarentur; nec pauci erant qui
manducaverant. Nam quattuor milia virorum, exceptis mulieribus
et parvulis, recensebantur:

154   Pisciculis paucis et septem panibus agmen
pavit inorme virum praeterque infirma secundi
sexus et aetatis saturavit quattuor illic
milia vescentum. Plus ut mireris, et auctas
disce fuisse dapes; epulas nutrivit edendo
vulgus et attritae creverunt morsibus escae.
Reliquiasque suas, sportarum culmina septem,
expavit fugitura fames, ubi fragmine sumpto
vidit abundantem modico de semine messem.

155   Cum deinde in Bethsaidam proficisceretur, caecum quemdam
sanandi causa ad eum adducebant. Iesus vero apprehensa manu
extra vicum ducens primo in oculos suos expuebat ac paulo post si
quid videret percontabatur. At ille hinc inde respiciens se homines
velut arbores ambulantes videre respondebat. Unde Iesus manibus

Hosts of lepers, crowds of the deaf, and bands of the infirm
And any ordinary person with an illness who had come,
By His ministrations He restored to his former state,
And gave their organs their former strength.[320]

Shortly thereafter, Jesus gathered His disciples and said "I have   153
compassion for the crowd, because they have already been with me
for three days and have nothing to eat. I do not want to send them
away hungry, lest they faint on the way."[321] The disciples replied to
Him, "Where shall we find enough bread in this wilderness to
feed such a large crowd?"[322] Jesus asked how many loaves they
had; and when He heard they had seven with a few small fish, he
bade the crowd sit down on the ground. When this was done, he
took the loaves and the fish, gave thanks, broke them, and gave
them to his disciples to distribute to the people.[323] And every one
of them was completely filled, although there were many who ate:
for they numbered four thousand men, not counting the women
and children,[324]

With a few small fish and seven loaves   154
He fed a vast host of men, four thousand mouths,
Besides those of lesser sex and age.
What is more wondrous, know that the feast
Grew larger: by eating, the mob
Nourished the banquet, and the food, though nibbled,
Grew, and the remnants, seven full baskets,
Chased famine away. For when He took and broke the bread
He saw an abundant harvest from modest seed.[325]

Then, when he journeyed to Bethsaida, they brought a blind   155
man to Him to be healed.[326] Jesus took his hand and led him
out of the village; then spitting on His eyes, he soon asked him
if he could see anything. The man looked here and there and replied that he saw people who looked like walking trees. So Jesus

suis eius oculos contingens ita repente sanavit ut clare et aperte—
mirabile dictu—omnia prospiceret, ceu poeta noster ad eum conversus his versibus expressit:

> Tu quoque virtutis sensisti munus erilis
> procumbens oculis, cuius in lumine Christus
> expuit et speciem simulatae mortis ademit.

156   Post haec assumpsit Iesus Petrum, Iacobum et Iohannem fratrem eius et duxit illos in montem excelsum seorsum et transfigu-
ratus est ante eos et resplenduit facies eius sicut sol et

>   velut igneus ardor
> solis, in aetheriam versus splendore figuram,
> vicerat ore diem vestemque tuentibus ipsam
> candida forma nivis Domini de tegmine fulsit.

Unde poeta noster se continere non potuit quin miranda huius
transfigurationis mysteria contemplatus in hunc modum exclamaret:

> O meritum sublime trium quibus illa videre
> contigit in mundo quae non sunt credita mundo!

157 Vestimenta autem sua facta sunt alba sicut nix et ita candida
effectu fuisse scribitur ut fullones hic in terris admirabilem
quemdam eorum candorem nullatenus adaequare possent. Et ecce
apparuerunt illis Moyses et Helias cum eo loquentes; unde Petrus
ad Iesum conversus 'Bonum est,' inquit, 'Domine, ut hic commore-
mur. Si vis itaque tria tabernacula constituamus, ut tibi unum,
Moysi unum et Heliae unum famuletur.' Adhuc Petro loquente
ecce nubes lucida obumbravit eos. Deus enim semper in nubibus
(sicut scriptum est: 'Nubes et caligo in circuitu eius') apparere
158 consuevit. Et ecce vox de nube dicens: 'Hic est Filius meus dilectus
in quo mihi bene complacuit. Ipsum audite' et audientes discipuli
ceciderunt in faciem suam et timuerunt valde. Et accessit Iesus et

touched his eyes with His hands and at once healed him so that —
wondrous to say! — he beheld everything clearly and plainly. Addressing this man, our poet expressed himself in these verses:

> You, too, have felt the gift of the Master's might,
> Brought low by blindness, in whose eyes Christ
> Spat and took away the appearance of seeming death.[327]

After this, Jesus took Peter, James, and his brother John, and 156
led them up into a high mountain apart; and He was transfigured
before them, and His face shone like the sun.[328]

> Like the sun's fiery blaze, changed by splendor
> Into an ethereal figure, His face surpassed the daylight,
> And as they beheld His garment, the Lord's form
> Shone from His garment like white snow.[329]

Contemplating the wondrous mystery of this transfiguration, our
poet could not refrain from exclaiming:

> O sublime reward for these three, to whom was granted
> A vision on earth of what is not entrusted to the earth![330]

His clothes became as white as snow,[331] and it is written that they 157
were, in fact, of such whiteness that no earthly launderers could
ever match their marvelous whiteness.[332] And behold, Moses and
Elijah appeared, speaking with Him.[333] So Peter turned to Jesus
and said: "It is good, Lord, for us to be here. If you wish, let us set
up three tabernacles, one for you; one for Moses; and one for Elijah."[334] While Peter was speaking, behold, a bright cloud over-
shadowed them.[335] For God always was wont to appear in clouds,
as it is written: "Clouds and thick darkness surround Him."[336]
And behold, a voice from the cloud said: "This is my beloved Son 158
in whom I am well pleased. Listen to Him." Hearing this, the
disciples fell on their faces and were greatly afraid.[337] But Jesus

tetigit ipsos dixitque eis: 'Surgite. Nolite timere.' Levantes autem
oculos suos neminem nisi Iesum solum videre potuerunt. Illis vero
de monte descendentibus[33] praecepit Iesus ne cui tam admirabilem
visionem revelarent donec Filius hominis ab inferis resurgeret.

159   Deinde ne publicani qui tributa et census exigebant forte scan-
dalizarentur, nisi ipse portionem quoque suam cum ceteris solvis-
set, Simon praecepit ut ad mare (volens ostendere quod mari et
piscibus dominaretur) piscandi gratia proficisceretur et eum piscem tolleret qui primus hamo[34] caperetur eiusque ore adaperto
staterem inveniret, que⟨m⟩ pro duplo utriusque tributo postea
160   solveret. Nam secundum legem quicumque primogeniti didrachma
vel potius unusquisque iuxta legem didrachma — quod duorum
denariorum pretium erat, unum pro animae alterum pro corporis
redemptione — solvere tenebantur. Petro igitur magistri sui mandatis obtemperante — mirabile dictu —

> incola mox pelagi pendentia fila momordit,
> iussa tributa ferens, graviorque onerante metallo
> vilis honor piscis pretio maiore pependit.

161   Paulo post accedens ad eum homo quidam devotissime obsecrabat ut filio suo lunatico misereretur, qui ita a daemonio vexabatur ut saepe in ignem et crebro in aquam caderet. Hunc a discipulis antea non curatum Iesus solo verbo curavit. Cum vero in
synagoga forte sabbatis doceret, incurvam quamdam mulierem
inde transeuntem vidit, quae decem et octo annis spiritum infirmitatis ita perpessa erat ut inclinata humi procumberet, nec aliquo
modo sursum prospicere valebat. Eam igitur Iesus conspicatus ad
se vocavit dixitque: 'Mulier, dimissa es ab infirmitate tua,' et im-
ponens illi manus ita continuo erexit ut laudaret et glorificaret
162   Deum. Quod cum archisynagogus moleste ferret, quoniam ea
mulier sabbato curaretur, a Iesu non immerito his verbis[35] redargu-
tus est: 'Hypocrita! Numquid unusquisque vestrum bovem aut
asinum suum e[t] praesepio diebus festis [ad] aquandi gratia non

approached and touched them, saying: "Arise. Fear not."[338] Raising their eyes, they could see no one but Jesus alone.[339] As they went down from the mountain, Jesus instructed them not to reveal this marvelous vision until the Son of Man had risen from the dead.[340]

Now, lest the tax collectors, who demanded duty and taxes, 159 take offense, unless He, too, pay His share with the others, Jesus bade Simon go to the sea (wanting to show that He ruled over the sea and its fish) and to fish. And when he had caught the first fish with his hook, he would open its mouth and find a silver shekel, which would pay the tax twice for both of them.[341] For according 160 to the Law, everyone was required to pay the two drachmas for the firstborn, or rather the two-drachma tax—the value of two denarii, one to redeem the soul, and one to redeem the body. Peter obeyed his master's command and—wondrous to say!—

soon the inhabitant of the sea bit the dangling line,
And heavier for being loaded with metal, the cheap fish,
Bearing the required tribute, paid it out at greater value.[342]

Soon thereafter a man approached Jesus and devoutly begged 161 him to take pity on his epileptic son, who was so tormented by a demon that he often plunged into the fire and into the water.[343] This boy, whom the disciples could not heal, was healed by Jesus with a single word. Now, when He chanced to be teaching in the synagogue on the Sabbath, He saw a hunchback woman passing by who had suffered a spirit of infirmity for eighteen years so that she was bent over and could not even look up.[344] When Jesus saw her, he called her to Him and said: "Woman, you are set free from your infirmity."[345] Then He put His hands on her, and she at once straightened so that she praised and glorified God. The leader of 162 the synagogue was indignant that this woman was healed on the Sabbath, but Jesus justly rebuked him with these words: "Hypocrite! Does not each one of you release his ox or ass from the stall on the holy days to take him to water? And this woman, a

solvit? Hanc vero mulierem Abrahae filiam, quam Satanas tam diu alligaverat, ecce decem et octo annis ab isto vinculo oppressam, die sabbati nonne solvi oportuit?' Quo dicto cuncti eius adversarii vehementer erubescebant; ceteri vero omnes populariter in multis gaudebantur quae ab eo mirabiliter glorioseque fiebant.

163   Et factum est, cum in domum cuiusdam Pharisaeorum principis manducandi causa sabbato ingrederetur, forte homo quidam hydropicus ante illum astabat, qui

> perspicuo distentus ventre tumebat
> plenus aquae gravidamque cutem suspenderat alvus,
> inclusam paritura necem. Iam membra fluebant
> arescente sinu miserosque infusa per artus
> turgida perflatum macies tenuaverat aegrum
> inque uteri[36] spatium totus convenerat hydrops.

At Iesus scribas et Pharisaeos percontabatur an sabbatis curare liceret. Obmutescentibus vero illis, apprehendit et sanavit eum. 'Cuius vestrum,' inquit, 'asinus aut bos in puteum cadet et non continuo abstrahet illum etiam in die sabbati?' Nec quidquam respondere poterant.

164   Et factum est, dum iret Iesus in Hierosolymam, transibat per mediam Samariam et Galilaeam et cum quoddam castellum ingrederetur decem viri leprosi occurrerunt ei, qui procul astantes vocem extulerunt certatim in hunc modum clamantes: 'Iesu, praeceptor, miserere nostri!' Quos ut Iesus vidit 'Ostendite,' inquit, 'vos sacerdotibus et lepra vestra continuo cessabit.'

> Cumque viam peterent, subito mundata vicissim
> mirantur sua membra viri variumque tuentes

daughter of Abraham, whom Satan bound so long that she was oppressed for eighteen years by his chains, should she not have been released on the Sabbath day?"[346] When He said this, all His adversaries were greatly ashamed; but everyone else universally rejoiced in the many things He so marvelously and gloriously accomplished.[347]

And it came to pass that, when He entered the house of a 163 leader of the Pharisees to take dinner on the Sabbath, a man with dropsy happened to be present.[348]

> Swollen with an enormous belly,
> Full of water, his belly supported bloated skin, as if it were
> About to give birth to death enclosed therein. His limbs drooped
> As his hollow belly dried them out, and throughout his wretched limbs
> Turgid consumption had weakened the gas-filled victim,
> While the entire dropsy converged on the space of the abdomen.[349]

Jesus asked the scribes and Pharisees if it was lawful to heal on the Sabbath. As they were silent, He touched and healed him. He said: "If your ass or ox falls into a well, which of you will not at once pull him out even on the Sabbath?" They could not answer Him.[350]

And it happened that as Jesus went to Jerusalem, He passed 164 through the region between Samaria and Galilee; and when he entered a village, ten lepers met him, who, standing at a distance, competed in shouting and crying out: "Jesus, Master, have mercy on us!"[351] When Jesus saw them, He said: "Show yourselves to the priests, and your leprosy will at once be ended."[352]

> And as they went their way, the men suddenly marvel
> At each other's limbs in turn, cleansed,

esse nihil pariter sese speculantur et omnes
explorant proprias alterno lumine formas.

Et ubi paulo post sese sacerdotibus ostenderunt, ita repente mutati
sunt ut universa lepra penitus evanesceret.

165   Dum autem Hiericho[37] appropinquaret Iesus, caecus quidam
Timaei filius secus viam, mendicandi gratia, sedebat. Hic cum
turbam praetereuntem strepitibusque—ut fit—frementem[38] audiret, quid illud esset forte interrogabat. Sed ubi Iesum Nazarenum
turba prope oppressum praetereuntem accepit, alta quantum potuit voce in hunc modum vociferans crebro lumen clamore petebat.
Sic enim aiebat: 'Iesu, Fili David, miserere mei!' Huiusmodi caeci
vocibus Iesus commotus, illum ad se statim duci iussit, quem ut
appropinquantem vidit quid sibi fieri vellet percontabatur. At ille
'Domine,' inquit, 'ut videam.' Et Iesus dixit illi: 'Respice! Fides
tua te salvavit.' Et confestim vidit. Et absque praevio ductore,
magnificans Deum, illum sequebatur; quod miraculum turbae
conspicatae ingentes Deo laudes et hymnos decantabant.

166   His igitur et multis aliis huiusmodi miraculis in Capharnaum
provincia perfectis, cum prope pascha Iudaeorum Hierosolymis
celebraretur eo contendit, ut in cunctis divinae legis mandatis ob-
temperaret. Sed cum de urbe Iericho egrederetur, multae eum
turbae sequebantur; magnum—ut fit—praetereuntium strepitum
duo caeci, qui mendicandi causa secus viam consedebant, forte
audiverunt. Sed quidnam id esset percontati, ut Iesum transeuntem perceperunt alta voce 'Miserere nostri, Fili David!' clamare coeperunt, de quo quidem a turbis increpabantur. At illi
eumdem miserandi versum vehementioribus clamoribus repetebant 'flebilibusque vagas implebant vocibus auras.' Horum misera-
bilibus vocibus Iesus commotus eos ad se stantem vocari iussit.
'Quid vultis,' inquit, 'ut fiat vobis?' At illi 'Ut aperiantur, Domine,
oculi nostri' responderunt. Unde Iesus misertus oculos eorum per

And seeing no motley skin, they inspect themselves,
All examining their own appearance in alternating light.[353]

Soon thereafter, when they showed themselves to the priests, they were so suddenly changed that every trace of leprosy had disappeared.

When Jesus was approaching Jericho, a blind man, the son of 165 Timaeus, sat begging by the roadside.[354] When he heard the crowd passing by and noisily clamoring, as is usual, he asked what was happening. When he heard that Jesus of Nazareth was passing by, nearly crushed by the crowd, he shouted in the loudest voice he could, asking for his sight in repeated cries, and said: "Jesus, son of David, have mercy on me."[355] Moved by the blind man's words, Jesus bade him be brought to Him at once; and seeing him approach, asked what he wanted. The blind man said: "Lord, let me see."[356] And Jesus said to him: "Look! Your faith has saved you."[357] And he immediately could see. Then, with no guide before him, he magnified God, and followed Jesus; and when the crowd beheld this miracle, they sang great praises and hymns to God.[358]

Now, when Jesus had performed these and other miracles in the 166 region of Capharnaum, since the Jewish Passover was close to being celebrated in Jerusalem, He went there in obedience to the commandments of God's Law. As He left the city of Jericho, many crowds followed Him; and two blind men sitting by the roadside to beg chanced (as happens) to hear the great clamor of the passersby.[359] When they asked what it was and learned that Jesus was passing by, they began to cry out in a loud voice "Have mercy on us, Son of David,"[360] for which the crowds reproached them. But the two wretches repeated their refrain in more powerful cries and "filled the shifting breezes with doleful words."[361] Moved by their pitiful words, Jesus bade them be brought to Him as He stood, and He asked: "What do you want done for you?"[362] They replied: "Let our eyes be opened, Lord."[363] Taking pity on them, Jesus

solam manuum suarum tactionem adaperuit ac protinus viderunt et secuti sunt eum.

167   Ac dum forte praeteriret, hominem quemdam a nativitate caecum conspexit, de quo cum a discipulis interrogaretur quisnam illorum — vel ipse vel parentes eius — peccavissent ut caecus nasceretur, 'Neque hic,' inquit, 'neque parentes eius peccaverunt, sed factum est ut in illo mirabilia omnipotentis Dei opera manifestarentur.' Et paulo post expuit in terram et lutum ex sputo factum super oculos eius linivit et iussit ei ut ad Siloam aquam, lavandi gratia, proficisceretur, quo turbae et coetus hominum ad natandum confluebant. Eo igitur ut imperatum erat facto 'mox gemellae

168 vultibus effulgent acies' adapertisque luminibus atque hinc inde prospectans magno cum gaudio revertebatur. Qui vero vicini erant eumque cognoverant ita intra se admirabantur ut nonnulli dubitare cogerentur an ipse esset is quem sedere et mendicare paulo ante conspexerant vel potius similis illi videretur; unde admirabundi percontabantur eum an ullo umquam tempore caecus fuisset et quonam modo adapertis oculis postea vidisset. At ille et se caecum fuisse et quemadmodum luminibus obortis paulo ante videre coepisset palam et aperte cunctis interrogantibus repondebat.

169   Accedens deinde Bethfage, oppidum Hierosolymis finitimum, ad Montem Oliveti duos ex discipulis suis in castellum quoddam — quod e regione situm astabat — pro asino et pullo eius nescio quibus transmisit. Qui cum asinam et pullum — ut eis fuerat imperatum — adduxissent, super tergis suis vestimenta ponebant, ut id quod a Domino per Zachariam prophetam dictum fuerat penitus adimpleretur, cuius haec erat sententia, ut a Mat⟨t⟩heo evangelista his verbis recitatur: 'Dicite filiae Sion: "Ecce rex tuus venit tibi mansuetus, sedens super asinam et pullum filium subiugalis."' Licet Zacharias ipse paulo expressius locutus fuisse videatur, cuius haec verba sunt: 'Exsulta satis filia Sion, iubila filia Hierusalem! Ecce rex tuus veniet tibi; iustus et salvator ipse, pauper et

merely touched their eyes with his hands, and at once they could see, and followed Him.[364]

As He passed by, He caught sight of a man blind from birth.[365] His disciples asked Him who had sinned that he should be born blind—he himself or his parents. Jesus said: "Neither this man nor his parents have sinned, but this was done so that the miraculous works of almighty God might be revealed in him."[366] Soon thereafter He spat on the ground; and making mud with the spittle, He smeared it on his eyes, and bade him go and wash at the pool of Siloam,[367] where crowds and parties of people gathered to swim.[368] When the man did as commanded, "his twin pupils soon blazed forth on his face."[369] And when his eyes were opened, he looked around, and came back with great joy. His neighbors and those who knew him were in such wonderment that some were compelled to doubt whether this was the man they had seen sit and beg not long before, or rather someone resembling him. In their wonder, they asked him if he had ever been blind, and how he could now see with opened eyes. To all who questioned him he replied clearly and plainly that he had been blind, and told how, when his eyes had been opened, he had begun to see a little while ago.[370]

Then, approaching Bethphage, a town near Jerusalem, close to the Mount of Olives, He sent two of his disciples to a nearby village in the region to find a donkey and its colt.[371] When they had brought the donkey and colt, as they had been ordered, they put cloaks on their backs, so that the Lord's words spoken by the prophet Zechariah would be completely fulfilled. The prophet's utterance is recorded by the evangelist Matthew in these words, "Tell the daughter of Zion: 'Behold your king comes to you tamely, seated on a donkey and on a colt, the foal of a donkey.'"[372] In fact, Zechariah himself spoke more clearly in these words, "Rejoice greatly, daughter of Zion! Shout aloud, daughter of Jerusalem! Behold, your king will come to you, the righteous Savior

167

168

169

170 ascendens super asinam et super pullum asinae' et reliqua. Per hunc igitur modum Rex et Salvator noster asinae tergo impositus equitabat. Et tamen tanta divinitatis suae fama erat ut tametsi spernendus vilissime incederet plurimae nihilominus turbae ipsum tamquam Deum venerabantur. Alii namque per vias sua vestimenta sternebant, alii autem palmarum ramos de arboribus caesos undique dispergebant. Qui vero praecedebant et qui sequebantur alta voce clamabant: 'Osanna Filio David! Benedictus qui venit in

171 nomine Domini! Osanna in excelsis!' Cum itaque eum summis quibusdam in caelum laudibus extollerent ac Pharisaei — gloriae suae invidentes — tantas et tam excellentes laudationes aequo animo tollerare non possent, ac propterea ab eo peterent ut huiusmodi laudatores obiurgaret, respondens ait illis: 'Non legistis quia scriptum est: "Ex ore infantium et lactentium perfecisti laudem?"' Et alibi de huiusmodi laudationibus inquit: 'Si isti tacuerint, lapides clamabunt,' quod licet plerique ita intelligendum putent: 'Si Iudaei tacuerint, multitudo gentium laudabit,' haec tamen est expressior et verior intelligentia: 'Etiam si homines taceant et signorum meorum magnitudinem invidentes eorum linguae non loquantur, ipsi tamen lapides et fundamenta murorum et parietum aedificio meam poterunt magnitudinem personare.'

172   Quae quidem expositio ut clarius appareat, non ab re visum est in hoc loco quaedam saecularium litterarum exempla proferre. A Crisippo historico nescio quo in historia sua sic scriptum fuisse accepimus: 'Saguntini, fide atque aerumnis incliti, pro mortali studio maiori quam op[er]ibus, quippe quin etiam tum semiusta moenia, domus intectae parietesque templorum ambusti manus Punicas ostentabant.' Simile quiddam et Tullius ad Caesarem pro Marcello loquens his verbis usus est: 'Parietes, medius fidius, ut mihi videtur, huius curiae tibi gratias agere gestiunt, quod brevi tempore futura sit illa auctoritas in his maiorum suorum et suis sedibus.' Sic Iesus super asina⟨m⟩ novo quodam et numquam alias

Himself, poor and riding on a donkey and on a colt, the foal of a
donkey," etc.[373] In this fashion, then, our King and Savior rode on   170
the back of a donkey. Yet so great was the fame of His divinity
that despite His lowly entry great crowds worshiped Him as God.
Some spread their cloaks on the road, and others cut branches
from palm trees and scattered them everywhere.[374] Those that
went ahead of Him and those that followed cried in a loud voice,
"Hosanna to the Son of David! Blessed is He who comes in the
name of the Lord! Hosanna in the highest!"[375] When the people   171
extolled Him to the heavens with the highest praises, the Pharisees, jealous of His glory, could not patiently endure such great
and excellent praise, and therefore asked Him to rebuke those who
praised Him.[376] He replied, saying, "Have you not read that it is
written: 'Out of the mouths of infants and nurslings, you have
perfected praise?'"[377] And another time He said of such praises, "If
these were silent, the very stones would cry out."[378] Many think we
should understand this to mean: "If the Jews were silent, the multitude of the nations would praise me." But the more explicit and
truer meaning is this, "Even if people keep quiet and, jealous of
the greatness of my signs, their tongues do not speak, the very
stones and foundations of the outer and inner walls will sound my
greatness throughout the building."[379]

In order to clarify our narrative, it seems appropriate here to   172
adduce some examples from secular literature. We read that a certain historian Chrysippus wrote as follows: "The people of Sagun-
tum were renowned for their fidelity and their misfortunes, and
more for their tenacity than for their riches: for their half-burnt
walls, their roofless houses, and their burnt temple walls showed
the handiwork of the Carthaginians."[380] Addressing Caesar in defense of Marcellus, Cicero spoke using similar words, "The walls
of the senate, by Jove, are eager (I think) to thank you because in
a short time its authority will return to its seat and that of their
forebears."[381] Just so, Jesus entered the city in a form of triumph

usitato more triumphantium urbem ingressus universam civitatem admirabundam in se convertit. Unde inquit poeta noster admirans: 'Dicite,' inquit,[39]

> gentiles populi cui gloria regi
> talis in urbe fuit? Cui palmis compta vel umquam
> frondibus arboreis laudem caelestibus hymnis
> obvia turba dedit domino nisi cum patre Christo,
> qui regit aeternum princeps in principe regno?

173   Paulo deinde post in templum intravit, in quo dum forte ambularet, boum, ovium, columbarum ac turturum et ceterorum omnium animalium quae ad immolandum[40] sacrificiis idonea putabantur venditores emptoresque conspexit. Hos omnes flagello quodam de resticulis effecto — sicut antea praediximus — inde iterato exegit. De hac tam repentina et tam subitan⟨e⟩a cunctorum mercatorum eiectione Iudaei vehementer admirati ab eo quaerebant unde sibi tantam potestatem arrogaret ut quoscumque libuisset de templo eiecisset. Ad eum igitur in templo stantem caeci et

174 claudi sanandi gratia accesserunt, quos cum repente sanasset lumina orbatis tribuens ac vestigia claudis, pueri catervatim versum illum de 'Osanna' — usque ad haec tempora nostra celebratum et decantatum — clamare non desinebant. Scribae vero et Pharisaei qui haec et alia similia eius miracula propriis oculis viderant et laudes ex ore infantium suis auribus audiverant mirum in modum indignabantur.

175   Unde Iesus ex urbe egressus in Bethaniam — quindecim circiter stadiis illinc distantem — venit, quo in loco illud ingens et celebratum de resurrectione quatriduani mortui miraculum magna cum admiratione omnium finitimorum palam ⟨et⟩ publice effecit. Quippe Lazarus quidam Bethaniensis ad mortem aegrotabat, quem Iesus plurimum diligebat. Proinde cum amicum suum graviter aegrotare ex Maria et Martha — duabus eius sororibus —

that was new and never practiced elsewhere, seated on a donkey, and turned all the wondering citizenry to Himself. Hence, in wonder our poet writes,

> tell me, peoples of the Gentiles, what king
> Enjoyed such glory in the city? Whom did the crowds ever
>   meet
> Adorned with palms and tree boughs, and praise
> In heavenly anthems? Only our Lord Christ with His Father,
> Who reigns eternal, a prince in the princely realm.[382]

Soon thereafter He entered the Temple; and as He walked about, He beheld people buying and selling oxen, sheep, pigeons and turtledoves, and other animals thought suitable for sacrifice.[383] Making a scourge of cords, as we said earlier,[384] he again drove them out.[385] The Jews marveled greatly at this sudden and immediate expulsion of all the merchants, and asked Him how he claimed such power to expel anyone He pleased from the Temple.[386] While He was standing in the Temple, the blind and the lame came to Him to be healed. When he immediately healed them, giving eyes to the blind and walking to the lame, crowds of children continued to cry the verse "Hosanna," which even today is celebrated and sung.[387] But the scribes and Pharisees, who had seen these and other similar miracles of His with their own eyes, and had heard the praises from the mouths of children with their own ears, were extraordinarily indignant.[388]

So Jesus left the city and came to Bethany, which was some two miles away.[389] And there He performed a prodigious and celebrated miracle by openly and publicly reviving a man dead for four days, to the great amazement of all the people nearby.[390] A man from Bethany named Lazarus, whom Jesus loved very much, was on his death bed. So when He heard from Lazarus' two sisters, Mary and Martha, that His friend was gravely ill, He went to that

accepisset, eo usque proficiscebatur. Martha vero altera soror ut Iesum venientem audivit, non cunctandum rata, statim ei occurrit dixitque: 'Si hic, Domine, apud nos fuisses profecto frater meus adhuc inter nos viveret. Et quamquam nunc defunctus hac luce careat, Deum tamen omnia tibi concessurum tributurumque intelligo quaecumque ab eo postulaveris.' Paulo post vero, ⟨cum⟩ fratrem a mortuis resurrecturum ex certis quibusdam Salvatoris nostri responsis cognovisset, exinde abiens domum propere remeavit ut Mariam, eius sororem, una secum ad Iesum duceret. Maria autem, ut de certo magistri sui adventu a sorore certior facta est, e vestigio conveniendi gratia surrexit celeriterque contendens ipsum in eodem prope loco repperit ubi Martha ei antea occurrerat. Qui vero domum consolandi causa venerant ipsam sectabantur, rati quod[41] ad monumentum plorandi causa proficisceretur. Ubi igitur Maria Salvatorem vidit, confestim ad pedes eius provoluta in hunc modum loquens 'Si hic,' inquit, 'Domine apud nos fuisses, frater meus non esset mortuus.' Iesus ergo, ut eam et Iudaeos qui secum venerant flentes conspexit, misericordia quadam commotus usque adeo turbatus est ut spiritu infremeret ac percontaretur ubinam[42] mortuum posuissent. Sed responsum[43] accipiens ut cum illis veniret et videret, secum tandem commeabat donec ad monumentum accederent. Ibi spelunca quaedam videbatur, cui lapis superpositus astabat; ut vero applicuerunt, subito astantibus imperavit ut lapidem tollerent. Qui vero astabant eius mandatis obtemperantes actutum lapidem inde amoverunt. Quo facto Iesus, suspiciens in caelum et elevatis sursum oculis, pro resuscitatione defuncti primum ad patrem oravit. Paulo deinde post voce magna sic 'Lazare, veni foras' exclamavit. Ad hanc ingentem Salvatoris nostri vocem — incredibile dictu —

magno concussa pavore
Tartara dissiliunt, Erebi patuere recessus,
extimuit letale chaos mortisque profundae

place. When Martha, the second sister, heard that Jesus was coming, she brooked no delay and at once met Him, saying, "Lord, if you had been here, my brother would still be alive and with us. Yet although he is now dead and sees not the light of day, I know that God will grant and give you whatever you ask of Him."[391] Soon thereafter she understood from our Savior's replies that her brother would rise again from the dead.[392] Going out, she swiftly returned home to bring her sister Mary with her to Jesus. And when Mary learned from her sister of her Master's arrival, she immediately rose up to meet Him, and walking in haste, she found Him where Martha had met Him earlier.[393] Now, those who had come to the house to comfort her followed her, thinking that she was going to the tomb to mourn.[394] When Mary saw the Savior, she at once fell at his feet and spoke in these words, "Lord, if you had been with us, my brother would not have died."[395] When Jesus saw her weeping, and the Jews who came with her weeping, He was moved by compassion and so greatly disturbed that He groaned in His spirit, and asked them where they had laid the dead man.[396] Hearing them reply that He should go with them and see,[397] He walked with them until they came to the tomb. They saw a cave with a stone placed over it; and when they got there, He immediately bade the bystanders remove the stone.[398] The bystanders immediately obeyed His command and at once removed it. When this was done, Jesus looked up to heaven and raising his eyes upward, he prayed to the Father to revive the dead man. Shortly thereafter He cried out in a loud voice, "Lazarus, come forth."[399] At this extraordinary utterance of our Savior— wondrous to say! —

176

177

178

struck with great fear,
The underworld bursts open, the depths of Erebus are
    revealed,
Deadly Chaos took fright, the law of profound death

lex perit atque anima proprias repetente medullas
cernitur ante oculos vivens astare cadaver.

Nam non aliter excitatus est qui mortuus per quatriduum fuerat
quam si e levi quodam somno expergisceretur. Statim enim, etsi
manus et pedes institis ligatus esset et facies eius sudario quodam
astricta teneretur, foras tamen prodiit, quem ut Iesus vidit mox
179   praecepit ut solutum abire sinerent. Quocirca multi ex Iudaeis qui
consolandi gratia ad Mariam et Martham venerant, et hoc prorsus
tam ingens et tam incredibile miraculum propriis oculis prospexe-
rant, ad eum conversi crediderunt. Quidam vero ex ipsis ad Pharisaeos abierunt ut quidquid viderent plane et aperte recitarent. Et
ne resurrectio eius ab incredulis[44] et perfidis aliquatenus phan-
tasma putaretur, cum Salvatore narratur iniisse convivium.

180   Post aliquot deinde dies, dum in Hierosolymam revertertur,
factum est ut in itinere esuriret. Proinde videns fici arborem secus
viam accessit ut fructus exinde perciperet. Sed cum in ea nihil nisi
folia invenisset, apprime indignatus 'Numquam,' inquit, 'ex te fructus in sempiternum nascatur'; quibus quidem verbis, cum admiratione omnium, continuo exaruit. Nam

confestim viduata suis ficulnea succis
aruit et siccis permansit mortua ramis.

In ficu vero hoc propterea fecisse creditur ut in arbore ceterarum
omnium humidissima maius atque evidentius tam subitae ac tam
repentinae arefactionis miraculum propalari appareret.

181   Cum Iesus discipulos eius et turbas unice edocebat, principes
vero sacerdotum et scribae, propter haec plurima et alia eius ingentia miracula sanamque doctrinam hinc inde dispersam, magno
eum odio habebant. Nam ut dictum est, quacumque iter faciebat
aegros ac debiles et omni genere laborantes uno verbo unoque
momento ita reddebat incolumes ut etsi membris omnibus cape-

Perishes, and as the soul reclaims its marrow,
A living corpse is seen standing before their eyes.[400]

The man dead for four days is thus roused as if awaking from a
light sleep. At once, even though bound hand and foot with strips
of cloth, and with his face covered with a shroud, Lazarus nonetheless came out; and when Jesus saw him, He bade them unbind
him and let him go.[401] Many of the Jews who had come to console   179
Mary and Martha, seeing this extraordinary and incredible miracle
with their own eyes, were converted and believed in Jesus.[402] But
some of them went to the Pharisees and plainly and openly recounted what they had seen.[403] And lest his resurrection be regarded as an illusion by unbelievers and the unfaithful, it is said
that Lazarus attended a banquet with the Savior.[404]

A few days later, while returning to Jerusalem, Jesus happened   180
to grow hungry on the way.[405] Seeing a fig tree by the roadside, he
went to pick its fruit. But when he found nothing on it but leaves,
he was very indignant and said, "May no fruit ever come from
you!"[406] At these words, the tree withered at once, to everyone's
amazement.[407] For

at once the fig tree, robbed of its sap, dried up
And was left dead with dry branches.[408]

It is thought that Jesus did this to the fig tree so that the miracle of this sudden and immediate withering would appear even
greater and more vivid in this most succulent of all trees.[409]

While Jesus offered singular teaching to His disciples and the   181
crowds, the high priests and scribes hated Him intensely on account of these many and other extraordinary miracles of His and
the sound doctrine He spread everywhere. For, as was said, wherever He traveled, with a single word and in a single moment He
made the sick, weak, and sufferers of all kinds whole: even if they
were crippled in all their limbs, they suddenly recovered their

251

rentur, receptis tamen repente viribus roborati ipsi[45] lectulos suos
182 reportarent in quibus fuerant paulo ante delati. Claudis vero ac
pedum vitio afflictis non modo gradiendi sed etiam currendi dabat
facultatem. Tum quorum caeca lumina in altissimis tenebris erant,
eorum oculos in pristinum restituebat aspectum. Mutorum quoque linguas in eloquium sermonemque solvebat. Surdorum insuper patefactis auribus insinuabat auditum, pollutos denique et as-
per⟨s⟩os maculis repurgabat et ad extremum quoscumque volebat
mortuos ab inferis ad vitam suscitabat. Et haec omnia pluraque
alia non manibus aut aliqua medela — quemadmodum cuncti sae-
culares medici tam physici quam chirurgici semper mederi consue-
183 verunt — sed verbis dumtaxat ac solis iussionibus faciebat. Quas ob
res Iudaei ipsum aliquotiens interemissent, nisi populum et plebem timuissent, qui eum velut verum Dei prophetam plurimum
venerabantur. Sed occasione hominis capiendi a quodam proditore
eius discipulo nomine Iuda sibi praestita, in ipsum tandem manus
iniecerunt, quemadmodum IIII[to] huius voluminis libro plane et
aperte declarabitur. Nam in tertio de salubri ac necessaria eius
doctrina tractare longe satius esse existimavimus. Quo facto, de
captivitate et morte sua quarto — ut diximus — libro postea narra-
bimus.

strength, and being strengthened, carried away the cots in which they had just been carried.[410] To the lame and others afflicted in 182 their feet, He not only gave the ability to walk, but even to run. And to those whose eyes were blind in deepest darkness, He restored their eyes to their former vision. The tongues of the mute He unloosed to give utterance and speech. He opened and instilled hearing in the ears of the deaf. He cleansed those infected and stained with spots,[411] and finally he raised whatever dead persons he wished from death to life. And He effected all these cures and many others without using his hands or any remedy — as all our worldly physicians, both general practitioners and surgeons, are wont to cure — but only with words and commands.[412] For these reasons, the Jews would have killed Him several times, 183 but they feared the people and the masses, who revered Him highly as a God's true prophet. But when His traitorous disciple Judas provided an opportunity for seizing the man, they finally laid hands on Him, as will be set forth plainly and openly in Book 4 of this work. In Book 3 we thought it preferable to discuss in detail His salutary and necessary teaching; and having done this, we shall next recount his captivity and death in Book 4, as we said.

LIBER TERTIUS[1]

De doctrina Christi

1 De saluberrima Iesu Christi Salvatoris Nostri doctrina hoc tertio libro tractaturi, primo de praeceptis eius, de responsionibus deinde, postremo de parabolis suis deinceps dicemus.

2 Ideoque a divino quodam sermone quem de industria in aliquo Galilaeae monte habuit non iniuria ordiemur. Iesus enim circumstantes turbas et coetus hominum conspicatus, in memoratum montem ascendit, ubi ad eum sedentem discipuli consecuti seorsum accesserunt. Hos adaperto ore non in fumo et caligine, non in tenebris et procellis, non in tubis terribiliter sonantibus, non cum tonitruis crebrius comminantibus, non coruscantibus denique fulgoribus, quemadmodum accidisse scribitur dum vetus lex traderetur, sed lucente prorsus die, cum pausa et quiete, non tamen sine plurium signorum ostensione, in hunc modum atque his verbis divinitus edocebat:

3 'Beati pauperes spiritu, quoniam ipsorum est regnum caelorum. Beati mites, quoniam ipsi possidebunt terram. Beati qui lugent, quoniam ipsi consolabuntur. Beati qui esuriunt et sitiunt iustitiam, quoniam ipsi saturabuntur. Beati misericordes, quoniam ipsi misericordiam consequentur. Beati mundo corde, quoniam ipsi Deum videbunt. Beati pacifici, quoniam ipsi filii Dei vocabuntur. Beati qui persecutionem patiuntur propter iustitiam, quoniam ipsorum est regnum caelorum. Beati estis cum maledixerint vobis homines et persecuti vos fuerint et dixerint omne malum adver-
4 sum vos propter me, mentientes. Gaudete et exsultate, quoniam merces vestra copiosa est in caelis. Sic enim et prophetas persecuti sunt qui ante vos fuerunt. Vos estis sal terrae; quod si sal evanuerit

BOOK THREE

Christ's Teaching

In this third book, we shall discuss the salutary teaching of Jesus 1
Christ, our Savior; we shall first discuss his precepts, then his answers to questions, and finally his parables.

We will begin most properly with the divine sermon that he 2
intentionally delivered on a mount in Galilee.[1] When Jesus saw
that He was surrounded by crowds of the assembled people, He
ascended the mount and sat down, joined by the disciples, who
followed separately. Then He opened His mouth, not in smoke
and gloom, not in darkness and storms, not amid terrifyingly
sounding trumpets, not with thunder frequently threatening, nor
with dazzling lightning bolts—as it is written happened when the
Old Law was handed down—but in peace and quiet, but not
without several signs being displayed,[2] and He divinely taught
them with these words:

"Blessed are the poor in spirit, for theirs is the kingdom of 3
heaven. Blessed are the meek, for they will inherit the earth.
Blessed are those who mourn, for they will be comforted. Blessed
are those who hunger and thirst for righteousness, for they will be
filled. Blessed are the merciful, for they will receive mercy. Blessed
are the pure in heart, for they will see God. Blessed are the peace-
makers, for they will be called children of God. Blessed are those
who are persecuted for righteousness' sake, for theirs is the kingdom of heaven. Blessed are you when people revile you and persecute you and utter all kinds of evil against you falsely on my account. Rejoice and be glad, for your reward is great in heaven. For 4
in the same way they persecuted the prophets who were before
you. You are the salt of the earth; but if the salt has lost its taste,

in quo salietur? Ad nihilum valet ultra nisi ut foras proiciatur et ab hominibus conculcetur. Vos estis lux mundi; non potest civitas urbsve abscondi supra montem posita neque lucernam accendunt et sub modio ponunt sed super candelabrum constituunt, ut omnibus domesticis luceat. Sic lux vestra coram hominibus luceat, ut vestra bona opera videant et patrem vestrum glorificent, qui in caelis est.

5   'Nolite putare quoniam veni legem solvere aut prophetas; non enim veni legem solvere sed adimplere. Amen: quippe dico vobis donec transeat caelum et terra iota unum aut unus apex non praeteribit a lege donec omnia fiant. Qui ergo solverit unum de mandatis minimis et sic homines docuerit ⟨minimus vocabitur in regno caelorum; qui autem fecerit et docuerit⟩, hic in regno caelorum magnus vocabitur. Dico autem vobis: nisi iustitia vestra plus quam scribarum et Pharisaeorum abundaverit non intrabitis in regnum caelorum. Audistis quia dictum est antiquis: "Non occides." Qui autem occiderit reus erit iudicio. Ego autem dico vobis quia omnis qui irascitur fratri suo reus erit iudicio; qui autem dixerit fratri suo "racha" reus erit concilio; qui autem dixerit "fatue" reus erit Gehen-

6   nae ignis. Si ergo offeres munus ad altare tuum et ibi recordatus fueris quia frater tuus habet aliquid adversum te, relinque ibi munus tuum ante altare et vade prius reconciliare fratri tuo et tunc veniens offeres munus tuum. Esto consentiens adversario tuo cito dum es in via cum eo, ne forte tradat te adversarius iudici et iudex tradat te ministris et in carcerem mittaris. Amen: dico tibi non exies inde donec novissimum quadrantem reddideris.

7   'Audistis quia dictum est antiquis: "Non moechaberis." Ego autem dico vobis quia omnis qui viderit mulierem ad concupiscen-

how can its saltiness be restored? It is no longer good for anything, but is thrown out and trampled underfoot. You are the light of the world. A community or city built on a hill cannot be hidden. No one lights a lamp and then puts it under a bushel basket, but rather on a lampstand, so that it gives light to all in the house. In the same way, let your light shine before others, so that they may see your good works and give glory to your Father, who is in heaven.

"Do not think that I have come to abolish the Law or the 5 prophets. I have come not to abolish, but to fulfill the Law. For truly I tell you, until heaven and earth pass away, not one iota, not one diacritic, will pass from the Law until all things come to pass. Therefore, whoever breaks one of the least of these commandments, and teaches others to do the same, will be called least in the kingdom of heaven; but whoever does them and teaches them will be called great in the kingdom of heaven. For I tell you, unless your righteousness exceeds that of the scribes and Pharisees, you will never enter the kingdom of heaven. You have heard that it was said to those of ancient times, 'You shall not commit murder'; and 'whoever commits murder shall be liable to judgment.' But I say to you that everyone who is angry with a brother, will be liable to judgment; and whoever insults a brother, will be liable to the council; and whoever says, 'You fool,' will be liable to the fire of hell. So if you are offering your gift at the altar, and there you re- 6 member that your brother has something against you, leave your gift there before the altar and go; first be reconciled to your brother, and then come and offer your gift. Come to terms quickly with your accuser while you are on the way with him, or your accuser may hand you over to the judge, and the judge to the guard, and you will be thrown into prison. Truly I say to you, you will never get out until you have paid the last penny.

"You have heard that it was said to those of ancient times, 'You 7 shall not commit adultery.' But I say to you that everyone who

dum eam iam moechatus est eam in corde suo. Quod si forte oculus tuus dexter scandalizat te, erue eum et proice abs te. Expedit enim tibi ut pereat unum membrorum tuorum quam totum corpus tuum in Gehennam mittatur. ⟨Et si dextera manus tua scandalizat te, abscide eam et proice abs te. Expedit tibi ut pereat unum membrorum tuorum quam totum corpus tuum eat in Gehennam⟩. Dictum est autem: "Quicumque dimiserit uxorem suam libellum repudii ei tradat." Ego autem dico vobis quia omnis qui uxorem suam—excepta causa fornicationis—dimiserit, eam moechari facit, et qui dimissam duxerit adulterat.

8   'Iterum audistis quia dictum est antiquis: "Non periurabis. Reddes autem Domino iuramenta tua." Ego autem dico vobis non iurare omnino neque per caelum, qui thronus Dei est, ⟨neque per terram, quia scabillum est pedum eius⟩, neque per Hierosolymam, quia civitas est magni regis, neque per caput tuum iuraveris, quia ne unum quidem capillum album aut nigrum facere potestis. Sermo autem vester vel aientis vel negantis esse debeat; quod autem his abundantius est a malo est.

9   'Audistis quia dictum est antiquis: "Oculum pro oculo et dentem pro dente." Ego autem dico vobis ne malo resistatis, sed si quis te in dexteram maxillam percusserit tu quoque alteram praebeas, et ei qui vult tecum in iudicio contendere et tunicam tuam tollere tu etiam et pallium ei dimittas. Et quicumque mille passus te angariaverit, cum eo et alia duo proficiscere. Qui abs te petit da ei et abs te mutuum capere volenti non avertaris.

10   'Audistis[2] quia dictum est antiquis: "Diliges proximum tuum et odio habebis inimicum tuum." Ego autem dico vobis diligite inimicos vestros, benefacite iis qui vos oderunt et pro persequentibus et calumniantibus[3] vos orate, ut sitis filii Patris vestri qui in caelis est, qui solem suum super bonos et malos exoriri facit et super iustos

looks at a woman with lust has already committed adultery with her in his heart. If your right eye offends you, tear it out and throw it away. It is better for you to lose one of your members than for your whole body to be thrown into hell. ⟨And if your right hand offends you, cut it off and throw it away; it is better for you to lose one of your members than for your whole body to be thrown into hell.⟩ It was also said that 'Whoever divorces his wife, let him give her a certificate of divorce.' But I say to you that anyone who divorces his wife, except on grounds of infidelity, causes her to commit adultery; and whoever marries a divorced woman commits adultery.

"Again, you have heard that it was said to those of ancient times, 'You shall not swear falsely. Carry out the vows you have made to the Lord.' But I say to you, Do not swear at all, either by heaven, for it is the throne of God; ⟨or by the earth, for it is His footstool,⟩ or by Jerusalem, for it is the city of the great King. And do not swear by your head, for you cannot make one hair white or black. Let your speech be 'Yes' or 'No.' Anything more than this comes from the evil one.

"You have heard that it was said to those of ancient times, 'An eye for an eye, and a tooth for a tooth.' But I say to you, Do not resist an evildoer, but if anyone strikes you on the right cheek, offer the other as well; and if anyone wants to sue you and take your coat, give your cloak as well. And if anyone forces you to go one mile, go with him two further miles as well. Give to everyone who begs from you, and do not turn your back on anyone who wants to borrow from you.

"You have heard that it was said to those of ancient times, 'You shall love your neighbor and hate your enemy.' But I say to you, Love your enemies. And do good to those who hate you, and pray for those who persecute and slander you, so that you may be children of your Father in heaven; for he makes His sun rise on the evil and on the good, and sends rain on the righteous and on the

et iniustos pluit. Si enim diligitis eos qui vos diligunt, quam mercedem habebitis? Nonne et publicani hoc faciunt? Et si vestros
fratres tantummodo salutaveritis, quid amplius facietis? Nonne et
ethnici hoc faciunt? Estote ergo perfecti, sicut et Pater vester caelestis perfectus est.

11   'Attendite ne iustitiam vestram coram hominibus faciatis, ut vi-
deamini ab eis, alioquin mercedem vestram apud Patrem vestrum
qui in caelis est non habebitis. Cum ergo facis elemosinam noli
ante te tubicinari, sicut publicani faciunt in synagogis et vicis ut
honorificentur ab hominibus. Amen dico vobis: receperunt mercedem suam. Te autem faciente elemosinam nesciat sinistra tua quid
faciat dextera tua, ut elemosina sit in abscondito et Pater tuus qui
videt in occultis reddet tibi.

12   'Cum autem orabitis nolite multum loqui, sicut ethnici faciunt.
In multiloquio enim suo sese exaudiendos putant. Nolite ergo eis
assimilari; scit enim Pater vester quid opus sit vobis antequam
petieritis. Sic ergo vos orabitis: "Pater noster, qui es in caelis, sanc-
tificetur nomen tuum. Adveniat regnum tuum, fiat voluntas tua,
sicut in caelo et in terra. Panem nostrum quotidianum da nobis
hodie et dimitte nobis debita nostra sicut et nos dimittimus debitoribus nostris; et ne nos inducas in temptationem sed libera nos a
malo. Amen."' Sic enim in evangeliis Latinis habetur, at in exemplaribus Graecis cum certa quadam horum paucorum verborum
adiectione fideliter reperitur. Ante namque ultimum verbum 'amen'
ita subiungitur: 'quoniam tuum est imperium et potestas et gloria
in saecula.'

13   'Si enim dimiseritis hominibus peccata vestra dimittet vobis
Pater vester caelestis; si autem non dimiseritis hominibus delicta,
nec Pater vester vobis peccata vestra dimittet. Cum autem ieiuna-
tis, nolite fieri sicut hypocritae tristes, qui exterminant facies suas
ut hominibus ieiunantes appareant. Amen dico vobis quia iam receperunt mercedem suam. Tu autem cum ieiunas unge caput tuum

unrighteous. For if you love those who love you, what reward do you have? Do not even the tax collectors do the same? And if you greet only your brothers, what more are you doing than others? Do not even the Gentiles do the same? Be perfect, therefore, as your heavenly Father is perfect.

"Beware of practicing your righteousness before men to be seen by them, for then you will not have your reward from your Father, who is in heaven. So whenever you give alms, do not sound a trumpet before you, as the tax collectors do in the synagogues and in the streets, so that they may be praised by men. Truly I tell you, they have received their reward. But when you give alms, do not let your left hand know what your right hand is doing, so that your alms may be done in secret. And your Father, who sees in secret, will reward you. 11

"When you are praying, do not go on at length as the Gentiles do. For they think that they have to be heard because of their many words. Do not be like them, for your Father knows what you need before you ask Him. Pray then in this way, 'Our Father, who are in heaven, hallowed be your name. Your kingdom come. Your will be done, on earth as it is in heaven. Give us this day our daily bread. And forgive us our debts, as we also forgive our debtors. And do not lead us into temptation, but deliver us from the evil one. Amen.'" (So read the Latin Gospels. But in the Greek copies it is reliably found with the certain addition of these few words: before the last word "Amen," there is added, "For yours is the kingdom and the power and the glory forever.") 12

"For if you forgive others their trespasses, your heavenly Father will also forgive you. But if you do not forgive others their trespasses, neither will your Father forgive you your trespasses. And whenever you fast, do not look gloomy, like the hypocrites, for they disfigure their faces so as to show others that they are fasting. Truly I tell you, they have already received their reward. But when you fast, put oil on your head and wash your face, so that your 13

et faciem tuam lava ne videaris hominibus ieiunans sed Patri tuo qui est in abscondito, et Pater tuus qui videt ab occultis reddet tibi.

14 'Nolite thesaurizare vobis thesauros in terra, ubi erugo et tinea demolitur et ubi fures effodiunt et furantur. Thesaurizate autem vobis thesauros in caelo, ubi neque erugo neque tinea demolitur et ubi fures non effodiunt nec furantur; ubi enim est thesaurus tuus ibi est cor tuum. Lucerna corporis tui est oculus tuus. Si oculus tuus fuerit simplex totum corpus tuum lucidum erit. Si autem oculus tuus nequam fuerit totum corpus tuum tenebrosum erit. Si ergo lumen quod in te est tenebrae sunt, ipsae tenebrae quantae

15 sunt! Nemo potest duobus dominis servire: aut enim unum odio habebit et alterum diliget aut unum sustinebit et alterum contemnet. Non potestis Deo servire et mamonae. Ideo dico vobis ne solliciti sitis animae vestrae quid manducetis aut corpori vestro quid induamini. Nonne anima vestra plus est quam esca et corpus plus quam vestimentum? Respicite volatilia caeli, quoniam non serunt neque metunt[4] neque congregant in horrea, et Pater vester caelestis nihilominus pascit illa. Nonne vos magis pluris estis illis?

16 'Quis autem vestrum cogitans potest adicere ad staturam suam cubitum unum? Et de vestimento quid solliciti estis? Considerate lilia agro quomodo crescunt; non laborant neque nent. Dico autem vobis quoniam neque Salomon in omni gloria sua coopertus est sicut unum ex istis. Si autem faenum agri quod hodie est et cras in clibanum mittetur Deus sic vestit quanto magis[5] vos modicae fi-

17 dei? Nolite ergo solliciti esse dicentes "Quid manducabimus?" aut "Quid bibemus?" aut "Quo operiemur?" Haec enim omnia gentes inquirunt. Scit Pater vester quia his omnibus indigetis. Quaerite ergo primum regnum Dei et iustitiam Eius et haec omnia adicientur vobis. Nolite ergo solliciti esse in crastinum. Crastinus enim dies sollicitus erit sibi ipsi; sufficit ergo diei malitia sua.

fasting may be seen not by men, but by your Father, who is in secret; and your Father, who sees in secret, will reward you.

"Do not store up for yourselves treasures on earth, where moth 14 and rust destroy and where thieves break in and steal; but store up for yourselves treasures in heaven, where neither moth nor rust destroys and where thieves do not break in and steal. For where your treasure is, there your heart is. Your eye is the lamp of your body. So if your eye is honest, your whole body will be full of light. But if your eye is wicked, your whole body will be full of darkness. If then the light which is in you is darkness, how great is the darkness! No one can serve two masters; for a slave will either 15 hate the one and love the other, or be devoted to the one and despise the other. You cannot serve God and wealth. Therefore I tell you, do not worry about your life, what you will eat, or about your body, what you will wear. Is not life more than food, and the body more than clothing? Look at the birds of the air; they neither sow nor reap nor gather into barns, and yet your heavenly Father feeds them. Are you not of more value than they?

"And can any of you by worrying add a single cubit to your 16 height? And why do you worry about clothing? Consider the lilies of the field, how they grow; they neither toil nor spin. Yet I tell you, even Solomon in all his glory was not clothed like one of these. But if God so clothes the grass of the field, which is today and tomorrow is thrown into the oven, will He not much more clothe you—you of little faith? Therefore do not worry, saying, 17 'What will we eat?' or 'What will we drink?' or 'What will we wear?' For the Gentiles inquire into all these things; and your heavenly Father knows that you need all these things. But first seek the kingdom of God and His righteousness, and all these things will be given to you as well. So do not worry about tomorrow, for tomorrow will worry about itself. Its own trouble is enough for the day.

18 'Nolite iudicare ut non iudicemini. In quo enim iudicio iudica-
bitis iudicabimini et in qua mensura mensi fueritis remetietur vobis. Quid autem festucam in oculo fratris tui intueris et trabem in
oculo tuo non vides? Aut quomodo dices fratri tuo "Frater, sine
eiciam festucam de oculo" [fratris tui] et ecce trabs est in oculo
tuo. Hypocrita! Eice primum trabem de oculo tuo et tunc ad ei-
ciendum festucam de oculo fratris tui speculaberis!

19 'Nolite sanctum dare canibus neque iactatis margaritas vestras
ante porcos, ne forte pedibus conculcarent et conversi disrumpant
vos. Vos petite et dabitur vobis. Quaerite et invenietis. Pulsate et
aperietur vobis. Omnis enim qui petit accipit et qui quaerit invenit
et pulsanti aperietur. Aut qui est ex vobis quem si petierit filius
suus panem numquid lapidem porriget illi aut si petierit piscem
numquid serpentem porriget ei? Si ergo vos cum sitis mali nostis
bona data dare filiis vestris quanto magis Pater vester caelestis dabit bona petentibus se? Omnia ergo quaecumque vultis ut faciant
vobis homines et vos facite illis. Haec est enim ⟨lex⟩ et prophetae.

20 'Intrate per angustam portam quia lata porta est et spatiosa via
quae ducit ⟨ad perditionem et multi sunt qui intrant per eam.
Quam angusta porta et arta via quae ducit⟩ ad vitam, et pauci sunt
qui inveniunt eam. Attendite a falsis prophetis qui veniunt ad vos
in vestimentis ovium; intrinsecus autem sunt lupi rapaces. A fruc-
21 tibus eorum cognoscetis eos. Numquid colligunt de spinis uvas aut
de tribulis ficus? Sic omnis arbor bona fructus bonos facit, mala
autem arbor malos fructus facit. Non potest arbor bona fructus
malos nec arbor mala fructus bonos facere. Omnis arbor quae non
facit fructum bonum excidetur et in ignem proicietur. Igitur ex
fructibus suis cognoscetis eos.

22 'Non omnis qui dicit mihi "Domine, Domine" intrabit in regnum caelorum, ⟨sed qui facit voluntatem Patris mei qui in caelis

"Do not judge, so that you may not be judged. For by the judg- 18
ment you make will you be judged, and the measure you give will
be the measure you get. Why do you see the straw in your brother's eye, but do not notice the beam in your own eye? Or how can
you say to your brother, 'Brother, let me take the straw out of your
eye,' but behold the beam is in your own eye? You hypocrite, first
take the beam out of your eye, and then you will see clearly to take
the straw out of your brother's eye.

"Do not give what is holy to dogs; and do not throw your pearls 19
before swine, or they will trample them under foot and turn and
maul you. Ask, and it will be given to you. Seek, and you will find;
knock, and the door will be opened for you. For everyone who
asks, receives; and everyone who searches, finds; and for everyone
who knocks, the door will be opened. Is there anyone among you
who, if your son asks for bread, will give him a stone? Or if he
asks for a fish, will give him a snake? If you, then, who are evil,
know how to give good gifts to your children, how much more
will your Father in heaven give good things to those who ask
Him? Everything you wish others to do to you, do the same to
them. For this is ⟨the Law⟩ and the prophets.

"Enter through the narrow gate; for the gate is wide and the 20
road is ample that leads ⟨to destruction, and there are many who
enter that way. How cramped is the gate, and narrow the road that
leads⟩ to life, and there are few who find it! Beware of false prophets, who come to you in sheep's clothing but inwardly are ravenous
wolves. You will know them by their fruits. Are grapes gathered 21
from thorns, or figs from thistles? In the same way, every good
tree bears good fruit, but the bad tree bears bad fruit. A good tree
cannot bear bad fruit, nor can a bad tree bear good fruit. Every
tree that does not bear good fruit will be cut down and thrown
into the fire. Thus you will know them by their fruits.

"Not everyone who says to me, 'Lord, Lord,' will enter the king- 22
dom of heaven. ⟨But only one who does the will of my Father in

est; ipse intrabit in regnum caelorum⟩. Multi dicent mihi in illa die "Domine, Domine nonne in nomine tuo prophetavimus et in nomine tuo daemonia eiecimus et in nomine tuo virtutes multas fecimus?" Et tunc confitebor illis: "Quia numquam novi vos discedite a me omnes qui operamini iniquitatem." Omnis ergo qui audierit verba mea et fecerit ea assimilabitur viro sapienti qui aedificavit domum suam supra petram et descendit pluvia et venerunt flumina et flaverunt venti et in domum illam irruerunt nec cecidit. Super petram enim fundata erat. Et omnis qui audierit verba mea haec et non fecerit ea similis erit viro stulto qui aedificavit domum suam super harenam et descendit pluvia et venerunt flumina et flaverunt venti et irruerunt in domum illam et ita cecidit ut magna eius ruina foret.'

23   Non multo post hunc tam prolixum et tam salutarem ac tam divinum sermonem factum est ut discipulos suos ad praedicandam evangelicam doctrinam per orbemque terrarum ceu necessaria quaedam salutis humanae semina undique dispergendam hinc inde transmitteret. Et mittens sic eis praecepit: 'In viam gentium ne abieritis et in civitates Samaritanorum ne intraveritis sed potius ite ad oves quae perierunt domus Israhel. Euntes autem praedicate dicentes quod appropinquavit regnum caelorum. Infirmos curate, mortuos suscitate, leprosos mundate, daemones eicite. Gratis accepistis, gratis date. Nolite possidere aurum neque argentum neque pecuniam in zonis vestris neque peram in via neque duas tunicas neque calciamenta[6] neque virgam. Dignus est enim operarius cibo suo.

24   'In quamcumque autem civitatem aut castellum intraveritis, interrogate quis in ea dignus sit et ibi manete donec exeatis. Intrantes autem in domum salutate eam et dicite "Pax huic domui,"' quod hebraice expressius dicitur. Sicut enim apud Graecos 'Chere,' hoc est 'Salve,' et apud Latinos eodem quoque modo sed aliis verbis 'Salve' dicitur, ita apud Hebraeos—⟨per⟩ uniuscuiusque lin-
25   guae proprietatem—'Scialom alach' 'Pax tecum' interpretatur. 'Et si

heaven will enter into the kingdom of heaven.) On that day many will say to me, 'Lord, Lord, did we not prophesy in your name, and cast out demons in your name, and do many deeds of power in your name?' Then I will declare to them, 'I never knew you; depart from me, all you who work iniquity.' Everyone then who hears these words of mine and acts on them will be like a wise man who built his house on rock. The rain fell, the floods came, and the winds blew and beat on that house, but it did not fall, because it had been founded on rock. And everyone who hears these words of mine and does not act on them will be like a fool- ish man who built his house on sand. The rain fell, and the floods came, and the winds blew and beat against that house, and it fell—and great was its fall!"

Not long after this elaborate, salutary, and divine sermon, it 23 came to pass that He sent His disciples in all directions to preach the Gospel teaching and to spread it everywhere throughout the earth as the necessary seeds of human salvation. In sending them, He instructed them thus: "Go nowhere among the Gentiles, and enter no town of the Samaritans, but go rather to the lost sheep of the house of Israel. As you go, proclaim the good news, 'The king- dom of heaven is near.' Cure the sick, raise the dead, cleanse the lepers, cast out demons. You received without payment; give with- out payment. Take no gold, or silver, or money in your belts, no bag for your journey, or two tunics, or sandals, or a staff. For the workman is worthy of his food.

"Whatever town or village you enter, find out who in it is wor- 24 thy, and stay there until you leave. As you enter the house, greet it, saying 'Peace to this house.'" (In Hebrew, they say this more pre- cisely. For the Greeks say *Chaire*,[3] which means "Greetings," which the Latins likewise say with another word: *Salve*. In Hebrew—for the idiom of each language—they say *Shalom alech*, which means "Peace be with you.")[4] "If the house is worthy, your peace will 25

quidem fuerit domus illa digna, veniet pax vestra super eam. Si autem non fuerit digna, pax vestra ad vos revertetur. Et quandocumque neque vos recipiemini neque sermones vestri recepti fuerint, exite foras de domo vel de civitate et excutite pulverem de pedibus vestris in testimonium illis. Amen: dico vobis tolerabilius erit terrae Sodomorum et Gomorraeorum in die iudicii quam illi civitati. Ecce, ego mitto vos sicut oves in medio luporum. Estote ergo prudentes sicut serpentes et simplices sicut columbae. Cavete autem ab hominibus; tradent enim vos in conciliis et synagogis suis, flagellabunt vos et ad reges ducemini propter me in testimonium illis et gentibus. Cum autem vos tradiderint, nolite cogitare quia aut quid loquamini; dabitur enim vobis in illa hora quid loquendum sit. Non enim vos estis qui loquimini sed Spiritus Patris vestri qui loquitur in vobis.

26　'Tradet enim frater fratrem in morte⟨m⟩ et pater filium et insurgent filii in parentes et eos morte afficient et eritis odio omnibus hominibus propter nomen meum. Qui autem perseveraverit usque in finem hic salvus erit. Cum autem persequuntur vos in aliqua civitate[7] fugite in aliam. Amen: dico vobis non consummabitis civitates Israhel donec veniat Filius hominis. Non est discipulus super magistrum nec servus super dominum suum. Sufficit enim discipulo ut sit sicut magister eius et servo satis est ut sit sicut dominus eius. Et si patrem familias Beelzebub[8] vocaverunt' (hoc erat idolum 'Acharon,' id est 'principem daemoniorum'; tam turpi et tam spurco cognomine vocaverunt, sic ob muscarum spur⟨c⟩itiam appellatum. 'Iebul' enim hebraice 'musca' interpretatur, 'bel' vero memorati idoli nomen habebatur ac Beelzebub[9] pro deo colebatur)

27　'quanto magis domesticos eius! Ne ergo timueritis eos; nihil enim opertum est quod non reveletur neque occultum quod ignoretur. Quod dico vobis in tenebris vos dicite in lumine et quod in aure auditis praedicate super tecta; et nolite timere eos qui corpus occidunt, animam autem non possunt occidere, sed potius eum timete qui potest animam et corpus perdere in Gehennam. Nonne

come upon it; but if it is not worthy, your peace will return to you. If anyone will not welcome you or listen to your words, leave the home or city and shake off the dust from your feet as a witness against them. Truly I tell you, it will be more tolerable for the land of Sodom and Gomorrah on the day of judgment than for that town. See, I am sending you out like sheep into the midst of wolves; so be wise as serpents and innocent as doves. Be wary of people, for they will hand you over to their councils and synagogues and flog you; and you will be dragged before their kings because of me, as a testimony to them and the Gentiles. When they hand you over, do not worry about how you are to speak or what you are to say. For what you are to say will be given to you at that time, since it is not you who speak, but the Spirit of your Father speaking through you.

"Brother will betray brother to death, and a father his child; 26 and children will rise against parents and have them put to death. And you will be hated by all because of my name. But the one who endures to the end will be saved. When they persecute you in one town, flee to the next. Truly I tell you, you will not have gone through all the towns of Israel before the Son of Man comes. A student is not above the teacher, nor a slave above the master. It is enough for the student to be like the teacher, and the slave like the master. If they have called the master of the house Beelzebub, how much more will they malign those of his household!" (Beelzebub is the idol Acharon, or the prince of demons, called by so foul and filthy a name because of the filthiness of flies: *iebul* in Hebrew means fly, and *Bel* was the name of the said demon; and they worshiped Beelzebub as a god.) "So have no fear of them; for nothing 27 is covered up that will not be uncovered, and nothing secret that will not become known. What I say to you in the dark, tell in the light; and what you hear whispered, proclaim from the housetops. Do not fear those who kill the body but cannot kill the soul; rather fear Him who can destroy both soul and body in hell. Are

duo passeres asse veneunt et unus ex illis non cadet super terram sine Patre vestro? Vestri autem et capilli omnes capitis numerati sunt. Nolite ergo timere: multis namque passeribus praestatis melioresque estis!

28 'Omnis ergo qui confitebitur me coram hominibus et ego eum coram Patre meo confitebor, qui in caelis est. Qui autem negaverit me coram hominibus negabo ⟨et⟩ ego illum coram Patre meo. Nolite ergo arbitrari quod veni pacem mittere in terram; non veni pacem mittere sed gladium. Veni enim separare hominem adversus patrem suum et filiam[10] adversus matrem suam et nurum adversus

29 socrum suam, et inimici hominis domestici[11] eius. Qui amat patrem aut matrem plus quam me non est me dignus et qui[12] amat filium aut filiam supra me non est me dignus. Et qui invenit animam suam perdet illam et qui perdiderit animam suam propter me inveniet eam. Qui enim recipit vos me recipit et qui me recipit, recipit eum qui me misit. Qui recipit prophetam in nomine prophetae mercedem prophetae accipiet et qui recipit iustum in nomine iusti mercedem iusti accipiet. Et quicumque potum dederit uni ex minimis istis calicem aquae frigidae tantum in nomine discipuli mei amen dico vobis: non perdet mercedem suam.'

30 Illis autem abeuntibus coepit Iesus dicere ad turbas de Iohanne: 'Quid existis videre in desertum? Arundinem vento agitatam? Sed quid existis videre? Hominem mollibus vestitum? Ecce, qui mollibus vestiuntur in dom[in]ibus regum sunt! Sed quid existis videre? Prophetam? Etiam dico vobis, et plus quam prophetam. Hic est enim de quo scriptum est: "Ecce ego mitto angelum meum ante faciem tuam qui praeparabit viam tuam ante te." Amen dico vobis: non surrexit inter natos mulierum maior Iohanne Baptista. Qui autem minor est in regno caelorum maior est illo. A diebus autem

not two sparrows sold for a penny? Yet not one of them will fall to the ground unperceived by your Father. And even the hairs of your head are all counted. So do not be afraid; you are greater and of greater value than many sparrows.

"Everyone therefore who acknowledges me before men, I also 28 will acknowledge before my Father, who is in heaven. But whoever denies me before men, I ⟨also⟩ will deny before my Father.[5] Do not think that I have come to bring peace to the earth. I have not come to bring peace, but a sword. For I have come to set a man against his father, and a daughter against her mother, and a daughter-in-law against her mother-in-law; and a man's household will be his enemies. Whoever loves father or mother more than 29 me is not worthy of me. And whoever loves son or daughter more than me is not worthy of me. ⟨And whoever does not take up the cross and follow me is not worthy of me.⟩ Whoever finds his life will lose it, and whoever loses his life for my sake will find it. Whoever welcomes you welcomes me, and whoever welcomes me welcomes Him who sent me. Whoever welcomes a prophet in the name of a prophet will receive a prophet's reward; and whoever welcomes a righteous person in the name of a righteous person will receive the reward of the righteous; and whoever gives even a cup of cold water to one of these little ones in the name of my disciple—truly I tell you, he will not lose his reward."

As they went away, Jesus began to speak about John to the 30 crowds, "What did you go to see in the wilderness? A reed shaken by the wind? What then did you go to see? A man dressed in soft robes? Look, those who wear soft robes are in royal palaces. What then did you go to see? A prophet? Yes, I tell you, and more than a prophet. This is the one about whom it is written, 'See, I am sending my messenger ahead of you, who will prepare your way before you.' Truly I tell you, among those born of women no one has arisen greater than John the Baptist; yet the least in the kingdom of heaven is greater than he. From the days of John the

Iohannis Baptistae usque nunc regnum caelorum vim patitur et violenti diripiunt illud. Omnes enim prophetae una cum lege usque ad Iohannem prophetaverunt. Si vultis recipere, ipse est Helias qui venturus est. Qui habet aures audiendi audiat.

31 'Cui autem similem existimabo generationem istam? Similis est pueris sedentibus in foro qui coaequalibus suis clamant et dicunt: "Cecinimus vobis et non saltastis, lamentavimus et non planxistis." Venit Iohannes, neque manducans neque bibens, et dicunt: "Daemonium habet." Venit et Filius hominis, manducans et bibens, et dicunt: "Ecce homo vorax et potator vini, publicanorum et peccatorum amicus" et iustificata est sapientia a filiis suis.'

32 Tunc coepit exprobare civitatibus in quibus plurimae virtutes eius factae fuerant, quod poenitentiam non egissent: 'Vae tibi, Corazain! Vae tibi, Bethsaida! Quia si in Tyro et Sidone factae fuissent virtutes quae factae sunt in vobis olim in cilicio et cinere poenitentiam egissent. Verumtamen dico vobis quia terrae Sodomorum remissius erit in die iudicii quam vobis! Et tu, Capharnaum, "Numquid usque in caelum exaltaberis, usque in infernum descendes?" Quia si in Sodomis factae fuissent virtutes quae apud te factae sunt, forte hactenus permansissent. Verumtamen dico vobis quia terrae Sodomorum remissius erit in die iudicii quam tibi.'

33 Ad turbas quoque et ad discipulos suos simul congregatos in hunc modum verba fecit: 'Super cathedram Moysi sederunt scribae et Pharisaei. Omnia ergo quaecumque dixerunt vobis servate et facite, secundum vero opera eorum ne faciatis. Dicunt enim et non faciunt. Alligant namque onera gravia et intollerabilia quae super umeros hominum imponunt; digito autem suo nolunt ea movere. Omnia vero opera sua propterea faciunt ut ab hominibus videantur; dilatant enim phylacteria sua et fimbrias magnificant,' in quibus ineffabile illud omnipotentis Dei nomen—quod graece

Baptist until now the kingdom of heaven has suffered violence, and the violent ravage it by force. For all the prophets and the Law prophesied until John came. And if you are willing to accept it, he is Elijah who is to come. Let anyone who has ears to hear listen!

"But to what will I compare this generation? It is like children 31 sitting in the marketplace and calling to one another and saying, 'We played the flute for you, and you did not dance; we wailed, and you did not mourn.' For John came neither eating nor drinking, and they say, 'He has a demon.' The Son of Man came eating and drinking, and they say, 'Look, a glutton and a drunkard, a friend of tax collectors and sinners!' Yet wisdom is vindicated by her sons."

Then he began to reproach the cities in which most of his 32 deeds of power had been done, because they did not repent. "Woe to you, Chorazin! Woe to you, Bethsaida! For if the deeds of power done in you had been done in Tyre and Sidon, they would have repented long ago in sackcloth and ashes. But I tell you, on the day of judgment it will be more tolerable for the land of Sodom than for you. And you, Capharnaum, will you be exalted to heaven? No, you will be brought down to Hades.[6] For if the deeds of power done in you had been done in Sodom, it would have remained until this day. But I tell you that on the day of judgment it will be more tolerable for the land of Sodom than for you."

Then Jesus spoke to the crowds and to His disciples gathered 33 together in the following words,[7] "The scribes and the Pharisees sit on Moses' seat; therefore, do whatever they teach you and follow it. But do not do as they do, for they do not practice what they teach. They tie up heavy burdens, hard to bear, and lay them on the shoulders of others. But they themselves are unwilling to lift a finger to move them. They do all their deeds to be seen by others. For they make their phylacteries broad and the fringes of their garments long"—on these they wore the unspeakable name of almighty God (called in Greek the *tetragrammaton*) written in

'tetragrammaton' appellatur—aureis scriptum litteris deferebant.
'Primos insuper recubitus in cenis et primas cathedras in synagogis
amant et salutari in foro et vocari cupiunt ab hominibus "rabbi,"'
quod verbum latine ex hebraeo interpretatum 'magistrum' significabat. '⟨Vos autem nolite vocari "rabbi"⟩. Unus enim est magister
vester; omnes fratres estis et patrem nolite vocare vobis super terram; unus enim est Pater, qui in caelis est, nec vocemini magistri
quia magister vester unus est Christus. Qui maior est vestrum erit
minister vester. Qui autem se exaltaverit humiliabitur et qui se
humiliat exaltabitur.

34   'Vae vobis, scribae et Pharisaei hypocritae, quia ante homines
regnum caelorum clauditis; vos enim ibi nec intratis nec alios in-
gressuros intrare sinitis. Vae autem vobis, scribae et Pharisaei hypocritae, qui circuitis mare et aridam et unum proselytum faciatis
et cum fuerit factus facitis eum Gehennae filium duplo quam vos.
Vae vobis, duces caeci, qui dicitis: "Quicumque iuraverit per templum Dei nihil est; quicumque autem iuraverit in auro templi debet." Stulti et caeci! Quid enim maius est: aurum an templum
quod sanctificat aurum? "Et quicumque iuraverit in altare nihil est;
qui autem iuraverit in dono quod est super illud debet." Caeci!
Quid enim est maius: donum an altare quod sanctificat donum?
Qui iurat in altari iurat in eo et in omnibus quae super illud sunt
et quicumque iuraverit in templo iurat in illo et in eo qui habitat
in ipso et quicumque iurat in caelo iurat in throno Dei et in eo qui
sedet super illud.

35   'Vae vobis, scribae et Pharisaei hypocritae, qui mentam, ane-
thum et cyminum decimatis et ceterarum rerum huiusmodi decimas datis; iudicium vero, misericordiam et fidem, quae longe
graviora sunt legis, reliquistis. Haec oportuit facere et illa non
omittere. O caeci duces! Nam camelum gluttientes culicem exco-
latis!

golden letters.[8] "They love to have the place of honor at banquets and the best seats in the synagogues, and to be greeted with respect in the marketplace, and to have people call them rabbi." (Translated from Hebrew into Latin, this word means "teacher.") "⟨But you are not to be called rabbi.⟩[9] For you have one teacher, and you are all brothers. And call no one your father on earth. For you have one Father, who is in heaven. Nor are you to be called teachers, for your one Teacher is Christ. The greatest among you will be your servant. All who exalt themselves will be humbled, and all who humble themselves will be exalted.

"But woe to you, scribes and Pharisees, hypocrites! For you 34 lock people out of the kingdom of heaven. For you neither enter yourselves, nor allow others to enter. Woe to you, scribes and Pharisees, hypocrites! For you cross sea and land to make a single convert, and when you have done so, you make him twice as much a child of hell as yourselves. Woe to you, blind guides, who say, 'Whoever swears by God's sanctuary is bound by nothing, but whoever swears by the gold of the sanctuary is bound by the oath.' You blind fools! For which is greater, the gold or the sanctuary that makes the gold sacred? And you say, 'Whoever swears by the altar is bound by nothing, but whoever swears by the gift that is on the altar is bound by the oath.' How blind you are! For which is greater, the gift or the altar that makes the gift sacred? So whoever swears by the altar, swears by it and by everything on it. And whoever swears by the sanctuary, swears by it and by Him who dwells in it. And whoever swears by heaven, swears by the throne of God and by Him who is seated upon it.

"Woe to you, scribes and Pharisees, hypocrites! For you tithe 35 mint, dill, and cumin and other such things, and have neglected the weightier matters of the Law, judgment and mercy and faith. It is these you ought to have practiced without neglecting the others. You blind guides! You strain out a gnat but swallow a camel!

36   'Vae vobis, scribae et Pharisaei hypocritae, quia mundatis[13] quod de foris est calicis et parapsidis, intus autem pleni estis nequitia et immunditia! Pharisaee caece,[14] munda prius quod intus est calicis et parapsidis ut fiat id quod de foris est mundum.

37   'Vae vobis scribae et Pharisaei[15] hypocritae, qui similes estis sepulchris dealbatis quae foris hominibus speciosa videntur, intrinsecus vero ossibus mortuorum omnique spurcitia plena sunt. Sic et vos quidem extrinsecus apparetis hominibus iusti, intus autem pleni estis hypocrisi et iniquitate. Vae vobis, scribae et Pharisaei hypocritae, qui aedificatis sepulchra prophetarum et ornatis monumenta iustorum et dicitis: "Si in diebus patrum nostrorum fuissemus utique non essemus socii eorum in sanguine prophetarum." Itaque in testimonio estis vobismet ipsis quia filii estis eorum qui prophetas occiderunt. Et vos implete mensuram patrum vestrorum! Serpentes, genimina viperarum, quo fugitis a iudicio Gehennae?

38   'Ecce ego mitto ad vos prophetas et sapientes et scribas et ex illis occidetis et crucifigetis et ex eis flagellabitis in synagogis vestris et persequemini de civitate in civitatem, ut omnis sanguis iustus super vos veniat qui effusus est super terram a sanguine Abel iusti usque ad sanguinem Zacchariae filii Barachiae, quem occidistis. Amen dico vobis: venient omnia haec super generationem istam.

39   Hierusalem, Hierusalem quae[16] occidis prophetas et lapidas eos qui ad te missi sunt, quotiens volui congregare filios tuos quemadmodum gallina congregat pullos suos sub alis et noluisti? Ecce relinquetur domus vestra deserta. Dico enim vobis, non me videbitis amodo donec dicatis: "Benedictus qui venit in nomine Domini."'

40   Adhuc autem clamavit et dixit: 'Qui credit in me non credit in me sed in eum qui misit me. Et qui videt me videt eum qui misit me. Ego lux veni in mundum ut omnis qui credit in me in tenebris non maneat. Et si quis audierit verba mea et non custodierit, ego

"Woe to you, scribes and Pharisees, hypocrites! For you clean   36
the outside of the cup and of the plate, but inside you are full of
wickedness and filth. You blind Pharisee! First clean the inside of
the cup and plate, so that the outside also may become clean.

"Woe to you, scribes and Pharisees, hypocrites! For you are like   37
whitewashed tombs, which on the outside present a beautiful appearance to observers, but inside they are full of the bones of the
dead and of all kinds of filth. So you also on the outside present
an appearance of righteousness to observers, but inside you are full
of hypocrisy and wickedness. Woe to you, scribes and Pharisees,
hypocrites! For you build the tombs of the prophets and decorate
the graves of the righteous and say, 'If we had lived in the days of
our ancestors, we would not have taken part with them in shedding the blood of the prophets.' Thus you testify against yourselves that you are descendants of those who murdered the prophets. Fill up, then, the measure of your ancestors. You snakes, you
brood of vipers! How can you escape being sentenced to hell?

"Behold, I send you prophets, sages, and scribes, some of whom   38
you will kill and crucify, and some you will flog in your synagogues
and pursue from town to town, so that upon you may come all the
righteous blood shed on earth, from the blood of righteous Abel
to the blood of Zechariah son of Barachiah, whom you murdered.
Truly I tell you, all these things will come upon this generation.
Jerusalem, Jerusalem, you that kills prophets and stone those who   39
are sent to you! How often have I desired to gather your children
together as a hen gathers her brood under her wings, and you refused! See, your house will be left desolate. For I tell you, you will
not see me again until you say, 'Blessed is the one who comes in
the name of the Lord.'"

And again He cried and said,[10] "Whoever believes in me be-   40
lieves not in me but in Him who sent me. And whoever sees me
sees Him who sent me. I have come as light into the world, so that
everyone who believes in me should not remain in the darkness. I

non iudico eum. Non enim veni ut mundum iudicarem sed ut salvarem. Qui spernit me et non accipit verba mea habet qui iudicet eum. Sermo quem locutus sum ille in novissimo die eum ipsum iudicabit, quia ego ex me ipso non sum locutus sed qui misit me Pater ipse mihi dedit mandatum quid dicam aut quid loquar. Et scio quod mandata eius vitam aeternam continent. Quae ergo loquor sicut dixit mihi Pater sic loquor.'

41   In cena insuper cenantibus illis accepit panem ac more suo benedixit et fregit deditque discipulis suis et ait: 'Accipite et comedite. Hoc est corpus meum.' Et accipiens calicem gratias egit et dedit illis dicens: 'Bibite ex hoc omnes. Hic est enim sanguis novi testamenti qui pro multis in remissionem peccatorum effundetur. Dico autem vobis, non bibam amodo de hoc genimine vitis usque in diem illum cum illud bibam novum vobiscum in regno Patris mei.' Et postquam exierunt in Montem Oliveti dixit eis: 'Omnes vos scandalum patiemini propter me in ista nocte. Scriptum est enim: "Percutiam pastorem et dispergentur oves gregis." Postquam autem surrexero praecedam vos in Galilaeam.'

42   Et paulo antequam pateretur, postremo ad discipulos conversus 'Non turbetur,' inquit, 'cor vestrum. Creditis in Deum et in me credite. In domo Patris mei mansiones multae sunt.' In hoc loco divinitus ac propterea obscurissime locutus est, ut mox luce clarius videbitur: 'Si quo minus, dixissem vobis: quia vado parare vobis locum; iterum veniam et accipiam vos ad me ipsum, ut ubi sum ego et vos sitis et quo ego vado scitis et viam cognoscitis. Ego sum via, veritas et vita. Nemo nisi per me ad Patrem venit. Si cognovissetis me utique et Patrem meum cognovissetis et amodo eum cog-
43   noscitis et vidistis eum. Verba quae ego loquor a me ipso non loquor. Pater autem in me manens ipse facit opera. Non creditis

do not judge anyone who hears my words and does not keep them, for I came not to judge the world, but to save the world. The one who rejects me and does not receive my words has a judge; on the last day the word that I have spoken will judge him, for I have not spoken on my own, but the Father who sent me has Himself given me a commandment about what to say and what to speak. And I know that His commandments are eternal life. What I speak, therefore, I speak just as the Father has told me."

While they were eating, Jesus took a loaf of bread, and, as was His wont, He blessed and broke it and gave it to His disciples and said, "Take, eat; this is my body."[11] Then he took a cup, and after giving thanks, He gave it to them, saying, "Drink from it, all of you; for this is the blood of the new covenant, which will be poured out for many for the forgiveness of sins. I tell you, I will never again drink of this fruit of the vine until that day when I drink it anew with you in my Father's kingdom." And after they had gone to the Mount of Olives, He said to them, "All of you will be offended because of me this night. For it is written, 'I will strike the shepherd, and the sheep of the flock will be scattered.' But after I am raised up, I will go ahead of you to Galilee." 41

And shortly before His passion, He turned to His disciples and said, "Do not let your hearts be troubled.[12] You believe in God, believe also in me. In my Father's house there are many dwelling places." (In this passage, He spoke divinely and therefore very obscurely, as we shall soon see, but soon more clearly than daylight.) "If it were not so, I would have told you, for I go to prepare a place for you. I will come again and will take you to myself, so that where I am, there you may be also, and you may know where I am going and the way. I am the way, the truth, and the life.[13] No one comes to the Father except through me. If you had known me, you would have known my Father also. From now on you do know Him and have seen Him. The words that I say to you I do not speak on my own. But the Father who dwells in me does the 42

43

quia ego in Patre et Pater in me est? Alioquin propter opera ipsa credite. Amen, amen dico vobis: qui credit in me, opera quae ego facio et ipse faciet et maiora horum faciet, quia ego vado ad Patrem. Et quodcumque petieritis in nomine meo hoc faciam ut glorificetur Pater in Filio. Si diligitis me, mandata mea servate et ego rogabo Patrem et alium Paracletum dabit vobis, ut maneat vobiscum in aeternum, Spiritum[17] veritatis quem mundus non potest accipere, quia nec videt nec cognoscit eum. Vos autem cognoscetis quia apud vos manebit et in vobis erit. Non relinquam vos orphanos; veniam ad vos. Adhuc modicum et mundus iam me non videt. Vos autem videtis me quia ego vivo et vos vivetis. In illo die vos cognoscetis quia ego sum in Patre meo et vos in me et ego in vobis. Qui habet mandata mea et servat ea, ille est qui diligit me. Qui autem diligit me diligetur a Patre meo, et ego diligam eum et manifestabo ei me ipsum. Si quis diligit me, sermonem meum servabit, et Pater meus diliget eum, et ad eum veniemus et mansionem apud eum faciemus. Qui non diligit me, sermones meos non servat. Et sermo⟨nem⟩ quem audistis non est meus, sed Patris, qui me misit. Haec locutus sum apud vos manens. Paracletus autem, Spiritus Sanctus[18] quem mittet Pater in nomine meo, ille vos docebit omnia et suggeret vobis omnia, quaecumque dixero vobis. Pacem relinquo vobis, pacem meam do vobis: non quomodo mundus dat ego do vobis. Non turbetur cor vestrum nec formidet. Audistis quod dixi vobis: "Vado et venio ad vos. Si diligeretis me, gauderetis utique quia vado ad Patrem, et Pater maior me est." Et nunc dixi vobis, priusquam fiat ut, cum factum fuerit, credatis. Iam non multa loquar vobiscum; venit enim princeps mundi huius

44

works Himself. Do you not believe me that I am in the Father and the Father is in me? But if you do not, then believe me because of the works themselves. Very truly, I tell you, the one who believes in me will also do the works that I do and will do greater works than these, because I am going to the Father. I will do whatever you ask in my name, so that the Father may be glorified in the Son. If you love me, keep my commandments. And I will ask the Father, and he will give you another Advocate, to be with you forever, the Spirit of truth, whom the world cannot receive, because it neither sees Him nor knows Him. But you will know Him, because He will abide with you, and He will be in you. I will not leave you orphaned; I will come to you. In a little while the world will no longer see me. But you will see me; because I live, you also will live. On that day you will know that I am in my Father, and you in me, and I in you. Whoever has my commandments and keeps them is one who loves me; and whoever loves me will be loved by my Father, and I will love him and reveal myself to him. Whoever loves me will keep my word, and my Father will love him, and we will come to him and make our home with him. Whoever does not love me does not keep my words; and the word that you hear is not mine, but is from the Father who sent me. I 44 have said these things to you while I am still with you. But the Advocate, the Holy Spirit, whom the Father will send in my name, will teach you everything, and remind you of all that I have said to you. Peace I leave with you; my peace I give to you. I do not give to you as the world gives. Do not let your hearts be troubled, and do not let them be afraid. You heard me say to you, 'I am going away, and I am coming to you.' If you loved me, you would rejoice that I am going to the Father, and the Father is greater than I. And now I have told you this before it occurs, so that when it has occurred, you may believe. I will no longer talk much with you, for the ruler of this world is coming. He has no

et in me non habet¹⁹ quidquam; sed, ut cognoscat mundus quod diligo Patrem, et sicut mandatum dedit mihi Pater, sic facio. Surgite, eamus hinc.

45 'Ego sum vitis vera, et Pater meus agricola est. Omnem palmitem in me non ferentem fructum purgabit eum, ut maiorem fructum afferat. Iam vos mundi estis propter sermonem, quem locutus sum vobis. Manete in me, et ego in vobis. Sicut palmes fructum a semet ipso facere non potest, nisi manserit in vite, sic nec vos fructificabitis nisi ⟨in⟩ me manseritis. Ego sum vitis, vos palmites. Qui manet in me, et ego in eo; hic affert fructum multum, quia sine me nihil potestis facere. Si quis in me non manserit, tamquam palmes foras proicietur et arescet, et arefactus colligetur et in ignem transmittetur, ut ardeat. Si manseritis in me, et verba mea in vobis manserint; quodcumque volueritis fiet vobis. In hoc clarificatus est Pater meus, ut fructum meum plurimum afferatis et efficiamini mei discipuli. Sicut dilexit me Pater, et ego di⟨le⟩xi vos; manete in dilectione mea. Si praecepta mea servaveritis manebitis in dilectione mea sic et ego Patris mei praecepta servavi et maneo in eius

46 dilectione. Haec locutus sum vobis, ut gaudium meum in vobis sit et gaudium vestrum impleatur. Hoc est praeceptum meum, ut diligatis invicem, sicut dilexi vos. Maiorem hac dilectione⟨m⟩ nemo habet quam ut animam suam ponat pro amicis suis. Vos amici mei estis, si feceritis quae ego praecipio vobis. Iam non dicam vos "servos," quia servus nescit quid faciat dominus eius; vos autem dixi "amicos," quia omnia quaecumque audivi a Patre meo nota feci vobis. Non vos me elegistis, sed ego elegi vos et posui vos, ut eatis et fructum afferatis et fructus vester maneat ut, quodcumque petieritis Patrem in nomine meo, det vobis. Et ego haec mando vo-

47 bis, ut diligatis invicem. Si mundus vos odit, scitote quia me priusquam vos odio habuit. Si de mundo fuissetis, mundus quod suum erat diligeret. Quia vero de mundo non estis, ⟨sed⟩ ego elegi

power over me; but I do as the Father has commanded me, so that the world may know that I love the Father. Rise up, and let us be on our way.

"I am the true vine, and my Father is the vintner.[14] Every   45
branch in me that bears no fruit he prunes to make it bear more fruit. You have already been cleansed by the word that I have spoken to you. Abide in me as I abide in you. Just as the branch cannot bear fruit by itself unless it abides in the vine, neither will you bear fruit unless you abide in me. I am the vine, you are the branches. Whoever abides in me, I also abide in him; he bears much fruit, because apart from me you can do nothing. Whoever does not abide in me will be thrown away like a branch and wither; and once withered will be gathered and thrown into the fire, and burned. If you abide in me, and my words abide in you, whatever you wish will be done for you. My Father is glorified by this, that you bear my fruit in abundance and become my disciples. As the Father has loved me, so I have loved you; abide in my love. If you keep my commandments, you will abide in my love, just as I have kept my Father's commandments and abide in His love. I have said these things to you so that my joy may be in you,   46
and that your joy may be complete. This is my commandment, that you love one another as I have loved you. No one has greater love than this, to lay down one's life for one's friends. You are my friends if you do what I command you. I do not call you servants any longer, because the servant does not know what his master is doing; but I have called you friends, because I have made known to you everything that I have heard from my Father. You did not choose me but I chose you. And I appointed you to go and bear fruit and for your fruit to last, so that the Father may give you whatever you ask Him in my name. I am giving you these commands so that you may love one another. If the world hates you,   47
be aware that it hated me before it hated you. If you belonged to the world, the world would love you as its own. But because you

vos de mundo, propterea odit vos mundus. Mementote sermonis
mei, quem ego dixi vobis: "Non est servus maior domino suo." Si
me persecuti sunt et vos etiam persequentur; si sermonem meum
servaverunt et vestrum servabunt. Sed haec omnia propter nomen
meum vobis facient, qui⟨a⟩ nesciunt eum qui me misit. Si non ve-
nissem et locutus eis non fuissem, peccatum non haberent; nunc
autem de peccato suo nullam excusationem habent. Qui me odit
et Patrem meum odit. Si opera non fecissem in eis, quae nemo
alius fecit, peccatum non haberent; nunc autem et viderunt et me
simul et Patrem meum oderunt. Sed ut impleatur sermo eorum,
qui in lege scriptus est: "Quia gratis me oderunt." Cum autem venerit Paracletus quem ego mittam vobis a Patre, Spiritum veritatis,
qui a Patre procedit, ille testimonium perhibebit de me et vos testimonium perhibebitis, quia ab initio mecum estis.

48   'Haec locutus sum vobis, ut non scandalizemini. Absque synagogis facient vos. Sed venit hora ut quicumque vos interfecerit se
Deo obsequium praestare arbitretur. Et haec vobis facient quia
neque Patrem neque me noverunt. Sed haec locutus sum vobis ut,
cum venerit hora eorum, reminiscamini quia dixi vobis. Haec autem ab initio non dixi vobis, quia vobiscum eram. Et nunc vado ad
eum qui me misit, et nemo ex vobis interrogat me quo ego vadam.

49   Sed quia haec locutus sum vobis, tristitia implevit cor vestrum.
Sed ego veritatem dico vobis: expedit vobis ut ego vadam. Si ego
non abiero, Paracletus non veniet ad vos; si autem abiero, mittam
eum ad vos et cum venerit ille arguet mundum de peccato et de
iustitia et de iudicio. De peccato quidem, quia in me non crediderunt; de iustitia vero, quia ad Patrem vado, et iam me non videbitis; de iudicio autem, quia princeps mundi huius iam iudicatus
est. Adhuc habeo multa vobis dicere, sed non potestis portare

do not belong to the world, but I have chosen you out of the world — therefore the world hates you. Remember the word that I said to you, 'A servant is not greater than his master.' If they persecuted me, they will persecute you also; if they kept my word, they will keep yours also. But they will do all these things to you on account of my name, because they do not know Him who sent me. If I had not come and spoken to them, they would have no sin; but now they have no excuse for their sin. Whoever hates me hates my Father also. If I had not done among them the works that no one else did, they would have no sin. But now they have seen and hated both me and my Father. It was to fulfill the word that is written in their Law, 'They hated me without a cause.' When the Advocate comes, whom I will send to you from the Father, the Spirit of truth who comes from the Father, he will testify on my behalf. You will also testify because you have been with me from the beginning.

"I have said these things lest you be offended.[15] They will put 48 you out of the synagogues. Indeed, the hour is coming when those who kill you will think that they are acting in obedience to God. And they will do this because they have not known the Father or me. But I have said these things to you so that when their hour comes you may remember what I said to you. I did not say these things to you from the beginning, because I was with you. But now I am going to Him who sent me; yet none of you asks me where I am going. But because I have said these things to you, sor- 49 row has filled your hearts. Nevertheless I tell you the truth: it is to your advantage that I go away, for if I do not go away, the Advocate will not come to you; but if I go, I will send him to you. And when he comes, he will prove the world wrong about sin and righteousness and judgment: about sin, because they did not believe in me; about righteousness, because I am going to the Father, and you will see me no longer; about judgment, because the ruler of this world has already been condemned. I still have many things to

modo. Cum autem venerit ille, Spiritus veritatis docebit vos omnem veritatem. Non enim a semetipso, sed[20] quaecumque audiet
loquetur et quae ventura sunt annuntiabit vobis. Ille me clarifica-
bit, quia de meo accipiet et annuntiabit vobis. Omnia quaecumque
habet Pater mea sunt; propterea dixi quia de meo accipiet et annuntiabit vobis. Modicum iam et non videbitis me; et iterum mo-
50 dicum et videbitis me, quia vado ad Patrem.' Hoc ergo 'modicum'
discipulis non intelligentibus in hunc modum explicavit: 'Amen,
amen dico vobis quia plorabitis et flebitis vos, mundus autem
gaudebit; vos vero contristabimini, sed tristitia vestra vertetur in
gaudium. Mulier cum parit, tristitiam habet, quia venit hora eius;
cum autem peperit puerum, iam non meminit pressurae propter
gaudium, quia natus est homo in mundum. Et vos igitur nunc
tristitiam habebitis; iterum autem videbo vos, et gaudebit cor vestrum, et gaudium vestrum nemo tollet a vobis. Et in illo die me
non interrogabitis quidquam. Amen, amen dico vobis: si quid petieritis Patrem in nomine meo, dabit vobis. Usque modo non pe-
tistis quicquam in nomine meo. Petite ut gaudium vestrum ple-
51 nius sit. Haec in proverbiis locutus sum vobis. Venit hora, cum
iam in proverbiis non loquar, sed palam de Patre meo annuntiabo
vobis. In illo die in nomine meo petitis; et modo dico vobis quia
ego rogabo Patrem de vobis. Ipse enim Pater amat vos, quia vos
me amatis et creditis quia a Deo exivi. Exivi a Patre et veni in
mundum; iterum relinquo mundum et vado ad Patrem. Ecce venit
hora, ut dispergamini unusquisque in propria et me solum relin-
quatis; et non sum solus, quia Pater meus est. Haec locutus
sum vobis, ut pacem habeatis. In mundo pressuram habebitis, sed
confidite, quia ego vici mundum.'

say to you, but you cannot bear them now. When he comes, the Spirit of truth, he will teach you the whole truth; for he will not speak on his own, but will speak whatever he hears, and he will declare to you the things that are to come. He will glorify me, because he will take what is mine and declare it to you. All that the Father has is mine. For this reason I said that he will take what is mine and declare it to you. A little while, and you will no longer see me, and again a little while, and you will see me, because I go to the Father." When His disciples didn't understand this "little while," He explained it in this way: "Very truly, I tell you, you will weep and mourn, but the world will rejoice; you will have pain, but your pain will turn into joy. When a woman is in labor, she has pain, because her hour has come. But when her child is born, she no longer remembers the stress, because of the joy of having brought a human being into the world. So you will have pain now. But I will see you again, and your hearts will rejoice, and no one will take your joy from you. On that day you will ask nothing of me. Very truly I tell you, if you ask anything of the Father in my name, He will give it to you. Until now you have not asked for anything in my name. Ask, so that your joy may be complete. I have said these things to you in proverbs. The hour is coming when I will no longer speak to you in proverbs, but will tell you plainly of the Father. On that day you will ask in my name; now I say to you that I will ask the Father on your behalf. For the Father Himself loves you, because you have loved me and have believed that I came from God. I came from the Father and have come into the world; I am leaving the world again and am going to the Father. See, the hour is coming when you will be scattered, each one to his home, and you will leave me alone. Yet I am not alone because the Father is with me. I have said this to you, so that in me you may have peace. In the world you face persecution. But be confident because I have conquered the world!"

50

51

52 Haec itaque est sana et salubris doctrina, quam Iesus turbis et discipulis sine ullis eius responsionibus et parabolis ad humani generis salutem reliquit et tradidit. Haec quidem doctrina quam facilis et quam expedita esset ipse vel tunc maxime declaravit, quando totam legem et prophetas ex his duobus mandatis, hoc est ex Dei et proximi caritate, pendere testatus est, et quando inquit: 'Quaecumque vultis ut faciant vobis homines, haec et vos facite illis.' Quae ad intelligendum ita facilia sunt ut omnibus cuiuscumque condicionis hominibus — servis et rudibus, viduis et pupillis, nedum eruditis omnibus — pateant.

53 Nunc autem ad responsiones et parabolas deinceps accedamus. Ad matrem igitur de vino quod in nuptiis deficiebat sibi annuentem plane et aperte respondit: 'Quid mihi et tibi, mulier? Nondum venit hora mea.' Pharisaeis quaerentibus quare cum publicanis et peccatoribus manducaret, 'Non est,' inquit, 'opus valentibus medicus, sed male habentibus. Euntes autem di⟨s⟩cite quid est: "Misericordiam volo et non sacrificium." Non enim veni vocare iustos sed peccatores.' Discipulis Iohannis petentibus quare ipsi et Pharisaei frequenter, discipuli autem sui non ieiunarent, 'Numquid,' ait, 'possunt filii sponsi lugere, quamdiu cum illis est sponsus? Venient autem dies cum auferetur ab eis sponsus, et tunc ieiunabunt. Nemo autem immittit commissuram panni rudis in vestimentum vetus; tollit enim plenitudinem eius a vestimento, et peior[21] scissura fit. Neque mittunt vinum novum in ut[e]res veteres, alioquin rumpuntur utres, et vinum effunditur, et utres pereunt. Sed vinum novum in utres novos mittunt et ambo conservantur.' Eisdem Baptistae discipulis an esset qui venturus erat quaerentibus an alium expectarent 'Euntes,' inquit, 'renuntiate Iohanni quae audistis et vidistis: caeci vident, claudi ambulant,

This, then, is the sound and salutary teaching that Jesus offered 52
the crowds and His disciples, besides His answers to questions
and parables, for the salvation of the human race. He Himself
declared how easy and effortless this teaching is when he asserted
that all the Law and the prophets depend on these two commandments — to love God and one's neighbor — and when He said, "Do
to others as you would have them do to you." These words are so
easy to understand that they are clear to all people of every condition, to all servants, uneducated folk, widows, and orphans, not to
mention the learned.

Now let us proceed to His answers to questions and to His 53
parables.[16] When His mother observed that the wine was running
out at the wedding, He plainly and explicitly replied, "Woman,
what concern is that to you and to me? My hour has not yet
come." When the Pharisees asked why He ate with publicans and
sinners, He said, "Those who are well have no need of a physician,
but those who are sick. Go and learn what this means: 'I desire
mercy, not sacrifice.' For I have come to call not the righteous, but
sinners."[17] When John's disciples asked Him why they and the
Pharisees often fasted, while His disciples did not, He said, "The
wedding guests cannot mourn as long as the bridegroom is with
them, can they? The days will come when the bridegroom is taken
away from them, and then they will fast. No one sews a piece of
unshrunk cloth on an old cloak, for the patch pulls away from the
cloak, and a worse tear is made. Neither is new wine put into old
wineskins; otherwise, the skins burst, and the wine is spilled, and
the skins are destroyed; but new wine is put into fresh wineskins,
and so both are preserved." When the Baptist's disciples asked
whether He was the one who was to come, or whether they
should wait for another, He replied, "Go and tell John what you
hear and see. The blind receive their sight, the lame walk, the

leprosi mundantur, surdi audiunt, mortui resurgunt, pauperes evan-
gelizantur. Et beatus erit qui non fuerit scandalizatus in me.'

54   Pharisaeis quod in principe daemoniorum daemonia eiceret
obicientibus, sic loquens respondebat: 'Omne regnum in se divisum desolabitur; et omnis civitas vel domus contra se non stabit.
Et si Satanas Satanam eicit, adversus se divisus est; quomodo ergo
stabit regnum eius? Et si ego in Beelzebub daemonia eicio, filii
vestri in quo eiciunt? Ideo ipsi iudices vestri erunt. Si autem ego in
Spiritu Dei daemones eicio, igitur pervenit in vos regnum Dei.
Aut quomodo potest quisquam in domum fortis intrare et vasa
eius deripere, nisi prius fortem alligaverit? Et tunc domum eius
diripiet. Qui non est mecum contra me est, et qui non colligit
mecum dispergit. Ideo dico vobis, omne peccatum et blasphemia[22]
remittetur hominibus; Spiritus autem blasphemiae non remittetur.
Et quicumque verbum dixerit contra Filium hominis, remittetur
ei; qui autem dixerit contra Spiritum Sanctum verbum, non remit-
55   tetur ei neque in hoc saeculo neque in futuro. Aut facite arborem
bonam et fructum eius bonum aut facite arborem malam ac fructum eius malum. Siquidem ex fructu arbor cognoscitur. Progenies
viperarum, quomodo potestis bona loqui cum sitis mali? Ex abundantia enim cordis os loquitur. Bonus homo de bono thesauro
profert bona, et malus de malo thesauro profert mala. Dico autem
vobis quod omne verbum otiosum quod locuti fuerint homines
reddent rationem de eo in die iudicii. Ex verbis enim tuis iustifica-
beris et ex verbis tuis condemnaberis.'

56   Scribis et Pharisaeis ab eo signum videre postulantibus et ef-
flagitantibus, 'Generatio,' inquit, 'mala et adultera signum quaerit;
et signum non dabitur ei nisi signum Ionae prophetae. Sicut enim
fuit Ionas in ventre ceti tribus diebus et tribus noctibus, sic erit

lepers are cleansed, the deaf hear, the dead are raised, and the poor have good news brought to them. And blessed is anyone who is not offended by me."

When the Pharisees reproached him for casting out demons by the prince of demons, He replied, "Every kingdom divided against itself will be brought to desolation, and every city or house divided against itself cannot stand. If Satan casts out Satan, he is divided against himself; how, then, will his kingdom stand? Now if I cast out the demons by Beelzebub, by whom do your children cast them out? Therefore they will be your judges. But if it is by the Spirit of God that I cast out the demons, then the kingdom of God has come to you. But how can one enter a strong man's house and plunder his goods unless he first binds the strong man? And then he will plunder the house. Whoever is not with me is against me, and whoever does not gather with me scatters. Therefore I tell you, people will be forgiven for every sin and blasphemy, but blasphemy against the Spirit will not be forgiven. Whoever speaks a word against the Son of Man will be forgiven, but whoever speaks against the Holy Spirit will not be forgiven, either in this age or in the age to come. Either make the tree good, and its fruit good; or make the tree bad, and its fruit bad; for the tree is known by its fruit. You brood of vipers! How can you speak good things, when you are evil? For out of the abundance of the heart the mouth speaks. The good person brings good things out of a good treasure, and the evil person brings evil things out of an evil treasure. I tell you that on the day of judgment people will have to give an account for every careless word they utter; for by your words you will be justified, and by your words you will be condemned."

When the scribes and Pharisees demanded and insisted on a sign from Him, He said, "An evil and adulterous generation seeks a sign, but no sign will be given to it except the sign of the prophet Jonah. For just as Jonah was in the belly of the whale for three days and three nights, so the Son of Man will be in the heart of

54

55

56

Filius hominis in corde terrae tribus diebus et tribus noctibus. Viri Ninivitae surgent in iudicio cum generatione ista et condemnabunt eam, quia poenitentiam egerunt in praedicatione Ionae; et ecce plus quam Ionas hic! Regina austri surge[n]t in iudicio cum generatione ista et condemnabit eam, quia venit a finibus terrae audire sapientiam Salomonis; et ecce plus quam Salomon hic! Cum autem spiritus immundus exierit ab homine, ambulat per loca arida quaerens requiem et non invenit. Tunc dicit: "Revertar in domum meam unde exivi." Et veniens invenit eam vacantem, scopis mundatam et ornatam. Tunc vadit et assumit septem alios spiritus nequiores se, et intrantes ibi habitant; et fiunt novissima hominis illius peiora prioribus. Sic erit et generationi huic pessimae.'

57   Et cuidam de matre eius et fratribus foris expectantibus dicenti sibi, 'Qui est,' inquit, 'mater mea, et qui sunt fratres mei?' extendens manus in discipulos suos dixit: 'Ecce mater mea et fratres mei. Quicumque enim fecerit voluntatem Patris mei, qui in caelis est, ipse meus frater et soror et mater est.' Pharisaeis autem de singulari quadam eius sapientia admirantibus et dicentibus: 'Nonne hic est fabri filius'? et reliqua, dixit: 'Non est propheta sine honore nisi in patria sua et in domo sua.' Et non fecit ibi virtutes multas propter incredulitatem illorum.

58   Scribis et Pharisaeis quare discipuli eius traditiones seniorum transgrederentur interrogantibus (non enim manus suas lavabant, cum panem manducarent), 'Quare et vos,' inquit, 'transgredimini mandatum Dei propter traditionem vestram? Nam Deus dixit: "Honora patrem tuum et matrem tuam et qui maledixerit patri vel matri, morte moriatur." Vos autem dicitis: "Quicumque dixerit patri vel matri: munus quodcumque est ex me tibi proderit, et non honorificaverit patrem suum aut matrem suam." Et irritum fecistis mandatum Dei propter traditionem vestram. Hypocritae, bene

the earth for three days and three nights. The men of Nineveh will rise up in judgment with this generation and condemn it, because they repented at the preaching of Jonah, and see, one greater than Jonah is here! The queen of the South will rise up in judgment with the people of this generation and condemn it, because she came from the ends of the earth to listen to the wisdom of Solomon, and see, one greater than Solomon is here! When the unclean spirit has gone out of a person, it wanders through waterless regions looking for a resting place, but it finds none. Then it says, 'I will return to my house from which I came.' When it comes, it finds it empty, swept, and put in order. Then it goes and brings along seven other spirits more evil than itself, and they enter and live there. And the last state of that person is worse than the first. So will it be also with this evil generation."

When someone told Him that His mother and brothers were 57 waiting outside, He said, "Who is my mother, and who are my brothers?" And extending His hand toward His disciples, he said, "Here are my mother and my brothers! For whoever does the will of my Father in heaven is my brother and sister and mother." When the Pharisees wondered at His singular wisdom and said, "Is not this the carpenter's son?" and so forth, He said "A prophet is only without honor in his own country and in his own house." And He did not do many deeds of power there because of their unbelief.[18]

When the scribes and Pharisees asked why His disciples vio- 58 lated the traditions of their elders (for they did not wash their hands before they ate bread), He said, "And why do you break the commandment of God for the sake of your tradition? For God said, 'Honor your father and your mother' and 'Whoever speaks evil of father or mother must be put to death.' But you say, 'Whoever tells his father or mother, "The gift you have comes from me," and he will not honor his father or mother.' So, for the sake of your tradition, you make void the word of God. You hypocrites!

prophetavit de vobis Esaias propheta dicens: "Populus hic labiis
me honorat, cor autem eorum longe est a me. Sine causa colunt
me docentes doctrinas et mandata hominum.'"

59   Et ad Petrum, qui sibi interroganti quis esset Christum filium
Dei vivi responderat esse,[23] 'Beatus es,' inquit, 'Simon Bar Iona,
quia caro et sanguis non revelavit tibi, sed Pater meus, qui in caelis
est. Et ego dico tibi quia tu es Petrus, et super hanc petram aedifi-
cabo ecclesiam meam, et portae inferi non praevalebunt adversus
eam. Et tibi dabo claves regni caelorum; et quodcumque ligaveris
super terram, erit ligatum et in caelis, et quodcumque solveris super terram, erit solutum et in caelis.'

60   Et ad discipulos 'Quis putas maior est in regno caelorum?' interrogantes, advocavit parvulum et statuit in medio eorum et dixit:
'Amen dico vobis, nisi conversi fueritis et efficiamini sicut parvuli,
non intrabitis in regnum caelorum. Quicumque ergo ut parvulus
iste se humiliaverit, hic maior est in regno caelorum. Et qui parvulum unum talem in nomine meo susceperit, me suscipit. Qui autem scandalizaverit unum de pusillis istis, qui in me credunt, expedit ei ut suspendatur mola asinaria in collo eius et demergatur in
profundum maris. Vae mundo a scandalis! Necesse est enim ut
veniant scandala. Verumtamen vae homini illi, per quem scandalum venit! Si autem manus tua vel pes tuus scandalizat te, abscide
eum et proice abs te: bonum est tibi ad vitam ingredi debilem vel
claudum, quam duas manus vel duos pedes habentem mitti in ignem aeternum. Et si oculus tuus scandalizat te, erue eum et proice
abs te: bonum est tibi luscum et cum uno oculo ad vitam intrare, quam duos oculos habentem in Gehennae ignem. Videte, ne
contemnatis unum ex his[24] pusillis; dico enim vobis quia angeli
eorum semper vident faciem Patris mei, qui in caelis est. Venit
enim Filius hominis salvare quod perierat.' Et ad Petrum quotiens
in[25] se frater suus peccaret, usque ne septies ei dimitteret pe-

Isaiah prophesied rightly about you when he said, 'This people honors me with their lips, but their hearts are far from me; in vain do they worship me, teaching human doctrines and commandments.'"[19]

And when Peter asked who He was, He replied that He was 59 Christ, the Son of God, and said, "Blessed are you, Simon son of Jonah! For flesh and blood have not revealed this to you, but my Father in heaven. And I tell you, you are Peter, and on this rock I will build my church, and the gates of Hades will not prevail against it. I will give you the keys of the kingdom of heaven, and whatever you bind on earth will be bound in heaven, and whatever you loose on earth will be loosed in heaven."[20]

When the disciples asked Him "Who do you think is the great- 60 est in the kingdom of heaven?" He called a child and stood him in their midst, and said, "Truly I tell you, unless you change and become like children, you will never enter the kingdom of heaven. Whoever becomes humble like this child is the greatest in the kingdom of heaven. Whoever welcomes one such child in my name welcomes me. If any of you offends one of these little ones who believe in me, it would be better for you if a great millstone were fastened around your neck and you were drowned in the depth of the sea. Woe to the world because of offenses! It must be that offenses come, but woe to the one by whom the offense comes! If your hand or your foot offends you, cut it off and throw it away; it is better for you to enter life maimed or lame than to have two hands or two feet and to be thrown into the eternal fire. And if your eye offends you, tear it out and throw it away; it is better for you to enter life with one eye than to have two eyes and to be thrown into the hell of fire. Take care that you do not despise one of these little ones; for, I tell you, in heaven their angels continually see the face of my Father in heaven. For the Son of Man has come to save what was lost." When Peter asked how many times he should forgive a brother sinning against him—

tentem, ait illi: 'Non dico tibi usque septies, sed usque septuagesies septies.'

61   Et ad Pharisaeos, temptantes et dicentes 'Si licet homini dimittere uxorem suam quacumque ex causa,' respondit: 'Non legistis quia, qui fecit ab initio masculum et feminam fecit eos et dixit: "Propter hoc relinquet homo patrem suum et matrem suam et adhaerebit uxori suae, et erunt duo in carne una"? Itaque iam non sunt duo, sed una caro. Quos Deus coniunxit, homo ne separet.' Et ulterius de libello repudii in lege permisso percontantibus ait: 'Quod Moyses ad duritiam cordis vestri permisit vobis dimittere uxores vestras; ab initio non sic fuit. Dico autem vobis, quod quicumque uxorem suam, nisi causa fornicationis, dimiserit et aliam duxerit, moechatur; et qui dimissam duxerit pariter moechatur.' Et ad discipulos, petentes 'Si ita est causa hominis cum uxore, non expedit nubere,' 'Non omnes,' inquit, 'verbum istud capiunt, sed quibus[26] est datum. Sunt enim eunuchi, qui seipsos propter

62   regnum caelorum castraverunt. Qui potest capere, capiat.' Et ad unum se ipsum bonum appellantem ac petentem quid se facere oporteret, ut aeternam vitam nancisceretur, dixit: 'Quid me interrogas de bono? Unus est bonus: Deus. Si autem vis ad vitam ingredi, serva mandata. Non homicidium facies, non adulterabis, non furaberis, non falsum testimonium dices, honora patrem tuum et matrem tuam, et diliges proximum tuum sicut te ipsum. Et si vis perfectus esse, vade et vende omnia quae habes et da pauperibus, et veni sequere me.' Quo audito, abiit tristis; erat enim locuplex et multas possessiones habebat. Iesus dixit discipulis suis: 'Amen dico vobis quod dives difficile intrabit in regnum caelorum. [Quis ergo potest salvus esse?] Iterum, dico vobis, facilius est camelum per foramen acus transire, quam divitem intrare in regnum

whether he should forgive his plea seven times — He said, "Not seven times, but, I tell you, seventy times seven."[21]

And when the Pharisees tested him by asking, "Is it lawful for a man to divorce his wife for any cause?" He answered, "Have you not read that the One who made them at the beginning 'made them male and female' and that 'For this reason a man shall leave his father and mother, and be joined to his wife, and the two shall become one flesh'? So they are no longer two, but one flesh. Therefore what God has joined together, let no man separate." And when they further asked Him why there was a certificate of divorce sanctioned by the Law, He said to them, "It was because you were so hard-hearted that Moses allowed you to divorce your wives, but at the beginning it was not so. And I say to you, whoever divorces his wife, except on grounds of infidelity, and marries another, commits adultery; and he who marries a divorced woman likewise commits adultery." When His disciples asked "If such is the case of a man with his wife, it is better not to marry," He said, "Not everyone can accept this teaching, but only those to whom it is given. For there are eunuchs who have made themselves eunuchs for the sake of the kingdom of heaven. Let anyone accept this who can." When a man who called Him good and asked what he should do to have eternal life, He said, "Why do you ask me about what is good? There is only One who is good, God. If you wish to enter into life, keep the commandments. You shall not murder; you shall not commit adultery; you shall not steal; you shall not bear false witness. Honor your father and mother, and love your neighbor as yourself. If you wish to be perfect, go, sell your possessions, and give the money to the poor, and come, follow me." When the man heard this, he went away sad, for he was rich and had many possessions. Jesus said to His disciples, "Truly I tell you, it will be hard for a rich person to enter the kingdom of heaven. Again I tell you, it is easier for a camel to go through the eye of a needle than for someone who is rich to enter the kingdom

61

62

caelorum.' 'Quis ergo potest salvus esse'?, interrogantibus discipulis, respondit Iesus: 'Apud homines hoc impossibile est, apud
63 Deum autem omnia possibilia sunt.' Et ad Petrum interrogantem
quid illis foret qui relictis omnibus eum secuti erant, Iesus dixit:
'Amen dico vobis quod vos, qui secuti estis me, in regeneratione,
cum sederit Filius hominis in sede maiestatis suae, sedebitis et vos
super sedes duodecim, iudicantes duodecim tribus Israhel. Et omnis, qui reliquerit domum vel fratres aut sorores aut patrem aut
matrem aut uxorem aut filios aut agrum propter nomen meum,
centuplum accipiet et vitam aeternam possidebit. Multi autem
erunt primi novissimi et novissimi primi.'

64 Et ad Solome, filiorum Zebedaei matrem, simul cum filiis pos-
tulantem, ut unus a dextris alter vero a sinistris sederet in regno
caelorum, respondit dicens: 'Nescitis quid petatis. Calicem quidem
meum bibetis; sedere autem ad dexteram meam vel ad sinistram
non est meum dare vobis, sed quibus paratum est a Patre meo.
Principes gentium dominantur eorum et qui maiores sunt potestatem exercent in eos. Non ita erit inter vos, sed quicumque inter vos praeesse voluerit minister vester sit. Et qui inter vos primus
esse voluerit, vester servus erit. Sicut Filius hominis non venit ut
ministraretur, sed ut ministraret et ut animam suam, redemptionem pro multis, traderet.'

65 Et ad principes sacerdotum et scribas de mirabilibus quae ipse
fecerat et de pueris in templo 'Osanna filio David' clamantibus
vehementer admirantibus, 'Numquid,' inquit, 'legistis "Quod ex
ore infantium et lactantium perfecisti laudem?"' Et ad discipulos
de repentina quadam ficulneae nescio cuius arefactione stupentes
'Amen,' inquit, 'dico vobis quod si habueritis fidem et non dubita-
veritis, non solum de ficulnea facietis, sed si monti huic dixeritis
66 "Tolle, iacta te in mare" fiet.' Et ad principes sacerdotum et seniores interrogantes in qua potestate tot tantaque miracula faceret,
respondens dixit: 'Interrogabo et ego vos unum sermonem, quem

of God." When the disciples asked, "Who then can be saved?" Jesus replied, "For mortals it is impossible, but for God all things are possible." When Peter asked what they would have after they had left everything to follow Him, Jesus said, "Truly I tell you, at the renewal of all things, when the Son of Man is seated on the throne of his glory, you who have followed me will also sit on twelve thrones, judging the twelve tribes of Israel. And everyone who has left his house or brothers or sisters or father or mother or wife or children or fields for my name's sake, will receive a hundredfold, and will inherit eternal life. But many who are first will be last, and the last will be first."[22]

When Salome, the mother of Zebediah's sons, demanded that they be seated on His right and His left in the kingdom of heaven, He answered, saying, "You do not know what you are asking. You will indeed drink my cup. But to sit at my right hand and at my left, this is not mine to grant; but it is for those for whom it has been prepared by my Father. The rulers of the Gentiles lord it over them, and their great ones are tyrants over them. It will not be so among you; but whoever wishes to be great among you must be your servant. And whoever wishes to be first among you must be your slave; just as the Son of Man came not to be served but to serve, and to give his life as redemption for many."[23]

When the chief priests and scribes wondered greatly at the miracles He had performed and at the children in the temple crying "Hosanna to the Son of David," He said, "Have you never read, 'Out of the mouths of infants and nursing babies, you have perfected praise?'"[24] When the disciples were amazed by the sudden withering of a fig tree, He said, "Truly I tell you, if you have faith and do not doubt, not only will you do what has been done to the fig tree, but if you say to this mountain, 'Be lifted up and thrown into the sea,' it will be done." When the chief priests and elders asked Him by what power He performed so many great miracles, He replied saying, "I will also ask you one question; if

63

64

65

66

si dixeritis mihi et ego vobis dicam in qua potestate hac facio:
Baptisma Iohannis e caelo erat an ex hominibus?' Et se nescire respondentibus ait: 'Nec ego dico vobis in qua potestate haec facio.'

67   Et ad discipulos Pharisaeorum cum Herodianis petentes an
Caesari censum dare liceret an non (de hoc enim multae et graves
inter Iudaeos seditiones intercesserant. Nam etsi quando Iudaea
sub Caesare Augusto subiecta Romanis eo maximo tempore, quo
in toto terrarum orbe est celebrata descriptio, stipendiaria facta
fuisset, non defuerunt tamen Pharisaei qui, sibi invicem applau-
dentes, populum Dei humanis legibus subiacere palam et aperte
inficiarentur cum decimas solveret et primitias daret et cetera
quae in divina lege scripta erant ad unguem servaret) respondens
Iesus: 'Quid me,' inquit, 'temptatis, hypocritae? Ostendite mihi
nomisma[27] census.' At illi obtulerunt ei denarium, et ait illis Iesus
cuius imago illa et superscriptio esset. Et dixerunt: 'Caesaris.' Tunc
ait illis: 'Reddite ergo quae sunt Caesaris Caesari et quae sunt Dei
68   Deo.' Et ad Sadduceos negantes resurrectionem et dicentes 'Magister Moyses dixit "Si quis mortuus fuerit non habens filium, ut
ducat frater eius uxorem illius et suscitet semen fratri suo." Erant
autem apud nos septem fratres et primus, ducta uxore, defunctus
est et non habens semen reliquit eam fratri suo. Similter secundus
et tertius usque ad septimum. Novissime autem omnium defuncta
est et mulier. In resurrectione ergo cuius erit de septem uxor?
Omnes enim habuerunt eam.' Respondens autem Iesus ait illis:
'Erratis nescientes Scripturas nec virtutem Dei. In resurrectione
enim, ut propriis Evangelii verbis utamur, neque nubent neque
nubentur sed erunt sicut angeli Dei in caelo. De resurrectione autem mortuorum non legistis quod dictum est a Deo dicente vobis:
"Ego sum Deus Abraham, Deus Isaac, Deus Iacob"? Non est

you tell me the answer, then I will also tell you by what authority I do these things. Did the baptism of John come from heaven, or was it of human origin?" When they replied that they did not know, He said, "Neither will I tell you by what authority I am doing these things."[25]

The disciples of the Pharisees and the Herodians asked if it 67 was lawful or not to pay the tribute to Caesar. (This subject had given rise to many grave dissensions among the Jews. For Judea, being subject to the Romans under Caesar Augustus, had been made liable for tribute precisely when the famous census was taken in the whole world. But there were Pharisees who encouraged one another to deny openly and publicly that God's people were subject to human laws, since they punctiliously paid the tithes, firstfruits, and other obligations prescribed by divine Law.) Jesus answered saying, "Why do you tempt me, you hypocrites? Show me the tribute money." And they brought him a penny. And Jesus asked them whose image and inscription it bore. They said, "Caesar's." Then He said to them, "Render therefore unto Caesar the things that are Caesar's; and unto God the things that are God's." The Sadducees denied the resurrection and said, "Teacher, 68 Moses said, 'If a man dies childless, his brother shall marry the widow, and raise up children for his brother.' Now there were seven brothers among us; the first married, and died childless, leaving the widow to his brother. The second did the same, so also the third, down to the seventh. Last of all, the woman died. In the resurrection, then, whose wife of the seven will she be? For all of them had married her." Jesus answered them, saying, "You are wrong, because you know neither the scriptures nor the power of God. For in the resurrection" — to use the Gospel's own words — "they neither marry nor are given in marriage, but are like God's angels in heaven. And as for the resurrection of the dead, have you not read what was said by God, who told you, 'I am the God of Abraham, the God of Isaac, and the God of Jacob'? He is God not

69   Deus mortuorum sed viventium.' Et ad unum Pharisaeorum legis doctorem quod esset magnum mandatum in lege interrogantem ait: 'Diliges Dominum Deum tuum ex toto corde tuo, ex tota anima tua et ex tota mente tua. Hoc est maximum et primum mandatum. Secundum autem huic simile est: diliges proximum tuum sicut teipsum. In his duobus mandatis tota lex pendet et prophetae.' Et ad Pharisaeos, de Christo quod esset filius David dum ab eo interrogarentur respondentes, obiecit: 'Quomodo ergo David in spiritu vocat eum "Dominum," quando filius eius est?' Et nemo poterat respondere ei verbum neque ausus fuit ex illa die quisquam amplius eum interrogare.

70   Et ad Pharisaeum quemdam, de Maria Magdalena peccatrice pedes Iesu osculante et pretioso unguento deungente admirabundum, dixit: 'Simon, habeo tibi aliquid dicere. Duo debitores erant cuidam feneratori; unus debebat denarios quingentos et alius quinquaginta. Non habentibus autem illis unde redderent, utrique debitum dimisit. Quis ergo eum plus diligit?' Respondens Simon dixit: 'Aestimo,' inquit, 'quod is cui plus donavit.' At ille dixit: 'Recte iudicasti.' Et conversus ad mulierem dixit Simoni: 'Vides hanc mulierem? Intravi in domum tuam, aquam pedibus meis non dedisti. Haec autem lacrimis rigavit pedes meos et capillis suis tersit. Osculum mihi non dedisti. Haec vero, ex quo intravi, non cessavit osculari pedes meos. Oleo caput meo non unxisti; haec autem unguento unxit pedes meos. Propter quod dico tibi: remittuntur ei peccata multa quoniam dilexit multum. Is autem cui minus dimittitur, minus diligit.' Ad illam autem conversus: 'Tibi,' inquit, 'remittuntur peccata tua' et 'Fides tua te salvavit; vade in pace.'

71   Et ad Iacobum et Iohannem interrogantes an diceret ut ignis de caelo descenderet, qui Samaritanos, Iesum in Samaria civitate sua non suscipientes, incendio consumeret, conversus increpavit illos,

of the dead, but of the living." When one of the Pharisees, a jurist, 69
asked Him which commandment in the law is the greatest, He
said to him, "You shall love the Lord your God with all your heart,
and with all your soul, and with all your mind. This is the greatest
and first commandment. And the second is like it: you shall love
your neighbor as yourself. On these two commandments hang all
the Law and the prophets." When He asked the Pharisees about
the Messiah, and they answered that he was the son of David, He
posed the objection, "How is it then that David by the Spirit calls
him Lord, when he is his son?" No one was able to give Him an
answer, nor from that day did anyone dare to ask Him any more
questions.[26]

When a Pharisee wondered that the sinful Mary Magdalene 70
kissed Jesus' feet and anointed them with precious ointment, He
said, "Simon, I have something to say to you. A certain creditor
had two debtors; one owed five hundred denarii, and the other
fifty. When they could not pay, he canceled the debts for both of
them. Now which of them will love him more?" Simon answered,
"I suppose the one for whom he canceled the greater debt." And
Jesus said to him, "You have judged rightly." Then turning toward
the woman, he said to Simon, "Do you see this woman? I entered
your house; you gave me no water for my feet, but she has bathed
my feet with her tears and dried them with her hair. You gave me
no kiss, but from the time I came in she has not stopped kiss-
ing my feet. You did not anoint my head with oil, but she has
anointed my feet with ointment. Therefore, I tell you, her sins,
which were many, have been forgiven, because she loved much.
But the one to whom little is forgiven, loves little." Then He
turned to her and said, "Your sins are forgiven" and "Your faith has
saved you; go in peace."[27]

When the Samaritans refused to receive Jesus in their city, 71
James and John asked if He would command fire to come down
from heaven and consume them. But He turned and rebuked

dicens: 'Nescitis cuius spiritus estis. Filius hominis non venit ut animas perderet sed ut salvaret.' Et ad quemdam in via dicentem 'Sequar te quocumque eris,' in hunc modum respondit: 'Vulpes foveas habent et volucres caeli nidos; filius autem hominis non habet ubi caput suum reclinet.'

72 Et ad illum qui petebat ut sibi, antequam ipsum sequeretur, patrem suum sepelire permitteret, 'Sine,' inquit, 'ut mortui sepeliant mortuos suos; tu autem vade et annuntia regnum Dei.' Et ad alium, priusquam sequeretur petentem ut renuntiaret domesticis suis, ait: 'Nemo mittens manus suas ad aratrum et respiciens retrorsum aptus est regno Dei.' Et ad quemdam de turba dicentem 'Magister, dic fratri meo ut dividat mecum hereditatem,' dixit ei hominem appellans: 'Quis me constituit iudicem aut divisorem super vos?'

73 Et, cum a quibusdam interrogaretur an pauci essent qui salvarentur, dixit ad illos: 'Contendite intrare per angustam portam; quia multi, dico vobis, quaerunt intrare et non poterunt. Cum autem pater familias ingressus ostium clauserit, rogantibus ut aperiat vobis respondens dicit: "Nescio vos unde sitis. Discedite a me, omnes operarii iniquitatis, in tenebras exteriores." Ibi erit fletus et stridor dentium, cum videritis Abraham, Isaac et Iacob et omnes prophetas in regno Dei, vos autem expelli foras. Et venient ab oriente et occidente, et aquilone et austro, et accumbent in regno Dei. Et ecce sunt novissimi qui erant primi, et sunt primi qui erant
74 novissimi.' Et ad quosdam Pharisaeos, exhortantes ut exinde recederet quoniam Herodes ipsum occidere cupiebat, 'Dicite,' inquit, 'vulpi illi: "Ecce, eicio daemonia et sanitates perficio hodie et cras et tertia die consumar. Verumtamen oportet me hodie et cras et nudius tertius ambulare, quia non capit prophetam perire extra Hierusalem." Hierusalem, Hierusalem, quae occidis prophetas et lapidas eos qui ad te missi sunt. Quotiens volui congregare filios

them, saying, "You know not of whose spirit you are. The Son of Man came not to destroy souls, but to save them." When someone on the road said to Him, "I will follow you wherever you go," Jesus said to him, "Foxes have holes, and birds of the air have nests; but the Son of Man has nowhere to lay his head."

When someone asked permission to bury his father before fol- 72 lowing Jesus, He said, "Let the dead bury their own dead; but as for you, go and proclaim the kingdom of God." And when another man asked to bid his servants farewell before following Jesus, He said, "No one who puts a hand to the plow and looks back is fit for the kingdom of God." When someone in the crowd said "Teacher, tell my brother to divide our inheritance with me," He called the man and said to him, "Who set me as judge or arbitrator over you?"

When some people asked Him if only a few would be saved, 73 He said to them, "Strive to enter through the narrow door; for many, I tell you, will try to enter and will not be able. When once the owner of the house has gone in and closed the door and you ask him to open for you, he will reply, 'I do not know you. Go away from me to the outer darkness, all you evildoers!' There will be weeping and gnashing of teeth when you see Abraham, Isaac, and Jacob and all the prophets in the kingdom of God, but you are thrown out. Then people will come from east and west, from north and south, and will feast in the kingdom of God. Indeed, some are last who were first, and some are first who were last." When some Pharisees urged Him to depart because Herod 74 wished to kill Him, He said, "Tell that fox, 'Behold, I am casting out demons and performing cures today and tomorrow, and on the third day I finish my work. Yet today, tomorrow, and the next day I must be on my way, because it is impossible for a prophet to be killed outside Jerusalem.' Jerusalem, Jerusalem, you who kill the prophets and stone those who are sent to you! How often have I desired to gather your children together as a hen gathers her brood

tuos, quemadmodum avis nidum suum sub pennis, et noluisti? Ecce, relinquetur domus vestra deserta. Dico autem vobis quod non videbitis me donec veniat cum dicatis: "Benedictus qui venit in nomine Domini.'"

75   Et ad turbas et coetus hominum, per naviculam ipsum in Capharnaum quaerentes interrogantesque quando illuc transfretasset, sic respondit: 'Amen, dico vobis, quaeritis me non quia vidistis signa, sed quia manducastis ex panibus et saturati estis. Operamini non cibum qui perit sed qui permanet in vitam aeternam, quem Filius hominis daturus est vobis. Hunc enim Pater signavit Deus.' Dixerunt ergo ad eum: 'Quid faciemus, ut opera Dei operemur?' Respondit Iesus et dixit: 'Hoc est opus Dei, ut credatis in eum quem ille misit.' Dixerunt ergo ei: 'Quod ergo signum facies, ut videamus et credamus tibi? Quid operaris? Patres nostri manducaverunt manna in deserto, sicut scriptum est: "Panem de caelo

76   dedit eis manducare.'" Dixit ergo eis Iesus: 'Amen, amen dico vobis, non Moses dedit vobis panem de caelo, sed Pater meus est qui dedit vobis panem verum de caelo. Panis enim verus est qui de caelo descendit et dat vitam mundo.' Dixerunt ergo: 'Da nobis semper hunc panem.' Dixit Iesus: 'Ego sum panis vitae: qui venit ad me non esuriet, et qui credit in me non sitiet umquam. Sed dixi vobis quia vidistis me et non credidistis. Omne quod dat mihi Pater ad me veniet; et omne quod venit ad me non[28] eiciam foras. Quia descendi de caelo non ut faciam voluntatem meam sed ut efficiam voluntatem eius qui misit me, Patris, ut omne quod dedit mihi non perdam ex eo sed suscitem illud in novissimo[29] die.'

77   Murmurabant ergo Iudaei de illo, quia dixisset: 'Ego sum panis, qui de caelo descendi.' Et Iesus: 'Nolite murmurare invicem; nemo potest venire ad me, nisi Pater meus traxerit eum; et ego resuscitabo eum in novissimo die. Scriptum est in prophetis: "Et erunt

under her wings, and you refused! See, your house will be left abandoned. And I tell you, you will not see me until the time comes when you say, 'Blessed is the one who comes in the name of the Lord.'"

When the crowds and groups of men took a boat to Caphar-   75
naum to look for Jesus, and asked when He had crossed over, He replied, "Truly, I tell you, you are looking for me, not because you saw signs, but because you ate your fill of the loaves. Do not work for the food that perishes, but for the food that endures for eternal life, which the Son of Man will give you. For it is on Him that God the Father has set His seal." Then they said to him, "What must we do to perform the works of God?" Jesus answered them, "This is the work of God, to believe in Him whom He has sent." So they said to Him, "What sign are you going to give us, then, so that we may see it and believe you? What work are you perform-ing? Our ancestors ate the manna in the wilderness; as it is writ-ten, 'He gave them bread from heaven to eat.'"[28] Then Jesus said to   76
them, "Very truly, I tell you, it was not Moses who gave you the bread from heaven, but it is my Father who gave you the true bread from heaven. For the true bread is the bread which comes down from heaven and gives life to the world." They said to Him, "Give us this bread always." Jesus said to them, "I am the bread of life. Whoever comes to me will never be hungry, and whoever be-lieves in me will never be thirsty. But I have told you because you saw me and did not believe. Everything that the Father gives me will come to me, and whatever comes to me I will not reject; for I have come down from heaven, not to do my own will, but the will of Him who sent me, the will of my Father, that I do not lose all that He has given me but raise it up on the last day."

When the Jews complained because He said "I am the bread   77
that came down from heaven," He said, "Do not complain among yourselves. No one can come to me unless drawn by my Father; and I will raise that person up on the last day. It is written in the

omnes docibiles Dei." Omnis qui audivit a Patre, et didicit, veniet
ad me. Non quia Patrem vidit quisquam; nisi qui est a Deo,
hic videt Patrem. Amen, dico vobis, quia qui credit in me, habet
vitam aeternam. Ego sum panis vitae. Patres vestri manducaverunt
manna in deserto et mortui sunt. Hic est panis de caelo descendens, ut si quis ex ipso manducaverit non moriatur. Ego sum panis vivus, qui de caelo descendi. Si quis manducaverit ex hoc
pane, vivet in aeternum; et panis, quem ego dabo, caro mea est

78   pro mundi vita.' Et de hoc invicem litigantibus discipulis inquit:
'Amen, amen dico vobis, nisi manducaveritis carnem Filii hominis
et bibetis eius sanguinem non habebitis vitam aeternam. Qui manducat meam carnem et bibit meum sanguinem, habet vitam aeternam, et ego resuscitabo eum in novissimo die. Caro enim mea vere
est cibus, et sanguis meus vere est potus. Qui manducat meam
carnem et bibit meum sanguinem, in me manet, et ego in illo.
Sicut misit me Pater vivens, et ego vivo propter ipsum. Hic est
panis qui de caelo descendit. Non sicut manducaverunt patres
vestri manna, et mortui sunt. Qui manducat hunc panem, vivet in
aeternum.'

79   Et ad fratres eius, quod de Galilaea in Iudaeam transiret postu-
lantes, ut discipuli eius opera sua propalam viderent, ita respondit:
'Tempus meum nondum advenit. Tempus autem vestrum semper
est paratum. Non potest mundus odisse vos; me autem odit, quia
ego testimonium perhibeo de illo, quoniam opera eius mala sunt.
Vos ascendite ad diem festum hunc; ego autem non ascendam ad
diem festum istum, quia tempus meum nondum impletum est.'

80   Et ad Iudaeos quonam modo litteras sciret, cum non didicisset,
admirantes 'Mea,' inquit, 'doctrina non est mea, sed eius qui misit
me. Si quis voluerit voluntatem eius facere, cognoscetur ex doctrina utrum ex Deo sit an ego ex meipso loquar. Qui a semetipso
loquitur, propriam gloriam quaerit; qui autem quaerit gloriam eius

prophets, 'And they shall all be taught by God.' Everyone who has heard from the Father and learned will come to me. Not that anyone has seen the Father except the one who is from God; he sees the Father. Truly, I tell you, whoever believes on me has eternal life. I am the bread of life. Your ancestors ate the manna in the wilderness, and they died. This is the bread that comes down from heaven, so that he who eats of it may not die. I am the living bread that came down from heaven. Whoever eats of this bread will live forever; and the bread that I will give for the life of the world is my flesh." When the disciples argued among themselves about 78 this, He said, "Very truly, I tell you, unless you eat the flesh of the Son of Man and drink his blood, you will not have eternal life. He who eats my flesh and drinks my blood has eternal life, and I will raise him up on the last day; for my flesh is truly food and my blood is truly drink. He who eats my flesh and drinks my blood abides in me, and I in him. Just as the living Father sent me, and I live because of the Father. This is the bread that came down from heaven, not like the manna which your ancestors ate, and they died. But the one who eats this bread will live forever."

When His brothers urged Him to leave Galilee for Judea so 79 that his disciples would manifestly see His works, He replied, "My time has not yet come, but your time is always here. The world cannot hate you, but it hates me because I testify against it that its works are evil. Go to the festival yourselves. I am not going to this festival, for my time has not yet been fulfilled."

When the Jews wondered how Jesus had such learning without 80 having been taught, He said, "My teaching is not mine but His who sent me. Anyone who wishes to do His will will know from the teaching whether it is from God or whether I am speaking on my own. He who speaks on his own seeks his own glory; but the one who seeks the glory of Him who sent him is true, and there is

qui misit illum, hic non est verax et iustitia in illo non est. Nonne
Moses dedit vobis legem et nemo ex vobis facit legem?'

81   Et ad scribas et Pharisaeos de adultera quadam in adulterio
deprehensa iudicium eius temptandi gratia efflagitantes, Iesus inclinans se deorsum scribebat in terram. Cum autem perseverantes
iterum interrogarent, erexit se et dixit: 'Qui sine peccato est vestrum, primus in illam lapidem mittat.' Et iterum se inclinans scribebat in terram. Audientes unus post alterum exibant, incipientes
a senioribus, et remansit Iesus solus et mulier in medio stans.
Erigens autem Iesus dixit ei: 'Mulier, ubi sunt qui te accusabant?
Nemo ne te condemnavit?' Quae respondens, 'Nemo,' inquit, 'Domine, me condemnavit.' 'Nec ego etiam te condemnabo: vade et
amplius noli peccare.' Haec quae de adultera superius scripta sunt,
licet nusquam in exemplaribus Graecis reperiantur, idcirco tamen
apposuimus,[30] quia in Evangeliis Latinis ea legisse memineramus.

82   Et ad Pharisaeos, quod de seipso falsum testimonium perhibe-
ret, ⟨dixit⟩:[31] 'De meipso verum est testimonium meum, quia scio
unde venio et quo vado; vos autem nescitis unde venio et quo
vado. Vos secundum carnem iudicatis, ego non iudico quemquam,
et si iudico ego, iudicium meum verum est. Ego sum qui testimonium perhibeo de meipso, et testimonium perhibet de me qui misit me, Pater.' Et ubi Pater suus esset interrogantibus quibusdam,
dicebat: 'Neque me scitis neque Patrem meum scitis; si me sciretis,
forsitan et Patrem meum sciretis.'

83   Et ad eos ipsos sciscitantes quonam modo diceret si in se crederent liberi essent, quoniam semen Abrahae erant et numquam
serviverant, respondit: 'Amen, amen dico vobis quod omnis qui
facit peccatum, servus est peccati. Scio quia filii Abrahae estis, et si
filii Abrahae estis, opera Abrahae facite. Nunc autem quaeritis me
interficere, hominem, qui veritatem locutus sum, quam audivi a
Patre: hoc autem Abraham non fecit. Vos facitis opera patris

nothing unrighteous in him. Did not Moses give you the Law? Yet none of you keeps the Law."

When the scribes and Pharisees had caught a woman in adul- 81 tery and demanded a judgment in order to test Him, Jesus bent down and wrote on the ground. When they persisted and asked Him again, He rose up and said, "Let anyone among you who is without sin be the first to throw a stone at her." And once again He bent down and wrote on the ground. When they heard it, they went away, one by one, beginning with the elders; and Jesus alone remained with the woman standing before him. Jesus straightened up and said to her, "Woman, where are they who accused you? Has no one condemned you?" She said, "No one, Lord." And Jesus said, "Neither do I condemn you. Go your way, and do not sin again." What is written above about the adulterous woman is not found in any Greek manuscripts, but we have added it because we remember reading it in the Latin Gospels.

When the Pharisees reproached Him for bearing false witness 82 about Himself, Jesus said, "Even if I testify on my own behalf, my testimony is true because I know where I have come from and where I am going, but you do not know where I come from or where I am going. You judge by human standards; I judge no one. Yet even if I judge, my judgment is true. I am the one who testifies about myself, and my Father, who sent me, testifies about me." When some asked Him where His Father was, He said, "You know neither me nor my Father. If you knew me, you would perhaps know my Father also."

When they asked why He said they would be free if they be- 83 lieved in Him, when they were descendants of Abraham and had never been slaves, Jesus answered, "Very truly, I tell you, everyone who commits sin is a slave to sin. I know that you are descendants of Abraham. If you are Abraham's children, do what Abraham did. But now you are trying to kill me, a man who has spoken the truth that I heard from my Father. Abraham did not do this. You

vestri.' Dixerunt itaque ei: 'Nos ex fornicatione non sumus nati: unde patrem habemus Deum.' Dixit eis: 'Si Deus pater vester esset, utique diligeretis me; ego enim a Deo processi et veni; neque enim a meipso veni, sed ille me misit. Quare loquelam meam non 84 cognoscitis? Quia non potestis audire sermonem meum. Vos ex patre diabolo estis et desideria patris vestri vultis facere. Ille homicida erat ab initio, et in veritate non stetit, quia non est veritas in eo: cum loquitur mendacium, ex propriis loquitur, quia mendax est et pater eius. Ego autem quia veritatem dico, non creditis mihi. Quis ex vobis arguet me de peccato? Si veritatem dico, quare non creditis mihi? Qui est ex Deo, verba Dei audit. Propterea vos non auditis, quia ex Deo non estis.' Responderunt ergo Iudaei et dixerunt: 'Nonne bene dicimus, quod Samaritanus es et daemonium habes?' Respondit Iesus: 'Ego daemonium non habeo, sed honorifico Patrem meum, et vos inhonoratis me. Ego non quaero gloriam meam; est qui quaerat et iudicet. Ego autem dico vobis, si quis sermonem meum servaverit, mortem non videbit in aeternum.'

85 Dixerunt ergo Iudaei: 'Nunc cognoscimus quia daemonium habes. Abraham mortuus est, et prophetae mortui sunt. Quem teipsum facis?' Respondit Iesus: 'Est Pater meus qui glorificat me, quem vos nescitis quia Deus vester est, et non cognovistis eum: ego autem novi eum; et si dixero quia non novi eum, ero similis vobis, mendax. Sed scio eum et sermonem eius servo. Abraham pater vester exultavit ut videret diem meum: vidit et gavisus est.' Dixerunt ergo ad eum Iudaei: 'Quinquaginta annos nondum habes et Abraham vidisti?' Dixit Iesus: 'Amen, amen dico vobis, antequam Abraham fieret, ego sum.' Tulerunt ergo lapidem, ut iacerent in eum; Iesus autem abscondit se et exivit de templo.

86 Et ad discipulos eius, de caeco nato interrogantes an ipse vel parentes eius peccassent ut caecus nasceretur, respondit: 'Neque hic peccavit neque parentes eius; sed ut manifestentur opera Dei

are doing what your father does." So they said to Him, "We are not illegitimate children; therefore we have God as our Father." Jesus said to them, "If God were your Father, you would love me, for I proceeded and came from God. I did not come on my own, but He sent me. Why do you not understand what I say? It is because you cannot accept my word. You are from your father the 84 devil, and you choose to do your father's desires. He was a murderer from the beginning and did not stand in the truth, because there is no truth in him. When he lies, he speaks according to his own nature, for he is a liar and the father of lies. But because I tell the truth, you do not believe me. Which of you convicts me of sin? If I tell the truth, why do you not believe me? Whoever is from God hears the words of God. The reason you do not hear them is that you are not from God." The Jews answered and said, "Are we not right in saying that you are a Samaritan and have a demon?" Jesus answered, "I do not have a demon; but I honor my Father, and you dishonor me. Yet I do not seek my own glory; there is one who seeks it and passes judgment. I tell you, whoever keeps my word will never see death." So the Jews said to him, 85 "Now we know that you have a demon. Abraham died, and so did the prophets. Who do you claim to be?" Jesus answered, "It is my Father who glorifies me, but you know not that He is your God, and you have not known Him. But I know Him; if I said that I do not know Him, I would be a liar like you. But I know Him and I keep His word. Your father Abraham rejoiced to see my day; he saw it and was glad." Then the Jews said to Him, "You are not yet fifty years old, and have you seen Abraham?" Jesus said, "Very truly, I tell you, before Abraham was, I am." So they picked up stones to throw at him, but Jesus hid himself and went out of the temple.

When His disciples saw a blind man and asked who had 86 sinned — the man or his parents? — so that he was born blind, Jesus answered, "Neither this man nor his parents have sinned; he

in illo. Me oportet operari opera eius qui me misit, donec dies est: veniet nox, quando nemo poterit operari. Quamdiu in mundo 87 sum, lux sum mundi.' Et cuidam ex Pharisaeis interroganti 'Numquid nos caeci sumus?,' dixit Iesus: 'Si caeci essetis, peccatum non haberetis; nunc vero dicitis quia videmus[32] peccatum vestrum manet. Amen, amen dico vobis, quia ego sum ostium ovium. Omnes quotquot venerunt, fures fuerunt et latrones, sed non audierunt eos oves. Ego sum ostium. Per me, si quis introierit, salvabitur, et egredietur et ingredietur et pascua inveniet. Fur non venit nisi ut furetur et mactet et perdat. Ego veni ut vitam habeant et abundan- 88 tius habeant. Ego sum pastor bonus. Bonus pastor animam suam dat pro ovibus suis. Mercenarius autem et qui non est pastor, cuius non sunt oves propriae, videt lupum venientem et dimittit oves et fugit; et lupus rapit et dispergit oves. Mercenarius autem fugit, quia mercenarius est et non pertinet ad eum de ovibus. Ego sum pastor bonus et cognosco oves meas, et cognoscunt me meae. Sicut novit me Pater, et ego agnosco Patrem et animam meam pono pro ovibus meis. Et alias oves habeo quae non sunt ex hoc ovili et illas oportet me adducere, et fiet unum ovile et unus pastor. Propterea me Pater diligit, quia ego pono animam meam, et iterum sumo eam. Nemo enim tollit eam a me, sed ego ponam eam a meipso. Potestatem habeo ponendi animam et potestatem habeo iterum sumendi eam; hoc mandatum accepi a Patre meo.'

89 Et ad Iudaeos, an esset Christus palam diceret interrogantes, sic respondit: 'Loquor vobis, et non creditis. Opera quae ego facio in nomine Patris mei haec testimonium perhibent de me. Sed vos non creditis, quia non estis ex ovibus meis. Oves meae vocem meam audiunt et ego cognosco eas, et sequuntur me, et ego vitam aeternam do eis, et non peribunt in aeternum, et non rapiet eas quisquam de manu mea. Pater meus quod dedit mihi maius omni-

was born blind so that God's works might be revealed in him. I must work the works of Him who sent me while it is day; night is coming when no one can work. As long as I am in the world, I am the light of the world." When one of the Pharisees asked "Surely we are not blind, are we?" Jesus said, "If you were blind, you would not have sin. But now because you say, 'We see,' your sin against God remains. Very truly, I tell you, I am the gate for the sheep. All who came before me were thieves and bandits; but the sheep did not listen to them. I am the gate. Whoever enters by me will be saved, and will go out and come in and find pasture. The thief comes only to steal and kill and destroy. I came that they may have life, and have it abundantly. I am the good shepherd. The good shepherd lays down his life for his sheep. The hired hand, who is not the shepherd and does not own the sheep, sees the wolf coming and leaves the sheep and runs away—and the wolf snatches the sheep and scatters them. The hired hand runs away because he is a hired hand and has no concern for the sheep. I am the good shepherd. I know my own sheep, and my own know me, just as the Father knows me and I know the Father. And I lay down my life for my sheep. I have other sheep that do not belong to this fold. I must bring them also, and there will be one flock, one shepherd. For this reason the Father loves me, because I lay down my life and take it up again. No one takes it from me, but I lay it down of my own accord. I have power to lay down my life, and I have power to take it up again. I have received this command from my Father."

When the Jews asked Him if He were the Messiah, Jesus answered, "I have told you, and you do not believe. The works that I do in my Father's name testify to me; but you do not believe, because you do not belong to my sheep. My sheep hear my voice. I know them, and they follow me. I give them eternal life, and they will never perish. No one can snatch them out of my hand. What my Father has given me is greater than all else, and no one can

87

88

89

bus est, et nemo potest rapere de manu Patris mei. Ego et Pater
90   unum sumus.' Et ad eos ipsos, sese Deum facere obicientes et
propterea lapidare volentes, huiusmodi responsum dedit: 'Nonne
scriptum est in lege vestra: "Ego dixi: dii estis"? Si illos dixit deos,
ad quos sermo Dei factus est, et non potest solvi scriptura, quem
Pater sanctificavit et misit in mundum, vos dicitis quia blasphemo
quia Filius Dei sum? Si non facio opera Patris mei, nolite credere
mihi. Si autem facio et si mihi non vultis credere, operibus credite,
ut cognoscatis et credatis quia in me est Pater et ego in Patre.'

91   Et ad Iudam proditorem quare unguentum, quo Iesus ipse a
Maria Magdalena ungebatur, potius non venundaretur et pretium
venditionis pauperibus daretur conquerentem, sic respondit: 'Sine
illam ut in die sepulturae meae servet illud. Pauperes enim semper
habebitis vobiscum, me autem non semper habebitis.'

92   Et ad Andream et Philippum, petentes de gentilibus quibusdam qui Iesum videre quaerebant, ita respondens ait: 'Venit hora
ut Filius hominis clarificetur. Amen, amen dico vobis, nisi granum
frumenti cadens in terram emarcuerit, ipsum solum manet; si autem mortuum fuerit, multum fructum afferet. Qui amat animam
suam perdet eam, et qui odit animam suam in hoc mundo, in vitam aeternam custodit eam. Si quis mihi ministrat, me sequatur;
et ubi ego sum, illic et minister meus erit. Si quis mihi ministrave-
rit, honorificabit[33] eum Pater meus. Nunc anima mea turbata est.
Et quid dicam? Pater, salvifica me ex hac hora. Sed propterea veni
in hanc horam. Pater, clarifica nomen tuum.'

93   Et ad turbam, quis esset Filius hominis petentem, dicebat: 'Adhuc modicum lumen in vobis est. Ambulate dum lucem habetis,
ne tenebrae vos comprehendant; et qui ambulat in tenebris nescit
quo vadat. Dum lucem habetis, credite in lucem, ut filii lucis sitis.'
Et ad Petrum, resistentem ne sibi ab eo pedes lavarentur ac dicen-

snatch it out of the Father's hand. The Father and I are one."
When the Jews reproached Him for making Himself God, and   90
wanted to stone Him, He gave this reply: "Is it not written in your
Law, 'I said, You are gods'? If those to whom the word of God
came were called 'gods,' and the scripture cannot be annulled, say
you of me whom the Father has sanctified and sent into the world
that I am blaspheming, because I said, 'I am God's Son'? If I am
not doing the works of my Father, then do not believe me. But if I
do them, even though you do not wish to believe me, believe the
works, so that you may know and believe that the Father is in me
and I am in the Father."

When Judas, who would betray Him, complained that the oint-   91
ment with which Mary Magdalene anointed Jesus was not sold
and the money given to the poor, Jesus answered, "Leave her alone
so that she may keep it for the day of my burial. You will always
have the poor with you, but you will not always have me."

When Andrew and Philip asked about some Gentiles who   92
wanted to see Him, Jesus answered, "The hour has come for the
Son of Man to be glorified. Very truly, I tell you, unless a grain of
wheat falls into the earth and dies, it remains just a single grain;
but if it dies, it will bear much fruit. He who loves his life loses it,
and he who hates his life in this world will keep it for eternal life.
Whoever serves me must follow me, and where I am, there will
my servant be also. Whoever serves me, my Father will honor.
Now my soul is troubled. And what should I say—'Father, save
me from this hour'? No, it is for this reason that I have come to
this hour. Father, glorify your name."

When the crowd asked who the Son of Man was, Jesus said,   93
"The light is with you for a little longer. Walk while you have the
light, so that the darkness may not overtake you. He who walks in
the darkness does not know where he is going. While you have the
light, believe in the light, so that you may be children of light."
When Peter resisted having Jesus wash his feet and said, "Lord,

tem 'Domine, non lavabis mihi pedes in aeternum,' sic respondit:
'Si non lavero, non habebis partem mecum.' Ad Petrum quoque,
quo ipse iret percontantem, ita dixit: 'Quo ego vado non potes me
modo sequi; sequeris autem postea.' Et 'Quare,' inquit, 'non possum te modo sequi? Animam meam pro te ponam.' Respondit:
'Animam tuam pro me pones? Amen, amen dico tibi, non cantabit
94   gallus, antequam ter me negaveris.' Et ad Thomam, dicentem 'Domine, nescimus quo vadas et quomodo possumus viam scire,' respondens ait: 'Ego sum via, veritas et vita. Nemo venit ad Patrem,
nisi per me. Si cognovissetis me, utique et Patrem meum cognovissetis; et amodo cognoscetis eum et vidistis eum.'

95   Et ad Pharisaeos, de discipulis eius per sata ambulantibus et
spicas frumenti ob esuriem undique vellentibus, quare ita sabbatis
facerent interrogantes 'Nonne,' inquit, 'legistis quid fecerit David,
quando esuriit et qui cum illo erant? Quomodo intravit in domum
Dei et panes propositionis manducavit, quos non licebat ei edere
neque etiam iis qui cum illo erant, nisi solis dumtaxat sacerdotibus? Aut non legistis in lege quia sabbatis sacerdotes in templo
sabbatum violant et sunt sine crimine? Dico autem vobis quia
templo maior est hic. Si autem sciretis quid est "Misericordiam
volo et non sacrificium," numquam condemnassetis innocentem.
Dominus enim est Filius hominis etiam sabbato.' Et cum inde
transisset, venit in synagogam[34] eorum. Et ecce homo manum
aridam habens et interrogabant eum dicentes si licet sabbatis curare, ut accusarent eum. Ipse autem dixit illis: 'Quis erit ex vobis
homo qui habeat ovem unam et, si ceciderit haec sabbatis in fo-
veam, nonne tenebit et levabit eam? Quanto magis melior homo
quam ovis est? Itaque licet sabbatis bene facere.'

96   Et ad Iudaeos, qui eum persequebantur, quod hominem in piscina sabbato sanum effecerat, utique ait: 'Pater meus usque modo
operatur et ego operor. Propterea dedit vobis Moses circumcisionem (non quia ex Mose est, sed ex patribus) in sabbato circumci-

you will never wash my feet," He replied, "Unless I wash you, you have no share with me." And when Peter asked Him where He was going, Jesus said, "Where I am going, you cannot follow me now; but you will follow afterward." When Peter said, "Lord, why can I not follow you now? I will lay down my life for you," Jesus answered, "Will you lay down your life for me? Very truly, I tell you, before the cock crows, you will have denied me three times." And when Thomas said, "Lord, we do not know where you are going, and how can we know the way?" Jesus replied: "I am the way, the truth, and the life. No one comes to the Father except by me. If you had known me, you would have known my Father also; and soon you will know Him and see Him." 94

When His disciples were walking through the fields and, being hungry, plucked ears of grain round about, the Pharisees asked why they did so on the Sabbath. Jesus said, "Have you not read what David did when he and his companions were hungry? He entered the house of God and ate the bread of the Presence, which it was not lawful for him or his companions to eat, but only for the priests. Or have you not read in the Law that on the Sabbath the priests in the temple break the Sabbath and yet are guiltless? I tell you, one greater than the temple is here. But if you had known what this means, 'I desire mercy and not sacrifice,' you would not have condemned the guiltless. For the Son of Man is Lord even on the Sabbath." And when He left, He came into their synagogue. There was a man there with a withered hand, and they asked Him, in order to accuse Him, if it was lawful to heal on the Sabbath. He said to them, "Is there any of you who has one sheep and if it falls into a pit on the Sabbath, will he not lay hold of it and lift it out? How much better is a human being than a sheep! So it is lawful to do good on the Sabbath."[29] 95

When the Jews persecuted Him for healing a man at the pool on the Sabbath, He said, "My Father is still working, and I am working. Moses gave you circumcision (not as if from Moses, but 96

ditis hominem. Si circumcisionem accipit homo in sabbato, ut non solvatur lex Mosi, mihi indignamini, quia totum hominem sanum feci in sabbato? Nolite iudicare secundum faciem sed iustum iudicium iudicate.'

97   Et ad discipulos eius, de signo adventus eius et consummatione saeculi seorsum, dum in Monte Oliveti remotis arbitris sederet, interrogantes 'Videte,' inquit, 'ne quis vos seducat. Multi enim venient in nomine meo dicentes: "Ego sum Christus," et multos seducent. Audituri enim estis proelia et opiniones proeliorum. Videte, ne turbemini; nam oportet haec et similia fieri, sed nondum est finis. Consurget enim gens contra gentem et regnum in regnum, et erunt pestilentiae et fames et terraemotus per loca. Haec autem omnia initia sunt dolorum. Tunc tradent vos in tribulationem[35] et occident, et eritis odio omnibus hominibus propter nomen meum. Et tunc scandalizabuntur multi et invicem tradent et odio habebunt invicem. Et multi pseudoprophetae surgent et seducent multos; et quoniam habundavit iniquitas, refrigescet caritas multorum. Qui autem perseveraverit usque in finem, hic salvabitur. Et praedicabitur hoc evangelium regni in universo terrarum orbe, in testimonium omnibus gentibus, et tunc veniet consum-

98   matio. Cum autem videritis abominationem desolationis, quae dicta est a Daniele propheta, stante in loco[36] sancto, qui legit intelligat: tunc qui in Iudaea sunt fugient ad montes; nec descendant, ut de domo sua quidquam auferant. Et qui in agro est, non revertatur, ut eius tunicam tollat. Vae autem praegnantibus et nutrientibus in illis diebus. Orate, ne fiat fuga vestra hieme vel sabbato. Erit enim tunc tribulatio magna, qualis non fuit ab initio mundi usque modo neque fiet. Et nisi brevitati fuissent dies illi, non fieret salva omnis caro; sed propter electos breviabuntur dies illi. Tunc si

from the patriarchs), and you circumcise a man on the Sabbath. If a man receives circumcision on the Sabbath in order that the Law of Moses may not be broken, are you angry with me because I healed a man's whole body on the Sabbath? Do not judge by appearances, but judge with righteous judgment."[30]

When His disciples were alone with Him as He sat on the Mount of Olives with no witnesses, and asked for a sign of His coming and the end of the age, He said, "Beware that no one leads you astray. For many will come in my name, saying, 'I am the Messiah!' and they will lead many astray. And you will hear of wars and rumors of wars; see that you are not alarmed; for these and similar things must take place, but the end is not yet. For nation will rise against nation, and kingdom against kingdom, and there will be plagues, famines, and earthquakes in various places, all this is but the beginning of the birth pangs. Then they will hand you over to be tortured and will put you to death, and you will be hated by all people because of my name. Then many will be offended, and they will betray and hate one another. And many false prophets will arise and lead many astray. And because of the increase of wickedness, the love of many will grow cold. But anyone who endures to the end will be saved. And this good news of the kingdom will be proclaimed throughout the world, as a testimony to all the nations; and then the end will come.[31] So when you see the desolating sacrilege which was spoken of by the prophet Daniel, standing in the holy place, let the reader understand: then those who are in Judea must flee to the mountains; let them not go down to take anything from their house; someone in the field must not turn back to get a coat. Woe to those who are pregnant and to those who are nursing infants in those days! Pray that your flight may not be in winter or on a Sabbath. For at that time there will be great suffering, such as has not been from the beginning of the world until now, no, and never will be. And if those days had not been cut short, no one would be saved; but for the sake of the

97

98

quis dixerit vobis: "Hic est Christus" aut "illic," nolite credere.
Exsurgent enim pseudochristi et pseudoprophetae et dabunt signa
magna et prodigia, ita ut in errorem ducantur, si fieri potest, etiam
electi. Ecce praedixi vobis. Si ergo dixerint vobis: "Ecce in deserto
est," nolite exire; "Ecce in penetrabilibus," nolite credere; sicut
enim fulgur exit ab oriente et paret usque in occidentem, ita erit
adventus Filii hominis. Ubicumque fuerit corpus, illic congrega-
99   buntur et aquilae. Statim autem post tribulationem dierum illorum, sol obscurabitur et luna non dabit lumen suum et stellae
cadent et virtutes caelorum movebuntur. Et tunc apparebit signum
Filii hominis in caelo, tunc quoque plangent omnes tribus terrae
et videbunt Filium hominis venientem in nubibus caeli cum virtute multa et maiestate. Et mittet angelos suos cum tuba et voce
magna, et congregabuntur electos eius a quattuor ventis, a summis
caelorum usque ad terminos eorum.

100   'Ab arbore autem fici discite parabolam: nam cum iam ramus
eius tener fuerit et folia nata, scitis quia prope est aestas. Ita et vos,
cum videritis haec omnia, scitote quia prope est in ianuis. Amen
dico vobis, quia non praeteribit generatio haec donec omnia fiant.
Caelum et terra transibunt, verba autem mea non praeteribunt. De
die autem et hora nemo scit, neque angeli caelorum, nisi Pater
solus; ut autem accidit in diebus Noe, ita erit adventus Filii hominis. Sicut enim erant in diebus ante diluvium comedentes et bi-
bentes, nubentes et nuptum tradentes, usque ad eum diem, quo
Noe ipse in archam ingrederetur et non cognoverunt, donec venit
diluvium et tulit omnes, ita erit adventus Filii hominis. Tunc duo
101   erunt in agro, unus assumetur, alter vero relinquetur. Vigilate ergo,
quia nescitis qua hora Dominus vester venturus est. Illud autem

elect those days will be cut short. Then if anyone says to you, 'Look! Here is the Messiah!' or 'There He is!' — do not believe it. For false messiahs and false prophets will appear and produce great signs and omens, to lead astray, if possible, even the elect. Take note, I have told you beforehand. So if they say to you, 'Look! He is in the wilderness,' do not go out. If they say, 'Look! He is in the inner rooms,' do not believe it. For as the lightning comes from the east and flashes as far as the west, so will be the coming of the Son of Man. Wherever the corpse is, there the vultures will gather. Immediately after the tribulation of those days 99 the sun will be darkened, and the moon will not give its light; the stars will fall, and the powers of heaven will be shaken. Then the sign of the Son of Man will appear in heaven, and then all the tribes of the earth will mourn, and they will see 'the Son of Man coming on the clouds of heaven' with great power and majesty. And He will send his angels with a trumpet call and a loud voice, and they will gather His elect from the four winds, from one end of heaven to the other.

"Learn a lesson from the fig tree: as soon as its branch becomes 100 tender and puts forth new leaves, you know that summer is near. So also, when you see all these things, know that He is near, at the door. Truly I tell you, this generation will not pass away until all these things have come to pass. Heaven and earth will pass away, but my words will not pass away. But about that day and hour no one knows, not even the angels of heaven, but only the Father. As happened in the days of Noah, so will be the coming of the Son of Man. For as in the days before the flood they were eating and drinking, marrying and giving in marriage, until the day Noah entered the ark, and they knew nothing until the flood came and swept them all away, so too will be the coming of the Son of Man. Then two will be in the field; one will be taken and one will be left. Keep awake therefore, for you do not know at what hour your 101 Lord is coming. But understand this: if the owner of the house

scitote, quoniam si sciret pater familias qua hora fur venturus esset, vigilaret utique et non sineret perfodi domum suam. Ideoque
parati estote, quia, qua hora non putatis, Filius hominis venturus
est. Quis putas est fidelis servus et prudens, quem dominus super
familiam suam constituit, ut illis cibum opportuno tempore ministraret?[37] Beatus servus ille, quem cum venerit dominus eius, sicut
sibi iniunctum erat, facientem invenerit. Amen dico vobis, ⟨quo-
niam⟩[38] super omnia bona sua constituet eum. Si autem, cogitans,
malus ille servus in corde suo ita dixerit: "Moram facit dominus
meus venire," et ideo coeperit percutere servos suos, manducet autem et bibat cum ebriosis; veniet dominus servi illius in die, qua
non sperat, et hora qua ignorat, et dividet eum partemque eius
ponet cum hypocritis: illic erit fletus et stridor dentium.'

102   Ceterum, cum de gravibus ac divinis Salvatoris nostri responsionibus suo ordine, ut potuimus, hactenus dixerimus, de parabolis eius deinceps pauca dicemus, ab illa de semine in terram
proiecto — ceterarum omnium celebratissima — initium sumentes.

103   'Ecce exiit, qui seminat, seminare semen suum et cum inter se-
minandum nonnulla secus viam forte cecidisset, supervenerunt
volucres caeli et comederunt ea. Alia autem in petrosa ceciderunt,
ubi cum terram multam non haberent, continuo exorta sunt, quia
non habebant altitudinem terrae; sole autem orto, aestuaverunt et,
quia radicem non habebant, confestim aruerunt. Quaedam vero in
spineta ceciderunt et creverunt spinae et suffocaverunt ea. Alia autem in terram bonam ceciderunt et varium cultum reddebant,
aliud namque centesimum, aliud sexagesimum, aliud trigesimum
104   dabat. Qui habet aures ad audiendum audiat.' Et paulo post, 'Vos,'
inquit, 'audite parabolam seminantis. Omnis qui audit verbum
regni et non intelligit, venit malus et rapit quod seminatum est in
corde eius; hic est, qui seminatus est secus viam. Qui autem seminatus est supra petrosa, hic verbum audit et continuo cum gaudio
accipit illud; non habet autem in se radicem, sed est temporalis.

had known at what hour the thief was coming, he would have stayed awake and would not have let his house be broken into. Therefore be ready, for the Son of Man is coming at an unexpected hour. Who do you think is the faithful and wise slave, whom his master has put in charge of his household, to give the other slaves their food at the proper time? Blessed is that slave whom his master will find at work, as he had been ordered, when he arrives. Truly I tell you, he will put that one in charge of all his possessions. But if that wicked slave, plotting, says to himself, 'My master is delayed,' and he begins to beat his fellow slaves, and eats and drinks with drunkards, the master of that slave will come on a day when he does not expect him and at an hour that he does not know. He will cut him in pieces and put part of him with the hypocrites: there will be weeping and gnashing of teeth."

Now that we have discussed our Savior's weighty and divine 102 answers to questions, so far as possible in proper order, we will say a few things about His parables, beginning with the most famous of all, the parable of the seed cast to earth.[32]

"Listen! A sower went out to sow his seed. And as he sowed, 103 some seed fell on the roadside, and the birds of heaven came and ate it up. Other seed fell on rocky ground, where it did not find much soil, and it sprang up quickly, since it had no depth of soil. And when the sun rose, it was scorched; and since it had no root, it quickly withered away. Other seed fell among thorns, and the thorns grew up and choked it. Other seed fell on good soil and brought forth grain, variously yielding a hundred- and sixty- and thirtyfold. Let anyone with ears to hear listen!"[33] And soon there- 104 after, He said, "Hear the parable of the sower. When anyone hears the word of the kingdom and does not understand it, the evil one comes and snatches away what was sown in his heart; this is the one sown on the path. The one sown on rocky ground is the one who hears the word and immediately receives it with joy but having no root in himself, he endures only for a while; and when

Facta autem tribulatione et persecutione propter verbum, continuo scandalizatur. Qui autem seminatur in spinetis, hic est qui verbum audit, et sollicitudo saeculi istius et fallacia divitiarum suffocat verbum, et sine fructu efficitur. Qui vero in terram bonam seminatus est, hic est qui audit verbum et intelligit et fructum affert et facit quidem aliud centesimum, aliud sexagesimum, alium trigesimum.'

105   Aliam deinde parabolam proponens, 'Simile factum est,' inquit, 'regnum caelorum homini qui seminat bonum semen in agro suo. Cum autem dormirent homines, venit inimicus eius et superseminavit zizania in medio tritici et abiit. Cum autem crevisset herba et fructum fecisset, apparuerunt et zizania. Accedentes autem servi patris familias dixerunt ei: "Domine, nonne bonum semen seminasti in agro tuo? Unde ergo habe[ba]t zizania?" Quibus inimicum hominem sic fecisse respondit.' Servi autem dixerunt: 'Si vis, ibimus et colligemus ea.' Et ait: 'Nolo, ne forte colligentes zizania eradicetis simul cum eis triticum. Sinite utraque crescere usque ad messem. In tempore messis dicam messoribus: "Colligite primum zizania et alligate ea in fasciculos ad comburendum; triti-
106   cum autem congregate in horreum meum."' Atque his dictis huius parabolae explicationem postulantibus discipulis ait: 'Qui seminat bonum semen, Filius hominis est, et ager autem est mundus; bonum vero semen, hii sunt filii regni. Zizania autem filii sunt nequam; inimicus vero qui seminat est diabolus. Messis autem consummatio saeculi est; messores vero angeli sunt. Sicut ergo zizania colliguntur et igni comburuntur, sic erit in consummatione saeculi. Mittet Filius hominis angelos eius, et colligent de regno eius omnia scandala et eos quoque congregabit qui iniquitatem operantur et mittent omnes in caminum ignis: ibi erit fletus et stridor dentium. Tunc iusti fulgebunt in regno patris eorum. Qui habet aures ad audiendum audiat.'

107   Aliam parabolam locutus est eis dicens: 'Simile est regnum caelorum fermento, quod acceptum mulier abscondit in farinae

trouble or persecution arises on account of the word, that person immediately falls away. As for the one sown among thorns, this is the one who hears the word, but the cares of the world and the lure of wealth choke the word, and it yields nothing. But the one who was sown on good soil is the one who hears the word and understands it and bears fruit and yields, in one case a hundred-, in another sixty-, and in another thirtyfold."

He then put forward another parable. "The kingdom of heaven 105 is like a man who sows good seed in his field; but while everybody was asleep, his enemy came and sowed weeds among the wheat, and went away. When the plants came up and bore grain, then the weeds appeared as well. And the slaves of the householder came and said to him, 'Master, did you not sow good seed in your field? Where, then, did these weeds come from?' He answered that an enemy did this. The slaves replied, 'If you like, we will go and gather them.' But he said, 'No; for in gathering the weeds you would uproot the wheat along with them. Let both of them grow until the harvest; and at harvest time I will tell the reapers, First collect the weeds and bind them in bundles to be burned, but gather the wheat into my barn.'" When this was said, His disciples 106 asked Him to explain the parable, and He answered, "The one who sows the good seed is the Son of Man; the field is the world, and the good seed are these children of the kingdom; the weeds are the children of the evil one, and the enemy who sows them is the devil; the harvest is the end of the age, and the reapers are angels. Just as the weeds are collected and burned up with fire, so will it be at the end of the age. The Son of Man will send His angels, and they will collect the evildoers out of His kingdom, and they will throw all of them into the furnace of fire, where there will be weeping and gnashing of teeth. Then the righteous will shine in the kingdom of their Father. Let anyone with ears listen!"

He told them another parable, saying "The kingdom of heaven 107 is like yeast that a woman took and mixed in with three *sata* of

satis tribus, donec fermentaretur totum.' ('Satum' autem est genus mensurae iuxta modum provinciae Palaestinae unum et dimidium modum capiens). 'Simile est etiam regnum caelorum thesauro abscondito in agro; quem cum invenerit homo recondit et pro gaudio illius vadit et vendit universa quae possidet et emit agrum illum. Iterum simile est regnum caelorum homini negotiatori quaerenti bonas margaritas; et cum quaesisset unam et quidem bonam invenisset, abiit et vendidit omnia quae habebat et emit eam.

108   'Iterum simile est regnum caelorum sagenae quae in mare mitteretur; ex omni genere piscium congregaret et, postquam impleta esset, educeretur et a secus litus sedentibus eligeretur et boni in vasa sua, mali autem foras mitterentur. Sic erit in consummatione saeculi: exibunt angeli et separabunt malos de medio iustorum et mittent eos in caminum ignis; ibi erit fletus et stridor dentium.' Iterum ait: 'Omnis scriba doctus in regno caelorum similis est homini patri familias, qui profert de thesauro suo nova et vetera.'

109   'Regnum insuper caelorum cuidam regi assimilatum esse,' dixit, 'qui a servis suis rationem administrationis exigens unum inter ceteros invenit, qui debebat decem milia talentorum. Cum autem non haberet, unde reddere posset, mox eum et uxorem suam et filios et omnia quae habebat venundari et exinde reddi iussit. Quod audiens, servus ille confestim genibus provolutus procidit in terram et rogabat eum, sic dicens: "Patientiam habe in me, et omnia reddam tibi." His servi sui praecibus dominus misericordia motus, universum debitum gratis remisit ei atque ideo ut relaxaretur edixit. Cum autem paulo post servus ille egrederetur atque in unum de conservis suis incideret, qui ei centum denarios debebat, apprehendens suffocabat eum dicebatque: "Redde quod debes." Unde procidens conservus eius in hunc modum rogabat: "Patien-
110   tiam habe in me, et omnia reddam tibi." Ille vero misit eum in carcerem, donec sibi satisfaceret (tantum abfuit ut ipsius miserere-

flour until all of it was leavened." (A *satum* is a kind of measure which, according to the standard of the region of Palestine, holds one and a half bushels.) "The kingdom of heaven is like a treasure hidden in a field. When a man found it, he reburied it and in his joy over this went and sold all his possessions and bought that field. Again, the kingdom of heaven is like a merchant seeking fine pearls; and when he had searched and found one fine one, he went and sold all his possessions and bought it.

"Again, the kingdom of heaven is like a net that was cast into 108 the sea and caught fish of every kind; and when it was full, they drew it up and sat down on the shore and put the good ones into baskets but threw out the bad. So it will be at the end of the age. The angels will come out and separate the evil from the righteous and throw them into the furnace of fire, where there will be weeping and gnashing of teeth." Again He said: "Every scribe who is learned in the kingdom of heaven is like a head of household who brings forth things new and old from his treasure."

"He also said that the kingdom of heaven is like a king who 109 demanded an accounting of their administration from his slaves and among them found one who owed him ten thousand talents; and as he could not pay, his master ordered him to be sold, together with his wife and children and all his possessions, and payment to be made from the proceeds. When he heard this, the slave immediately fell on his knees and begged him, saying, 'Have patience with me, and I will pay you everything.' Moved to pity at his slave's entreaties, the master released him and forgave him the debt and therefore ordered him to be released. But a little later, as that same slave went out, he came upon one of his fellow slaves who owed him a hundred denarii; and seizing him by the throat, he said, 'Pay what you owe.' Then his fellow slave fell down and pleaded with him, 'Have patience with me, and I will pay you everything.' But he threw him into prison pending repayment of the 110 debt (he was so far from feeling pity for him). When his fellow

tur). Ubi autem conservi eius conspexerunt quae hinc inde fiebant, contristati sunt valde. Proinde illinc abeuntes accesserunt et domino suo omnia quaecumque acciderant fideliter retulerunt. Quibus auditis, illum ad se dominus acciri iussit et ait: "Serve nequam! Ideo omne debitum remisi tibi, quoniam rogasti me; nonne ergo oportuit te miserere conservi tui, tibi supplicantis, sicut ego tui, mihi obsecrantis, misertus sum?" Ira deinde motus, tradidit eum tortoribus, quoadusque reddens universum debitum satisfaceret. Sic et Pater meus caelestis faciet vobis, nisi unusquisque fratri suo de cordibus vestris remiseritis.'

111 'Simile est propterea regnum caelorum homini patri familias, qui exiit primo mane, ut operarios in vineam suam conduceret. Cum quibus conventione facta, ex denario diurno, misit eos in vineam, ut operarentur. Et tertia circiter hora postea ingressus, vidit alios otiosos qui in foro stabant et dixit illis: "Ite et vos in vineam meam et operamini, et quod iustum fuerit dabo vobis." Ubi vero illi abierunt, exiit iterum inter sextam circiter et nonam horam et fecit similiter ut antea fecerat. Circa undecimam denique horam egressus est et alios stantes invenit et dixit illis: "Quid hic statis tota die otiosi?" "Quia nemo," inquiunt, "nos conduxit." Dixit illis:

112 "Ite et vos in vineam meam." Cum sero autem factum esset, dicit dominus vineae procuratori: "Voca operarios et redde illis mercedem incipiens a novissimis usque ad primos." Cum accessissent ergo, qui circa horam undecimam ad operandum venerant, denarios singulos acceperunt. Venientes autem proximi, et solutionem factam conspicati, arbitrabantur quod plus essent accepturi; sed cum et ipsi singulos denarios accepissent, inter accipiendum adversus patrem familias sic dicentes, murmurabant: "Hii novissimi una hora tantum operati sunt, et pares nobis fecisti, qui pondus diei et

113 aestus continue portavimus!" At ille respondens uni eorum dixit: "Amice, non facio[39] tibi iniuriam; nonne ex denario diurno convenisti mecum? Tolle quod tuum est et vade; volo autem dare et huic

slaves saw what had happened in both cases, they were greatly distressed, and they went and approached their master and reported faithfully all that had taken place. When he heard this, his master summoned him and said to him, 'You wicked slave! I forgave you all that debt because you pleaded with me. Should you not have had mercy on your fellow slave when he begged you, as I had mercy on you when you beseeched me?' And in anger his master handed him over to be tortured until he should pay his entire debt. So my heavenly Father will also do to you, if every one of you does not forgive your brother from your heart."[34]

"For the kingdom of heaven is like a landowner who went out 111 early in the morning to hire laborers for his vineyard. After agreeing with the laborers on a denarius for the day, he sent them into his vineyard to work. When he went out about nine o'clock, he saw others standing idle in the marketplace; and he said to them, 'You also go into my vineyard, and I will pay you whatever is fair.' When they went, he went out again about noon and about three o'clock, he did the same as before. And about five o'clock he went out and found others standing around; and he said to them, 'Why are you standing here idle all day?' They said, 'Because no one has hired us.' He said to them, 'You also go into my vineyard.' When 112 evening came, the owner of the vineyard said to his manager, 'Call the laborers and give them their pay, beginning with the last and then going to the first.' When those who had arrived to work about five o'clock came, they received one denarius each. Now when the next ones came, seeing the payment that was made, they thought they would receive more; but they also received one denarius each. And when they received it, they grumbled against the landowner, saying, 'These last worked only one hour, but you have made them equal to us who have continuously borne the burden of the day and the scorching heat.' But he replied to one of them, 113 'Friend, I am doing you no wrong; did you not agree with me on a denarius for the day? Take what belongs to you and go; I want

novissimo sicut et tibi. Nonne licet mihi quod volo facere? An oculus tuus nequam est quia ego bonus? Sic ergo erunt novissimi primi, et primi novissimi." Multi autem sunt vocati, pauci vero electi.'

114 'Homo quidam habebat duos filios et accedens ad primum dixit: "Vade hodie operare in vinea mea." At ille se ire nolle respondit. Postea vero poenitentia motus abiit et fecit quod sibi iniunctum erat. Accessit deinde ad alterum et dixit similiter. Ille autem se ire velle respondit, et tamen, ut promiserat, non ivit. Quis ergo ex his duobus voluntati patris oboedivit?' Illis de primo respondentibus dicit Iesus: 'Amen dico vobis, quia publicani et meretrices praecedunt vos in regnum Dei.'

115 'Homo erat pater familias qui plantavit vineam et saepibus circumdedit eam et ibidem torcular effodit et turrem in medio eius aedificavit et locavit eam agricolis; et postquam haec omnia fecit, peregre profectus est. Cum autem opportunum vindemiarum tempus appropinquasset, servos suos ad agricolas mittere constituit, ut fructus exinde susciperent. Ceterum agricolae, apprehensis servis eius, alios vendiderunt, alios occiderunt, alios vero lapidaverunt. Iterum misit alios servos plures prioribus, et cum illos similiter ab eis tractatos fuisse accepisset, novissime misit et filium suum, ratus quod illum venerarentur. Agricolae autem ubi filium viderunt, intra se dixerunt: "Hic est heres. Eamus et occidamus eum et nostra erit hereditas." Et apprehenderunt eum et extra vineam

116 eiecerunt et demum occiderunt. Cum ergo venerit dominus vineae, quid faciet agricolis illis?' Dicunt: 'Malos male perdet et vineam suam aliis locabit qui reddent ei fructum temporibus suis.' Dicit illis Iesus: 'Numquam legistis in Scripturis: "Lapidem quem reprobaverunt aedificantes, hic factus est in caput anguli.[40] A Domino factum est istud et est mirabile in oculis nostris"? Ideo dico vobis, quia auferetur a vobis regnum Dei et dabitur gentibus quae fruc-

to give to this last one the same as I give to you. Am I not allowed to do what I want? Or are you envious because I am generous? So the last will be first, and the first will be last.' Many are called, but few are chosen.

"A man had two sons; he went to the first and said, 'Go and 114 work in my vineyard today.' He answered that he did not wish to. But later he changed his mind and went and did as he had been ordered. The father then went to the second and said the same; and he said that he was willing to go, but he did not go as he had promised. Which of the two did the will of his father?" When they said, "The first," Jesus said to them, "Truly I tell you, the tax collectors and the prostitutes are going into the kingdom of God ahead of you."

"There was a householder who planted a vineyard, put a fence 115 around it, dug a wine press in it, and built a watchtower in the middle of it and leased it to tenants; and after he did this, he traveled to another country. When the harvest time had come, he decided to send his slaves to the tenants to collect his produce. But the tenants seized his slaves and sold some and killed others, and stoned others. Again he sent other slaves, more numerous than the first; and when he learned that they had treated them in the same way, he finally sent his son to them, thinking that they would respect him. But when the tenants saw the son, they said to themselves, 'This is the heir; come, let us kill him and get his inheritance.' So they seized him, threw him out of the vineyard, and killed him. Now when the owner of the vineyard comes, what will 116 he do to those tenants?" They said, "He will put those wretches to a miserable death, and lease the vineyard to other tenants who will give him the produce at the harvest time." Jesus said to them, "Have you never read in the scriptures, 'The stone that the builders rejected has become the cornerstone; this was the Lord's doing, and it is amazing in our eyes'?[35] Therefore I tell you, the kingdom of God will be taken away from you and given to peoples who will

tum eius efficient. Et qui ceciderit super lapidem istud confringe-
tur; super quem vero ceciderit, conteret eum.'

117 'Simile factum est regnum caelorum cuidam regi, qui—cum
nuptias filio suo solemniter celebraret—misit servos suos tempore
opportuno, ut invitatos ad nuptias vocarent. Quos ubi frustra revertisse accepit, iterum misit alios servos ut prandium paratum
tauros et altilia occisa et cetera omnia invitatis similiter praeparata
esse nuntiarent atque ad nuptias adducerent. Illi vero quod nuntiatum erat neglexerunt et alii in villam, alii in negotiationem suam
abierunt; reliqui vero servos eius tenuerunt et contumeliis affectos
occiderunt. Quod cum regi nuntiatum esset, iratus est et, missis
exercitibus suis, perdidit homicidas illos et civitates eorum succen-
dit. Quo facto, servis suis "Nuptiae," inquit, "paratae sunt, sed qui
invitati erant, non fuerunt digni. Ite ergo ad exitus viarum et
quoscumque inveneritis invitate ad nuptias." Unde servi, regio
edicto parentes, in vias egressi congregarunt omnes quos invenerunt, bonos pariter et malos, et impletae sunt nuptiae discum-
118 bentibus. Et ingressus est rex, ut videret discumbentes, et vidit ibi
hominem non vestitum veste nuptiali et ait illi: "Amice, quomodo
huc intrasti non habens vestem nuptialem?" Et cum obmutuisset,
confestim rex ministris suis edixit ut, ligatis pedibus et manibus,
in tenebras exteriores eicerent, ubi erat fletus et stridor dentium.
Multi autem sunt vocati, pauci vero electi.

119 'Simile est regnum caelorum decem virginibus, quae acceptis
lampadibus suis obviam sponso sponsaeque exiverant. Ex quibus
quinque fatuae et totidem prudentes erant; sed quinque fatuae acceptis lampadibus secum oleum non sumpserunt;[41] prudentes vero
oleum in vasis suis simul cum lampadibus acceperunt. Commo-
rante autem sponso, dormitaverunt omnes et dormierunt. Media
vero nocte clamor factus est sponsi eis obviam exeuntis. Unde
omnes illae virgines surrexerunt et ubi lampades suas ornaverunt,
fatuae sapientibus dixerunt: "Date nobis, quaesumus, de oleo

produce the fruits of the kingdom. Anyone who falls on this stone will be broken to pieces; and it will crush anyone on whom it falls.

"The kingdom of heaven is like a king who celebrated his son's 117 wedding with a feast. He sent his slaves in good time to call those who had been invited to the feast. When he learned that they had returned in vain, he again sent other slaves to announce to those who had been invited that the dinner was prepared, the oxen and the fat calves had been slaughtered, and everything else was ready and to bring them to the feast. But they made light of the report and went away, one to his farm, another to his business, while the rest seized his slaves, maltreated them, and killed them. When this was reported to the king, he was enraged. He sent his troops, destroyed those murderers, and burned their cities. Then he said to his slaves, 'The feast is ready, but those invited were not worthy. Go therefore to the crossroads, and invite everyone you find to the feast.' So in obedience to the royal edict, those slaves went out into the streets and gathered all whom they found, both good and bad, and the feast was filled with guests. But when the king came in to 118 see the guests, he noticed a man there who was not wearing a wedding robe, and he said to him, 'Friend, how did you get in here without a wedding robe?' When he made no reply, the king immediately ordered his attendants to bind him hand and foot, and throw him into the outer darkness, where there was weeping and gnashing of teeth. Many are called, but few are chosen.

"The kingdom of heaven is like ten bridesmaids who took their 119 lamps and went out to meet the bride and groom. Five of them were foolish, and five were wise. When the five foolish ones took their lamps, they took no oil with them; but the wise took oil in their flasks with their lamps. As the bridegroom was delayed, all of them became drowsy and fell asleep. But at midnight there was a shout of the groom coming out to meet them. Then all those bridesmaids got up and trimmed their lamps. The foolish ones said to the wise, 'Give us some of your oil please, for our lamps

vestro, quia lampades nostrae extinguuntur." At illae respondentes: "Ite," inquiunt, "potius ad venditores et quod expedit vobis emite, ne — si ⟨de⟩ nostro vobis traderemus — forte utrisque non sufficeret." Dum autem, emendi causa, proficiscerentur, accessit sponsus et quae paratae erant cum eo ad nuptias e vestigio intraverunt, et mox clausa est ianua. Novissimae vero reliquae virgines venerunt etiam atque etiam obsecrantes ut eis aperiret. At ille respondens ait: "Amen dico vobis, nescio vos." Vigilate itaque, quia nescitis diem nec horam.

120   'Homo quidam peregre profecturus, antequam proficisceretur, servos suos ad se vocavit et, secundum propriam cuiuscumque virtutem, singulis bona sua distribuit. Nam uni quinque talenta, alii vero duo, alii denique unum dedit, et statim peregre profectus est. Qui autem quinque talenta acceperat, abiens ita in eis operatus est, ut totidem superlucraretur; similiter et qui duo acceperat totidem comparavit. Qui autem unum acceperat, abiens in terram fo-

121   dit et domui suae pecuniam abscondit. Post multum vero temporis dominus servorum illorum ex ea peregrinatione reversus est, et rationem administrationis pecuniae suae ab illis repetens. Et accessit qui quinque talenta acceperat et totidem referens: "Domine," inquit, "quinque talenta tradidisti; ecce alia quinque superlucratus sum." Ait illi dominus eius: "Euge, serve bone et fidelis, quia super pauca fidelis fuisti, super multa te constituam: intra in gaudium domini tui." Accedens deinde et qui duo talenta acceperat: "Domine," inquit, "duo talenta tradidisti mihi; ecce alia duo superlucratus sum." Ait illi dominus eius: "Euge, serve bone et fidelis, quia super pauca fidelis fuisti, super multa te constituam; intra in gau-

122   dium domini tui." Accessit denique et qui unum talentum accepe-rat et ait: "Domine, scio quia homo durus es: metis ubi non

are going out.' But the wise ones replied, 'Go rather to the vendors and buy some for yourselves lest if we share from our supply we both run out.' And while they were going to buy it, the bridegroom came, and those bridesmaids who were ready immediately went with him into the feast; and the door was shut. The other bridesmaids came last, begging repeatedly for the door to be opened for them. But he replied, 'Truly I tell you, I do not know you.' Keep awake therefore, for you know neither the day nor the hour.

"For it is as if a man, on the eve of a trip to a foreign country, 120 before departing summoned his slaves and divided his property among them according to the ability of each: to one he gave five talents, to another two, to another one; and he immediately departed. The one who had received the five talents went off and traded with them, and made five more talents. In the same way, the one who had received the two talents made two more talents. But the one who had received the one talent went off and dug a hole in the ground and hid the money at his home. After a long 121 time the master of those slaves came back from his journey and demanded from them an accounting of their management of his money. Then the one who had received the five talents came forward, bringing five more talents, saying, 'Master, you handed over five talents to me; see, I have made five more talents.' His master said to him, 'Well done, good and trustworthy slave; since you have been trustworthy in a few things, I will put you in charge of many things; enter into the joy of your master.' And the one with the two talents also came forward, saying, 'Master, you handed over two talents to me; see, I have made two more talents.' His master said to him, 'Well done, good and trustworthy slave; since you have been trustworthy in a few things, I will put you in charge of many things; enter into the joy of your master.' Finally the one 122 who had received the one talent also came forward, saying, 'Master, I knew that you are a harsh man, reaping where you did not

seminasti et congregas ubi non sparsisti. Et timens abii et abscondi talentum in terra. Ecce habes quod tuum est." Cui dominus respondens sic dixit: "Serve male, serve nequam et piger! Scire aiebas quia meto ubi non seminaveram et congrego ubi non sparseram. Oportebat ergo te pecuniam meam committere nummulariis, ut — postquam ego reversus essem — quod meum erat utique cum usura recepissem." Et iniungens ut ab eo talentum tolleretur eique daretur qui decem talenta habebat, "Omni," inquit, "habenti dabitur, et abundabit; ei autem, qui non habet, et quod videtur habere, auferetur ab eo. Et inutilem servum eicite in tenebras exteriores: ibi erit fletus et stridor dentium."

123 'Cum autem Filius hominis et omnes angeli cum eo in maiestate sua venerint, tunc sedebit super sedem maiestatis suae. Et congregabuntur ante eum omnes gentes et separabit eos ab invicem, sicut pastor segregat oves ab haedis et statuet oves quidem a dextris, haedos autem a sinistris. Tunc dicet Rex illis, qui a dextris eius erunt: "Venite, benedicti Patris mei, possidete vobis regnum paratum a constitutione mundi. Esurivi enim et dedistis mihi manducare; sitivi et dedistis mihi bibere; hospes eram et collegistis me; nudus et coperuistis me; infirmus, et visitastis me; in carcere eram, et venistis ad me." Amen, dico vobis, quamdiu fecistis uni ex his fratribus meis, mihi fecistis. Tunc dicet his qui a sinistris eius erunt: "Discedite a me, maledicti, in ignem aeternum, qui paratus est diabolo et angelis eius. Esurivi enim et non dedistis mihi manducare."' Et illos a ceteris omnibus praedictarum misericordiarum generibus longe abhorruisse exprobavit quibus priores usos fuisse praedixerat.

124 'Hominis cuiusdam divitis ager quidem erat, qui quotannis uberes fructus afferebat. Unde intra se cogitans dicebat: "Quid

sow, and gathering where you did not scatter seed; so I was afraid, and I went and hid the talent in the ground. Here you have what is yours.' The master replied to him and said, 'You wicked and worthless and lazy slave! You said you know that I reap where I did not sow, and gather where I did not scatter seed. Then you ought to have invested my money with the bankers, so that on my return I would have received what was my own with interest.' So he ordered that the talent be taken from him, and given to the one with the ten talents. 'For to all those who have,' he said, 'more will be given, and they will have an abundance; but from those who have nothing, even what they seem to have will be taken away. As for this worthless slave, throw him into the outer darkness, where there will be weeping and gnashing of teeth.'

"When the Son of Man comes in his glory, and all the angels 123 with him, then he will sit on the throne of his glory. All the nations will be gathered before him, and he will separate them one from another as a shepherd separates the sheep from the goats, and he will put the sheep at his right hand and the goats at the left. Then the King will say to those at his right hand, 'Come, you that are blessed by my Father, inherit the kingdom prepared for you from the foundation of the world; for I was hungry and you gave me food, I was thirsty and you gave me something to drink, I was a stranger and you welcomed me, I was naked and you clothed me, I was sick and you cared for me, I was in prison and you visited me. Truly I tell you, just as you did it to one of these my brothers, you did it to me.' Then he will say to those at his left hand, 'You that are accursed, depart from me into the eternal fire prepared for the devil and his angels; for I was hungry and you gave me no food.'" And He reproached those who shunned all other forms of mercy which He said that their ancestors had practiced.

"The land of a rich man produced abundant crops every year. 124 And he thought to himself, 'What should I do, for I have no place

faciam? Locum enim non habeo quo fructus meos recondere et collocare valeam." Et, paulo post, hoc se facturum aiebat: "Destruam horrea mea et maiora efficiam et in illis, capacioribus factis, congregabo omnia quaecumque nata sunt mihi et bona mea. Et postea dicam animae meae: 'Nunc, anima, quando habes bona multa in annos plurimos servata et posita: requiesce, comede, bibe, epulare quaeso.'" Illi autem, sic secum cogitanti, Deus "Stulte!" ait, "Hac nocte animam tuam abs te repetent; cuius ergo erunt quae parasti?" Sic est qui sibi thesaurizat et non est in Deum dives.'

125   Et ad discipulos conversus: 'Estote,' inquit, 'similes hominibus qui dominum suum a nuptiis revertentem propterea praestolarentur, ut cum venerit et pulsaverit confestim aperiatur ei. Beati servi illi, quos, cum reverterit dominus, utique vigilantes invenerit. Amen dico vobis, quod se praecingens faciet illos discumbere et ministrabit illis. Et, si vel secunda vel tertia vigilia venerit, et ita invenerit, beati erunt servi illi. Hoc autem scitote quia, si sciret pater familias qua hora fur venturus esset, vigilaret utique et non sineret perfodi domum suam. Itaque parati estote, quia hora qua non putatis Filius hominis veniet.'

126   'Quis est fidelis dispensator aut prudens quem dominus super familiam suam constituet, ut domesticis suis tritici mensuram opportuno tempore exhiberet? Beatus ille servus, quem, cum venerit dominus, ita facientem invenerit. Vere dico vobis quia super omnia quae possiderit constituet illum. Si quis vero, intra seipsum cogitans, sic dixerit: "Reversionem suam morabitur dominus," et ideo servos et ancillas percutere, edere quoque et bibere et insuper inebriari coeperit, veniet dominus servi illius in die, qua non sperat, et hora, qua ignorat, partemque eius cum infidelibus ponet. Ille autem servus, qui cognovit voluntatem domini sui et tamen non praeparavit neque fecit secundum voluntatem eius, vapulabit multis; qui vero non cognovit et digna plagis operatus est, paucis

to store and keep my crops?' A little later he said he would do this: 'I will pull down my barns and build larger ones, and once they have been enlarged, I will gather all my grain and my goods there. And afterward I will say to my soul, "Soul, you now have ample goods saved and laid up for many years; relax, eat, drink, be merry."' But as he thought this to himself, God said to him, 'You fool! This very night your life is being demanded of you. And the things you have prepared, whose will they be?' So it is with those who store up treasures for themselves but are not rich toward God."[36]

Turning to His disciples, He said, "Be like those who are wait- 125 ing for their master to return from the wedding feast, so that they may open the door for him as soon as he comes and knocks. Blessed are those slaves whom the master finds alert when he returns; truly I tell you, he will fasten his belt and have them sit down to eat, and he will serve them. If he comes during the middle of the night, or near dawn, and finds them so, blessed are those slaves. But know this, if the owner of the house had known at what hour the thief was coming, he would have been awake and would not have let his house be broken into. You must therefore be ready, for the Son of Man is coming at an unexpected hour."

"Who then is the faithful and prudent manager whom his mas- 126 ter will put in charge of his slaves, to give them their allowance of food at the proper time? Blessed is that slave whom his master will find at work when he arrives. Truly I tell you, he will put that one in charge of all his possessions. But if anyone says to himself, 'My master's return is delayed,' and if he begins to beat the other slaves, men and women, and to eat and drink and get drunk, the master of that slave will come on a day when he does not expect him and at an hour that he does not know, and will put part of him with the unfaithful. That slave who knew what his master wanted, but did not prepare or do what was wanted, will receive a severe beating. But one who did not know and did what deserved

utique vapulabit. Omnibus autem quibus multum datum est, et multum quaeritur ab eis. Ignem veni mittere in terram, et quid volo nisi ut accendatur et ardeat?

127 'Arborem fici habebat quidam plantatam in vinea sua et accessit ut ex illa fructum quaereret. Et cum nullum in ea fructum invenisset ad cultorem vineae conversus, "Ecce," inquit, "iam tres anni sunt ex quo nemo in ficulnea fructum quaerens carpere potuit. Ut quid amplius terram occupat?" At ille respondens dixit: "Dimitte quaeso illam etiam hoc anno donec circa eam effodero et stercoravero et nisi fructum fecerit succides eam."

128 'Homo quidam ab Hierusalem in Hiericho descendebat et, descendens, incidit in latrones, qui non modo ipsum depraedantes despoliaverunt, sed etiam usque adeo verberaverunt ut abeuntes semivivum hominem relinquerent. Forte accidit ut quidam sacerdos eadem via descenderet et viso illo tacitus praeteriit. Similiter et Levita, nescio quis, cum esset secus locum, ubi ille iacebat in terra, et videret eum, transivit velut mutus. Samaritanus autem quidam iter faciens dum prope accederet et videret eum misericordia motus est eique appropinquans se continere non potuit quin vulnera sua alligaret atque oleum et vinum desuper infunderet et illum in iumentum suum imponeret et demum in stabulum duceret et 129 curam eius ageret. Postridie namque duos denarios protulit et stabulario tradens ait: "Curam, quaeso, illius habe et quodcumque supererogaveris ego, cum rediero, restituam tibi." "Quis illorum trium," inquit Iesus, "videtur tibi proximus fuisse illi qui in latrones inciderat?" At ille dixit: "Is qui misericordiam fecit." Et ait illi Iesus: "Vade et similiter operare."

130 'Homo quidam duos filios aetate dispares habebat, et adolescentior ait patri: "Pater, da mihi, quaeso, portionem patrimonii quae me contingit." Unde pater, adolescentulo morem gerens, utrique substantiam eius aequis portionibus partitus est. Non multo post, qui minor natu erat, congregatis omnibus suis, in regionem longinquam peregre profectus est, ubi libidinibus indulgens, univer-

a beating will receive a light beating. From everyone to whom much has been given, much will be required. I came to bring fire to the earth. What can I wish but that it kindles and burns?

"A man had a fig tree planted in his vineyard; and he came to 127 gather fruit from it. When he found no fruit on it, he turned to the gardener and said, 'See here! For three years no one has been able to pluck fruit from this fig tree. Why should it be wasting the soil?' He replied, 'Please let it alone for one more year, until I dig round it and put manure on it. If it does not bear fruit next year, cut it down.'

"A man was going down from Jerusalem to Jericho, and en route 128 fell into the hands of robbers, who not only stripped him of his goods but also beat him so severely that, when they went away, they left him half dead. By chance a priest was going down that road; and when he saw him, he passed by without a word. So likewise a Levite, when he came to the place where he lay on the ground and saw him, passed by in silence. But a traveling Samaritan came near and saw him and was moved to pity. When he approached he could not but bandage his wounds, having poured oil and wine on them. Then he put him on his own animal, brought him to an inn, and took care of him. The next day he took out 129 two denarii, gave them to the innkeeper, and said, 'Take care of him; and when I come back, I will repay you whatever more you spend.' 'Which of these three,' Jesus asked, 'do you think, was a neighbor to the man who fell into the hands of the robbers?' He said, 'The one who showed him mercy.' Jesus said to him, 'Go and do likewise.'"

"There was a man who had two sons of different ages. The 130 younger of them said to his father, 'Father, please give me the share of the property that will belong to me.' So, to satisfy the young man, the father divided his property in equal shares between them. A little later the younger son gathered all he had and traveled to a distant country, and there he squandered his entire share

sam patrimonii sui portionem erogavit. Postquam vero omnia sua consumpsisset, factum est ut fames valida regionem illam vehementer urgeret. Quocirca, egestate quadam coactus, cuidam regionis illius incolae adhaesit, qui mox illum in villam suam misit, ut porcos pasceret. Et paulo post tanta ciborum penuria premebatur, ut ventrem suum de siliquis, quas porci manducant, implere cupe-
131 ret, et nemo illi dabat. Unde, poenitentia ductus atque in se reversus, sic secum ipse dicebat: "Quanti mercenarii in domo patris mei abundant panibus, ego autem hic fame pereo. Surgam et ibo ad patrem meum et dicam illi: 'Pater, peccavi in caelum et coram te: et iam non sum dignus vocari filius tuus; sed me sicut unum de mercenariis tuis facias quaeso.'" His dictis, inde abiens, domum ad patrem suum tendebat. Pater autem illius, ipsum longe ad se venientem conspicatus, misericordia motus est et accurrens cecidit super collum eius et osculatus est eum. Atque mox, inter osculandum, filius "Peccavi," inquit, "in caelum et coram te; et iam non
132 sum dignus vocari filius tuus." Audiens vero pater quae a filio dicebantur, ad servos suos conversus "Cito," ait, "proferte stolam primam et induite illum et date anulum in manu eius et calciamenta in pedes et adducite vitulum saginatum et occidite, ut manducemus et epulemur; quia filius mortuus fuerat et revixit, perierat et inventus est." Quibus omnibus — ut imperatum erat — expletis, epulari ac diem festum solemniter celebrare coeperunt. Cum autem alter filius senior ex agro, ubi erat, domum reverteretur, mox ut appropinquavit symphoniam et chorum audivit. Unde, quid illud esset ignorans, servum quemdam ad se accitum quae-
133 nam illa essent interrogavit. A quo cum fratrem suum ex peregrinatione domum revertisse atque propterea patrem, inter cetera, vitulum saginatum mactari fecisse, ut omnes epularentur et dies festos solemniter celebrarent, in responsis accepisset, ita indignatus est ut introire nollet. Pater ergo foras egressus rogabat illum ut ingrederetur. At ille patri suo in hunc modum respondebat: "Ecce tot annis serviens tibi, numquam mandatum tuum praeterivi et

on dissolute living. When he had spent everything, it happened that a severe famine ravaged that country. So goaded by need, he hired himself out to one of the local residents, who sent him to his country house to feed the pigs. A little later, he suffered from such lack of food that he would gladly have filled his belly with the silage that the pigs were eating; and no one gave him anything. Then, feeling regret and coming to his senses, he said to himself, 131 'How many of my father's hired hands have bread enough and to spare, but here I am dying of hunger! I will get up and go to my father, and I will say to him, "Father, I have sinned against heaven and before you; I am no longer worthy to be called your son; please treat me like one of your hired hands."' This said, he set off and went home to his father. But while he was still far off, his father saw him and was filled with compassion; he ran and put his arms around him and kissed him. Then the son said to him, 'I have sinned against heaven and before you; I am no longer worthy to be called your son.' But upon hearing his son's words, the father 132 turned to his slaves and said, 'Quickly, bring out the best robe and put it on him; put a ring on his finger and sandals on his feet. And get the fatted calf and kill it, so that we can eat and feast; for my son was dead and is alive again; he was lost and is found!' When these orders had been carried out, they began to feast and celebrate a holiday. The elder son returned home from the field, where he had been; and as he approached, he soon heard music and dancing. Not knowing the cause, he called one of the slaves and asked what was going on. When he learned from him that his 133 brother had returned home from his travels, and that his father had therefore, among other things, had the fatted calf killed, so that all could feast and solemnly celebrate a holiday, he became so angry that he refused to go in. His father therefore came out and asked him to come in. But he answered his father, 'Listen! For all these years I have been working like a slave for you, and I have never disobeyed your command; yet you have never given me even

tamen haedum numquam dedisti mihi, ut cum amicis meis epula-
rer. Sed postquam hic filius tuus, qui universam patrimonii sui
substantiam cum meretricibus in lupanaribus et postribulis degens
erogaverat, reversus est, illi vitulum saginatum occidisti." Pater
vero respondens, sic ei dicebat: "Tu, fili, semper mecum es, et omnia mea tua sunt. Nunc autem epulari et gaudere oportebat, quia
hic frater tuus mortuus fuerat et revixit, perierat et inventus est."

134   'Homo quidam erat dives et habebat vilicum, qui cum apud
eum diffamatus esset, quasi bona ipsius dissipasset, illum ad se
vocavit dixitque: "Quid hoc audio de te? Redde rationem vilicatio-
nis tuae; iam enim amplius vilicare non poteris." Audiens autem
vilicus quod sibi a domino dicebatur, intra se aiebat: "Quid faciam
nescio quando dominus meus a me vilicationem abstulerit. Nam
fodere non valeo et mendicare erubesco." Et paulo post inquit: "Id
profecto agam, ut cum amotus fuero a vilicatione me in domos
135   suas recipiant." Convocatis itaque singulis domini sui debitoribus,
dicebat primo: "Quantum debes domino?" Cum autem ille "Centum cados olei," respondisset, "Accipe," inquit, "cautionem tuam et
sede cito et scribe quinquaginta." Deinde alii aiebat: "Tu vero
quantum debes?" Qui "Centum choros tritici" respondebat, et ille
"Accipe," inquit, "litteras tuas et scribe octuaginta." Atque haec
cum dominus ab eo facta rescisset, laudavit vilicum iniquitatis,
quoniam prudenter fecisset; quia filii huius saeculi prudentiores
136   sunt filiis lucis in generatione sua. Ideo dico vobis: Facite vobis
amicos de mamona iniquitatis, ut—cum forte defeceritis—recipiant vos in aeterna tabernacula. Qui enim in minimis fidelis est,
et in maioribus fidelis est, et qui in modicis iniquus est, in maioribus quoque iniquus est. Si ergo in iniquo mamona fideles non
fuistis, quod vestrum est quis dabit vobis? Nemo potest duobus
dominis servire: aut enim unum odio habebit et alterum diliget,

a young goat so that I might feast with my friends. But when this son of yours came back, who has devoured his entire inheritance with prostitutes, spending his time in brothels and dens of vice, you killed the fatted calf for him!' The father replied, 'Son, you are always with me, and all that I have is yours. But now we had to celebrate and rejoice, because this brother of yours was dead and has come to life again; he was lost and has been found.'

"There was a rich man who had a manager, and charges were 134 brought to him that this man was squandering his property. So he summoned him and said to him, 'What is this that I hear about you? Give me an accounting of your management, because you cannot be my manager any longer.' Upon hearing his master's words, the manager said to himself, 'I do not know what to do, now that my master has taken the position away from me. I am not strong enough to dig, and I am ashamed to beg.' A little later he said, 'I will bring it about that, when I am dismissed as manager, people may welcome me into their homes.' So, summoning 135 his master's debtors one by one, he asked the first, 'How much do you owe my master?' He answered, 'A hundred jugs of olive oil.' He replied, 'Take your bill, sit down quickly, and make it fifty.' Then he asked another, 'How much do you owe?' He replied, 'A hundred bushels of wheat.' He said to him, 'Take your bill and make it eighty.' And when his master learned that he had so acted, he commended the dishonest manager because he had acted shrewdly; for the children of this age are more shrewd in dealing with their own generation than are the children of light. And I tell 136 you, make friends for yourselves by means of dishonest wealth so that when it is gone, they may welcome you into the eternal homes. Whoever is faithful in small matters is faithful also in large matters; and whoever is dishonest in modest matters is dishonest also in great matters. If, then, you have not been faithful with the dishonest wealth, who will give you what is your own? No slave can serve two masters; for a slave will either hate the one and love

aut uni adhaerebit et alterum contemnet. Non potestis Deo servire
et mamonae.

137   'Homo insuper quidam erat dives, qui purpura et bysso induebatur et quotidie splendide epulabatur. Et alter quidam erat pauper et mendicus nomine Lazarus, qui ulceribus plenus ad ianuam
eius iacebat ac de micis saturari cupiebat, quae de mensa illius divitis quotidie cadebant et nemo ei dabat; sed et canes veniebant et
iacentis pauperis ulcera lingebant. Non multo post factum est ut
moreretur mendicus et in sinum Abrahae ab angelis portaretur.
Mortuus est etiam et dives et sepultus est in inferno. Et, cum in
tormentis esset, elevans oculos suos vidit Abraham a longe et La-
138   zarum in sinu eius exsistentem recognovit. Unde ad Abraham clamans "Pater," inquit, "Abraham, miserere mei, et mitte, quaeso,
Lazarum, ut intingat extremum digiti sui in aquam, ut refrigeret
linguam meam, quia crucior in hac flamma." Abraham autem respondens illi "Recordare," inquit, "fili, qui recepisti bona in vita
tua, Lazarus vero mala perpessus est; nunc autem hic consolatur,
tu vero cruciaris. Et in his omnibus inter nos et vos chaos magnum firmatum est, ut hii qui volunt hinc transire ad vos non pos-
139   sint neque istinc huc ad nos transmigrare." Cui ita respondenti ait
dives: "Rogo ergo te, pater, ut mittas eum in domo patris mei (habeo enim quinque fratres), ut testetur illis ne et ipsi in hunc tormentorum locum veniant." Et ait illi Abraham: "Mosen et prophetas habent: eos audiant." At ille dixit: "Non, pater Abraham, sed
si quis ex mortuis resurgens ierit ad eos, poenitentiam agent."
Ait autem Abraham: "Si Mosen et prophetas non audient, neque
etiam credent si quis ex mortuis resurrexerit."

140   'Iudex quidam erat in quadam civitate, qui nec Deum timebat
nec homines reverebatur, et vidua quoque in civitate illa similiter
exsistebat, quae ad eum quotidie accedebat dicebatque "Vindica

the other, or be devoted to the one and despise the other. You cannot serve God and wealth.

"There was a rich man who was dressed in purple and fine linen 137
and who feasted sumptuously every day. There was another man, a poor man and beggar named Lazarus, who was covered with sores and lay at his door, who longed to satisfy his hunger with the scraps that fell each day from the rich man's table, but no one gave to him; even the dogs would come and lick his sores as he lay. Shortly thereafter the poor man died and was carried away by the angels to be with Abraham. The rich man also died and was buried in Hades. When he was being tormented, he looked up and saw Abraham far away and recognized Lazarus by his side. So he 138
called out to Abraham, 'Father Abraham, have mercy on me, and send Lazarus to dip the tip of his finger in water and cool my tongue; for I am in agony in these flames.' But in reply Abraham said to him, 'my son, remember that during your lifetime you received good things, and Lazarus suffered evil things; but now he is comforted here, and you are in agony. Besides, in all these matters a great chasm has been fixed between you and us, so that those who want to pass from here to you cannot do so, and no one can cross here to us from there.' So when he replied thus, the wealthy 139
man said to him, 'Then, father, I beg you to send him to my father's house—for I have five brothers—that he may warn them, so that they will not also come into this place of torment.' Abraham replied to him, 'They have Moses and the prophets; they should listen to them.' But the other said, 'No, father Abraham; but if someone rises from the dead and goes to them, they will repent.' Abraham said to him, 'If they will not listen to Moses and the prophets, neither will they be convinced even if someone rises from the dead.'

"In a certain city there was a judge who neither feared God nor 140
had respect for people. In that city there was also a widow who kept coming to him every day and saying, 'Grant me justice against

me de adversario meo." Quod iudex per multum tempus facere recusabat. Paulo post, poenitentia ductus, sic intra se dicebat: "Etsi Deum non timeo, homines non revereor, quia tamen haec vidua mihi molesta est, illam de adversario suo vindicare constitui, ne me forte in novissimo die veniens suggillaret." Ait autem Dominus: 'Audite quid iudex iniquitatis dixerit. Deus vero non faciet vindictam electorum suorum die noctuque ad se clamantium et patientiam habens in illis tollerabit? Amen dico vobis quia cito vindictam illorum faciet. Verumtamen Filius hominis veniens, putas ne inveniet fidem in terra?

141 'Duo homines, unus Pharisaeus alter publicanus, orandi gratia in templum ascendebant. Pharisaeus autem stans apud se orabat dicebatque: "Deus, gratias ago tibi, quia non sum sicut ceteri homines: raptores, iniusti, adulteri, neque sum etiam sicut publicanus iste. Ieiuno bis in sabbato, decimas do omnium quae possideo." Publicanus vero, a longe stans, ne⟨c⟩ oculos ad caelum levare audebat, sed percutiebat pectus suum dicens: "Deus, propitius esto mihi peccatori." Amen dico vobis, quia publicanus, Pharisaeo iustificatior, de templo in domum suam descendit, quoniam omnis qui se exaltat humiliabitur et qui se humiliat exaltabitur.'

142 Haec igitur Christi tam salubris, tam sancta catholicaque doctrina, quam piscatores (sine ullo scribendi cultu et arte verborum) litterarum monumentis ad salutem humani generis tradiderunt, paulatim usque adeo invaluit ut cuncti fere populi — mirabile dictu — docti pariter et indocti, servi et liberi, reges et principes, Graeci et barbari (praeter admodum paucos) omni cum reverentia summaque devotione iamdudum non immerito suscepisse videan-

143 tur. Nam quicumque hanc salutarem disciplinam servaverit, non olearum ramis, non coronis oleastri foliis intextis coronabitur, non opiparibus conviviis, non aereis statuis, non imaginibus variis coloribus adumbratis exornabitur, quemadmodum fortibus viris ex proeliis et agonibus victoriam antiquitus reportantibus in praecipuum quoddam virtutum suarum praemium donari consuevit;

my opponent.' For a long time the judge refused to do so; but later, regretting it, he said to himself, 'Though I have no fear of God and no respect for people, yet because this widow keeps bothering me, I have decided to grant her justice against her opponent, so that she may not finally wear me out with her visits.'" And the Lord said, "Listen to what the unjust judge says. And will not God grant justice to His chosen ones who cry to Him day and night? Will he delay long in helping them? Truly, I tell you, he will quickly grant justice to you. And yet, when the Son of Man comes, do you think he will find faith on earth?

"Two men went up to the Temple to pray, one a Pharisee and 141 the other a tax collector. The Pharisee, standing by himself, prayed saying, 'God, I thank you that I am not like other people, thieves, rogues, adulterers, or even like this tax collector. I fast twice a week; I give a tenth of all my income.' But the tax collector, standing far off, did not dare even to raise his eyes to heaven, but was beating his breast and saying, 'God, be merciful to me, a sinner!' Truly, I tell you, the tax collector went down from the Temple to his home more justified than the Pharisee; for all who exalt themselves will be humbled, but all who humble themselves will be exalted."

This, then, is Christ's salutary, sacred, and catholic teaching 142 which fishermen with no training in letters or rhetoric passed on through written texts for the salvation of humankind. And this teaching gradually gained strength until nearly all people — wondrous to say! — have long since rightly embraced it with the greatest reverence and devotion — people learned and unlearned, slaves and freeborn, kings and princes, Greeks and (with a few exceptions) barbarians. Whoever observes this salutary teaching will not 143 be crowned with olive branches or crowns plaited with fronds of oleaster, nor celebrated with sumptuous banquets, bronze statues, or colorful paintings, which were customarily bestowed as a special reward for their prowess on the brave men of old who won victory

non denique terra lacte et melle fluente potietur, velut Moses Iudaeis veteris legis praecepta servantibus pollicebatur, sed vita nullo umquam fine claudenda, cumque angelorum choris iugenda laetitia et ante regale thronum secura ac beata, omnipotentis Dei Patris et Filii et Spiritus Sancti praesentia perfruetur. Praevaricatores vero — ut verissime simul ac brevissime dixerim — cunctis tormentorum generibus cruciabuntur atque perpetuis et aeternis Gehennae suppliciis absque ulla umquam evadendi spe miserabiliter damnabuntur.

144

in battles and contests. Nor will he possess the land flowing in milk and honey, as Moses promised to the Jews who observed the precepts of the ancient Law. Rather, he will enjoy a life unbounded by any termination, a life of happiness joined with choirs of angels and secure and blessed before the royal throne in the presence of God the Father, Son, and Holy Spirit. But transgressors, to put it with the utmost truth and brevity, will be tortured by all kinds of torments and will be damned to the perpetual and eternal punishments of hell with no hope of escape. 144

LIBER QUARTUS

De morte Christi[1]

1   Cum ergo de praeparatione evangelica primo, de miraculis deinde ac postea de doctrina Iesu Christi, humani generis Salvatoris, tribus prioribus libris pro modulo nostro satis abundeque tractarimus, reliquum est ut de passione eius et morte ac resurrectione deinceps dicamus.

2   Itaque pontifices et scribae, propter miracula ab ipso variis regionibus celebrata sanamque doctrinam hinc inde publice seminatam, exardescebant atque usque adeo interdum effervescebant, usque adeo concitabantur, usque adeo fremebant, ut ipsum nonnumquam interemissent nisi forte populum timuissent, quoniam eum tamquam certum quemdam ac verum omnipotentis Dei prophetam vulgo haberi ac venerari intelligebant.

3   Non multo post occasione hominis capiendi a quodam Iuda proditore discipulo suo sibi praestita, in eum per hunc modum manus iniecerunt. Quippe Iudas, Simonis cuiusdam filius, cognomento Scarioth ab insula vel a villa quadam sic nuncupata, unde oriundus erat, instigante diabolo, paucis antequam azymorum festivitas Hierosolymis celebraretur (quae Pascha dicebatur) diebus intercedentibus, ducentesimo trigesimo secundo supra quinquies mille a creatione mundi, quarto vero ducentesimae secundae Olympiadis anno, ingenti avaritia simul et insania commotus, in atrium summi pontificis ad pontifices et scribas furibundus

4   fanaticusque contendit. Cum quibus triginta dumtaxat argenteos pro digna vel potius pro indignissima quadam tantae proditionis mercede pactus, sese magistrum suum in manibus eorum traditurum sponte sua pollicebatur. Hac igitur cum pontificibus et scribis conventione facta ictisque foederibus, sceleris perpetrandi oppor-

BOOK FOUR

On the Death of Christ

In the previous three books we have, according to our modest abil- 1
ity, sufficiently and amply treated, first, the preparation for the
Gospel, then the miracles, and finally the teaching of Jesus Christ,
the Savior of the human race. It now remains to discuss His passion, death, and resurrection.

Now, the priests and scribes were incensed by the miracles per- 2
formed by Him in various places and by His sound teaching so
widely disseminated in public. At length, they were so angry,
aroused, and indignant that they would have killed Him on several occasions, had they not feared the people: for they saw that
the public viewed and venerated Him as the reliable and true
prophet of God almighty.

Within a short time, the treacherous disciple Judas provided an 3
opportunity for arresting Him, and they laid hands on Him in
this way. Incited by the devil, this Judas, a son of Simon called
Iscariot after his native island or town, was overcome with enormous greed and madness. A few days before the feast of unleavened bread, which was called Passover, was celebrated in Jerusalem, the furious and frenzied Judas entered the chief priest's
courtyard to find the priests and scribes. (This was in the year
5232 since the creation of the world, or the fourth year of the
202nd Olympiad.) With the priests he agreed upon a payment of 4
a mere thirty pieces of silver as the worthy, or rather unworthy,
price for so great a betrayal, and promised of his own accord to
deliver his teacher into their hands. Having struck this deal and
made this pact with the priests and scribes, Judas sought an

tunitatem quaerebat. Proinde ad collegas suos—ne si forte abfuisset illis scrupulum suspicionis iniecisset—reversus, prima azymorum die una cum Iesu et cum discipulis suis paschales de more dapes comedebat.

5   Ac Iesus, qui occultas cordis sui cogitationes noverat, ad discipulos conversus 'Unus,' inquit, 'vestrum me traditurus est.' Quo verbo omnes, praeter Iudam, velut ingenti quodam ictu ac pavore percussi, quisque singillatim an ipse esset proditor Iesum interrogabat. At ille eis in hunc modum respondebat: 'Qui mecum,' inquit, 'in parapside manum intingit, hic me traditurus est. "Sed vae illi," sicut de eo scriptum est, "per quem Filius hominis tradetur, quippe longe ei melius erat si natus non fuisset" atque

> utinam sterili damnatus matre nequisset
> natalem sentire diem, nec luminis huius
> hausisset placidas flabris vitalibus auras.'

6   Ceterum proditor, huiusmodi terribilibus verbis nequaquam commotus, quasi hoc nihil ad se attineret vel potius quasi parvula quaedam ac frivola et omnino contemnenda res ageretur, 'Numquid,' ait, 'ego sum, Rabi?' Quod Iesus non palam, sed latenter per haec verba 'Tu dixisti' confessus est. Cenantibus autem illis, accepit Iesus panem atque de more benedixit et fregit deditque discipulis suis et ait: 'Accipite et comedite: hoc est corpus meum.' Similiter quoque de vino faciens 'Accipite,' inquit, 'et bibite: hic est
7   sanguis meus,' et reliqua. Proditori vero panis buccellam tradidit; quam cum accepisset, a daemone vehementius quam antea agitabatur. Sed cum discipulorum omnium pedes, ob nimiam quamdam ac paene incredibilem eius in omne genus hominum humilitatem, postea lavisset Iesus, confestim Iudas exinde abiit, ut eum proderet, indeque abiens a Domino audivit ut cito faceret quod facturus erat.

8   Paulo post ipse et discipuli ex urbe egredientes in Montem Oliveti contenderunt. Ibique parum commoratus, cunctos discipulos

opportunity to commit his crime. Accordingly, he returned to his fellow disciples, lest his absence arouse any suspicion in them; and on the first day of Passover he ate the traditional paschal meal together with Jesus and His disciples.

Now, Jesus, knowing the secret thoughts of his heart, turned to   5
his disciples and said, "One of you will betray me." At these words all the disciples but Judas were struck as if by a terrifying blow; and each of them singly asked Jesus if he was the traitor. And He replied to them in this way: "The one who dips his hand in the bowl with me will betray me. 'But,' as is written, 'woe to him by whom the Son of Man is betrayed! For it would have been far better for him had he not been born.'[1] And

> if only, condemned by a barren mother,
> He never experienced his natal day, nor inhaled
> With vital breath the peaceful air of this world."[2]

But the traitor was in no way moved by these terrible words. As if   6
they had nothing to do with him, or rather as if a small, trivial, and contemptible matter were at issue, he said, "Surely not I, Rabbi?" Jesus did not admit it openly, but cryptically in these words, "You have said so."[3] Now, as they ate, Jesus took bread and after the traditional blessing, He broke it and gave it to His disciples, saying, "Take this and eat: this is my body." And doing similarly with the wine, He said "Take this and drink: this is my blood," and so forth. He gave a morsel of bread to the betrayer,   7
who, upon receiving it, was even more violently tormented by the devil than before. Moved by His great and nearly incredible humility toward the entire human race, Jesus washed the feet of all His disciples; after Jesus had done so, Judas at once departed to betray Him, and as he departed heard the Lord tell him that he should quickly do what he planned to do.

Soon thereafter, Jesus and the disciples left the city and went   8
out to the Mount of Olives. After a brief pause there, He pre-

illa nocte propter se scandalum palam et aperte passuros esse
praedixit, ita scriptum esse testatus: 'Percutiam pastorem et dispergentur oves gregis.' Cui Petrus respondens: 'Et si omnes,' inquit, 'ut dicis, in te scandalum patientur, ego vero usque ad mortem
numquam scandalizabor.' Iesus autem illum ea nocte, antequam
gallus cantaret, se ter negaturum fore pronuntiavit:

> Namque illi, clara iamdudum voce fatenti,
> cum Domino se velle mori, 'Prius alliger,' inquit,
> 'quam gallus cantet, hac me ter nocte negabis.'

At Petrus constanter affirmabat etiamsi ipsum mori oporteret se
numquam id negandi sui scelus perpetraturum.

9   In quamdam deinde villam nomine Gethseman devenerunt,
quae trans torrentem Cedron ad radices Montis Oliveti sita erat,
ubi ortum quemdam esse constabat. Ibique ut sederent discipulos
admonuit eousque commoraturos quo ad orandi gratia parumper
secederet atque ad eos reverteretur. Tunc assumpto Petro et duobus aliis discipulis eius Iohanne et Jacobo, Zebedaei filiis, ob
propinquitatem mortis quam propemodum sibi affuturam atque e
vestigio tergo suo invasuram praevidebat, ita pavescere coepit ut
animam suam usque ad mortem tristem esse commemoratis[2] discipulis palam et aperte protestaretur, quibus praecepit ut secum
vigilarent. Et paululum progressus, in faciem suam, ut praedixerat,
orandi causa procubuit atque ita procumbens 'Pater,' inquit, 'si fieri
potest, calix iste praetereat; verumtamen iuxta placita tua fiat.'

10   Ad tres illos postea reversus, eos dormientes invenit. De quo
Petrum prae ceteris obiurgavit, una tantum hora secum vigilare
non potuisse redarguens. Deinde: 'Vigilate,' inquit, 'et orate, ne
intretis in temptationem; spiritus quidem promptus est, caro autem infirma.' Paulo deinde post illinc abiit atque eamdem sicut
prius fecerat orationem peroravit. Et iterum ad tres reversus, ad-

dicted that all the disciples would clearly and openly be scandalized because of Him that night, calling to witness that it is written: "I shall strike the shepherd, and the sheep of the flock will be scattered."[4] Peter answered Him, saying, "Even if all will be scandalized because of you, as you say, I shall never be scandalized even to my death." But Jesus foretold that he would deny Him three times that night before the cock crowed:

> For when he declared in a loud voice that he was willing
> To die with the Lord, "Before the winged cock crows,"
> Jesus said, "this night you will deny me three times."[5]

But Peter stoutly asserted that, even if he had to die, he would never commit the sin of denying Him.

Then they came to a place called Gethsemane, which lay across   9
the brook of Cedron at the foot of the Mount of Olives, where there was a garden. There He bade the disciples to sit and wait while He withdrew briefly to pray until He returned to them. Then He took with Him Peter and two other disciples of His, John and James, the sons of Zebedee. And foreseeing the imminence of His death, which was approaching and would soon arrive and suddenly assail Him from behind, He began to be so fearful that He plainly and openly declared to these disciples that His soul was sorrowful unto death, and He told them to stay awake with Him. Then He went a little farther and prostrated Himself to pray, as he had said; and thus prostrate, He said, "Father, if it is possible, let this cup pass from me; but let it be done according to your will."

Later, he returned to the three, and found them asleep. He re-   10
buked Peter more than the others, reprimanding him because he could not stay awake even a single hour with Him. Then He said, "Stay awake and pray that you are not led into temptation. The Spirit is willing, but the flesh is weak." Then a little later, He left and completed the prayer that he had begun earlier. And coming

huc dormitantes reperit (oculi namque eorum prae nimio somno oppressi ac gravati erant) et, relictis illis, tertio abiit eumdemque sermonem oraturus. Cum prolixius oraret, prae nimio sudore sanguineas guttas e toto corpore emittebat; atque ad perpetuam quamdam huius dominicae orationis commemorationem postea, eo loco ubi oraverat, basilicam condiderunt.

11   Postremo, angelicis exhortationibus adiutus, ad eos remeavit ac per haec verba eos a somno et sopore excitavit: 'Ecce appropinquat hora et Filius hominis tradetur. Vos autem dormitis et requiescitis, quasi ad vos haec personae meae traditio nihil attinere videretur. Surgite, eamus! Nam prope est qui me tradet.' Dum haec igitur ad discipulos loqueretur, ecce Iudas proditor, triginta argenteorum mercede corruptus, magna cum turba non inermi sed gladiis et fustibus armata adventabat, quos pontifices et seniores populi ad Iesum capiendum de industria mittebant.

12   Sed proditor, ne in magistro capiendo ob similitudinem Iacobi forte aberraretur—qui propterea frater Domini dicebatur, quoniam ei ceteris similior videbatur—satellitibus suis osculum signum dederat, ut scilicet quemcumque osculatus fuisset, illum repente apprehenderent. Et confestim appropinquans, ei salutem simul cum amaro et pernicioso vel potius cum suavissimo atque saluberrimo osculo hebraice dixit: 'Ave,' enim inquit, 'Rabbi' et osculatus est eum. At Iesus dicebat ei: 'Amice, ad quid venisti?' Tertio ad ceteros qui cum eo venerant conversus: 'Quid quaeritis?' interrogabat. Illi vero se Iesum Nazarenum quaerere respondebant. Et ille: 'Ego sum,' inquit.

13   Quo dicto, velut subita quadam epilepsia vel potius apoplexia illi correpti, abierunt retrorsum et ceciderunt in terram donec iterum interrogaret quem quaererent. Qui cum Iesum Nazarenum se iterato quaerere asseverassent et ille 'Ego sum' respondisset, in eum tanto impetu irruerunt, ut quasi in frustra dilaniaturi certatim comprehenderent. Ita enim mentibus consternati erant, ut quem Iudas osculatus fuisset minime recognoscerent.

to the three again, He found them asleep again, for their eyes were heavy and overwhelmed by great somnolence. So leaving them, He went away a third time to say the same prayer. Having prayed at great length, His entire body gave off drops of blood from his excessive sweat, and in the place where He had prayed they built a basilica as a perpetual memorial of the Lord's praying.

At length, comforted by angelic exhortations, He returned to   II them and woke them from their sleep and slumber with these words, "Behold, the hour is approaching, and the Son of Man will be betrayed. But you sleep and rest, as if this betrayal of me meant nothing to you. Rise up, let us go. For my betrayer is at hand." As he said this to His disciples, behold Judas the traitor, suborned by thirty pieces of silver, approached with a great crowd (not unarmed, but armed with swords and clubs) which the priests and elders of the people had purposely sent to seize Jesus.

But in order not to be misled in his Master's arrest because he   12 resembled James (who was afterward called the Lord's brother because he resembled Him more closely than the others), the traitor had given a kiss as a sign to his henchmen, that is, that they should at once seize whatever man he kissed. Quickly approaching Jesus, he greeted Him with a kiss that was bitter and deadly, or rather sweet and salutary, and said in Hebrew, "Hail, Rabbi!" And he kissed Him. But Jesus said to him, "Friend, why have you come?" A third time, He turned to the others who had come with Judas and asked, "What do you seek?" They replied that they sought Jesus of Nazareth. And He said, "It is I."

At these words, they fell back as if seized by sudden epilepsy or   13 rather apoplexy, and fell to the ground, until He again asked them whom they sought. When they had once more declared that they sought Jesus of Nazareth, and He had replied, "It is I," they rushed at Him so violently that they competed in seizing Him as if to tear Him to pieces. Their minds were so disturbed that they barely recognized the man whom Judas had kissed.

14   O impiam et sceleratam vel potius o impiissimam et scelestissi-
mam et omnibus saeculis detestandissimam et, si quid ultra dici
potest, exsecrandissimam omnipotentis Dei et innocentis hominis
proditionem simul atque capturam! Teque divinarum et humanarum rerum proditor appello, cuius perversissimam simul atque
stolidissimam mentem nunc etiam atque etiam intuens nec satis
admirari neque satis intelligere possum. Dic mihi, quaeso, quid
consequi putabas, scelestissime ac nimirum ceterorum omnium
infelicissime, si praeceptorem tuum non solum probum, sed etiam
divinum hominem vel, ut expressius dixerim, humanum deum,
hac iniquissima proditione in saevissimorum hostium suorum
15   manus coniecisses? Aut enim emolumentum aut voluptatem aliquam aut gloriam aut honorem consequi putabas, quandoquidem
homines huiusmodi rerum blandimentis ad peragenda et perpe-
tranda quaecumque mala facinora inducuntur? Non emolumentum, ut de singulis brevissime simul ac verissime dixerim; nam
pecunia, pro pretio venditionis vel potius proditionis accepta, ita
parva et vilis erat, ut ea causa te dumtaxat adductum scelestum et
antehac inauditum facinus perpetrasse non credam. Non voluptatem etiam, quae pessimo et iniquissimo sceleri nulla inesse poterat.
Relinquitur igitur ut gloria et honore adductus fecisse existimeris.
16   Sed qualis haec tua inanis gloria fieri valuerit, mecum ipse
etiam atque etiam cogitans, non sane intelligo, nisi forte eam
te gloriosam laudem ex hoc scelestissimo et iniquissimo facinore
consecuturum putasses, ut omnibus saeculis nomen tuum aeternis
litterarum monumentis damnatum memoraretur, ut quando virtutibus et benemeritis ac beneficiis honorem et gloriam consequi
non poteras, saltem inusitatis et inauditis proditionibus et sceleribus aeternum nomen nanciscereris, quemadmodum de duobus
scelestis perditisque hominibus apud idoneos auctores legisse meminimus.
17   Quorum alter Pausanias dicebatur: 'Is Hermoclem quemdam
percontatus quonam modo clarus subito posset evadere, cum in

O impious and wicked deed, or rather, most detestable in all 14
the ages, most execrable beyond words — the betrayal and capture
of almighty God and an innocent man! I call on you, betrayer of
things human and divine, for when I repeatedly contemplate your
most perverse and brutish mind, it exceeds my amazement and
comprehension. Tell me, please, what you thought you would gain,
most wicked and most wretched of all men, if by this base treachery you cast Him into the hands of His most savage enemies —
this man who was not only your upright Teacher, but even a divine human being, or, to speak more accurately, a human god?
Did you think to gain some reward or pleasure or glory or honor? 15
For such are the blandishments that lead men to perform and
perpetrate all kinds of evil misdeeds. Let me briefly and truthfully
address each one. It was not a reward, for the money that you took
as the price of your sale, or rather betrayal, was so small and contemptible that I cannot believe it alone led you to commit such a
wicked and unprecedented crime. Nor was it pleasure, since this
base and wicked crime could offer none. It remains, then, to consider that you acted for glory and honor.

Yet as I ponder repeatedly what would have been the nature of 16
that empty glory of yours, I fail to understand, unless perhaps you
thought to win glorious praise by this most wicked and base
crime, so that your name would be damned for all the ages in the
eternal records of history. Hence, when you could not attain honor
and glory by virtues and meritorious services and benefactions,
you would at least acquire eternal renown through unusual and
unparalleled betrayals and crimes, just as we recall reading in the
best authors concerning two wicked and depraved men.

One of these was named Pausanias. "He asked Hermocles how 17
he could suddenly become famous. As an answer, he learned that,

responsis accepisset si aliquem illustrem virum occidisset, futurum
ut gloria illius ad ipsum redundaret, continuo Philippum interemit
et quidem quod petierat assecutus est, siquidem tam se parricidiis
quam Philippum virtutibus notum posteris reddidit.' Alter quoque
inventus est qui Dianae Ephesiae templum incendere vellet, ut —
opere pulcherrimo consumpto — 'nomen eius per totum terrarum
orbem diffunderetur; quem quidem mentis furorem, eculeo postea
distentus, se eo incendio habuisse palam et aperte confessus est.'

18   His duobus tam perditis hominibus tu, Iuda, tertius ob nefarium proditionis tuae facinus non immerito ascriberis.[3] Quibus te
tanto scelestiorem non immerito fuisse et esse foreque censemus
quanto hoc tuum ineffabile scelus commemoratis duobus scelestis
facinoribus excellere ac praestare intelligimus. Quod si huius ne-
fandi sceleris memoria forte ulla umquam oblivione deleri potuisset — quandoquidem non virtutibus sed facinoribus gloriam quaes-
isse videbaris — equidem nomen tuum de litterarum monumentis
(non secus quam de libro vitae abrasum esse conspicimus)[4] auferre
abolereque temptarem, quemadmodum Ephesii publico civitatis
decreto de commemorata[5] templi sui eversione decrevisse narrantur.

19   Sed ceu Ephesii id, quod cupiebant, consequi non potuerunt,
quoniam Theopompus historicus ea ipsa historiis suis adnotaverat,
sic nos etiam multo minus optata nostra consequi valeremus,[6]
quoniam ⟨per⟩[7] et evangelistas et plures alios scriptores eccle-
siasticos ⟨diffamata⟩[8] singularis quaedam huius scelestissimae proditionis infamia nulla aetate, ceterorum omnium consumptrice,
aboleri poterat, non alienum forte putavimus si paucis verbis tum
soluta oratione, ut paulo ante feceramus, tum etiam carminibus, ut
mox apparebit, aliquatenus adaugeremus:

20   'Tune,' perditionis fili,

        cruente, ferox, audax, insane, rebellis
    perfide, crudelis, fallax, venalis, inique,

if he killed some illustrious man, that man's glory would pass to him. Pausanias immediately killed Philip, and indeed got what he wanted, for it made him as famous to posterity for his murder as Philip had been for his virtues."[6] The second man chose to burn down the temple of Diana at Ephesus, so that by the destruction of this beautiful work "his name would be spread throughout the entire world. For when he was later placed on the rack, he confessed clearly and openly that this mad scheme had driven him to set the fire."[7]

To these two depraved men, Judas, you may rightly be added as 18 a third for the vile crime of your betrayal. But we shall rightly deem that you were, are, and will be all the more wicked since we see that your unspeakable crime excelled and surpassed these two wicked misdeeds. Now, if the memory of this heinous crime could ever be erased and forgotten, since you obviously sought to win glory by misdeeds rather than by virtues, I would try to strike and strip your name from the history books—just as we see it has been erased from the book of life—just as the people of Ephesus are said to have published a city decree about the destruction of their temple.[8]

But just as the people of Ephesus could not get what they 19 wanted, since the historian Theopompus recorded the deed in his histories,[9] so even less can we attain what we wish, since the disgrace of this wicked betrayal, spread abroad by the evangelists and many other ecclesiastical writers, could not be erased by time, which destroys all other things. Hence we thought it appropriate to dilate on this briefly in prose, as we have just done, and in verse, as follows:

"Do you," O son of perdition, 20

bloodthirsty, savage, rash, insane, rebellious,
Faithless, cruel, deceitful, venal, unjust,

traditor[9] immitis, fere proditor, impie latro,
praevius[10] horribiles comitaris signifer enses
sacrilegamque aciem gladiis, sudibusque minacem
cum moveas, ori ora premis mellique venenum
inseris et blanda Dominum sub imagine prodis?
Quid socium simulas[11] et amica fraude salutas?
Numquid terribiles aut pax coniurat in enses
aut truculenta pio lupus oscula porrigit agno?

21 Quod quia tu nimis nefarie fecisti, aeternis et intollerabilibus cruciatibus torqueberis, quos ita magnos itaque ingentes esse puto, ut nullatenus adaugeri posse videantur. Sed redeamus unde digressi sumus, quandoquidem nos, sceleste proditor, indignabundi adversus te gladium orationis nostrae vel paululum vibravimus.

22 Interea, dum haec agerentur, Petrus, Christi discipulus, hanc magistri sui capturam permoleste ferens, gladio quo forte accinctus erat extemplo (iam paulo ante paschales de more dapes duobus gladiis abscisas comederant ac deinde id quod futurum de proditione audiverant extimescentes secum, si forte opus esset, se defendendi gratia[12] tulerant) Malcum, quemdam servum pontificis, in dextera eius auricula adeo percussit, ut eam penitus abscideret

23 atque a reliquo corpore avelleret. De quo quidem Iesus iam saevorum hostium suorum manibus deprehensus Petrum vehementer redarguebat admonebatque ut gladium in vagina sua reconderet. 'Qui enim,' inquit, 'alios gladio feriunt, ipsi gladio peribunt.' Et confestim abscisam auriculam memorato servo solo tactu ita restituit ac si numquam amputata fuisse videretur:

Nec enim vindicta Tonanti
conveniens humana fuit, qui milia Patrem

Harsh traitor, beastly betrayer, impious thief,
As the leading ensign do you escort dreadful swords?
When you lead sacrilegious troops, menacing with swords and
  stakes,
Do you press your face to His, and mix your poison with His
  honey,
And betray the Lord with a beguiling visage?
Why pretend to be an ally, and greet Him with friendly
  deceit?
Will peace conspire with grim swords,
Or a wolf give grim kisses to a pious lamb?[10]

Since you acted so nefariously, you will be tormented by eternal 21
and unbearable tortures, which I consider so great and enormous
that nothing could possibly add to them. But let us return where
we left off, since, wicked traitor, we have briefly wielded the sword
of our speech in outrage against you.

Meanwhile, while this was going on, Christ's disciple Peter was 22
greatly vexed by his Master's capture. He happened to be wearing
a sword, for a little earlier the disciples had eaten the Passover
meal in the customary way, slicing the food with two swords, and
then they bore them to defend themselves, if need be, since they
feared what they had heard was going to happen about the betrayal. With the sword Peter struck Malchus, a servant of the
priest, with such force on his right ear, that he sliced it completely
off. Jesus, who was already in the hands of his fierce enemies, 23
strongly reprimanded Peter and warned him to put his sword back
in its sheath, saying, "Those who wound others with the sword
will perish by the sword." Instantly, with a mere touch He restored the servant's severed ear so that it seemed never to have
been cut off:

  For human vengeance ill suited the Thunderer,
  Who could have asked His Father send Him angels,

angelicas sibimet legiones poscere posset
plus duodena dari, si vellet sumere poenas
de meritis quam sponte sua ignoscere plagas.

24 Paulo post ad turbas conversus: 'Tamquam ad latronem,' inquit,
'cum gladiis et fustibus comprehendendi causa venistis. Numquid
quotidie in templo docens apud vos sedebam?' Quod totum factum est ut scripturae prophetarum adimplerentur, ut 'illa foderunt
manus meas et pedes meos'; et alibi: 'Sicut ovis ad victimam ductus est'; et in alio loco: 'Ab iniquitatibus populi mei ductus est ad
mortem' ac sexcenta huiusmodi, quae quidem a nobis propriis locis
latius et opportunius explicabuntur.

25 Omnes vero eius discipuli quid ageretur conspicati, velut timore quodam perterriti postmodum—praeter unum solum ado-
lescentem, qui succinctus syndone eum sequebatur—aufugerunt.
Sed cum non multo post ipsum per syndonem apprehendissent,
reiecto et ipse syndone instar ceterorum repente nudus effugit.
Satellites autem Iesum per hunc modum captum ligatumque ad
Annam pontificem, Iosephi cuiusdam cognomento Caiaphae so-
cerum, qui et ipse anni illius pontifex erat (nam Iosephus, Hebraeus historicus, istum Caiapham unius tantum anni pontifica-
tum pretio redemisse testatur), cum tamen Moses Deo iubente
praecepisset ut pontifices patribus succederent atque ita generationis series in sacerdotibus texeretur, primum adduxerunt quod scri-
26 bae et Pharisaei iam pridem convenerant. Petrus vero et alter discipulus, qui pontifici notus erat, eum a longe sequebantur, donec
alter ille discipulus in atrium pontificis ingrederetur; qui, atrium
ingressus, hostiario persuasit ut Petrum introduceret. Per hunc
igitur modum Petrus in atrium pontificis introductus, cum ministris quibusdam ad ignem forte—frigus quippe erat—sedentibus
consedebat, ut exitum rei conspicaretur.

More than twelve thousand legions of them,
If He chose to punish the guilty as they deserved,
Rather than freely forgive His wounds.[11]

A moment later, He turned to the crowd, and said, "Have you   24
come out with swords and clubs to seize me as if I were a bandit?
Did I not sit with you daily teaching in the temple?" All this took
place so that the scriptures of the prophets might be fulfilled:
"They have pierced my hands and my feet."[12] In another place,
"He was brought as a lamb to slaughter."[13] And again, "For the
transgressions of my people was he led to death."[14] There are
countless passages like these, which we shall explain more fully
and appropriately in their place.

Now, when all the disciples saw what was happening, as if   25
struck with terror, they immediately fled, except for one young
man wearing a linen cloth, who followed Him. The mob soon
caught hold of his cloth, but he let it go and, now naked, at once
ran off like the others. The henchmen, who had in this manner
seized and bound Jesus, first led Him to Annas the chief priest,
the father-in-law of Joseph, known as Caiaphas, who was the
priest for that year (the Jewish historian Josephus writes that this
Caiaphas had purchased his priesthood for that one year alone,[15]
even though by God's commandment, Moses had laid it down
that priests should succeed their fathers, and thus create a succession of generations in the priesthood), where the scribes and
Pharisees had assembled. Peter and another disciple, who was   26
known to the chief priest, followed Jesus at a distance, until this
other disciple entered the courtyard of the chief priest. And having entered, he persuaded the janitor to admit Peter. In this way,
then, Peter entered the courtyard of the chief priest, where he
took his seat with some attendants who sat warming themselves
by a fire—for it was cold—to see what would happen.

27   Pontifices autem et universum concilium contra Iesum falsa testimonia quaerebant, ut eum interimerent. Sed cum multi falsi testes ad ipsum accessissent, quod cupiebant invenire non poterant. Novissime et duo falsi testes in publicum prodeuntes, saepe sese templum Dei destruere et post triduum reaedificare posse ipsum dixisse testificati sunt. Quibus Iesus nihil respondebat. Unde pontifex, quasi indignatus quod nihil responderet, actutum surrexit et 'Nihil,' inquit, 'ad ea respondes quae isti adversum te testificantur?' Iesus tamen tacebat. At ille: 'Per Deum verum,' ait, 'ad-

28 iuro te ut dicas nobis si tu es Christus Filius Dei!' Ad quod cum ipsum dixisse respondisset, statim adiecit: 'Verumtamen dico vobis, Filium hominis a dextris virtutis Dei sedentem et in nubibus caeli venientem paulo post videbitis.' Tunc pontifex, utpote capta hominis interimendi opportunitate quod se filium Dei fecisset, quasi magno dolore exasperatus, veteri et usitato lamentantium Iudaeorum ritu vestimenta sua rescidit, 'Quid amplius,' dicens, 'nobis opus est testibus? Nos ipsi ex ore eius manifestam Dei blasphemiam nuper audivimus; quid ergo vobis videtur?' At illi Iesum propterea reum mortis esse palam responderunt. Proinde quasi in reum capitis ultimoque supplicio dignum, cuncta tunc probrorum

29 genera exercebant. Alii namque in faciem suam quadam fiscicula velatam involutamque—vetusto quodam Iudaeorum more deperditis atque similibus ultimo supplicio damnatis hominibus—expuebant, alii colaphis caedebant, alii palmis percutiebant. Ceteri vero omnes ad unum illudebant, et 'Si tu es Filius Dei,' dicebant, 'prophetiza nobis qui te percutiebant.'

Heu mihi quantis
impedior[13] lacrimis rabidum[14] memorare tumultum,
sacrilegas movisse manus, non denique passis
⟨vel⟩[15] colaphis pulsare caput vel caedere palmis

The priests and the entire council sought false witnesses against 27
Jesus in order to have Him killed. Yet although many false witnesses approached Him, they could not find what they wanted. In
the end, two false witnesses came forth in public, and testified that
He had said He could destroy God's temple and rebuild it in three
days. Jesus did not reply to them. The chief priest was indignant
at His silence, and suddenly stood up, saying "Do you say nothing
in reply to the testimony these men bear against you?" But Jesus
remained silent. And the priest said "By the true God, I adjure
you to tell us if you are Christ, the Son of God." Now when He 28
had replied that he himself had said it, He added at once, "Nevertheless, I say to you that soon you shall see the Son of Man seated
at the right hand of God's power and coming in the clouds of
heaven." Then the chief priest seized this opportunity for putting
the man to death because He had claimed to be God's Son; and as
if exasperated by great indignation, he tore his garments in the
ancient and customary manner of Jews in mourning.[16] And he
said, "Why do we still need witnesses? We have just heard his
clear blasphemy of God from his own mouth. What then is your
verdict?" They openly replied that on this account Jesus was guilty
of a capital crime. So they subjected Him to every kind of insult,
as one condemned of a capital crime and worthy of the ultimate
punishment. Some of them spat in His face, which they had cov- 29
ered with a blindfold, according to the ancient Jewish custom for
men who were wicked and the like and condemned to death. Others struck Him with their fists, and others slapped Him. All the
rest, to a man, kept mocking Him, and saying "If you are the Son
of God, prophesy to us who they were who struck you."

Alas, how many tears
Prevent me from recounting that the crazed throng
Raised its sacrilegious hands? When they had
Struck blows to his head and slapped him with their palms,

371

aut spuere in faciem plebs execranda quievit!
Ille tamen patiens subiecto corpore totum
sustinuit nostraeque dedit sua membra saluti.
Namque per hos colaphos caput est sanabile nostrum,
haec sputa per Dominum nostram lavere figuram,
his alapis nobis libertas maxima crevit.

30   Dum haec igitur et cetera huiusmodi probrorum genera in
contumeliam[16] et illusionem Iesu Christi, Domini nostri, agerentur, ad Petrum in atrio pontificis prope ignem (frigus quippe erat,
ut diximus) sedentem ancilla quaedam accedebat ac sibi statim, ut
recognovit, ipsum cum Iesu Galilaeo fuisse exprobabat. At ille
coram omnibus quod ab ancilla obiciebatur, tametsi verum esse
cognosceret, negare tamen non dubitabat. Atque propterea inde
abiens, cum ex atrio egrederetur, forte eum alia ancilla in ianua
egredientem vidit, quae ibidem pluribus forte assistentibus plane
et aperte dixit: 'Et hic etiam cum Iesu Nazareno erat.' At ille in
iurando praestito sese hominem illum ullo umquam tempore cog-
31   novisse inficiabatur. Et paulo post qui illic assistebant, ei appropinquabant quasi ipsum ex facie recognoscerent. 'Vere,' inquiunt, 'et tu
de illis es, nec negare potes; nam et loquella tua manifestum te
faciet.' Non quia ipse alterius sermonis esset quam qui percontra-
rentur, omnes quippe Hebraei erant, sed quoniam unaquaque
provincia et omnis regio habet proprietates suas et vernaculum
loquendi sonum tenet, unde a ceteris discernitur. Quae cum natu-
32   ralia sunt, vitari non possunt. Petrus vero, quasi in manifesto quodam scelere ac flagranti crimine deprehensus, quid ageret nesciebat; sed ad negationes conversus, velut incertum quemdam salutis
suae portum ex magna tempestate confugeret, detestari et iurare
coepit expressisque iuramentis affirmabat quod nullis umquam
temporibus hominem cognovisset; et continuo gallus vocem suam
emittebat, quasi de industria cantaret, quod et Petrus auribus hau-
sit. Mox divini verbi recordabatur. Nam Iesus Petro paulo ante

And spat in His face, the accursed mob would not rest.
But He patiently bore every blow with his suffering body,
And offered up His limbs for our salvation.
By these blows our head may be healed;
Through the Lord this spittle has washed our face;
By these slaps our greatest freedom was born.[17]

While they practiced these and other kinds of insults to affront 30
and mock our Lord Jesus Christ, a servant girl came up to Peter as
he was sitting in the chief priest's courtyard near the fire (it was
cold, as we said) and, recognizing him, at once reproached him as
a companion of Jesus of Galilee. In front of everyone, Peter did
not scruple to deny the servant girl's accusation, even though he
knew it was true. As a result, he now left the place, but while he
was leaving the courtyard, another servant girl saw him coming
out the gate, and plainly and openly declared to the many people
there present, "This man, too, was with Jesus of Nazareth." But
swearing an oath, he kept denying that he had ever known Him.
A little later, the bystanders approached him, and seemed to rec- 31
ognize his face. "Truly," they said, "you are also one of them, and
cannot deny it; for your speech gives you away." It was not that his
language was different from theirs — since they were all Jews — but
each single province or region has its own peculiarities as well as a
local pronunciation that distinguishes it from others. This is both
natural and inevitable.[18] As if caught red-handed in an egregious 32
misdeed and a flagrant crime, Peter knew not what to do. He re-
sorted to denials, and as if fleeing from a great tempest to a doubtful port of safety, he began to deny and swear, and asserted by explicit oath that he had at no time known the man. Immediately, as
though intentionally, the cock crowed. Peter heard it, and at once
recalled the divine saying. For a little earlier Jesus had predicted to

praedixerat: 'Priusquam gallus cantaret, tertio me negabis.' Unde foras egressus et poenitentia ductus, usque adeo amare flebat, ut non indignam trinae negationis veniam mereretur.

33   Pontifex deinde Iesum de discipulis et de doctrina eius percontabatur. Iesus autem sese mundo palam praedicasse atque in synagoga semper docuisse respondebat. Proinde 'Quid me interrogas?' dicebat; 'Interroga illos, qui memet ipsum saepenumero audierunt.' Quod cum unus ex assistentibus audisset, quasi indigne admodum pontifici respondisset, confestim alapam dabat atque exprobabat quod sic (hoc est, parum reverenter) pontifici respondisset.

34   Postridie vero, mane facto, pontifices et seniores in domum Caiaphae convenerunt, quo Iesus ducendus erat. Qui quidem omnes in eodem maligno ac perverso innocentis hominis interimendi proposito, ceu in certa coniuratione, persistentes rursus adversus Iesum consilium inierunt, ut ubi ductus esset ad Caiapham, quasi certus et non dubitatus mortis reus ad Pontium Pilatum—tunc forte eius provinciae praesidem—mitteretur, ut praeses ipsum, iam mortis reum et ab illis propemodum ante damnatum, demum occideret. Hic Pilatus, cognomento Pontius (ex Ponto insula oriundus erat), Tiberio Caesare, qui Augusto successerat, duodecimo imperii sui anno Iudaeorum provinciam gubernabat. Nam tunc legatus Syriam regebat. Hunc enim de condemnandis reis morem servabant, ut quoscumque morti adiudicassent, eos idoneo iudici vinctos traderent, quatenus capitalem illorum sententiam exsequeretur.

35   Interea Iudas proditor Iesum iam prope morte damnatum cernens, poenitentia ductus triginta argenteos retulit, quos pro mercede proditionis—quemadmodum supradiximus—a pontificibus et senioribus acceperat: 'Pretium iniquitatis,' inquit, 'recipite. Nam ego in hac mea scelesta proditione sanguinem iusti hominis vendidi,' quasi in potestate sua, quandocumque vellet, iniquam illam et iniustam malignorum persecutorum mutare sententiam remaneret. At illi dixerunt: 'Quid hoc ad nos? Tu videris!' Et proiec-

Peter, "Before the cock crows, you will deny me three times." Peter went out, seized with remorse, and wept so bitterly that he deserved pardon for his triple denial.

The chief priest then questioned Jesus about His disciples and His teaching. Jesus replied that he had always preached openly to the world and taught in the synagogue. So He said, "Why do you ask me? Ask those who so often heard me." Hearing this, one of the bystanders thought that Jesus had answered the chief priest insolently, and immediately slapped Him, reproaching Him for answering the chief priest in this irreverent way. 33

On the morning of the next day, the priests and elders gathered in the house of Caiaphas, where Jesus was to be brought. Sticking to their malign and perverse design to kill an innocent man, as if in a set conspiracy, they all formed this plot against Jesus: as soon as He was brought before Caiaphas, He would be sent to Pontius Pilate, then the provincial governor, as clearly and indubitably guilty and deserving death and virtually condemned by them in advance, so that the governor might put him to death. Now, Pilate — known as Pontius after his native island Pontus — was governing the province of Judea in the twelfth year of his command in the interest of the emperor Tiberius, the successor to Augustus; at the time Syria was governed by a legate. The Jews observed this custom for condemning the guilty: whenever they assigned capital punishment, the condemned would be bound and handed over to the competent judge to carry out the death sentence. 34

Meanwhile, when Judas, His betrayer, saw that Jesus was virtually already sentenced to death, he repented and returned the thirty pieces of silver that, as related above, he had received from the priests and elders as payment for his betrayal. "Take this price of wickedness," he said. "For by my wicked betrayal I have sold the blood of a righteous man." He spoke as if it remained in his power, whenever he wished, to change the wicked and unjust verdict of Jesus' malign persecutors. But they said, "What is that to 35

tis argenteis in templo, exinde recessit ac mox eodem scilicet
daemone impulsus quo paulo ante inspiratus vel potius concitatus
nefarium tantae et tam immanis proditionis scelus perpetraverat,
laqueo se suspendit. Per hunc igitur modum

> infelicem animam laqueo suspendit ab alto.
> Lenior illa quidem tanto pro crimine culpa,
> cunctorum cui nulla foret par poena malorum.

36 Pontifices autem argenteis acceptis eos mittere in corbona (quod
hebraice 'sacramentum' significat, quoniam a corbam, quod latine
'sacrificium' interpretatur, ubi apud Iudaeos sacer thesaurus conde-
batur et sacrum aerarium dicebatur) minime licere dixerunt quod
pretium humani sanguinis esset; sed consilio quid de illis agi oporteret inito, exinde agrum quemdam figuli in sepulturam peregrino-
rum redemerunt. Propterea cognominatus postea fuit ager ille,
hebraice vel potius lingua Syrorum vel Chaldaeorum, 'Hachelde-
37 mach,' quod latine 'agrum sanguinis' significat. Id proptera divina
providentia factum esse videbatur, ut et pretium Salvatoris nostri
nullum peccatoribus illis et scaelestis ac perditis hominibus ad-
miniculum auxiliumque praeberet sed peregrinis potius requiem
aliquam consolationemque subministraret; et huiusmodi quoque
Hieremiae prophetae dictum adimpleretur: 'Qui acceperunt,' inquit, 'argenteos, pretium adpretiati, quem adpretiaverunt a filiis
Israhel; et dederunt eos in agrum figuli, sicut constituit mihi Dominus.'

38   Iesus igitur postremo ad Caiapham perductus, ad quem ab initio ducebatur, exinde postea ad memoratum Pilatum — provinciae,
ut diximus, praesidem — e vestigio transmittitur; ad quem iam
antea propterea transmittendus fuisse videbatur, ut morti traderetur. Per hunc itaque modum ad praesidem ductus, ante eum
stabat; praeses vero pro tribunali sedens, sic eum examinabat
dicebatque: 'Tu ne es rex Iudaeorum?' At Iesus nihil aliud quam
'Tu dicis' respondebat. Cum vero a principibus populi et seniori-

us? See to it yourself." Throwing down the pieces of silver in the temple, he departed. Then driven by the same demon that had earlier inspired, or rather inflamed him, to commit the nefarious crime of this great and monstrous betrayal, he hanged himself with a noose. In this way,

> he hanged his wretched soul from a noose on high,
> A mild guilt for so great a crime,
> For which no punitive evils sufficed.[19]

But the priests, taking the pieces of silver, said they could in no way be placed in the *corbona* (which in Hebrew means "sacrament," so called from *corbam*—or "sacrifice" in Latin—where the Jews hid their sacred treasure and sacred treasury), for it was blood money.[20] So conferring about what should be done with them, they bought a potter's field as a place to bury foreigners. Later this field was called *Hacheldemach* in Hebrew (or rather, in Syrian or Chaldean), which in Latin means "Field of Blood." Divine providence apparently arranged this so that the money for our Savior offered no aid or assistance to those wicked and depraved men, but rather offered some rest and consolation to foreigners. And this saying of the prophet Jeremiah was also fulfilled, "And they took the pieces of silver, the price of the one on whom the people of Israel had set a price, and they gave them for the potter's field, as the Lord determined for me."[21]

Brought at last before Caiaphas, to whom He was first led, Jesus was immediately thereafter taken before Pilate, the governor of the province, as we said; for He had to be taken first to him in order to be put to death. Thus Jesus was brought to the governor and stood before him. Seated before the tribunal, the governor examined Him and said, "Are you the king of the Jews?" But Jesus would only reply, "You say it." The leaders of the people and elders

36

37

38

bus accusaretur quod legem Iudaeorum subverteret et quod tributa dari Caesari prohiberet et quod regem et filium Dei se faceret, quasi mutus esset vel potius quasi huiusmodi Iudaeorum tam
nefaria ac tam scelesta accusatio nihil ad se attineret, perpetuo
silebat.

39   Pilatus vero illi placide humaneque dicebat: 'Non audis quanta
adversum te dicunt testimonia?' Iesus autem tacebat. Praeses vero
de tanta ac tam incredibili eius taciturnitate atque constantia vehementer admirabatur. Paulo post in praetorium venit et ad Iesum
iterum conversus an rex Iudaeorum esset interrogabat. Iesus autem
respondebat: 'A temet ipso hoc dicis an ab aliis audistis?' Cum autem Pilatus sic dixisset 'Numquid ego Iudaeus essem? Gens tua
et pontifices tui te mihi tradiderunt,' ait Iesus: 'Regnum meum
non est de hoc mundo. Si enim regnum meum de hoc mundo esset, ministri mei, ne Iudaeis traderer, utique decertarent.' Pilatus:
'Ergo,' inquit, 'rex es tu?'

40   His dictis ad turbas exibat et dicebat: 'Ego nullam in hoc homine causam invenio, quo crucifigi oporteat. Itaque crucifigite eum
vos.' At illi: 'Nos legem habemus,' responderunt, 'et secundum legem nostram debet mori, quia Filium Dei se fecit; quod quidem
prae ceteris capitali poena prohibetur, ut nostris legibus cavetur.'
Interea dum huiusmodi inter Iudaeos et Pilatum altercationes agerentur, intonuit praesidi quod Iesus vir Galilaeus erat et quod illius
causae cognitio ad Herodis tetrarchae potestatem dictionemque
pertinebat. Unde statuit ad eum, tunc per id tempus forte Hierosolymis commorantem, Iesum vinctum trasmittere.

41   Quo facto Herodes ob hanc ipsam Iesu Christi trasmissionem
admodum gavisus est, quod hominem illum fama undique increbrescente mirabilium atque incredibilium rerum effectorem diutius
convenire et alloqui concupiverat et signa ac miracula ab eo videre
apprime cupiebat sperabatque. Tum etiam cum Pilato, cui antea
infensus erat, in gratiam reverterat; ut autem satellites praesidis sui

accused Him of subverting Jewish law, of refusing to pay tribute to Caesar, and of claiming to be a king and the Son of God. But He still remained silent, as if He were mute or rather as if this wicked and nefarious accusation of the Jews had nothing to do with Him.

Pilate then said to Him calmly and humanely, "Don't you hear 39 how many testimonies are brought against you?" But Jesus remained silent. The governor was greatly amazed by such firm and incredible reticence and constancy. A little later he returned to his headquarters, and turning again to Jesus, asked if He was the king of the Jews. Jesus answered, "Do you say this on your own, or did you hear this from others?" Pilate said, "Am I a Jew? Your nation and priests have handed you over to me." Jesus said, "My kingdom is not of this world. If my kingdom were of this world, my followers would have fought to keep me from being handed over to the Jews." Pilate said, "Are you, then, a king?"

After he had said this, he went out to the crowd and said, "I 40 find in this man no ground for which he should be crucified. Therefore, crucify him yourselves." But they replied, "We have a Law, and according to our Law he must die because he claimed to be the Son of God. This crime above all others is prohibited by capital punishment as our laws prescribe." Now while the Jews and Pilate were thus disputing with each other, it dawned on the governor that Jesus was a man from Galilee, and therefore that the hearing of the case belonged to the power and jurisdiction of Herod the tetrarch. So he decided to send Jesus bound to Herod, who happened to be in Jerusalem at the time.

When this was done, Herod rejoiced that Jesus Christ was be- 41 ing handed over to him, for he had long desired to meet and speak with this man, whose fame had spread everywhere as one who performed miraculous and incredible feats. And he eagerly wished and hoped to see Him produce signs and miracles. At the same time, Herod became friends again with Pilate, who had previously been his enemy. When in obedience to the governor's command

imperio parentes ipsum ad Herodem adduxerunt, Herodes ipse de variis rebus multifariam illum interrogabat. At cum Iesus, velut mutus quidam, nihil ad eius interrogata respondisset, paulo post ipsum—veste alba illudendi gratia indutum—ad Pilatum remisit.

42   Pilatus autem, ad pontifices et scribas et plebem conversus, quid de Iesu facturus esset plane et aperte interrogabat. Vetus enim apud Iudaeos consuetudo erat, iam inde usque ab Aegyptiaca libertate repetita, ut hac anniversaria[17] azymorum solemnitate provinciarum praesides ex omnibus vinctis et in carceribus trusis quemcumque vellent populo liberandum dimitterent. Forte eo tempore unus et quidem insignis vinctus habebatur qui Barabbas dicebatur. Hic propter seditionem nescio quam homicidii scelere conditam trusus in carceres fuerat. Congregatis ergo illis, dixit Pilatus, ut veteri eorum consuetudini obsequeretur: 'Quem vultis dimittam vobis, Barabban an Iesum qui dicitur Christus?' Nam per invidiam ab eis illum insimulatum et traditum ac diversis capitalium iniuriarum generibus affectum fuisse intelligebat, quamvis eum de multis falso accusarent.

43   Forte praesidis uxor ad virum pro tribunali adhuc sedentem, antequam condemnaretur, admonitum veniebat, ne de iusto illo aliquid condemnandi gratia iudicaret, quod multa in somnis propter eum se vidisse asseverabat. Pontifices autem et seniores populi iam plebi persuaserant ut Barabban dimittendum, Iesum vero perdendum peterent efflagitarentque. Per hunc itaque modum ab illis persuasi, Barabban sibi dimittendum atque e carceribus liberandum postularunt. At praeses quid ergo de Iesu faceret, qui dicebatur Christus, interrogabat. Ad quod omnes, una paene et alta quidem voce, ut crucifigeretur respondebant.

44   Hic vero quid mali hunc hominem perpetrasse ut crucifigeretur percontabatur. At illi vehementius hac ipsa praesidis resistentia ac repugnatione irritati, ut crucifigeretur altius clamabant. Qua de re praeses aperte cernens quod suis interrogationibus non modo

his attendants had brought Jesus to Herod, Herod himself questioned Him on various subjects. But when Jesus, as if dumb, answered none of his questions, he soon put a white robe on him in mockery, and sent Him back to Pilate.

Pilate turned to the priests, the scribes, and the people, and 42 plainly and directly asked what he should do with Jesus. Now, ever since they had regained their freedom from Egypt, the Jews had an ancient custom that on the annual feast of unleavened bread the provincial governors would release to the people whatever man they chose from all those imprisoned and incarcerated. It happened that at the time there was a notorious prisoner named Barrabas. He had been incarcerated for fomenting a revolt involving the crime of murder. When the Jews now gathered, Pilate sought to comply with their ancient custom, and said, "Whom do you want me to release to you, Barrabas or Jesus, who is called the Christ?" For he realized that it was out of jealousy that Jesus had been accused by them, handed over to him, and charged with various kinds of capital offenses, although many of their accusations were false.

It happened that the governor's wife came to her husband still 43 seated before the tribunal, warning him not to condemn an innocent man; for she said that in dreams she had seen many visions on account of Him. But the priests and elders of the people had already persuaded the mob that they should ask and insist that Barrabas be released, but Jesus condemned. Thus persuaded by their leaders, the mob demanded that Barrabas be released to them and freed from prison. But the governor asked what he should do with Jesus, who was called the Christ. To which they all replied loudly and virtually in unison that He should be crucified.

Pilate asked what evil this man had committed that He should 44 be crucified. The masses were even more violently enraged by the governor's resistance and recalcitrance, and kept shouting even more loudly that He should be crucified. As a result, the governor

nihil proficeret sed potius obesset, quoniam propterea magis tu-
multuabant, accepta aqua, manus suas, coram omni populo, his
verbis palam et aperte parlavit: 'Innocens ego sum a sanguine iusti
huius; vos videritis,' quasi per hunc modum ab iniqua et impia
innocentis hominis condemnatione et quidem capitali per hunc

45   modum sese excusaret. At universus populus dicebat: 'Sanguis
eius, ne forte dubites, praeses, super nos et super filios nostros
corruens descendat.' Haec Iudaeorum imprecatio in universo eorum genere, illis dumtaxat exceptis qui ad Christianam et Catholi-
cam fidem mirabiliter convertuntur, incredibile dictu, hactenus
perseverat, necdum sanguis Domini ab eis aufertur, ut quotidie
in singulis quibusque Iudaeorum synagogis ubique exsistentibus
plane et aperte videmus.

46   Quo circa cum per duarum circiter horarum spatium in huiusmodi altercationibus ipse et Iudaei perstitissent, tandem et variis
illorum clamoribus et pluribus Herodis tetrarchae instigationibus
(metuentis ne forte regno tamquam alienigena pelleretur) commotus, victus superatusque, iuxta postulata eorum, sive ipse sententiam protulerit sive potius concesserit, ut ipsi de illo secundum legem suam iudicarent, Barabban e carceribus dimisit. At deinde
Iesum, iuxta Romanas leges, flagellandum eis tradidit ut, si liberet,
postea crucifigeretur. Romanorum enim legibus sancitum erat ut
qui crucifigeretur prius nonnullis flagellorum generibus verberare-
tur. Unde praesidis milites satellitesque, universa cohorte congre-
gata, ipsum in praetorio susceperunt eumque exuentes coccineam
chlamydem circumdederunt et plectentes coronam de spinis super
caput eius posuerunt atque in dextera eius harundinem dederunt
genibusque ante eum flexis ridiculis verbis illudebant dicebantque:
'Ave, rex Iudaeorum.' Et expuentes in eum, harundinem capiebant

47   et caput eius percutiebant. Haec autem omnia idcirco faciebant
quoniam rex Iudaeorum appellabatur. Et hoc ei velut abhomina-
bile quoddam crimen scribae et sacerdotes frequenter obiecerant,
quod sibi in populum Israhel usurparet imperium. Unde ante

clearly saw that his questions did more harm than good, only increasing the uproar; so taking water, he washed his hands before all the people, speaking these words clearly and openly, "I am innocent of the blood of this just man; see to it yourselves," as if in this way he would excuse himself from an innocent man's unjust and impious condemnation, and a capital sentence at that. But all the people said, "If perhaps you are in doubt, governor, let His blood flow rushing down on us and our children." Except only for those who are miraculously converted to the Christian Catholic faith, this curse of the Jews on all their race persists — incredible to say — to this day, and the blood of the Lord is not yet removed from them, as every day we plainly and clearly see in every single existing Jewish synagogue everywhere. 45

After Pilate and the Jews had spent about two hours in such disputing, moved at last by the various shouts of the crowd and the repeated urging of Herod the tetrarch (who feared being expelled from his realm as a foreigner), Pilate, defeated and conquered, acceded to their demands — whether he himself pronounced the verdict, or merely allowed them to judge him according to their own Law — and released Barrabas from prison. Then, according to Roman law, Pilate gave Jesus to them to be flogged and later crucified, if they wished. For Roman laws prescribed that one condemned to be crucified should first be subject to various forms of flogging. Hence, when the entire cohort had gathered, the governor's soldiers and attendants took Jesus to the headquarters. They stripped Him and put a purple robe on Him, and wove a crown of thorns that they put on His head. They put a reed in his right hand and knelt before Him and mocked and taunted Him, saying: "Hail, King of the Jews!" They spat on Him, and took the reed and struck Him on the head. They did all this because He was called king of the Jews. Indeed, the scribes and priests often reproached Him with the abominable crime of usurping power over the people of Israel. Hence, first of all He 46

47

omnia ipsum pristinis vestibus nudatum, pro rufo lembo, quo veteres reges utebantur, coccineam chlamydem induerunt, pro dya-
demate insuper coronam spineam eius capiti iniunxerunt, pro
sceptro deinde regali in manu sua calamum et harundinem tradiderunt. Et denique ipsum quasi regem illudendi gratia adorarunt.

48   Postea vero quam variis eorum illusionibus satis — ut sibi videbatur — illuserant, exuta chlamyde, prioribus suis vestibus indue-
bant. Postremo eum crucifigendi gratia ducebant; sed dum forte
ductores sui de urbe egrederentur, hominem quemdam Cyrenen-
sem, peregrinum et alienigenam, nomine Simonem, Alexandri et
Rufi patrem, convenerunt, qui forte de villa sua revertebatur. Hunc
igitur quasi opportuno tempore repertum, quoniam Iesus usque
assiduis adeo flagris verberibusque defessus erat quod patibulum
ulterius ferre ac portare non poterat, nimirum angariaverunt coe-
geruntque ut eius crucem baiulandi et adiuvandi gratia tolleret.

49   Per hunc itaque modum citius in Golgotha devenerunt, quod
ex Hebraea in Latinam linguam interpretatum 'Calvariae locus' ferebatur, ubi scilicet sontes puniebantur et ultima de eis supplicia
sumebantur et damnatorum capita abscindebantur; ex quo Calvariae, id est decollatorum, nomen assumpserat. Proinde vulgatus illorum error, quamquam aures populi mulcere videatur, plane et
aperte convincitur, qui primum hominem hoc in loco sepultum
fuisse atque propterea Calvariae nomen suscepisse testatur. In quo
numero Hieronymus noster, ceu in quadam eius epistola evidenter
apparet, exstitisse creditur. De quo quidem satis admirari cogimur.
Namque per ea, quae sacris litteris traduntur, Adam quodam loco
sepultum fuisse constat, ubi post multa temporum curricula oppidum condiderunt, quod idcirco Caria Tharben hebraice appellarunt, quoniam Abraham, Ysaac et Iacob, primi omnium patriar-
charum, una cum memorato humani generis conditore sepulti
fuisse narrantur. Id enim nomen 'quattuor virorum urbem' latine
significat.

was stripped of His former clothes, and instead of a red cloak (which ancient kings wore), they clothed Him in a purple robe, and instead of a diadem they set a crown of thorns on His head; and instead of a royal scepter they put a reed or cane into His hand. And then in mockery they worshiped Him as a king.

After they had mocked and taunted Him sufficiently, as they thought, they took off the robe, and clothed Him in His previous garments. Finally, they led Him out to crucify Him. But as his escort was leaving the city, they happened to meet with a man from Cyrene, a foreigner and alien, named Simon, father of Alexander and Rufus, who chanced to be returning from his country house. The encounter was quite timely, since Jesus was by now so exhausted by the unremitting lashes and blows that he could no longer bear the cross. So they pressed Simon into service and compelled him to take up and help carry His cross. 48

In this way, they soon came to Golgotha, which translated from Hebrew into Latin means the place of Calvary, where, that is, the guilty were punished, the final penalty was exacted from them, and the heads of the condemned men were cut off; hence it had taken the name of Calvary, that is, of the decapitated. Thus is plainly and clearly confuted the widespread error that seems to beguile the masses' ears, namely, that the first man was buried in this place and for that reason it received its name of Calvary. Among such people some have believed that our own Jerome was counted, as is manifestly clear from one of his epistles.[22] We can only find this quite surprising. According to what the Holy Scriptures record, Adam was buried in a place where, after the course of many years, they founded a city that was called Caria Tharben [Kiryat Arba] in Hebrew, because Abraham, Isaac, and Jacob—the first of the patriarchs—were said to have been buried there with the founder of the human race: for in Latin this name means the City of Four Men. 49

50   Hic ergo in medio duorum latronum crucifixus, cum se ardore quodam sitire significaret, vinum felle mixtum sitienti sibi barbara et inhumana crudelitate porrexerunt. Quod gustatum, velut amarum respuebat.

51   Quid ergo nos hic in tanto ac tam scelesto facinore, ut ait quidam vir eloquentissimus, deploremus aut quibus verbis tantum et tam immane nefas conqueremur? Non enim Gabinianam crucem describimus, quam Marcus Tullius, universis eloquentiae suae verbis ac viribus velut effusis totius ingenii fontibus, persecutus est, facinus indignum esse clamans civem Romanum contra omnes leges esse sublatum. Qui, quamvis innocens fuerit et illo supplicio indignus, mortalis tamen et ab homine scelesto qui iustitiam ignoraret patibulo affixus est. Quid de huius crucis indignitate dicemus, in qua Deus a cultoribus Dei suspensus fuit atque suffixus? Quis tam facundus et tanta rerum verborumque copia instructus exsistet? Quae oratio, tam affluente ubertate decurrens, ut illam crucem merito deploret, quam mundus ipse et tota—ut paulo post apparebit—mundi elementa luxerunt?

52   Postea vero quam milites qui ministrabant, hoc est carnifices, Iesum inter duos latrones medium—ut diximus—crucifixerunt, eius vestimenta acceperunt atque de omnibus indumentis suis, excepta dumtaxat tunica, contentione habita, pariter partientes, quattuor particulas constituerunt, ut unusquisque portionem attingentem carperet. Tunica vero quoniam inconsutilis desuper contexta per totum a militibus divisoribus reperiebatur, de non dividenda ea convenerunt. Itaque super illa sortem miserunt, cuius tota esse deberet. Hoc autem factum est, ut adimpleretur quod dictum est a Domino per prophetam David, qui 'Diviserunt,' inquit, 'vestimenta mea et super vestem meam miserunt sortem.' Quo facto servandi et custodiendi gratia sedebant.

53   Interea Iesus turpissime simul atque crudelissime patibulo—ut diximus—affixus, Mariam matrem suam iuxta crucem cum quibusdam aliis mulieribus astantem ac magno merore confectam

So it was here that Jesus was crucified between two bandits. 50
When He said that He was thirsty from the heat, with barbarous
and inhuman cruelty they offered the thirsty man wine mixed with
gall, which he tasted and spit out as bitter.

What can we here lament in such a great and wicked crime, as 51
a most eloquent man says, or with what words can we lament such
a great and monstrous sacrilege?[23] We are not describing the cross
on which Gabinius[24] died. Using a vast arsenal of eloquence drawn
from his deep founts of wit, Cicero denounced it, decrying as a
base crime the slaying of a Roman citizen against all laws. Now,
although Gabinius was innocent and undeserving of that punishment, he was still mortal and fastened to the cross by a wicked
man who knew no justice.[25] What shall we say about the indignity
of Christ's cross, on which God was suspended and nailed by the
worshipers of God? Who could be found so eloquent and possessing so great a wealth of ideas and words? Whose speech flows
with such rich amplitude that it could justly deplore Christ's cross,
which was mourned by the whole world and by all the elements of
the world, as we shall soon see?

Now, after the soldiers on duty — that is, the executioners — had 52
crucified Jesus between two bandits, as we said, they took his
clothes, and since there was a dispute, divided them equally, creat-
ing four parts (except only for his tunic), so that each got his
share. But the soldiers dividing the spoils found that the tunic was
seamless, and woven in one piece, so they agreed not to divide it.
They cast lots to see who would get the whole tunic. This was
done to fulfill what the Lord said through his prophet David, saying: "They divided my clothes, and for my clothing they cast
lots."[26] After this, they sat down to guard and keep watch.

Meanwhile, after Jesus was most basely and cruelly nailed to the 53
cross, as we said, He saw his mother Mary, afflicted with great
grief, standing near the cross together with some other women.
Also standing there was His disciple John, the son of Zebedee,

conspicatus, Iohanni, Zebedaei filio, eius discipulo similiter assistenti, quem ob virginitatem suam prae ceteris arctius ac vehementius diligebat, plurimum ac non immerito utpote virginem virgini commendavit. Nam ad eam conversus 'Mulier,' inquit, 'ecce filius tuus.' Similiter et ad Iohannem quoque ait: 'Ecce mater tua.' Et ex illa dominicae commendationis hora Iohannes eam velut propriam matrem accipiens semper tamquam verus eius filius postea veneratus est.

54   Super caput igitur Iesu Christi, per hunc modum crucifixi, eiusmodi mortis sui causam hebraice, graece et latine — secundum veterem Iudaeorum de omnibus ultimo supplicio damnatis consuetudinem — inscripserunt: 'Hic Iesus Nazarenus, Rex Iudaeorum,' ne forte ab aliquo eorum idiomatum vel paululum perito ac mediocriter erudito ignorari posset.

> Scribitur et titulus: *Hic Est Rex Iudaeorum*,
> quo nihil a deitate vacet. Nam caelitus actum
> hoc Hebraea refert, hoc Graeca Latinaque lingua,
> hoc docet una fides, unum ter dicere regem.

55   Hoc ego quotienscumque mecum ipse inter cogitandum etiam atque etiam considerabam, satis digne pro magnitudine rei admirari non poteram, stupens quonam modo falsis testibus, pretio ac mercede redemptis, et infelici populo ad seditionem clamoremque concitato, nullam aliam nisi quod rex Iudaeorum esset interfectionis ac mortis suae causam reperirent. Quod Iudaei paulo post accuratius legentes diligentiusque considerantes, a Pilato efflagitabant[18] ut eiusmodi inscriptionem, si exinde amovere nollet vel saltem immutaret, ut non *Rex Iudaeorum*, sicut scriptum erat, sed quod ipse se Iudaeorum regem fecerat,[19] mutatione facta, inscriberetur.

56   Pilatus vero eorum postulata iterum atque iterum conspicatus, non modo non admisit, sed etiam palam et aperte his verbis infitiatus repudiavit atque ita respondere non dubitavit: 'Quod scripsi,

whom He loved intimately and more strongly than the others because of his chastity. So He rightly commended His virgin mother to His virgin disciple. Turning to her, He said, "Woman, here is your son." Then He spoke in the same way to John, "Here is your mother." And from this hour of the Lord's commendation John embraced Mary as his own mother, and thenceforth honored her as her true son.

Thus they crucified Jesus Christ in this way, and above His 54 head they wrote the cause of His death, in accordance with the ancient Jewish custom for all those condemned to die, "This is Jesus of Nazareth, King of the Jews." This was written in Hebrew, Greek, and Latin, so that it could be read by anyone with even a little knowledge or learning in one of those languages.

> An inscription is written: "This is the King of the Jews."
> And it lacks not divinity, for by divine power it reports this
>   fact
> In the Hebrew, Greek, and Latin tongues.
> One faith teaches us to name one King three times.[27]

Now, I have repeatedly considered and pondered this, but I 55 could never feel astonishment adequate to the scale of this fact: after producing false witnesses suborned by bribes, and goading the miserable mob to clamorous riot, they found no other cause for Jesus' murder and death than his claim to be King of the Jews. A little later, when the Jews read the inscription more closely and reflected more carefully, they demanded that, if he refused to remove it, Pilate should at least to change it. Instead of "King of the Jews," as was written, he should change the inscription to say that "He *claimed* to be the King of the Jews."

Pilate considered their demands at length, but not only did 56 he not accept them, but he clearly and openly rejected them, and did not hesitate to reply as follows: "What I have written, I have

scripsi,' quasi ad hoc responsum faciendum divino spiritu ageretur atque id tunc ei diceretur quod in libro *Psalmorum* tanto ante praedictum fuerat: 'Ne corrumpas tituli inscriptionem.'

57   Qui autem praeteribant variis eum detestationibus blasphemabant eique illudentes capita sua movebant dicebantque: 'Vah, qui destruis templum Dei et post triduum illud reaedificas: salva temet ipsum! Si Filius Dei es, descende de cruce!' Similiter et pontifices cum scribis et senioribus his verbis illudebant: 'Alios salvavit, seipsum vero non potest salvare,' et cetera huiusmodi exprobabant. Eadem unus ex latronibus improperabat. Quem cum alter audiret, vehementer increpabat; et paulo post ad Iesum conversus: 'Memento,' inquit, 'mei, cum in regnum tuum veneris.' Quod adeo devote et humiliter postulavit ut a Iesu audire mereretur: 'Hodie, mecum eris in paradiso.'

58   Ante vero quam Iesus patibulo turpissime, ut diximus, affixus exspiraret, tenebrae inter sextam et nonam horam super universam[20] terram, ob admirabilem quamdam solis per tres horas obscurationem, extemplo apparuerunt. Quo quidem nonae horae tempore Iesus voce magna miserabilem vigesimi primi secundum Graecos ac Latinos, secundum vero Hebraeos vigesimi secundi *Psalmi* versum his verbis hebraice recitavit, atque 'Heli! Heli,' inquit, 'lama sabacthani?'[21] Quod enim in medio versiculi apud nos legitur ('Respice in me'), superfluum esse ii soli intelligunt qui linguam Hebraeam aliqua ex parte noverunt, quippe ad verbum ita in Hebraeo scriptum est, ut Domini noster—propriis vocibus suoque divinae maiestatis oraculo—expressisse legitur. Id latine interpretatur: 'Deus meus, Deus meus, ut quid dereliquisti me?'

59   Et statim sese sitire adiecit. Unde continuo unus ex eis cursim spongiam accepit, quam aceto infusam harundini superimposuit, ut huiusmodi tam dulcem ac tam suavem potum in extremo mortis articulo recreandi animi gratia porrigeret! Atque simul cum quibusdam Romanis—ut aiunt—militibus ac per hoc Hebraeae linguae expertibus et illic forte astantibus, dicebat 'Sinite, videamus si

written." It was as if the Holy Spirit moved him to give this reply and told him what had been foretold in the book of Psalms: "Do not destroy the writing of the inscription."[28]

Those who passed by cursed and mocked Him with various 57 oaths, shaking their heads and saying, "You who would destroy the temple of God and rebuild it in three days, save yourself! If you are the Son of God, come down from the cross." In the same way the priests, along with the scribes and elders, mocked Him, saying, "He saved others, but He cannot save Himself," and other such reproaches. One of the bandits rebuked Him in this way. When the other bandit heard this, he upbraided him loudly, and then soon turning to Jesus he said, "Remember me, when you come into your kingdom." He said this so devoutly and humbly that he deserved to hear Jesus say, "Today you will be with me in paradise."

Now before Jesus expired, basely nailed to the cross (as we 58 said), darkness suddenly covered the entire earth, between noon and three in the afternoon, caused by a miraculous darkening of the sun that lasted three hours. At the three o'clock, Jesus cried with a loud voice the pitiable verse in Hebrew, *Eli, eli, lama sabachtani*. (For the Greeks and Latins, this is Psalm 21; for the Jews, Psalm 22.) In the middle of the Latin verse, the phrase "Look upon me" is superfluous, as those are aware who know the Hebrew language to some extent.[29] For it is literally written in Hebrew as our Lord is said to have expressed it in His own voice and with the oracle of His divine majesty. In Latin this translates as "My God, my God, why have you forsaken me?"

He quickly added that He was thirsty. One of the soldiers ran 59 and got a sponge, soaked it in vinegar, and placed it on a reed. And they offered this sweet and pleasant drink to refresh Him in the final throes of death! And together, they say, with some Roman soldiers who stood by and knew Hebrew, the soldier said, "Let us

veniat Helias ad deponendum eum,' ignarus illius Hebraici verbi
quod Iesus afflictus paulo ante praedixerat.

60   Per hunc igitur modum gustato et abdicato aceti potu, 'Con-
summatum,' inquit, 'est.' Et paulo post, alta voce verum clamans,
'Pater,' ait, 'in manus tuas commendo spiritum meum.' Quo dicto,
mox inclinato capite xxxiii aetatis suae, eo vero a creatione mundi
quem supra diximus anno, octavo kalendas aprilis, Tiberio Caesare
imperante ac xviii imperii sui anno, extremum efflavit spiritum.

61   Unde in hac ultima eius acclamatione apertissime se verum
Deum esse omnibus paulo diligentius consuetas morientium hominum voces considerantibus ostendit, qui — dum moriuntur —
vix tenuem vocem emittere posse videntur. Defuncto igitur per
hunc modum humani generis Salvatore, plurima et varia miracula
e vestigio subsecuta sunt. Nam

> horrendae subito venere tenebrae,
> et totum tenuere polum maestisque nigrantem
> exsequiis traxere diem. Sol nube coruscos
> abscondens radios, taetro velatus amictu,
> delituit tristemque infecit luctibus orbem.

62   Et velum templi a summo usque deorsum in duas partes con-
fractum est, quod quidem omnia Iudaeorum secreta tunc primum
patuisse significabat. Quippe[22]

> ovans templum, maioris culmine templi
> procubuisse videns, ritu plangentis alumni,
> saucia[23] discusso nudavit pectora velo,

quod inter templum et sanctas sanctorum interponebatur, et terra
mota:

> Nec enim tellus sine clade fuit, quae talia cernens
> funditus intremuit dubioque in fine supremum
> expavit natura modum.

see whether Elijah will come to bring Him down." For he mistook the Hebrew word that the suffering Jesus had said shortly before.

Having tasted and rejected the drink of vinegar, Jesus said, "It is 60 finished." A little later, He cried in a loud voice, "Father, into your hands I commend my spirit." Having said this, He bowed His head and breathed His last, in the thirty-third year of his life, in the year of the creation that we have said above, on March 25, in the eighteenth year of the rule of the Emperor Tiberius.

By His last outcry, Jesus showed most clearly that He was the 61 true God to all those who have duly considered the usual words of dying men, who, at the point of death, can barely utter a faint sound. When the Savior of the human race had died in this way, many and various miracles immediately ensued. For

> horrible darkness suddenly descended,
> And occupied the whole sky, covering the blackened day
> With woeful obsequies; the sun, hiding its flashing rays
> In a cloud, and veiled under a foul mantle,
> Vanished and darkened the sad world with laments.[30]

And the curtain of the temple was torn in two from top to bot- 62 tom. This meant that all the secrets of the Jews were then revealed for the first time. In other words,

> the Temple triumphant, seeing Him fall from the top
> Of the great Temple, like one bewailing a nursling,
> Bared its wounded breast and tore its veil.[31]

This curtain separated the temple from the holy of holies, and there was an earthquake:

> Nor was the earth unscathed; beholding such things,
> It trembled from deep within, and in this dubious outcome
> Nature feared the final end.[32]

63 Et petrae scissae et monumenta aperta sunt et multa corpora sanctorum a mortuis resurrexerunt, qui de apertis monumentis exeuntes post resurrectionem suam in sanctam Hierosolymae civitatem
convenerunt et apparuerunt multis. Namque

> ruptae fatiscunt
> divisa compage petrae, rediviva iacentum
> corpora sanctorum fractis abiere sepulchris,
> in cineres animata suos.

64 Ceterum de tenebris exortis, quonam modo tam repente orien-
tur,[24] diversae sanctorum doctorum sententiae reperiuntur. Quidam namque huiusmodi obscuritatem per solarium radiorum sub-
tractionem divinitus factam, quidam vero per nubium densarum
intercessionem, nonnulli etiam per lunae inter solem et terram
non naturalem sed miraculosam interpositionem provenisse putaverunt. Nam Origenes, Hieronymus et Augustinus de hoc ipso
65 ab invicem dissenserunt. Sed Augustini opinio de solis defectione
ceteris praefertur. Quarto namque *De civitate Dei* libro ita ferme
inquit: 'Hanc solis defectionem, quae nimirum accidit cum Dominus et Salvator humani generis crudelitate atque impietate Iudaeorum crucifigeretur, non ex canonico siderum cursu accidisse manifestum est, quoniam tunc erat Pascha Iudaeorum, quod plena luna
solemniter agebatur.'

66 'Regularis autem solis defectio non nisi lunae fine contingit,'
propter quod Dionysius Areopagita, tunc forte in Aegypto degens,
ubi nubes caelorum aspectum nullatenus impediebant quominus is
solis defectus prospiceretur, quemadmodum ipse in epistola quadam palam et aperte commemorat ideoque huiusmodi eclipsim
plane et aperte conspiciens, admirabundus dixisse fertur, ut testatur astrologus: 'Aut Deus naturae patitur aut mundi machina dis-
solvetur.' Quod si, ut in fabulis legitur, solem (nefariis Atrei caedi-
bus nepotum suorum carnibusque eorum pro inhumanis dapibus,
coram Thyeste comedente, conspectis) usque adeo indignatum

Rocks were split, and tombs were opened, and many bodies of the   63
saints were raised from the dead. After His resurrection, they
came out of the open tombs and entered the holy city of Jerusalem
and appeared to many. For

> broken rocks gaped,
> As their fabric split, and the revived bodies
> Of saints that lay dead left the broken tombs,
> With life restored to their ashes.[33]

Now, we find various opinions of holy scholars concerning how   64
the looming darkness could arise so suddenly. Some thought that
this darkness was divinely caused by the withdrawal of the sun's
rays; others by the intervention of dense clouds; and still others by
the unnatural and miraculous interposition of the moon between
the sun and the earth. Indeed, on this point Origen, Jerome, and
Augustine disagree. But Augustine's theory of the solar eclipse is   65
preferred to the others. In Book 4 of the *City of God*, he writes
roughly as follows, "It is clear that the solar eclipse, which happened when the Lord and Savior of the human race was crucified
through the cruelty and impiety of the Jews, did not occur by the
natural course of the heavenly bodies, because it was then the Jewish Passover, which is solemnly celebrated with a full moon."[34]

"But a natural eclipse of the sun occurs only during a new   66
moon."[35] Now, at this moment Dionysius the Areopagite happened to be in Egypt, where (as he expressly states in a letter) no
clouds at all blocked the view of the heaven so as to prevent the
solar eclipse from being seen.[36] Hence, when he viewed the eclipse
plain and clear, he is said to have exclaimed in wonder, "Either the
God of nature is suffering, or the mechanism of the world will be
dissolved," as an astronomer informs us.[37] As one reads in dramas,
poets imagine that, upon seeing Atreus monstrously slaughter his
nephews and serve their flesh as an inhuman feast for their father
Thyestes to eat, the sun, with good reason, was so indignant as to

fuisse non sine certa quadam ratione poetae fingunt, ut radios suos ab usitato terrarum cursu rapuerit secumque continuerit, minime—ut arbitror—quamquam gentiles essent mirarentur si sol, decor caelorum et splendor orbis, in tantis ac tam immanibus et tam inauditis impiorum Iudaeorum adversus Creatorem suum facinoribus, ne conspicaretur, lucis defectum pateretur.

67   Non enim in cruce pendentem Dominum suum aspicere ausus est. Quod si etiam in morte Romuli, primi Romanorum regis, ipsum defecisse legimus, longe secus quam cum Dominus noster exspiraverit contigisse non dubitamus. Forte enim mortis suae tempore acciderat et solis defectio, quam certa ratione sui cursus effectam imperita nesciens multitudo eius meritis tribuebat putabatque ipsum in deorum numero collocatum, cum subito sole obscurato nequaquam comparuisset.

68   Nec solum haec et huiusmodi ingentia et inusitata miracula in sacris libris istac divinae passionis tempestate propalam apparuisse legimus, sed in ethnicorum quoque commentariis scripta reperiuntur. Nam et solis facta defectio adeo magna ut stellae in caelo viderentur et Bithynia terraemotu concussa et in urbe Nicaea aedes plurimae corruisse traduntur. Etenim Phlegon, ut ait Eusebius, egregius Olympiadum supputator, haec omnia eisdem temporibus palam et aperte accidisse testatur. Et Iosephus etiam, vernaculus Iudaeorum scriptor, circa haec tempora sacerdotes commotiones locorum et quosdam sonos sensisse confirmat. Deinde ex adito templi repentinam subito erupisse vocem dicentium: 'Transmigremus ex his sedibus.'

69   Centurio autem et ceteri crucifixorum custodes haec tanta et tam stupenda miracula conspicati vehementer admirabantur et usque adeo admirabantur ut magno quodam timore attoniti et perterriti illum Dei filium aperte cum magna nominis sui gloria fuisse faterentur. Cum vero non multo post crucifixorum corpora de

withhold its rays from their usual course over the earth and restrain them in his sphere. If that is so, in my opinion, even the Gentiles would scarcely wonder if the sun—the glory of the sky and splendor of the earth—amid the enormous, monstrous, and unprecedented crimes of the impious Jews toward their Creator, suffered an eclipse in order to avoid viewing them.

The sun, then, dared not view his Lord hanging on the cross. 67
When we read that the sun was eclipsed at the death of Romulus, the first king of the Romans,[38] we cannot doubt that the event occurred far differently from when our Lord expired. For at the time of Romulus' death, an eclipse of the sun occurred by chance. But the ignorant masses, not knowing that it was produced by the fixed system of its course, attributed it to his achievements, and thought he had taken his place among the gods, because after the sun suddenly darkened he could no longer be found.

At the time of the divine Passion, we not only read in Holy 68
Scripture that these and similar momentous and unusual miracles were made manifest; they are also found recorded in the histories of the Gentiles. For there was a solar eclipse so vast that the stars could be seen in the sky, Bithynia was shaken by an earthquake, and several buildings are said to have collapsed in Nicaea.[39] According to Eusebius, the distinguished calculator of the Olympiads, Phlegon clearly and openly attests that all these events took place at the same time.[40] The writer Josephus, a native Jew, confirms that around this time the priests felt the earth move and heard certain sounds. And from the inner sanctum of the temple a sound suddenly burst out of people saying: "Let us move out of this place."[41]

Now, when the centurion and other guards of the crucified men 69
saw these great and stupendous miracles, they were so powerfully amazed that in their astonishment and utter terror they openly confessed Him to be the Son of God to the great glory of His name. The bodies of the crucified ones had by law to be removed

cruce, iuxta id quod statutum erat, propter parasceven tolleren-
tur (nam postridie anniversariam paschatis solemnitatem celebrari
oportebat), milites praesidis latronum crura nondum penitus defunctorum quibusdam clavis perfregerunt, ut propterea citius mo-
rerentur. Quod itidem in Christo conficere cupientes, minime
confecerunt, quoniam ipsum iam antea exspirasse deprehenderent.

70   Quod idcirco factum esse videtur ut Scripturae prophetarum,
quae de ossibus eius non comminuendis loquebantur, penitus im-
plerentur. Sed quidam ex militibis, nescio quis, lancea latus eius
iam praemortuui percutiens, ita perforavit, ut aqua et sanguis —
mirabile dictu — continuo effluentes effunderentur. Quod ideo de
aqua factum esse videtur, ut ob id palam omnibus corpus eius
ex quattuor elementis compositum fuisse ostenderetur ac propterea detestabilis quorumdam haereticorum error convinceretur,
qui Christum caeleste vel fantasticum corpus habuisse tradiderunt.

71   De hac igitur tam impia et tam scelesta, vel potius tam pia et
tam gloriosa, Salvatoris nostri morte multum admodum lamenta-
rer. In quo quidem mihi — ut arbitror — non deesset oratio, nisi
eam solam humanae salutis causam plane et aperte exstitisse cog-
noscerem. Quod si Romanarum rerum scriptores de Caesaris per-
cussoribus quemquam neque triennio amplius supervixisse neque
etiam sua morte defunctum fuisse memoriae prodiderunt (omnes
namque damnatos, alios aliis casibus periisse memorantes, partim
naufragio, partim proelio occubuisse, nonnullos semetipsos eodem

72   illo pugione quo Caesarem violaverant interemisse scribunt) quid
de Iesu Christi, humani generis Salvatoris, interemptoribus existi-
mandum est? An eis secus quam Caesaris peremptoribus accidisse existimabimus? De Iuda enim proditore ac de Pontio Pilato,
qui iniqui iudicis est functus officio, utrumque mortem sibi ipsi
co⟨n⟩sciisse non dubitamus. Iudas quippe ita laqueo se suspendit,
ut medius crepuerit et viscera eius turpiter exciderint. Pilatus
quoque variis calamitatum casibus agitatus, tandem de salute sua

73   desperans, propriis manibus sese transverberavit. De reliquis inter-

from the cross because it was the day of Preparation—on the next day the Passover feast had to be celebrated—so the governor's soldiers broke the legs of the bandits, who were not quite dead, with clubs to finish them off. They wished to do the same to Christ, but did not do so, since they found that He had already died.

This seems to have been done so that the scriptures of the prophets might be completely fulfilled that said that His bones were not to be broken.[42] But one of the soldiers pierced his side with a lance so that water and blood—wondrous to say—immediately flowed out. He was seen to be made of water so that it would be clearly shown that His body was composed of the four elements, and so as to refute the detestable error of some heretics who have taught that Christ had a celestial or fantastic body.   70

I would greatly lament our Savior's death, so impious and wicked—or rather, so pious and glorious—and would not, I think, lack things to say on the subject, if I did not know that it was plainly and clearly the sole cause of human salvation. Now, apropos of Caesar's assassins, Roman historians record that none of them survived by more than three years, and none died a natural death. For they write that all of them were condemned, recording that they perished in various accidents, some in shipwrecks, some in battles, and some killed themselves by the very dagger with which they murdered the Caesar.[43] What then are we to think of   71

the slayers of Jesus Christ, the Savior of the human race? Shall we think they escaped the fate of Caesar's assassins? We do not doubt that Judas, His betrayer, and Pontius Pilate, who played the part of His unjust judge, both committed suicide. Judas hanged himself with a noose, so that his abdomen ruptured and his guts foully spilled forth. Pilate was tormented by various calamities, despaired of his survival, and ran himself through with his own hands. We can only believe that Jesus' other slayers perished har-   72

  73

emptoribus suis ipsos variis casibus actos interiisse credendum est, quandoquidem duos Herodes, patrem et filium alterum, ob saevam illam et inhumanam eius tunc forte pueri exsistentis persecutionem, xvii *Antiquitatum* libro variis diversarum calamitatum casibus agitatum, semetipsum interimere voluisse ac demum ita interisse legimus, ut super omnes, ceu Iosephus ipse testatur, infelicissimus moreretur; alterum vero ob persuasiones Pontio Pilato de morte Christi factas, una cum nefaria illa et scelesta Iohannis Baptistae decollatione, quemadmodum iure arbitror, a C. Caligula tetrarchia privatum ac Lugduni simul cum Herodiade, uxore sua, ex decimoctavi *Antiquitatum* libri lectione in exsilium actum fuisse

74 non dubitamus, quando insuper universae Iudaeorum genti maximas diversasque clades ab eius morte usque ad haec nostra tempora in dies semper supervenisse cognovimus. Nam, ut paucis ab initio repetamus, et temporibus Tiberii Romae et in Iudaea gentes novarum rerum turbationes, ita paulo post imperante C. Caligula varia mala et deinceps, defuncto Caligula, sub Claudii imperio validam et vehementem famem et seditionem insuper in paschatis solemnitate ita magnam omnibus Hierosolymis commorantibus provenisse accepimus, ut ii soli qui in foribus templi necati fuisse

75 dicuntur, triginta milia Iudaeorum numerarentur. Quid plura? Omissis Iudaeorum cladibus, quas saevis Neronis et ceterorum impiorum imperatorum temporibus sibi accidisse legimus, post commissum de nece Iesu Christi sacrilegium illud scelestum ac nefarium numquam ab eis seditiones, numquam bella, numquam mortes (per ea quae a diversis profanis sacrisque historicis scripta

76 sunt) cessasse manifestum est. Unde si Iudas, si Herodes, si Pilatus, particulares homines plus ceteris in mortem Christi machinati, semetipsos occiderunt; si universum insuper Iudaeorum genus qui tunc temporis vivebant; si non solum praedicti, sed omnes etiam qui postea usque ad tempora nostra nefariis illis et scelestis maioribus suis successerunt variis ac paene infinitis calamitatibus excruciati sunt—quemadmodum supra plane et aperte probasse

ried by various misfortunes, as did both Herods, father and son. In Book 17 of the *Jewish Antiquities*, we read that for his savage and inhumane persecution of the Christ child Herod the father was tormented by various calamities, wanted to kill himself, and finally died the most wretched death of all, as Josephus attests.[44] For persuading Pontius Pilate to kill Christ as well as for the impious and wicked decapitation of John the Baptist, Herod the son was rightly dismissed as tetrarch by Gaius Caligula and banished to Lyon with his wife Herodias—as we cannot doubt when we read Book 18 of the *Jewish Antiquities*.[45] Moreover, we know what great 74 and varied slaughters have continually plagued the entire Jewish nation from Jesus' death down to our own times. To cite only a few examples starting from the beginning, during the reign of Tiberius there were revolutionary riots in both Rome and Judea, and soon thereafter under Gaius Caligula there were various disasters. Then after Caligula's death, under Claudius there was a mighty and severe famine; and during the Passover feast so vast a revolt occurred among all those lodging in Jerusalem that the Jews killed on the steps of the Temple alone amounted to thirty thousand.[46] In short, leaving aside the slaughters of the Jews that we read had 75 occurred in the savage times of Nero and other impious emperors, the writings of diverse authors both sacred and profane make clear that, ever since the wicked and nefarious sacrilege of Christ's murder was committed, the Jews have not been free from revolts, wars, and murders. Hence, Judas, Herod, and Pilate—the individuals 76 who more than any others engineered Christ's death—took their own lives. Moreover, the entire Jewish race—both those already mentioned and all who succeeded their nefarious and wicked ancestors down to our time—was plagued by various and nearly innumerable disasters, as we have clearly and explicitly shown above.

videmur—nequaquam dubitari potest quin impiis Christi interemptoribus longe peiora quaedam quam Caesaris occisoribus, de
quibus ab idoneis auctoribus—quasi miraculi loco—scribitur, accidisse et evenisse intelligimus. Sed redeamus unde digressi sumus.

77   Interea Ioseph, quidam nobilis decurio, ab Arimathia civitate
Iudaeae oriundus, Christi ob metum Iudaeorum, ne forte de synagoga amoveretur, latens et occultus discipulus corpus eius iam antea praemortuui a Pilato sepeliendi gratia postulavit. Quod sicut
petierat, a praeside facile impetravit, ubi praeses ipsum a centu-
rione quodam cohortis praetoriae praefecto iam exspirasse rescivit,
quamquam de celeritate mortis eius miraretur. Unde Ioseph ipse
et Nicodemus quoque, vir nobilis ac legis et prophetarum peritis-
simus, de cruce primum corpus eius deposuerunt; variis deinde
aromatibus condiverunt, suspicantes ne forte putresceret, linteis et
institis eum sudario capiti adhibito, iuxta veterem Iudaeorum se-
78   peliendi ritum, ligaverunt. Postremo in monumento quodam novo,
quod Ioseph ex lapide quadrato in eodem loco exciderat ubi crucifixus fuerat, ipsum sepelierunt. Nam ibi forte ortus erat et in
orto memoratum monumentum exstabat. Ubi igitur ipsum hu-
maverunt, magno quodam saxo ad ostium monumenti advoluto,
confestim abierunt. Quod quidem monumentum paulo post pontifices et scribae armatis custodibus—non sine praesidis consensu—ideo munierunt, quoniam timebant ne eius discipuli noctu
corpus de sepulchro tollerent, et cum postea non inveniretur, ipsum a mortuis resurrexisse palam et aperte testarentur, sicut ipsum post tertium mortis suae diem se resurrecturum dicentem
audiverant, quasi parum in scelesta immensi facinoris perpetrati-
one, dum viveret, antea fecissent nisi etiam postquam ipsum mortuum ac sepultum esse cognovissent seductorem detrahendi gratia
appellarent.

79   Post haec ingens terraemotus ob angelos de caelo ad sepulchrum descendentes ita repente auditus est ut, lapide de sepulchro

As a result, no one can doubt that Christ's murderers suffered far worse fates than Caesar's assassins, about whom the best authors have written—a virtual miracle. But let us return now to the point where this digression began.

In the meantime, a certain Joseph, a respectable member of the 77 council who came from the Judaean city of Arimathea, had become Christ's disciple, but confidentially and in secret for fear of the Jews, so as to avoid expulsion from the synagogue. Before Christ died, he had asked Pilate to give him His body for burial. The governor readily granted the request, for he had learned from the centurion leading the praetorian cohort that Christ had expired, although he was surprised at the speed of His death. So Joseph, together with Nicodemus, a distinguished man and great expert in the Law and the Prophets, first took His body down from the cross. Then they applied various spices lest the corpse decay; and according to the ancient Jewish rite of burial, they bound His body with linen wrappings and bands and placed a cloth over His head. Finally, they buried Him in a new tomb that 78 Joseph had had carved from a square rock near the place where He had been crucified. For there was a garden in that place, and the tomb was in that garden. After burying Him, they rolled a large stone in front of the opening to the tomb, and immediately went away. A little later, with the governor's consent, the priests and scribes posted armed guards to secure the tomb, because they feared that His disciples might steal the body from the tomb at night and later, when the body was not found, they might publicly and openly claim that He was risen from the dead, just as they had heard Him say he would, on the third day after His death— as if they had done too little by wickedly committing an enormous crime while He lived, unless they were also to slander Him as a seducer, even after they knew Him to be dead and buried.

After this, there was the sudden sound of a great earthquake 79 caused by angels descending from heaven to the tomb, and the

revoluto, alter angelus supersederet adeo splendidus adeoque ornatus ut et aspectus eius instar fulguris appareret et vestimenta eius
candida ad similitudinem nivis viderentur.

Nam missus ab astris
angelus amoti residebat vertice saxi,
flammeus adspectu, niveo praeclarus amictu,
qui gemina specie terrorem et gaudia portans
cunctaque dispensans, custodibus igne minacem
venerat in formam Christum quaerentibus albam.

80 Custodes autem sepulchri, quamquam armati essent et ut delecti
milites audaces et intrepidi, prae magno tamen timore ita exterriti
sunt ut velut mortui iacerent. Itaque Golgothana rupe et antro illo
per hunc modum, avulsis inferni claustris, denuo corpus reddidit
animatum, quod exinde post quadragesimum resurrectionis suae
diem in caelum ascendit.

81   Maria vero Magdalena et nonnullae aliae mulieres videndi gratia ad monumentum venerant. Quae quidem, ut lapidem revolu-
tum conspexerunt, repente, quasi corpus inde ablatum fuisse minime dubitantes, recurrerunt atque Petro et Iohanni sublatum
Iesum renuntiarunt. Quo audito, statim ambobus ad monumentum cernendi causa currentibus, Iohannes iunior praecesserat; hic
festinabundus monumentum non ingrediebatur, sed sese inclinans,
diligenter intuens linteamina sola respexit. Hunc e vestigio Petrus
cursim assecutus intravit linteaminaque, uno cum sudario sui capitis velamento seorsum involuto, repente conspicatus est. Similiter
et Iohannes postea intravit et vidit et credidit quod a Maria antea
audiverat.

82   His visis, Maria Magdalena et ceteris mulieribus quae secum ad
sepulchrum venerant relictis, ad socios reverterunt. Maria autem
ad monumentum foris, ante illum saxei sepulchri locum stabat
plorabatque. Paulo post angelum quemdam, super lapidem revolu-
tum, a dextris sedentem, aperte viderunt, qui eas consolari cupiens

stone was rolled away from the tomb, and one of the angels sat above it so radiant and beautifully clothed that his appearance seemed like lightning, and his clothing white as snow.

> For sent from the stars
> The angel sat on top of the removed stone,
> Flaming in appearance, and shining in a snowy robe.
> His double aspect brought terror and joy,
> Dispensing all things. He came to the guards in the shape
> Of menacing fire, but seemed white to the seekers of Christ.[47]

The guards of the tomb were armed and, being select soldiers, 80 were bold and fearless. Yet even so, they were so struck with terror that they lay as if dead. Thus, on the hill of Golgotha and in that cave, the gates of the underworld were torn away, and His body was again revived,[48] which then ascended into heaven forty days after His resurrection.

Mary Magdalene and several other women came to see the 81 tomb. When they saw that the stone had been rolled away, they did not doubt that the body had been removed, but at once ran to tell Peter and John that Jesus had been taken away. When they heard this, both of them ran to the tomb to take a look. Being younger, John got there first; though he hurried, he did not enter the tomb, but stooping and carefully looking in, he saw only the linen cloths. Peter quickly caught up with him, and entering at once saw the linen wrappings, and the cloth that been on His head rolled up to one side. John, too, entered afterward and saw and believed what he had heard from Mary.

Upon seeing this, the disciples left Mary Magdalene and the 82 other women who had come with them to the tomb and returned to their companions. But Mary stood outside the tomb, in front of the site of the stone sepulcher, and wept. A little later, the women clearly saw an angel above the rolled-away stone and sitting on the

'Nolite,' inquit, 'timere; nam scio quod Iesum quaeritis, qui a Iudaeis crucifixus est. Non est hic. Surrexit enim sicut iam antea
praedixerat. Venite et videte locum ubi positus fuerat, et cum videritis discipulis eius renuntiate.'

83   Maria vero ad haec angelica verba lacrimabunda sese in monumentum prospiciendi gratia inclinabat. Hoc eius aspectu duos angelos albis vestimentis indutos conspexit, alterum ad caput, alterum ad pedes loci ubi divinum corpus collocaverant astantes; et
dicunt ei: 'Mulier, quid ploras?' 'Ideo,' inquit, 'ploro, quia tulerunt
Dominum meum, et nescio ubi posuerunt eum.' Et paulo post
angeli surrexerunt et ad commemoratas mulieres iam timentes et
vultum in terram declinantes conversi 'Quid viventem,' inquiunt,
'intra mortuos quaeritis? Non est hic, quoniam surrexit. Quod
facilius credetis, si verborum suorum, dum de hac eius resurrectione inter vos vivens loqueretur, recte memineritis.'

84   Maria autem retrorsum conversa, Iesum stantem vidit, quem
non cognoscebat, hortulanum esse rata. Et dicit ei Iesus: 'Mulier,
quid ploras? Quem quaeris?' Illa vero hortulanum esse, ut diximus, arbitrata 'Si tu, domine,' inquit, 'sustulisti eum, dicito —
quaeso — mihi ubi ipsum posuisti, ut ego tollere possim.' Dicit ei
Iesus: 'Maria.' Ad haec suavissima magistri sui verba conversa, eum
loquentem et nomen suum exprimentem recognovit. Et subito
amplectens, 'Rabboni' hebraice dixit (quod 'magistrum' latine significat). Dicit ei Iesus: 'Ne me tangas! Nondum enim ad Patrem
meum ascendi. Vade ad fratres meos et dic eis quod ascendo ad
Patrem meum.'

85   Unde confestim a monumento, hoc est ab illo ubi erat spatium
horti ante lapidem effossum, una cum aliis mulieribus egrediebа-
tur. Euntibus ergo ut discipulis nuntiarent, Iesus in itinere occurrit. Quae salute ab eo impartitae, ad illum accesserunt et pedes
eius tenuerunt et adoraverunt. Iesus vero exhortans eas ait: 'Ne

right. He sought to console them, saying, "Fear not; for I know you are looking for Jesus, who was crucified by the Jews. He is not here, for He is risen, as He foretold. Come and see the place where they laid Him, and when you have seen this, tell His disciples."

At these words of the angel, Mary, weeping, stooped to look   83
into the tomb. She beheld two angels in white clothes, one standing at the head and the other at the foot of the place where the divine body had been placed. They said to her, "Woman, why are you weeping?" She said, "I am weeping because they have taken my Lord, and I don't know where they have laid Him." And soon the angels stood up and turned to the women, who were frightened and staring at the ground, and said, "Why are you looking for the living among the dead? He is not here, for He is risen. You will easily believe this if you correctly recall the words He spoke about His resurrection when He lived among you."[49]

When Mary turned back, she saw Jesus standing there, but did   84
not recognize Him and thought He was the gardener. And Jesus said to her, "Woman, why are you weeping? Whom are you looking for?" Supposing Him to be the gardener, as we said, she said, "Sir, if you have carried Him away, please tell me where you have laid Him, so that I can take Him away." Jesus said to her, "Mary!" At these sweet words of her Master, she turned to Him, and hearing Him speak and say her name, she recognized Him. Embracing Him at once, she said in Hebrew *Rabboni* (which means "Master" in Latin). Jesus said to her, "Do not touch me, because I have not yet ascended to my Father. Go to my brothers, and tell them that I am ascending to my Father."

Together with the other women, she at once left the tomb, that   85
is, the place in the garden hollowed out in front of the stone. As they went to tell the disciples. Jesus met them on the way. When He had greeted them, they approached Him and held His feet and worshiped Him. Jesus exhorted them, saying, "Fear not; go,

timete; ite, nuntiate fratribus meis, ut in Galilaeam proficiscantur. Nam ibi me videbunt.' Quod a mulieribus factum sicut a Domino fuerat imperatum, discipuli non crediderunt. Hoc idem quidam ex custodibus, qui exterriti velut mortui iacuerunt, pontificibus nun-

86   tiaverunt, narrantes scilicet ea que ipsi audire poterant. Quo audito pontifices consilio[25] cum senioribus inito copiosam pecuniam militibus haec ipsa nuntiantibus propterea dederunt, ut discipulos eius intempesta nocte dormitantibus custodibus ipsis ad sepulchrum venisse indeque ipsum abstulisse testarentur. Ideo iterum atque iterum mirandum est quonam modo pontifices (qui saltem, ubi Christum a mortuis vere surrexisse cognoverant, ad poenitentiam erroris sui converti debuerant) in obstinata quadam mentis suae perversitate pertinaciter nimis insistere potuerunt ac pecuniam, quae ad usum templi designata fuerat, in mendacii redemptionem pervertere praesumpserunt, sicut triginta argenteos Iudae proditori antea tradiderant. Quo circa huius mendacii fama in dies, ut fit, increbrescens, usque adeo hactenus invaluit ut inveteratae Iudaeorum perfidiae vel sola vel certe propria causa fuisse videatur.

87   Deinde Simoni, cognomento Petro, discipulo suo, dum solus esset, apparuit. Eadem forte huius solitariae — ut ita dixerim — apparitionis die duo ex discipulis suis, Cleopas et Lucas, in castellum quoddam nomine Emmaus tendebant, et graece a veteribus Nicopolis appellabatur, quod sexaginta circiter stadia a Hierosolymis distabat. Euntes autem de his, quae nuper acciderant, ut fit, in itinere ad invicem confabulabantur. Iesus vero dum illis peregrini hominis habitu appareret eisque appropinquaret,[26] quales eorum sermones essent et cur ita tristes esse viderentur interrogare coepit.

88   Cui Cleopas: 'Tu solus,' inquit, 'peregrinus es in Hierusalem et quae ibi facta sunt de Iesu Nazareno ignoras, qui maximus prophetarum fuit in opere et sermone, cum Deo et hominibus praepotens? Et quemadmodum deinde pontifices eum crucifigendum tradiderunt?' Postremo de mulieribus referebat, quae ex monu-

tell my brothers to go to Galilee. They will see me there." This was done by the women, as the Lord had commanded. But the disciples did not believe them. Some of the guards who had lain as if dead from fear reported the same thing to the priests, relating what they themselves had been able to hear. When the priests heard this, they hatched a plot with the elders and gave a large sum of money to the soldiers who had reported this, so that they would attest that His disciples came to the tomb in the middle of the night while the guards were asleep, and carried off the body. One cannot sufficiently marvel at the priests. For when they had learned that Christ had truly risen from the dead, they should at least have been changed and repented of their error. Instead, they were able to persist in their stubborn perversity, and presumed to divert money destined for use in the Temple in order to purchase a lie, just as they had earlier given Judas the betrayer thirty pieces of silver. As a result, the fame of this lie grew daily, as happens, to such a degree that it seems to be the sole or at least the essential source of the ancient perfidy of the Jews. 86

Then Jesus appeared to His disciple Simon, called Peter, when he was alone. Now on the day of this solitary appearance, as it were, two of His disciples, Cleopas and Luke, happened to be going to a village called Emmaus—which in Greek was called Nicopolis by the ancients—that lay about sixty stades[50] from Jerusalem. As they walked, they talked on the way—as is usual—about recent events. Jesus appeared before them in foreign garb; and approaching them, He began to ask what they were discussing, and why they seemed so sad. Cleopas replied, "Are you the only stranger in Jerusalem who does not know about the events there concerning Jesus of Nazareth, who was the greatest prophet in deed and word, and mighty before God and men, and how the priests then handed Him over to be crucified?" Finally, he told 87 88

mento redeuntes ipsum e mortuis resurrexisse asseverabant, quod
a quibusque condiscipulis, qui eo videndi gratia accesserant, repertum fuisse affirmabatur, et cetera huiusmodi enarrabant ut illis
89 diebus nuper acciderant. At ipse eos stultos et tardos in omnibus
de credendis[27] quae de eo fuerant prophetata testatus, 'Nonne,' inquit, 'Christum pati passumque in gloriam suam intrare oportebat?' Et a Mose incipiens et per singulos tendens prophetas qui de
eo loquebantur illis divina veterum sanctorum scriptorum oracula
interpretabatur. Dum haec igitur ad invicem confabularentur, memorato castello appropinquabant, at Iesus ulterius se tendere pro-
ficiscique dissimulabat. Illi vero ut secum commoraretur, quoniam
sol iam in occasum vergebat, peregrinum hominem arbitrati, etiam
90 atque etiam rogabant. Itaque eorum precibus obsecutus, una cum
ipsis in castellum ingrediebatur. Omnibus autem postea come-
dendi causa discumbentibus, iuxta consuetudinem suam, panem
accepit, benedixit et fregit. At vero dum illis fragmenta porrigeret,
ob haec consueta magistri sui signa ipsum adapertis repente oculis
agnoverunt. Quo facto confestim evanuit nec amplius in conspectu
eorum apparuit. Illi autem haec omnia conspicati, invicem prae-
terita repetebant intra sese, non sine singulari admiratione dicentes: 'Nonne cor nostrum ardens erat in nobis dum in via nobiscum
loqueretur prophetarumque scripturas interpretaretur?' Ac e vestigio surgentes Hierosolymam reverterunt atque ad discipulos suos
contendentes, ipsos cum plurimis aliis una congregatis de memo-
rata magistri sui ad Simonem apparitione invicem disserentes invenerunt.

91   Haec ergo ubi ipsi ab illis invicem confabulantibus acceperunt,
ea etiam quae sibi in via acciderant omnia enarrarunt atque plane
et aperte retulerunt quemadmodum eum tandem in fractione panis secum discumbentes cognoverunt. Cum autem haec et huiusmodi de variis Christi apparitionibus invicem loquerentur, Iesus
repente (dum quidam nomine Thomas, qui Didymus dicebatur,
forte abesset), in medio eorum stetit, et salute impertita dixit eis:

Him about the women who, returning from the tomb, asserted that He had risen from the dead. Some of their fellow disciples had gone to see, and affirmed that they found this true. And they told Jesus other such things that had recently happened in those days. Calling them foolish and slow to believe all that had been 89 prophesied about Him, Jesus said, "Was it not necessary that Christ should suffer and by suffering enter into His glory?" Then beginning with Moses and continuing one by one through all the prophets who had spoken about Him, He interpreted to them all the divine prophecies of the ancient Holy Scriptures. As they talked among themselves, they neared the town. But Jesus pretended that He set out bound for a further destination. Since the sun would soon set, thinking Him a foreigner, they repeatedly asked Him to stay with them. So yielding to their entreaties, he 90 entered the town together with them. When all reclined at dinner, as was His custom, Jesus took bread, blessed it, and broke it. As He offered them the pieces of bread, this customary gesture of their Master suddenly opened their eyes, and they recognized Him. At this, He immediately vanished, and appeared no more in their sight. Having seen all this, they recalled to each other the past events, and with singular amazement said, "Wasn't our heart burning within us when He spoke to us on the road, and interpreted the writings of the prophets?" At once, they rose up and returned to Jerusalem to join the other disciples, and found them, with many others who had gathered together, discussing their Master's appearance to Simon.

When they heard this from the others, they in turn related ev- 91 erything that had happened to them on the way and reported plainly and clearly how at supper they had finally recognized Him at dinner in the breaking of bread. While they were talking about this and other appearances of Christ (the disciple named Thomas, called Didymus,[51] happened to be absent), Jesus suddenly stood

'Pax vobis. Ego sum, nolite timere.' Conturbati vero et exterriti, se spiritum videre existimabant. Qua de re, 'Quid,' inquit, 'turbati estis, et quales in corda vestra cogitationes ascendunt? Videte manus meas et pedes meos, quia ego ipse sum. Palpate et videte quia
92   spiritus carnem et ossa non habet, sicut me videtis habere.' Et cum haec dixisset ostendit eis manus et pedes. Adhuc autem illis non credentibus et prae gaudio mirantibus, 'Habetis hic aliquid,' inquit, 'quod manducetur?' At illi partem piscis assi et favum mellis obtulerunt. Et cum coram eis manducasset, reliquias assumpsit eisque dedit. Discipuli itaque, viso Domino, supra quam dici potest gavisi sunt. At Iesus iterum dixit eis: 'Pax vobis. Sicut misit me Pater et ego mitto vos.' Atque his dictis paulo post insufflavit et dixit: 'Accipite Spiritum Sanctum; quorum remiseritis peccata, remittuntur eis, et quorum retinueritis, retenta sunt.'

93   Insuper ad eos conversus 'Haec,' inquit, 'sunt verba quae vobiscum loquar, quoniam necesse est impleri omnia quae scripta sunt in lege prophetis et *Psalmis* de me.' Et illis abstrusum scripturarum sensum aperuit, ut plane et aperte intelligerent sic scriptum esse testatus quoniam sic oportebat Christum pati et tertia die a mortuis resurgere et praedicari in nomine eius poenitentiam et remissionem primo omnibus Hierosolomitanis, deinde ceteris gentibus. 'Vos autem horum omnium testes ac martires estis. Ego vero promissum Patris mei in vos mittam; vos autem sedete, quoadusque virtutem ex alto induamini.'

94   Post octo quoque dies omnes forte discipuli una cum Thoma, qui eum prius — ut diximus — ceteris condiscipulis apparentem non viderat aliisque de apparitione Domini quae eis nuper acciderat referentibus non crediderat, intus commorabantur. Et Iesus potentia maiestatis suae clausis ingressus ianuis — mirabile dictu! — in medium accessit. In medio quoque consistens 'Pax vobis,'

among them, and greeted them, saying, "Peace be with you. It is I; fear not." They were startled and terrified, and thought they saw a ghost. So He said, "Why are you frightened, and what thoughts are arising in your minds? Look at my hands and my feet; see that it is I myself. Touch me and see, for a ghost does not have flesh and bones, as you see that I have." And when He had said this, 92 He showed them His hands and His feet. While they were still disbelieving and marveling in their joy, He said, "Have you anything here to eat?" They gave Him a piece of broiled fish, and a honeycomb. And after He had eaten in their presence, He took what was left and gave it to them. Seeing the Lord, the disciples were joyous beyond words. Then Jesus again said to them, "Peace be with you. As the Father has sent me, so I send you." When He had said this, He breathed on them and said, "Receive the Holy Spirit. If you forgive anyone's sins, they are forgiven; if you retain their sins, they are retained."

Next, turning to them, He said, "These are the words that I 93 speak to you, since everything written about me in the Law, the prophets, and the psalms must be fulfilled." Then He opened to them the hidden meaning of the scriptures, so that they plainly and clearly understood. For thus it is written, He declared, that Christ had to suffer and rise again from the dead on the third day, and that repentance and forgiveness should be proclaimed in His name first to all in Jerusalem, and then to the other nations. "You are the witnesses and martyrs of all these things. I am sending you what my Father promised; so stay here until you have been clothed with power from on high."

A week later all the disciples happened to be together inside 94 with Thomas, who had not previously seen Jesus appear with the other disciples, as we have said, and who did not believe the others' report of what had recently happened to them. And by the power of His majesty Jesus entered the closed doors—wondrous to say!—and came into their midst. Standing there, He said,

inquit. Et paulo post, ad Thomam conversus, 'Infer,' ait, 'digitum tuum huc et vide manus meas, et affer manum tuam et mitte in latus meum et ne sis incredulus sed fidelis.' Ad haec dominica verba Thomas humiliter fideliterque respondens 'Dominus,' inquit, 'meus et Deus meus.' Dicit ei Iesus: 'Quia vidisti me, Thoma, credidisti; beati qui non viderunt et crediderunt.'

95   Septem etiam ex discipulis dumtaxat ad mare Tiberiadis piscandi gratia commorantibus Iesus in litore mane iam facto luceque exorta manifestatus est. Nondum tamen ipsum cognoverunt. Sed cum paulo post numquid pulmentarium haberent interrogasset eos, illis sese non habere respondentibus quod tota illa nocte piscantes nihil capere potuissent, 'Mittite,' inquit, 'in dexteram navigii rete et invenietis et capietis.' Quo sicut eis iniungebatur repente facto, rete prae magnitudine piscium trahere non poterant. At Iohannes prae ceteris recognoscens confestim 'Dominus,' inquit, 'est.' Cum vero Petrus Dominum esse audisset, mox tunica
96   (erat enim nudus) se subcinxit in mareque intravit. Alii autem discipuli navigio venerant, ut rete, tanta piscium multitudine refectum, attraherent. Ut ergo in terram descenderunt, dixit eis Iesus: 'Afferte de piscibus quos nunc apprehendistis.' Ascendit Petrus ut rete attraheret traxitque magnis piscibus plenum numero tres supra centum quinquaginta; et tamen rete ob multitudinem tantorum piscium minime scindebatur. Dicit illis Iesus, parato prandio: 'Venite et prandete.'[28] Et cum paulo post discubuissent, nemo discumbentium eum interrogare audebat quis esset, quia ex his quae viderant Dominum esse non ignorabant. Accepit deinde Iesus panem similiter et piscem et dabat eis.
97   Postea vero quam prandissent, Iesus Petrum interrogabat an se plus ceteris discipulis suis diligeret. Quod cum in responsis illum plus ceteris omnibus ipsum diligere accepisset, respondit Iesus: 'Pasce agnos meos.' De quo cum Iesus iterum ac tertio interrogasset, ipsum et idem responsum ab eo retulisset, demum innuens

"Peace be with you." Then, turning to Thomas, He said, "Put your finger here, and see my hands. And reach out your hand and put it in my side. Do not doubt, but believe." To these words of the Lord, Thomas replied humbly and faithfully, "My Lord, and my God!" Jesus said to him, "You have believed me because you have seen me, Thomas. Blessed are those who have not seen and have believed."

Now, seven of the disciples went fishing in the Sea of Tiberias. 95 Jesus showed Himself to them on the shore just after daybreak. But they did not yet recognize Him. Soon He asked them if they had caught any food, and they replied that they had fished all night but had been able to catch nothing. He said, "Cast your net to the right side of the boat, and you will find and catch some." So they immediately did as He bade them, and because of the number of fish they could not haul in the net. But John, recognizing Him before the others, quickly said, "It is the Lord!" When Peter heard that it was the Lord, he put on some clothes—he was naked—and jumped into the sea. But the other disciples came in a 96 boat, to haul the net, which was filled with such a great number of fish. When they landed, Jesus said to them, "Bring some of the fish you have just caught." Simon Peter went aboard to haul the net in, and hauled in more than one hundred fifty-three large fish. Yet despite the great number of fish the net was not broken. When the meal was prepared, Jesus said to them, "Come and eat." And when they had then taken their places, none of them dared to ask Him who He was, because they knew from what they had seen that He was the Lord. Then Jesus again took the bread and the fish and gave it to them.

When they had finished their meal, Jesus asked Peter whether 97 he loved Him more than the other disciples. After He heard Peter answer that he loved Him more than all the others, Jesus replied: "Feed my lambs." When Jesus asked him a second and third time, and heard the same answer from him, then hinting at the death

qua morte esset moriturus sibi clanculum praedixit. Postremo 'Sequere,' inquit, 'me.' Conversus Petrus Iohannem, eius condiscipulum, vidit et interroganti 'Domine, hic autem quid?,' respondit ei Iesus. 'Sic eum volo manere donec veniam; quid ad te?'

98   Undecim insuper discipulis in quodam Galilaeae monte forte consistentibus apparens Iesus manifeste ac propalam visus est, quem ubi aperte viderunt, confestim adoraverunt. Unde accedens Iesus eis in hunc modum loquebatur: 'Data est' dicens 'mihi omnis potestas in caelo et in terra. Euntes ergo docete omnes gentes, eos in nomine Patris et Filii et Spiritus Sancti baptizantes et docentes eos probare omnia quaecumque mandavi vobis. Et ecce ego vobiscum sum omnibus diebus usque ad consummationem saeculi.'

99   Novissime commemoratis eisdem undecim, dum forte simul recumberent, in propatulo apparuit et incredulitatem et duritiem cordis sui palam et aperte exprobavit, quoniam iis qui eum viderant resurrexisse non crediderant. Et dixit eis: 'Euntes in universum mundum, praedicate Evangelium omnibus gentibus. Quicumque crediderit et baptizatus fuerit hic profecto salvus erit; qui autem non crediderit procul dubio condemnabitur. Signa vero haec et huiusmodi eos qui crediderint consequentur; in nomine meo daemonia eicient, linguis loquentur novis, serpentes tollent, et, si mortiferum quid biberint non nocebit eis, super aegros quoque manus imponent et bene habebunt, convalescent et sanabun-

100   tur.' Ceterum postquam haec et alia huiusmodi admonendi gratia locutus est, videntibus discipulis non amplius in terra sed elevatum in nube atque in caelos corporali specie ascendentem plane et aperte suspicientibus verissime simul ac certissime ascendisse manifestum est.

101   Discipuli autem post claram et indubitatam eius ascensionem, ut eius mandatis obtemperarent, per varias orbis terrarum regiones profecti, iuxta mandata Domini, evangelicam doctrinam ubique praedicaverunt praedicationibusque suis mundum dominicis et salutaribus praeceptis referserunt, quemadmodum plurimis ante

that he would die, He secretly foretold it to him. At last He said, "Follow me." Peter turned and saw John, his fellow disciple, and asked "Lord, what about him?" Jesus replied to him, "It is my will that he remain until I come. What is that to you?"

Now when the eleven disciples were on a mountain in Galilee, 98 Jesus appeared to them manifestly and openly; and when they clearly saw Him, they at once worshiped Him. Jesus came to them and said, "All power in heaven and on earth has been given to me. Go therefore and teach all the nations, baptizing them in the name of the Father and of the Son and of the Holy Spirit, and teaching then to obey everything that I have commanded you. And behold, I shall be with you all the days until the end of the age."

At the end, when the eleven were at supper, he openly appeared 99 to them, and plainly and openly reproved their incredulity and the hardness of their hearts, because they had not believed those who had seen that He had risen. And He said to them, "Go into all the world and preach the Gospel to all the nations. Whoever believes and is baptized will be saved; but whoever does not believe will surely be condemned. And these signs will accompany those who believe: by using my name they will cast out demons; they will speak in new tongues; they will pick up snakes, and if they drink any deadly thing, it will not hurt them; they will also lay their hands on the sick, and they will recover and be restored to health." Then, after He had spoken these things as instructions to them, 100 as the disciples watched, He was no longer on the earth, but was taken up in a cloud, and in his bodily form plainly and openly ascended into heaven, as was both truly and certainly manifest to the disciples who beheld it.

After His clear and indubitable ascension, in order to obey 101 His commandments, the disciples went out to the various regions of the world, according to the Lord's commandments, and everywhere preached the Gospel teaching, and by their preaching filled the world with the Lord's salutary precepts, just as was

saeculis a David propheta his verbis prophetatum esse constabat: 'In omnem terram exivit sonus eorum, et in fines orbis terrae verba eorum'; et plura praeterea miracula signaque fecerunt, velut Iesus antea praedixerat.

102   Per quadraginta ergo commemorationis suae dies ubi a mortuis resurrexerat (totidem enim in terris habitavit antequam in caelum ascenderet), decies ipsum, per ea quae superius commemorata sunt, variis hominibus diversisque temporibus visum fuisse manifestum est.

103   Et post non parum ascensionis suae tempus, Saulo, cognomento Paulo, dum primitivam Christi ecclesiam utpote capitalis et acerrimus hostis enixe persequeretur, ut eius verbis utar, tamquam abortivo novissime apparuit. Haec eius ultima apparitio tantarum virium fuisse creditur, ut ille primo ex infesto christiani nominis persecutore domesticus et familiarius, ex lupo deinde agnus, ex martyrum denique interfectore pretiosus Christi martyr fieri meruerit.

prophesied in these words centuries before by the prophet David, "Their sound is gone out into all the earth, and their words to the ends of the world."[52] And in addition they performed many miracles and signs, as Jesus had foretold.

During the forty days commemorating His resurrection from the dead (for He lived that many days on earth before He ascended into heaven), it is clear from what was reported above that Jesus appeared ten times to various people "at different times." 102

Sometime after His Ascension, Saul, who was known as Paul, was vigorously persecuting the early church of Christ like a fierce and deadly enemy, when, last of all, Jesus appeared to Paul, as to "one untimely born," to use his own expression.[53] This last appearance is believed to have possessed so much power that Paul deserved to change from a hostile persecutor of Christ's name to a family friend, from a wolf to a lamb, from a killer of martyrs to Christ's precious martyr. 103

Note on the Text

🎕🎕🎕

Manetti's Latin treatise *Adversus Iudaeos et gentes* survives in a single manuscript, Vatican City, Biblioteca Apostolica Vaticana, Urb. lat. 154, a
parchment manuscript of the fifteenth century bearing the title *Iannotii
Manetti Adversus Iudaeos et gentes libri X ad Alfonsum clarissimum Aragonum
regem.*[1] Written in humanistic script—*littera antiqua* with some Gothic
features—the manuscript measures 335 × 233 mm (written area 205 ×
130 mm) and consists of 215 folios, plus a single flyleaf at the front and
back; each leaf has 38 long lines, ruled in ink. It was prepared by the
workshop of Manetti's Florentine friend Vespasiano da Bisticci for the
library of Federico da Montefeltro in Urbino, the only one that today
preserves all of Manetti's Latin works. The manuscript was made between 1475 and 1482, that is, about twenty years after the death of the
Florentine humanist. The date is confirmed by Federico's coat of arms on
f. 1r, indicating his rank as Gonfaloniere of the Holy Roman Church, an
office he held from August 1474 to his death on September 10, 1482.
Given the amount of time needed to copy such a long text, it is unlikely
to have been finished before 1475. In 1657, the codex passed into the
Vatican Library with the rest of the Urbino library; its leather binding
now carries the coat of arms of Pope Alexander VII (1655–67). The same
anonymous scribe also copied the first part of the codex San Marco 456
in the Biblioteca Medicea Laurenziana, which contains Manetti's *De dignitate et excellentia hominis* (ff. 1–51). These folia are numbered in red ink
from 215 to 265, which suggests that they were originally intended to
follow the text of the *Adversus* in Urb. lat. 154, which ends with f. 214.[2]

As is often the case with Vespasiano's workshop, the elegant appearance of the codex is not matched by a scrupulous transcription of the
text; and the uniqueness of Urb. lat. 154 in fact complicates the task of
editing *Adversus Iudaeos et gentes.*[3] Given the friendship between Manetti
and Vespasiano, we believe that the author's original text passed into the
collection of his son Agnolo, who was also a friend of Vespasiano and
supplied him with various manuscripts, sometimes as outright gifts, as

was probably the case with *Adversus Iudaeos et gentes*. After the sumptuous decoration of the first pages,[4] the text of *Adversus Iudaeos et gentes* raises several questions, for two reasons. First, the author never revised the work, as has been shown in detail with respect to Book 6.[5] The errors we have registered in our notes may belong to the archetype or to the copyist, but in the absence of other witnesses, it cannot be decided which is the case. For example, there are omissions due to homoteleuton (similar endings) that may derive from Manetti's dictation, as we see in the recent edition of his *Historia Pistoriensis*.[6] Citations from the New Testament or the *Carmen Paschale* of Sedulius pose difficult questions, especially since Manetti was in this period making a new version of the former that often differs from the version of St. Jerome.[7] Given the large number of discrepancies between the Vulgate and *Adversus Iudaeos et gentes*, we have only recorded the most significant cases. It is important to note that Manetti did not in fact use his new translation of the Scriptures, and that most of the variants we find can be traced to the tradition of the so-called *Editio Clementina* and are not the result of the translator's choice.[8] Since the copyist was evidently not very sophisticated, we have had to correct numerous readings, which the punctuation of the text makes clear.

Various scholars have addressed the question of Manetti's orthographic practice.[9] Recent work by Daniela Pagliara synthesizes the conclusions of scholarship in the past thirty years.[10] Since the practice of Manetti and his copyist conforms to contemporary standards, it is difficult to distinguish between them; but we are inclined to attribute most of the spellings to Manetti himself.[11] We believe that the copyist generally respected Manetti's practice, as suggested by the scarcity of diphthongs. Yet things are complicated by the fact that—as Pagliara has shown— Manetti was not consistent in his Latin spelling. For instance, in his autograph manuscripts we find frequent inconsistencies, such as *y* for *i*, *f* for *ph*, *mn* for *nn*, *mpn* for *mn* (*columna* / *columpna*), *ci* for *ti* before a vowel (*negocia*, *preciosum*, etc.), variations between possessive adjectives and such nouns as *dicio* and *dictio*.[12] Furthermore, Manetti observes the so-called rule of Priscian ("ante *c*, *d*, *t*, *q*, *f* non est scribenda *m* sed *n*"), as is clear from forms such as *plerunque*, *nanque*, *quecunque*, *quanquam*, *ubicunque*, etc.

In view of such uncertainties and inconsistencies, we have chosen to follow the common practice of the I Tatti Renaissance Library and adopt the reconstructed classical orthography of the *Oxford Latin Dictionary*, ed. P. G. W. Glare (Oxford: the Clarendon Press, 1982), except that the distinction between *u* and *v* has been preserved. Punctuation and capitalization have been modernized.

In Books 2 and 4, Manetti inserts frequent quotations from Sedulius' *Paschalis carminis libri V.* We have not noted individually the many discrepancies between Manetti's text and modern texts of the poem. Interested readers may consult the edition of Johannes Huemer in the *Corpus scriptorum ecclesiasticorum latinorum* (Vienna, 1885), recently reprinted with supplements by Victoria Panagl (Vienna, 2007).

CONVENTIONS

⟨/⟩   Editorial additions to the text
[/]   Editorial deletions

NOTES

1. C. Stornajolo, *Bibliothecae Apostolicae Vaticanae Codices Urbinates latini, I (codices 1–500)* (Rome: Typis Vaticanis, 1902): 160–61, and Baldassarri, "Scolastica e umanesimo," ,"25–26. For bibliography on this codex, see Michelangiola Marchiaro's precise description in *Coluccio Salutati e l'invenzione dell'Umanesimo*, ed. T. De Robertis, G. Tanturli, S. Zamponi (Florence: Mandragora, 2008), 61–62.

2. The second part of the San Marco codex contains Manetti's *Oratio ad Calixtum tertium*, written in a different hand. The scribe of Urb. lat. 154 and the first part of San Marco 456 copied some twenty-two manuscripts for Federico's library: see A. C. de la Mare, "Vespasiano da Bisticci e i copisti fiorentini di Federico," in *Federico di Montefeltro. Lo stato, le arti, la cultura*, vol. III: *La cultura*, ed. G. Cerboni Baiardi, G. Chittolini, P. Floriani (Rome: Bulzoni, 1986), 81–96 at 88–90. For another codex containing works by Manetti copied by the same scribe and decorated by the same illuminator, see the description of Urb. lat. 387 by Marchiaro in *Coluccio Salutati e l'invenzione dell'Umanesimo*, 60–61.

3. In the ducal medallion on fol. IIv, the work is called *Contra Iudeos et gentes* (see note 4 below), but the title *Adversus Iudaeos et gentes* is found in the rubrics to the individual books. The following variant titles are given by Vespasiano da Bisticci: *Contra Judeos et gentes* in his *Vita di meser Giannozo Manetti, fiorentino*, in idem, *Le vite*, 1:534 and 537; *Contra gl'impii et scelerati Giudei* and *Contra Judeos* in his *Comentario della vita di messer Giannozo Manetti*, in idem, *Le vite*, 2:623 and 626.

4. The initial capitals at the beginning of each book are in gold and decorated with floral patterns in red and light blue. On fol. IIv, in keeping with the tradition of books owned by the dukes of Urbino, we find a green crown bordered with gold and decorated with flowers and golden spheres, and in the center the title in blue and gold: *In hoc codice contine⟨n⟩tur Iannozi Manetti florentini ad Alfonsum Aragonum regem Contra Iudeos et Gentes libri X.*

5. See Baldassarri, "Scolastica e umanesimo."

6. See the remarks of Baldassarri in Manetti, *Historia Pistoriensis*, 90–92.

7. On Manetti's use of the *Carmen Paschale*, see Baldassarri, "Conferme e novità." We have recorded variants (noted in Huemer's critical edition of the *Carmen Paschale*) and obvious errors. On Manetti's translation of the New Testament, see Baldassarri, "Riflessioni preliminari." See now the excellent dissertation of Annet den Haan, *Manetti's New Testament*.

8. Cf. *Biblia Sacra Iuxta Vulgatam Versionem*, ed. R. Weber, R. Gryson et al., 4th ed. (Stuttgart: Deutsche Bibelgesellschaft, 1994).

9. See the critical editions of Alfonso De Petris, Anna Modigliani, and Daniela Pagliara cited in the Bibliography.

10. Cf. Manetti, *De terremotu*, ed. Pagliara, 83–86.

11. Naturally, we cannot attribute to Manetti the numerous errors in proper names found in Book 1; these must be the responsibility of the copyist or another intermediary scribe. The text of Urb. lat. 154 consistently uses the medieval forms *michi* and *nichil*, which is contrary to Manetti's known practice.

12. See note 56 on *Adversus Iudaeos et gentes* (1.86).

Notes to the Text

❧❧❧

1. LIBER PRIMUS INCIPIT *MS*

2. aliis *MS*

3. iniustitia *MS*

4. in hunc mundum *MS*

5. trucidatur *MS*: trucidatus *Cicero*

6. et tot *MS*: etiam tot *Cicero*

7. praestantissimum *MS*: praestantissima *Cicero*

8. *Modern texts of Cicero have* tam feliciter *after* Marius

9. sua *supplied, following modern texts of Seneca*

10. sint *MS*: *corrected to* sicut

11. Calipho *MS*

12. tanto *MS*; *better,* tauro

13. cassiis *MS*; *better,* casiis: *cf. Vergil,* Eclogues *2.49*

14. cocodrillum *MS, for* crocodilum

15. ibin *MS, a Greek accusative*

16. venerabantur *MS*

17. Rufinam *MS*; Rusinam *Augustine*

18. Florea *MS*; Flora *Augustine*

19. Nascionem *MS*

20. Nascio *MS*

21. ⟨qui culmis⟩ *supplied*

22. temperantia *MS*; intemperantia *Cicero*

23. ignorantie *MS*; ignoratione *Cicero*

24. Aegyptus *MS; perhaps* Aegyptii *should be read*

25. Sanctum *MS;* Sancum *Lactantius*

26. studeamus *MS; corrected to* sileamus *by the scribe*

27. Ameti *MS*

28. Damnem *MS* (= Danaem); *but cf.* Danes *in Boccaccio* Genealogiae 7.27.1, 7.29.1–2, 9.4.2

29. Coronidam *MS; perhaps* Calydoniam *should be read*

30. natum *MS*

31. *See note 28 above.*

32. modestas *MS*

33. *corrected*: incoloratam pluviam *MS*

34. Alcineam *MS; better,* Alcmenam *or* Alcumenam

35. Agotode *MS; better,* Agathocle

36. discurrebantes *MS*

37. saltationibus *MS*

38. atque usus *MS*

39. ⟨memoretur⟩ *supplied*

40. consulturi *MS*

41. erudiendi *MS*

42. Acon *MS*

43. Neptalim *MS*

44. mane *MS*

45. ⟨et⟩ *supplied*

46. quid *MS*

47. amigdolas *MS*

48. ex scriptis *MS*

49. Tarbi *MS*

50. Syna *MS*

51. minis *MS*

52. cynifum *MS; but cf. Exodus* 8:16: *"Et sint scinifes in universa terra Aegypti."*

53. cynifes *MS: see previous note*

54. praecedentibus *MS*

55. Syna *MS; cf. n. 50*

56. dictionem *MS*

57. et *MS*

58. et mittet *MS*

59. *In the rest of Book 1, the departures and omissions from the Vulgate are too numerous to list individually. Only significant variants are noted.*

60. aenea *MS:* ferrea *Vulgate Deut.* 27:23

61. egeruntur *MS, Editio Clementina:* digeruntur *Vulgate Deut.* 28:27

62. descendet *MS*

63. fetus *MS:* fructum *Vulgate Deut.* 27:51

64. eosdem *MS*

65. Gagirum *MS*

66. Gargalim *MS*

67. prevationis *MS*

68. abrupto *MS*

69. Domino *MS*

70. simile *MS*

71. similia *MS:* persimilia *is a conjecture*

72. animam *MS:* arvinam *Vulgate Lev.* 3:15

73. Cyrogallus *MS:* chyrogryllius *Vulgate Lev.* 11:5

74. ghriphum *MS*

75. de morticinis *MS:* de morticinis eorum *Vulgate Lev.* 11:32

76. protendebant *MS*

77. *Latin* euceria *transliterates Greek* εὐκαιρία, *"the fullness of time" or "the right time"*

BOOK II

1. LIBER SECUNDUS INCIPIT *MS*

2. Cyrino *MS*: *sc.* Quirino; *cf. Josephus*, Antiquities *18.1.1*

3. Bethlehem *MS*; Bethleem *Vulgate*

4. Esaiam *MS*; Isaiam *Vulgate*

5. Tecuites *MS, apparently Manetti's coinage for "the man from Tekoa"*

6. Tecua *MS*; *cf.* Thecua *Vulgate Amos 1:1*

7. tempore *MS*

8. immortali *MS*

9. Inventus *MS*

10. veramque *MS*

11. gererentur *MS*

12. Aegyptiis *MS*

13. tam et tanta *MS*

14. necatu *MS*

15. nos *MS*

16. natum *MS*

17. toloneo *MS*

18. Benarges *MS*

19. ipse *MS*

20. provolutis *MS*

21. prorumperunt *MS, corrected to* proruperunt

22. ⟨exstitit⟩ *supplied*

23. solemni *MS*

24. praecipit *modern texts of Sedulius*

25. in miraculis in parabolis *MS*

26. ponticus *MS*

27. apertae *MS*

28. populo *MS*

29. fantasmate *MS*

30. fere *MS*

31. inlotis *MS*

32. ⟨morbis⟩ *supplied*

33. descentibdentibus, *corrected by the scribe*

34. homo *MS,* hamo *in marg.*

35. verbis Dei *MS*

36. veteri *MS*

37. Hiericho *MS;* Iericho *§166 and Vulgate*

38. frementem *repeated in MS*

39. *This second* inquit *is superfluous.*

40. ymmolandum *MS, here with interlinear correction to* immolandum

41. ratique *MS*

42. ubi iam nam *MS*

43. respondens *MS*

44. ab incredibilis et dulis *MS*

45. ipsis *MS*

BOOK III

1. LIBER TERTIUS INCIPIT *MS*

2. Audistis ei *MS*

3. calumpnientibus *MS*

4. nent *MS*

5. quanto magis vos magis *MS*

6. caltiamenta *MS*

7. in aliquam civitatem *MS*

8. Belgebud *MS*

9. Belzebud *MS*

10. filium *MS*

11. domesticis *MS*

12. et qui invenit animam suam *MS*

13. manducatis *MS*

14. ecce *MS*

15. Pharisaei et *MS*

16. qui *MS*

17. Spiritus *MS*

18. sancti *MS*

19. non habet *repeated in MS*

20. sed sed *MS*

21. peri perior *MS*

22. blasfemia *MS*

23. *Corrected from* esse responderat *by the scribe.*

24. *Here and elsewhere the MS reads* hiis.

25. inter *MS*

26. quibus dictum *MS*

27. nummisma *MS*

28. non et *MS*

29. novissimo Dei die *MS*

30. apposiimus *sic MS*

31. ⟨dixit⟩ *supplied*

32. in Deum *MS*

33. honorificavebit *sic MS*

34. synagogas *MS*

35. tribulatione *MS*

36. stante in loco stan *MS*

37. ministrabit *MS*

38. ⟨quoniam⟩ *supplied*

39. non faciam ti facio *MS*

40. angeli *MS*

41. susceperunt sumpserunt *MS*

BOOK IV

1. DE MORTE CHRISTI LIBER QUARTUS INCIPIT FELICITER *MS*

2. commeratis commemoratis *MS*

3. asscriberis *MS*

4. conspacimus *sic MS*

5. commemorato *MS*

6. velleremus *MS*

7. ⟨per⟩ *supplied*

8. ⟨diffamata⟩ *supplied*

9. traditur *MS*

10. pervius *MS*

11. similas *sic MS*

12. defendendi gratiam *MS*

13. imperior *MS*

14. rapidum *MS*

15. ⟨vel⟩ *supplied*

16. contumelia *MS*

17. animadver anniversaria *MS*

18. aff efflagitabant *MS*

19. fac fecerat *MS*

20. universam u *MS*

21. azantani *MS*

22. Quippe in *MS*
23. santia *MS*
24. oricentur *MS*
25. concilio *MS*
26. appinquaret *sic MS*
27. credendum *MS*
28. prandite *MS*

Notes to the Translation

꿍꿍꿍

BOOK I

1. Book subtitle supplied by the editors; this is the only book missing
such a subtitle. In 1.112 and 2.1 Manetti uses the expression, borrowed
from the title of Eusebius' work, *The Preparation for the Gospel.*

2. Genesis 1:26–28.

3. On the angels, see Augustine, *City of God* 9.13.22–23 and 9.9–21.

4. Jerome, *On Hebrew Names* 4 and 105, and Isidore, *Etymologies* 7.6.4. Cf.
Manetti, *On the Dignity and Excellence of Man* 1.1, a passage that also cites
Josephus, *Jewish Antiquities* 1.1.2.

5. Genesis 2:15.

6. Genesis 2:17.

7. Genesis 3:1–5.

8. Eusebius, *Chronicle* (PL 27: 71A).

9. Genesis 5:29 (King James version): "And he [Lamech] called his name
Noah, saying, This same shall comfort us"; ibid. (Vulgate): "vocavitque
nomen eius Noe, dicens: Iste consolabitur nos" By contrast, in *On Hebrew
Names* 14 (PL 23: 826/838), Jerome writes that Noah means "rest" (*re-
quies*).

10. Genesis 6:11–22.

11. Genesis 9:1–7.

12. Eusebius, *Chronicle* (PL 27: 68A).

13. Galatians 4:4.

14. Hebrews 1:9.

15. As the son of Seth, Enos was a grandson of Adam.

16. Genesis 4:26.

17. Eusebius, *Chronicle*, *Canon chronicus* (PL 27: 266).

18. Genesis 10:9.

19. The Peripatetic doctrine of three goods (those of the mind, the body, and the external goods) and the Stoic theory of a single good (virtue) are debated extensively in Cicero, *On Ends* 3–5.

20. Cicero, *On Divination* 1.36.

21. Diogenes Laertius, *Lives of the Philosophers*, preface 2.

22. Cicero, *On the Nature of the Gods* 3.80–81.

23. The reference is to Seneca, *On Providence*.

24. Lactantius, *Divine Institutes* 5.23.

25. Eusebius, *Preparation for the Gospel* 10.4 and 14.4, and Augustine, *City of God* 8.2.

26. Cicero, *Tusculan Disputations* 5.8.

27. Cicero, *On the Nature of the Gods* 1.27; see also Lactantius, *Divine Institutes* 1.5.

28. Manetti's account of the pre-Socratic philosophers is indebted to Lactantius, *Divine Institutes* 1.5, and Augustine, *City of God* 8.2.

29. On Anaxagoras, cf. Manetti, *On the Dignity and Excellence of Man* 2.4.

30. On Archelaus, cf. Manetti, *On the Dignity and Excellence of Man* 2.5.

31. On Democritus, cf. Manetti, *On the Dignity and Excellence of Man* 2.5.

32. Each point mentioned by Manetti contradicts the idea of *ex nihilo* creation.

33. On Empedocles and Lucretius, cf. Manetti, *On the Dignity and Excellence of Man* 2.5.

34. On Socrates, cf. Manetti, *On the Dignity and Excellence of Man* 2.6.

35. No Peripatetic of this name is known; perhaps Manetti is thinking of Eudemus.

36. Excerpted verbatim from Cicero, *Tusculan Disputations* 1.18–19; see also Manetti, *On the Dignity and Excellence of Man* 2.5.

37. On Zeno, see note 39.

38. On Aristoxenus, see note 39.

39. On Xenocrates, see Cicero, *Tusculan Disputations* 1.20, the excerpting of which continues.

40. On Plato, cf. note 42.

41. On Aristotle, cf. Cicero, *Tusculan Disputations* 1.22, and Manetti, *On the Dignity and Excellence of Man* 2.7.

42. Cicero, *On Ends* 5.7.

43. Cicero, *On Ends* 2.19.

44. As a Stoic, Cleanthes is wrongly classified with the hedonists here; the reason is that Manetti takes Cleanthes' simile of Pleasure and the virtues as straightforward, rather than ironic (see next paragraph).

45. Aristotle, *Nicomachean Ethics* 10.2.

46. Cicero, *On Ends* 2.69.

47. On Hieronymus, cf. Cicero, *On Ends* 2.19.

48. Cicero, *On Ends* 2.42–43.

49. On Callipho and Diodorus, see Cicero, *On Ends* 2.19.

50. For the crocodile, cf. Pliny, *Natural History* 8.37; for the ibis, *Natural History* 8.41; for the ox Apis, *Natural History* 8.71. Adopting the conjecture of Stefano Ugo Baldassarri, I have translated the odd noun *peles* as "falcon," since Pliny, *Natural History* 10.21 mentions an *epileus* (a hawk or falcon), a bird sacred to the Egyptian god Horus.

51. On Atlas, cf. Boccaccio, *Genealogy of the Pagan Gods* 4.31, trans. Jon Solomon in this I Tatti series (Cambridge, MA, 2011), 1:508–11.

52. For the minor Roman deities that follow, see Augustine, *City of God* 4.8, and Lactantius, *Divine Institutes* 1.20. For the idea of all things being

filled with gods, see Thales *apud* Cicero, *On Laws* 2.26; cf. also Vergil, *Eclogues* 3.60.

53. For Venus Cluacina (or Cloacina), cf. Livy, *History of Rome* 2.44–48.

54. Cicero, *On the Nature of the Gods* 3.47.

55. Augustine, *City of God* 4.8

56. Cf. Cicero, *On the Nature of the Gods* 2.66; Firmicus Maternus, *On the Error of Profane Religions* 17.2.

57. On the major Roman deities, see Augustine, *City of God* 4.9.

58. Cicero, *On the Nature of the Gods* 1.42.

59. Lactantius, *Divine Institutes* 1.11.

60. Cf. Cicero, *On the Nature of the Gods* 1.42.

61. Cicero, *On the Nature of the Gods* 1.43.

62. Cicero, *On the Nature of the Gods* 1.46–49.

63. Lactantius, *Divine Institutes* 1.15.

64. Lactantius, *Divine Institutes* 1.9.

65. Manetti mistakenly writes that Omphale was the daughter of Eurystheus, probably misled by the the mention of the two names in Lactantius, *Divine Institutes* 1.9.

66. Lactantius, *Divine Institutes* 1.10.

67. Ibid.

68. On Daphne and Apollo, see Ovid, *Metamorphoses* 1.452–567.

69. On Hyacinth and Apollo, see Ovid, *Metamorphoses* 10.162–219, and cf. Lactantius, loc. cit.

70. Lactantius, loc. cit.

71. Reading "Calydoniam" for "Coronidem" (found two sentences later), we identify the virgin with Althea, queen of Calydon, who bore Meleager: cf. Hyginus, *Genealogies* 171.

72. On Mars and Venus, cf. Homer, *Odyssey* 8.266–366, and Ovid, *Metamorphoses* 4.171–89.

73. On Pluto and Proserpina, cf. Ovid, *Metamorphoses* 5.341–71.

74. Ovid, *Metamorphoses* 2.736–59.

75. Ovid, *Metamorphoses* 2.572–95.

76. Cf. §26. A citation of Lactantius, *Divine Institutes* 1.10.

77. Ovid, *Metamorphoses* 2.846–75; Lactantius, *Divine Institutes* 1.11.

78. Ovid, *Metamorphoses* 2.846–51 (trans. Anthony S. Kline).

79. Terence, *Eunuch* 584–91.

80. Ovid, *Metamorphoses* 10.155–61; Lactantius, *Divine Institutes* 1.11.

81. Seneca, *Hercules furens* 1–5 (Loeb Classical Library translation by Frank Justus Miller).

82. For Omadius as an epithet of Dionysus, cf. Boccaccio, *Genealogy of the Pagan Gods* 12.24.

83. Lactantius, *Divine Institutes* 1.20.

84. Lactantius, *Divine Institutes* 1.21.

85. Ibid.

86. On Cybele, see Lactantius, *Divine Institutes* 1.11, 1.14; Augustine, *City of God* 7.26; Boccaccio, *Genealogy of the Pagan Gods* 1.8.3 and 3.2.8 (trans. Solomon, 1:87 and 1:325).

87. Vergil, *Aeneid* 6.784–85.

88. Cicero, *On the Orator* 2.168.

89. Romans 1:20.

90. Isidore, *Etymologies* 5.39.5; 7.6.23; 9.2.5,51.

91. Jerome, *On Hebrew Names* 9; and Isidore, *Etymologies* 7.6.10.

92. Cf. Eusebius, *Demonstration of the Gospel* 3.2.39–42.

93. Jerome, *On Hebrew Names* 4.33; and Isidore, *Etymologies* 7.6.4. Cf. Manetti, *On the Dignity and Excellence of Man* 1.1, a passage that also cites Josephus, who glosses the name Adam as "formed of red earth" (*Jewish Antiquities* 1.1.2.34).

94. Isidore, *Etymologies* 5.39.2.

95. Jerome, *On Hebrew Names* 9.94; and Isidore, *Etymologies* 7.6.11.

96. Jude 14.

97. Genesis 6:9.

98. Genesis 6:6–9:26.

99. Jerome, *On Hebrew Names* 14.114; and Isidore, *Etymologies* 7.6.25.

100. See §44 and the source identified in note 90.

101. Jerome, *On Hebrew Names* 53.110; and Isidore, *Etymologies* 7.6.23.

102. Isidore, *Etymologies* 7.7.1–21.

103. Genesis 15:6; Romans 4:3; Galatians 3:6; James 2:23.

104. Genesis 17:10–14.

105. Jerome, *On Hebrew Names* 91; and Isidore, *Etymologies* 7.7.5.

106. Jerome, *On Hebrew Names* 20, 108, 110; and Isidore, *Etymologies* 7.7.6. For Jacob wrestling with the angel — the origin of his name "Israel" — see Genesis 33:25–33.

107. On Reuben, see Genesis 37:4–36; Josephus, *Jewish Antiquities* 2.20–34; and the *Testament of Reuben* in the so-called *Testaments of the Twelve Patriarchs* (see next note).

108. §§49–65 rely on the apocryphal Greek text known as the *Testaments of the Twelve Patriarchs*, a work that also survives in Armenian, Slavonic, and Latin translations (the last by Robert Grosseteste, ca. 1170–1253). See Robert Henry Charles, ed. and trans., *The Testaments of the Twelve Patriarchs* (London, 1908); Paolo Sacchi, ed., *Apocrifi dell'Antico Testamento* (Turin, 2006); and Fubini, "Ancora sul 'Testamento' di Niccolò V." On Reuben, see *Testament of Reuben* 1.6–10 and 3.11–15.

109. Genesis 34:1–31.

110. *Testament of Simeon* 3–4.

111. *Testament of Simeon* 5.4–5 and 7.1–2.

112. *Testament of Simeon* 6.5–7.

113. *Testament of Levi* 1.

114. *Testament of Levi* 2.10–11, 4.1–5, 10.1–3, 14.1–2, 16.3–5, 18.1–14.

115. *Testament of Judah* 1.

116. *Testament of Judah* 2.3–5.

117. *Testament of Judah* 2.7.

118. *Testament of Judah* 3.1–2.

119. Actually, Jashub.

120. *Testament of Judah* 3.3–4.

121. *Testament of Judah* 3.3–7.

122. *Testament of Judah* 3.16–19.

123. *Testament of Judah* 3.21.1–5.

124. *Testament of Judah* 3.24–25.

125. *Testament of Issachar* 1 and 3–5. Cf. also Job 1:1, "In the land of Uz there lived a man whose name was Job. This man was blameless and upright; he feared God and shunned evil."

126. *Testament of Issachar* 3–5.

127. *Testament of Issachar* 7.1.

128. *Testament of Zebulun* 1 and 6.4–7.

129. *Testament of Zebulun* 7.3–4.

130. *Testament of Zebulun* 9.8–10.2.

131. *Testament of Dan* 5.4–13 and 7.3.

132. *Testament of Naphtali.*

133. *Testament of Gad* 1.2–3.

134. *Testament of Gad* 1.3–7.

135. *Testament of Asher* 1.2.

136. *Testament of Asher* 1.3–9.

137. *Testaments of the Twelve Patriarchs.* Cf. ibid., 7:887–88, with the notes on the interpolations in this prophetic text.

138. Genesis 39–47. Manetti also consulted the *Testament of Joseph,* and Josephus, *Jewish Antiquities* 2.7–200.

139. Jerome, *Hebrew Questions on Genesis* 49:22.

140. John Cassian, *Conferences* 6.10.7.

141. *Testament of Benjamin.*

142. *Testament of Benjamin* 9–11.

143. Exodus 1:5. Cf. Genesis 46:27 and Deuteronomy 10:22.

144. Acts 7:14–15.

145. Numbers 17:16–25.

146. Numbers 16:1–33.

147. Numbers 17:6–14.

148. Numbers 17:1–11.

149. Exodus 28.

150. Exodus 2:1–10; and Josephus, *Jewish Antiquities* 2.217–31.

151. Josephus, *Jewish Antiquities* 2.232–36.

152. Josephus, *Jewish Antiquities* 2.239–55.

153. Josephus, *Jewish Antiquities* 2.241–42,

154. Josephus, *Jewish Antiquities* 2.245–47.

155. Josephus, *Jewish Antiquities* 2.247–52.

156. Exodus 2:11–15; Josephus, *Jewish Antiquities* 2.253.

157. Exodus 2:15 and 3:1.

158. Exodus 2:23–4:17.

159. Exodus 5:1–5.

160. Exodus 5:5–23.

161. Exodus 7:14–12:30.

162. Exodus 12:31–40:38.

163. Exodus 14:5–9.

164. Exodus 14:10–31.

165. Exodus 15:1.

166. Exodus 19–34.

167. Not Athanasius, but Philo, *Life of Moses.*

168. Deuteronomy 24; Josephus, *Jewish Antiquities* 4.320–30.

169. Eusebius, *Demonstration of the Gospel* 1.6.1–30, 3.3.3.

170. Deuteronomy 28:1–13.

171. Deuteronomy 28:15–53.

172. Deuteronomy 28:56–57.

173. Deuteronomy 11:26–31.

174. Leviticus 1:4–7.

175. Leviticus 1:10–17.

176. Leviticus 2:10.

177. Leviticus 3:1–16 with some variants: for *animam*, I read *arvinam* (Vulgate).

178. Leviticus 3:3–7.

179. Leviticus 7:37.

180. Leviticus 11:1–20 (with variants and omissions indicated in the Notes to the Text).

181. Leviticus 11:47.

182. Leviticus 11:31–33.

183. Cicero, *On the Nature of the Gods* 2.160.

184. Juvenal 1.141.

185. Manetti here echoes Eusebius, *Demonstration of the Gospel* 1.8.3, 1.10.14, and 1.10.39.

186. Galatians 2:24.

187. Galatians 4:4.

188. That is, both laws deal with important moral precepts, but the Old Law contains more detailed provisions.

189. Manetti's characterization of his work as a difficult and arduous task (*difficile opus et arduum*) echoes the preface of Augustine, *City of God* (*magnum opus et arduum*), which is also echoed in Lorenzo Valla, *On Pleasure* (*magnum opus profecto et arduum*); cf. also Cicero, *Tusculan Disputations* 3.84 (*magnum opus et difficile*).

441

BOOK II

1. Manetti follows Eusebius' *Chronology* as translated by Jerome.

2. Romans 3:2. It is worth noting that the Gospel passages translated in *Against the Jews and the Gentiles* often differ both from the Vulgate and from Manetti's later complete translation: see Baldassarri, "Riflessioni preliminari." A critical edition of Manetti's New Testament is available in Den Haan, *Manetti's New Testament*.

3. Genesis 22:15–18.

4. Genesis 32:23–29.

5. Here Manetti repeats the distinction between Hebrews and Jews outlined in Book 1.

6. Galatians 4:4–5 (with variants indicated in notes on Latin text).

7. Manetti cites Isaiah 7:14 with the verb *vocabitur* rather than the variant *vocabitis*.

8. Matthew 1:23. Cf. Jerome, *On Hebrew Names* 73; Isidore, *Etymologies* 7.2.10.

9. Isaiah 11:1, a passage discussed in Eusebius, *Demonstration of the Gospel* 2.3.40 and 2.4.110.

10. Luke 1:26–38.

11. Jerome, *On Hebrew Names* 95; Isidore, *Etymologies* 7.5.10–11.

12. Matthew 1:1–16 and Luke 3:23–28.

13. 2 Timothy 2:8.

14. Luke 1:36.

15. Luke 1:5.

16. Isidore, *Etymologies* 7.2.2. Cf. Jerome, *On Hebrew Names* 97.

17. Isaiah 45:1 (Cyrus); 1 Samuel 24:7 and 2 Samuel 1:4 (Saul).

18. Psalm 104(105):15.

19. Sedulius, *Easter Poem* (*Carmen Paschale*) 2.63. During the Middle Ages, this passage (2.63–69) entered the Roman liturgy and was sung to

plainchant. On Manetti's use of Sedulius, see Baldassarri, "Conferme e novità."

20. Theologians in the later Middle Ages debated the question of the Virgin's immaculate conception. After the doctrine had been staunchly defended by the Franciscan Duns Scotus, Franciscans generally affirmed it, whereas Dominicans rejected it. It was held as a pious opinion until its definition as an orthodox doctrine (*de fide*) in 1854.

21. A rare instance of Manetti's use of apocryphal Gospels, namely, the *Passing of the Blessed Virgin Mary* by pseudo-Joseph of Arimathea. Cf. M. Craveri in *I vangeli apocrifi* (Turin: Einaudi, 2005), 447–48 and 465–74.

22. Dionysius the Areopagite, *On Divine Names* 3.2, a text translated into Latin by Manetti's contemporary and friend Ambrogio Traversari.

23. The Annunciation is recounted in Luke 1:26–38.

24. Matthew 1:21; Jerome, *On Hebrew Names* 21, 28, 91, 112; Isidore, *Etymologies* 7.2.7–8.

25. Matthew 1:21; cf. Luke 1:31 and 2:21.

26. Matthew 1:20–21.

27. Luke 1:34.

28. Ibid.

29. Isaiah 7:14; Matthew 1:23.

30. Until the eighteenth century, March 25, the feast of the Annunciation, marked the beginning of the new year in Florence and many other Italian cities.

31. Manetti seems here to confuse Zachariah, a priest of the Temple, with the prophet Zechariah. In §78, he correctly calls him a high priest.

32. Luke 1:41–42.

33. Luke 1:46.

34. The Feast of the Visitation, celebrated on July 2, was reaffirmed by the Council of Basel in 1441. Manetti's words here may commemorate the fact.

35. Matthew 1:19–21.

36. Josephus, *Jewish Antiquities* 18.1.1.

37. Luke 2:1–20.

38. Some apocryphal accounts report the presence of a midwife named Salome at the Nativity.

39. Psalm 117(118):24, a text that is sung as a gradual for Easter.

40. Manetti echoes Sallust, *Jugurtha* 19.2: "About Carthage, I think it better to remain silent than to say too little."

41. Isaiah 53:8.

42. The Marian hymn, "Virgo Dei Genitrix," sung for the Assumption and for the Nativity of the Blessed Virgin Mary: August 15 and September 8, respectively.

43. This passage dates the first books of Manetti's work to 1454.

44. Cf. §2 above on Manetti's adoption of Eusebius' chronology, which places the Creation 5,199 years before the Nativity.

45. Amos 1:1.

46. To be precise, the village of Tekoa was located five miles south of Bethlehem on the road to the Dead Sea.

47. Luke 2:8–9.

48. Luke 2:14.

49. Jerome, *On the Location and Names of Hebrew Places* 167.

50. On the name Eder, see Jerome, *On Hebrew Names*, and *Hebrew Questions on Genesis* 35:21.

51. Luke 2:15–18.

52. Sedulius, *Easter Poem* 2.35–72.

53. Luke 2:21.

54. Emmanuel is the name foretold in Isaiah 7:14 and cited in Matthew 1:22–23.

55. Matthew 1:1; Mark 1:1; Luke 2:11; John 1:17.

56. Exodus 39:7.

57. Leviticus 10:7 and 21:10.

58. 1 Kings 19:16.

59. Psalm 44(45):8.

60. John Chrysostom, *Homilies on Matthew* 6.2, a passage quoted by Thomas Aquinas in his *Catena aurea. Glossa continua super Evangelia* (Bologna: ESD, 2007), 1:162.

61. Church Fathers cited Numbers 24:17 and Isaiah 11:1 as proof of the descent of the Magi from Balaam: cf. Eusebius, *Demonstration of the Gospel* 9.1–10.

62. Sedulius, *Easter Poem* 2.73–75.

63. Juvencus, *Gospels* 1.224–28.

64. Eusebius, *Ecclesiastical History* 1.6.1.

65. Josephus, *Jewish Antiquities* 14.8–9, 14.121.

66. Eusebius, *Ecclesiastical History* 1.6.1.

67. Matthew 2:7–8.

68. Matthew 2:9–10.

69. Ibid.

70. John Chrysostom, *Homilies on Matthew* 6.2

71. Ibid., with reference to Exodus 13:21 and Numbers 9:15–23.

72. Matthew 2:11.

73. Juvencus, *Gospels* 1.250–51.

74. Ambrose, *Exposition of Saint Luke* 2:44.

75. Sedulius, *Easter Poem* 2.95–96.

76. Matthew 2:12.

77. Matthew 2:16.

78. Psalm 47(48):8. Cf. Psalm 71(72):1, "The kings of Tarshish and of distant shores will bring tribute to him."

79. 2 Chronicles 37:22–23; Ezra 1:1–4.

80. Leviticus 12:2–4.

81. Leviticus 12:6–8; Luke 2:24.

82. This is the feast known as Candlemas, celebrated on February 2, which originally fell on February 14, forty days after Epiphany.

83. Luke 2:25–26.

84. Luke 2:27–28.

85. Luke 2:29–32.

86. 2 Corinthians 5:15.

87. Luke 2:34–35.

88. Luke 2:36.

89. Juvencus, *Gospels* 1.251–54; cf. Luke 2:36–38.

90. Ambrose, *Exposition of Saint Luke* 2:58.

91. Luke 1:22.

92. Luke 1:67.

93. Ambrose, *Exposition of Saint Luke* 2:58.

94. Josephus, *Jewish Antiquities* 16.90–126.

95. Micah 5:2. Cf. Matthew 2:7–16, and Eusebius, *Ecclesiastical History* 1.8.1.

96. Matthew 2:13–14.

97. For Egyptian taboos about leeks and onions, cf. Juvenal, *Satires* 15.9: *Porrum et caepe nefas violare et frangere morsu* ("It's a violation and a sin to crunch your teeth into a leek or an onion." Loeb translation by Susanna Morton Braund).

98. John Chrysostom, *Homilies on Matthew* 8:4. Manetti is referring to the reputation of Egypt in antiquity as the original home of hermits and monks, foreshadowed by the flight of Joseph and Mary into Egypt.

99. Josephus, *Jewish Antiquities* 17.169–92.

100. Josephus, *Jewish Antiquities* 17.183–84.

101. Josephus, *Jewish Antiquities* 17.168–70.

102. Eusebius, *Ecclesiastical History* 1.8.16.

103. Sedulius, *Easter Poem* 2:121–26.

104. Jeremiah 31:15, cited in Matthew 2:18.

105. Sedulius, *Easter Poem* 2.127–33.

106. Matthew 2:19–21.

107. Matthew 2:22–23.

108. Josephus, *Jewish Antiquities* 1.668–69, 2.93–100.

109. Matthew 2:22.

110. Manetti here rejects the apocryphal Gospels called *The Childhood of Jesus*.

111. Jerome, *Commentary on Matthew* 2:86.

112. Luke 2:41–42.

113. Exodus 12:12–13.

114. Luke 2:43–44.

115. Luke 2:45–46.

116. Jerome, *Epistles* 53.3

117. Luke 2:48.

118. Luke 2:49–51.

119. Luke 2:51.

120. Cf. notes 112 and 113 above.

121. Luke 3:2; Josephus, *Jewish Antiquities*, 18.33–35.

122. This lengthy sentence exceeds even the standard of Manetti's most ponderous prose, which suggests that the author failed to revise it.

123. Luke 1:41.

124. The description of St. John the Baptist follows the passage in Matthew 3:4.

125. Juvencus, *Gospels* 1.323–26.

126. Josephus, *Jewish Antiquities* 18.118.

127. Josephus, *Jewish Antiquities* 18.116, 18.119.

128. Josephus, *Jewish Antiquities* 18.109–12; Eusebius, *Ecclesiastical History* 1.11.1–2.

129. Matthew 3:11; Mark 1:7; Luke 3:16; John 1:27.

130. Luke 1:44, 1:76.

131. Matthew 3:5–6; Mark 1:5; Luke 3:3; John 1:28.

132. Matthew 3:13; Mark 1:9; Luke 3:3; John 1:29.

133. Luke 1:5.

134. John 1:29.

135. Matthew 3:14.

136. Actually, the rite of baptism was performed by Christ's disciples: John 1:33–34, 4:1–2.

137. Luke 3:21.

138. Manetti may have in mind the hymn of St. Thomas Aquinas, *Sacris solemniis*, which reads, "Let the old give way, / Let all things become new" (*Recedant vetera, / nova sint omnia*).

139. This passage echoes the distinction of Eusebius between the Law of Moses and the Gospel of Christ.

140. Psalm 113(114):3.

141. Sedulius, *Easter Poem* 2.162–65.

142. Joshua 4:7, 4:22–24; 2 Kings 2:8.

143. Matthew 3:16; Mark 1:10; Luke 3:21–22; John 1:32.

144. Matthew 3:17; Mark 1:11; Luke 3:22.

145. Lactantius, *Divine Institutes* 4.5.

146. Matthew 3:16; Mark 1:10; Luke 3:23.

147. Genesis 8:10–11.

148. Sedulius, *Easter Poem* 2.166–69.

149. Matthew 4:1; Mark 1:12–13; Luke 4:1–2.

150. Exodus 34:28 (Moses); 1 Kings 19:8 (Elijah). The forty-day fasting of Moses and Christ is noted by Eusebius, *Demonstration of the Gospel* 3.2.12–13.

151. Manetti emphasizes Christ's physical weakness, perhaps in reply to the Docetist notion that his suffering was merely apparent.

152. Cf. Ambrose, *Exposition of Saint Luke* 4.2 (PL 15: 1617).

153. Cf. note 146 above.

154. Matthew 4:3; Luke 4:3. Although Manetti translated the New Testament into Latin (Vatican Library, MS Pal. lat. 45; see Den Haan, *Manetti's New Testament*), he seldom uses his new version in this work. See Baldassarri, "Riflessioni preliminari."

155. Matthew 4:4; Luke 4:4.

156. Matthew 4:5.

157. Matthew 4:6.

158. Matthew 4:7.

159. Matthew 4:8–9.

160. Matthew 4:9.

161. Manetti here corrects the reading of some manuscripts (*vade retro*). On Peter, see Matthew 16:23; Mark 8:33.

162. Matthew 4:10; Luke 4:8.

163. Matthew 4:11.

164. Sedulius, *Easter Poem* 2:175–219.

165. On Andrew and John, see Matthew 4:18; John 1:40.

166. Manetti follows John 1:41, rather than Matthew 4:18 and Mark 1:16, in which Jesus finds them fishing.

167. John 1:43–44.

168. John 1:45–46.

169. John 1:47.

170. John 1:48.

171. John 1:49.

172. Luke 4:14–16; Matthew 13:54.

173. Luke 4:16–30.

174. Luke 4:31.

175. Manetti is unclear at this point whether the wedding was that of John the future evangelist, as is asserted in the next paragraph.

176. John 2:1–10.

177. Jerome, *Preface to Saint John*.

178. John 2:1–10.

179. Sedulius, *Easter Poem* 3.3–7.

180. Cf. note 177 above.

181. Luke 5:1–11; John 21:1–6.

182. Luke 5:4.

183. Luke 5:5.

184. Luke 5:8.

185. Sedulius, *Easter Poem* 4.119–21.

186. Matthew 9:9; Mark 2:14; Luke 5:27–28; John 1:43.

187. Matthew 16:17–18; John 1:42.

188. Jerome, *On Hebrew Names* 89; Isidore, *Etymologies* 7.9. 4.

189. Jerome, *On Hebrew Names* 97, where the author refers to his own *Commentary on Daniel* 1.7.

190. Mark 3:17; Jerome, loc. cit.; Isidore, *Etymologies* 7.9.13.

191. Matthew 10:1; Mark 3:13–14; Luke 6:13.

192. Matthew 10:2–4; Mark 3:16–19; Luke 6:14–16; Acts of the Apostles 1:13. (The scribe apparently omitted James, the son of Alpheus.)

193. John 2:12.

194. Matthew 21:12–13; Mark 11:15–17; Luke 19:45–46; John 2:14–16.

195. John 2:15.

196. Matthew 21:12; Mark 11:17; Luke 19:46.

197. Matthew 21:15; Mark 11:18; Luke 19:47–48, 20:1–2.

198. John 3:1–21.

199. John 3:22.

200. John 3:23–24.

201. John 4:1–2.

202. John 4:3–5.

203. John 4:5–6.

204. John 4:8.

205. John 4:7–26.

206. John 4:9.

207. Ibid., with Manetti's parenthetical comment.

208. John 4:10–27 and 29.

209. John 4:29.

210. John 4:30 and 39.

211. John 4:40–41.

212. John 4:43 and 45.

213. John 4:46; the cross-reference is to §94.

214. Matthew 8:5–13; Luke 7:2–10; John 4:47–54 (Manetti's principal source).

215. John 4:48.

216. John 4:50.

217. Sedulius, *Easter Poem* 3:20–22.

218. John 4:51.

219. John 4:52–53.

220. John 4:53.

221. Sedulius, *Easter Poem* 3.23–25.

222. For the Sermon on the Mount, see Matthew 5–7; Luke 6:20–49. Manetti cites the whole text in Book 3, §§3–22.

223. Matthew 8:2–4 (Manetti's prinicpal source); Mark 1:40–44; Luke 5:12–14.

224. Sedulius, *Easter Poem* 3.26–32.

225. Matthew 8:4; Mark 1:44; Luke 5:14.

226. Leviticus 14:2–8.

227. Matthew 9:1–8; Mark 2:1–5; Luke 7:1–10.

228. Luke 4:33–37.

229. Luke 4:34. Curiously, Manetti has added the phrase "before the time" (*ante tempus*), which is found in the story of the demons related in Matthew 8:29 (n. 241 below).

230. Luke 4:35.

231. Matthew 8:14–15; Mark 1:32–34; Luke 4:38–39.

232. Sedulius, *Easter Poem* 3.33–39.

233. Mark 1:32–34; Matthew 8:16; Luke 4:40–41.

234. Matthew 8:18.

235. Matthew 8:23–27; Mark 4:35–40; Luke 8:22–25.

236. Matthew 8:27; Mark 4:40; Luke 8:25.

237. Sedulius, *Easter Poem* 3.59–63.

238. Gerasenes, *sc.* Gadarenes. Matthew 8:28–34 (Manetti's principal source); Mark 5:10; Luke 8:26–37.

239. Matthew 8:29.

240. Sedulius, *Easter Poem* 3.78–85.

241. Matthew 8:32.

242. Matthew 8:33–34.

243. Matthew 9:1–8; Mark 2:1–12; Luke 5:18–26.

244. Matthew 9:2; Mark 2:5; Luke 5:20.

245. Matthew 9:4–6; Mark 2:8–11; Luke 5:23–24.

246. Matthew 9:7–8.

247. Matthew 9:18–26; Mark 5:22; Luke 8:41–56.

248. Eusebius, *Ecclesiastical History* 7.18.1–3.

249. Matthew 9:20–22; Mark 5:25–34; Luke 8:43–48.

250. Sedulius, *Easter Poem* 3.117–19, reading *tenuarat* for the unmetrical *tenuerat*.

251. For the story of the Veronica, see note 250 above.

252. Matthew 9:23–26; Mark 5:35–43; Luke 8:49–56.

253. Sedulius, *Easter Poem* 3.129–33.

254. Matthew 9:24; Mark 5:39; Luke 8:52.

255. Sedulius, *Easter Poem* 3.135–37.

256. Matthew 9:25; Mark 5:40.

257. Luke 8:54; Mark 5:41.

258. Mark 5:41. Manetti replaces the Aramaic word *tabitha* with Hebrew *iaalda*. On this emendation of the text, see Manetti, *Apologeticus* 5.62 (ed. De Petris, p. 123 = ed. McShane and trans. Young, 254–57); Paul Botley, *Latin Translation in the Renaissance: The Theory and Practice of Leonardo Bruni, Giannozzo Manetti and Desiderius Erasmus* (Cambridge, 2004), 98; and an Italian translation of *Apologeticus* 5 in Stefano Ugo Baldassarri, *Umanesimo e traduzione da Petrarca a Manetti* (Cassino: Pubblicazioni dell'Università di Cassino, 2003), 219–36, at 230. See also Den Haan, *Manetti's New Testament*, 48.

259. Sedulius, *Easter Poem* 3.138–42.

260. Mark 5:43; Luke 8:55.

261. Matthew 9:26.

262. Matthew 9:27–31.

263. Sedulius, *Easter Poem* 3.148–51.

264. Matthew 9:32–33; Luke 11:14.

265. Sedulius, *Easter Poem* 3.155–57.

266. Luke 7:11–17.

267. Luke 7:13.

268. Sedulius, *Easter Poem* 4.132–36.

269. Matthew 10:1; Mark 6:7; Luke 9:1.

270. Matthew 10:7–8.

271. Matthew 11:2–3.

272. Matthew 11:4–5.

273. Matthew 12:1; Mark 2:23: Luke 6:1.

274. Matthew 12:9–13; Mark 3:1–5; Luke 6–10.

275. Sedulius, *Easter Poem* 3.186–87.

276. Matthew 12:22.

277. Sedulius, *Easter Poem* 3.196–97.

278. Matthew 12:23.

279. Mark 4:2.

280. Luke 4:16–30, commenting on a passage in Isaiah 61:1–2.

281. Matthew 14:1–2; Mark 6:14–16; Luke 9:9.

282. John 5:1–13.

283. Cf. the gloss to the *Vulgata*, 1665.

284. John 5:5–9.

285. John 5:9–18.

286. John 5:11.

287. John 5:14.

288. Matthew 14:13–21 (Manetti's principal source); Mark 6:30–44; Luke 9:10–17; John 6:1–13.

289. Sedulius, *Easter Poem* 3.214–18.

290. Matthew 14:22–27; Mark 6:45–50; John 6:15–20.

291. Jerome, *Commentary on Matthew* 2.14; St. Thomas Aquinas, *Golden Chain. Continuous Gloss on the Gospels* (Bologna: ESD, 2007), 1:134. The reasoning is, of course, faulty: the storm could have arisen suddenly.

292. Matthew 14:26; Mark 6:49.

293. Matthew 14:27–28; Mark 6:50.

294. Matthew 14:30.

295. Matthew 14:31.

296. Sedulius, *Easter Poem* 3.234–35.

297. Matthew 14:31.

298. Sedulius, *Easter Poem* 3.229–30.

299. Matthew 14:33.

300. Matthew 14:34–36; Mark 6:53–56.

301. Sedulius, *Easter Poem* 3.236–41.

302. Matthew 15:1–20; Mark 7:1–23.

303. Matthew 15:21–22; Mark 7:24–26.

304. Matthew 15:23; Mark 7:27.

305. Matthew 15:23.

306. Matthew 15:24.

307. Matthew 15:25.

308. Matthew 15:26.

309. Ibid.

310. Matthew 15:28.

311. Ibid.

312. Sedulius, *Easter Poem* 3.242–50.

313. Mark 7:32–36.

314. Mark 7:34.

315. Mark 7:35.

316. Sedulius, *Easter Poem* 4.62–63.

317. Mark 7:36.

318. Mark 7:36–37.

319. Matthew 15:29–31.

320. Sedulius, *Easter Poem* 3.251–56.

321. Matthew 15:32; Mark 8:2–3.

322. Matthew 15:33; Mark 8:4.

323. Matthew 15:34–37.

324. Matthew 15:38.

325. Sedulius, *Easter Poem* 3.264–72.

326. Mark 8:22–26.

327. Sedulius, *Easter Poem* 4.106–8.

328. Matthew 17:1–9 (Manetti's principal source); Mark 9:1–8; Luke 9:28–36.

329. Sedulius, *Easter Poem* 3.279–82.

330. Sedulius, *Easter Poem* 3.283–84.

331. Matthew 17:2; Mark 9:2.

332. Mark 9:2.

333. Matthew 17:3; Mark 9:3; Luke 9:30.

334. Matthew 17:4 (Manetti's principal source); Mark 9:4; Luke 9:33.

335. Matthew 17:5; Mark 9:6; Luke 9:34.

336. Psalm 97:2.

337. Matthew 17:5.

338. Matthew 17:7.

339. Matthew 17:8.

340. Ibid.; Mark 9:8.

341. Matthew 17:23–26.

342. Sedulius, *Easter Poem* 3.317–19.

343. Matthew 17:14–17 (Manetti's prinicpal source); Mark 9:16–26; Luke 9:37–43.

344. Luke 13:10–13.

345. Luke 13:12.

346. Luke 13:14–16.

347. Luke 13:17.

348. Luke 14:1–6.

349. Sedulius, *Easter Poem* 4.175–80.

350. Luke 14:3–6.

351. Luke 17:11–13.

352. Luke 17:14.

353. Sedulius, *Easter Poem* 4.198–201.

354. Mark 10:46–52; Luke 18:35–42 (Manetti's principal source).

355. Luke 18:38; Mark 10:47.

356. Luke 18:41; Mark 10:51.

357. Luke 18:42; Mark 10:52.

358. Luke 18:43.

359. Matthew 20:29–34.

360. Matthew 20:31

361. Cf. the verse in Dado (Audoenus), *Life of St. Eligius* 37 (PL 87: 568C).

362. Matthew 20:32.

363. Matthew 20:33.

364. Matthew 20:34.

365. John 9:1–12.

366. John 9:3.

367. Cf. Sedulius, *Easter Poem* 4.259.

368. John 9:6.

369. Sedulius, *Easter Poem* 4.261–62.

370. John 9:13–34.

371. Matthew 21:1–9 (Manetti's principal source); Mark 11:1–10; Luke 19:28–39; John 12:14–15.

372. Matthew 21:5; John 12:15.

373. Zechariah 9:9; cf. John 12:15.

374. Matthew 21:8; Mark 11:8; Luke 19:36.

375. Matthew 21:9.

376. Luke 19:39.

377. Matthew 21:16.

378. Luke 19:40.

379. Ambrose, *Commentary on Saint Luke* 9.15.

380. Sallust, *Histories* 2.25. *Crisippus historicus* is a mistake for Gaius Sallustius Crispus.

381. Cicero, *In Defense of Marcellus* 10.

382. Sedulius, *Easter Poem* 4.304–8.

383. Matthew 21:12–13; Mark 11:15–17; Luke 19:45–46; John 2:14–16.

384. Manetti recounted the expulsion of the merchants at §109.

385. John 2:15.

386. Matthew 21:23; Mark 11:27–28; Luke 20:1–2.

387. Matthew 21:14–15.

388. Matthew 21:15.

389. Matthew 21:17; Mark 11:11–12. The distance between Jerusalem and Bethany is given in John 11:18.

390. John 11:1–44.

391. John 11:21–22.

392. John 11:23–27.

393. John 11:28–30.

394. John 11:31.

395. John 11:32.

396. John 11:33–34.

397. John 11:34.

398. John 11:38–39.

399. John 11:41–43.

400. Sedulius, *Easter Poem* 4.284–88.

401. John 11:44.

402. Ibid.

403. John 11:46.

404. John 12:1–9.

405. Matthew 21:17–22; Mark 11:12–14.

406. Matthew 21:19.

407. Matthew 21:19–20.

408. Sedulius, *Easter Poem* 4.50–51.

409. John Chrysostom, *Homily on Matthew* 67.2.

410. Cf. Lactantius, *Divine Institutes* 4.15.

411. That is, lepers.

412. Lactantius, loc. cit.

BOOK III

1. The first twenty-two paragraphs of Book 3 paraphrase the Sermon on the Mount recorded in Matthew 5:1–7:28. Manetti often slightly rewords the text of the Vulgate: see Baldassarri, "Riflessioni preliminari." These variants are not recorded in the following notes. We have supplied in brackets a number of omissions of the Gospel text when they seem to reflect a scribal rather than an authorial oversight.

2. Manetti contrasts the humility of Christ on the Mount to the "fireworks" of God's appearance to Moses on Mount Sinai in Exodus 19:16–19.

3. Greek χαῖρε.

4. After his linguistic digression, Manetti resumes the Gospel account at Matthew 10:13.

5. Supplying the Vulgate's "also" in brackets.

6. The citation in Matthew 11:23 paraphrases Isaiah 14:13–15.

7. Manetti now picks up with Jesus' teaching in Matthew 23:1–39, paraphrasing the Gospel down to the end of §39.

8. The comment on the tetragrammaton is Manetti's addition.

9. The words in parenthesis are an addition by Manetti; the bracketed phrase — *Vos autem nolite vocari rabbi* in the Vulgate — was omitted, probably by scribal error.

10. Manetti now turns to John 12:44–50.

11. Manetti now returns to Matthew 26:26.

12. Manetti now resumes the words of Christ in John 14, continuing down to the end of §44.

13. In this place, Manetti omits John 14:5, a verse in which Thomas asks how they shall know the way; it is reserved for §94.

14. Manetti now begins to paraphrase John 15, continuing to the end of §47.

15. The next four paragraphs follow John 16:1–33.

16. See above, §1.

17. Manetti now turns back to Matthew, chapters 9 and 12.

18. The last two sentences are paraphrased from Matthew 13:54–58.

19. Matthew 15:1–9; Isaiah 29:13.

20. Following Matthew 16.

21. §§60–69 cite Matthew 18–22.

22. Following Matthew 19.

23. Following Matthew 20:20–28.

24. Cf. Psalm 8:2.

25. Following Matthew 21.

26. Following Matthew 22.

27. §§70–74 cite passages in Luke 7–13.

28. §§75–94 follow John 6–14.

29. §95 follows Matthew 12:1–12.

30. §96 follows John 5 and 7.

31. §§97–102 follow Matthew 24.

32. See above, §1.

33. §§103–8 follow Matthew 13.

34. §§109–23 paraphrase passages from Matthew 18, 20, 21, 22, and 25.

35. Manetti quotes four lines from Psalm 118:22–24, following Mark 12:10–11.

36. §§124–41 paraphrase passages in Luke 12–18.

BOOK IV

1. Manetti's account of the Last Supper, Passion, and Resurrection in Book 4 largely follows Matthew 26–28, with some parallels in the other Gospels.

2. Sedulius, *Easter Poem* 5.50–53.

3. Manetti paraphrases Matthew 26:25.

4. For the prophecy, see Zechariah 13:7.

5. Sedulius,, *Easter Poem*, 5.79–81.

6. Valerius Maximus, 8.14. *Ext. 4*.

7. Valerius Maximus, 8.14. *Ext. 5*.

8. Ibid.

9. Ibid.

10. Sedulius, *Easter Poem* 5.59–68.

11. Sedulius, *Easter Poem* 5.72–76.

12. Psalm 21:17.

13. Isaiah 53:7.

14. Isaiah 53:8.

15. Josephus, *Jewish Antiquities* 18.35 (18.2.2.35). The source is also referred to in St. Thomas Aquinas, *Golden Chain. Continuous Gloss on the Gospels* (Bologna: ESD, 2007), 2:872 (on Matthew 26:55–58).

16. Thomas Aquinas, *Golden Chain*, 2:880 (on Matthew 26:59–68).

17. Sedulius,, *Easter Poem* 5.95–103.

18. Manetti adds this linguistic reflection based on his own knowledge.

19. Sedulius, *Easter Poem* 5.131–33.

20. Matthew 27:6 in the Vulgate reads *corbana*, but Manetti's Latin version (Vatican City, Biblioteca Apostolica Vaticana, MS Pal. lat. 45, f. 19v) has *corbona*. For the etymology, Manetti may have recalled Josephus, *The Jewish War* 2.9.4.175, which alludes to the *korbonàs*.

21. Matthew 27:9. Cf. Jeremiah 32:6–9; Zechariah 11:12–13.

22. Jerome, *Epistle* 46 (to Marcella): see *PL* 22: 435A.

23. Lactantius, *Divine Institutes* 4.18. Lactantius in turn borrows this formula from Cicero, *Defense of Roscius* 37. Interestingly, the issue at stake in that oration is parricide.

24. A mistake on Manetti's part for Gavius (see next note); possibly he was influenced by Cicero, *Against Piso* 42, where the orator hopes to see Piso and Gabinius hanging on crosses.

25. In the Verrine orations, Cicero repeatedly excoriates Gaius Verres' venal justice both as praetor in 74 BCE and governor of Sicily in 73 to 71. On Gavius, cf. Cicero, *Against Verres* 2.5.165 and 168, but the whole passage is basically a quotation from Lactantius, *Divine Institutes* 4.18.10–11.

26. Psalm 21(22):19.

27. Sedulius, *Easter Poem* 5.196–99.

28. Psalm 58:1. See Augustine, *Commentary on the Psalms* 58:1 (PL 36: 692); Augustine, *Tractates on the Gospel of John* 117.5, on John 19:17–22 (PL 35: 1946); and Isidore, *On the Catholic Faith* 1.41 (PL 83: 487). Cf. Thomas Aquinas, *Golden Chain*, 19:19–22, citing Augustine, *Tractates* 117.5.

29. This point is repeated from Manetti, *Apologeticus* 3.8 (ed. McShane-Young, 115).

30. Sedulius, *Easter Poem* 5.232–36.

31. Sedulius, *Easter Poem* 5.270–72.

32. Sedulius, *Easter Poem* 5.245–47.

33. Sedulius, *Easter Poem* 5.266–69.

34. Augustine, *City of God*, 3.15 (PL 41: 92A).

35. Ibid. Manetti's discussion of the eclipse is repeated in his treatise on earthquakes, including the citations to Augustine, Dionysius, Sacrobosco, Livy (Romulus), Bithynia, and Phlegon (notes 31–37 here). See the critical edition of *De terremotu* by Daniela Pagliara, 132–34.

36. Dionysius the Areopagite, *Epistle* 7 (PG 3: 1081B).

37. The astronomer is Johannes de Sacrobosco (d. 1256). The quotation is from the closing statement in his *On the Sphere of the World*. On this treatise see Lynn Thorndike, *The* Sphere *of Sacrobosco and Its Commentators* (Chicago: University of Chicago Press, 1949).

38. Livy, *History of Rome* 1.16.1.

39. The earthquake that hit Bithynia and destroyed Nicaea occurred on November 24, 29 CE. Christian authors often associated it with the portents that accompanied Christ's crucifixion. On it see, E. Guidoboni, *I terremoti prima del mille in Italia e nell'area mediteranea. Storia, archeologia, sismologia* (Bologna: ING-SGA, 1989), 660.

40. Cf. Jerome's Latin translation of Eusebius' *Chronicle* 2.1.203 (*PG* 19: 535–36).

41. Cf. Josephus, *The Jewish War* 6.5.3.298–99. This passage, too, is an almost literal quotation from Jerome's Latin translation of Eusebius, *Chronicle* 2.1.203 (*PG* 19: 535–36). Cf. also Jerome, *Epistle* 46.4 (to Marcellam); and Peter Comestor in his *Scholastic Investigation on the Gospels* 178 (*PL* 198: 1633B). It should be noted, however, that the anecdote reported by Josephus occurred when Titus besieged Jerusalem.

42. For the prophecy, see Exodus 12:46.

43. Cf. Suetonius, *Caesar* 89.

44. Cf. Josephus, *Jewish Antiquities* 17.6.5.168–70.

45. Cf. Josephus, *Jewish Antiquities* 18.7.2.252.

46. On the disasters at Jerusalem, see Josephus, *Jewish Antiquities* 20.5.2–3.

47. Sedulius, *Easter Poem* 5.326–31.

48. The words "Thus, on the hill of Golgotha . . . revived" echo a passage from the *Oration for Our Faith* sometimes attributed to Rufinus. See T. Christensen, *Rufinus of Aquileia and the Historia Ecllesiastica (Lib. VIII–IX) of Eusebius* (Copenhagen: The Royal Danish Academy of Sciences and Letters, 1989), 252.

49. The account of the risen Christ in §§83–97 relies mainly on Luke and John.

50. Equal to seven miles.

51. That is, "the Twin."

52. Psalm 18:5 (Vulgate).

53. 1 Corinthians 15:8.

Bibliography

꿎ᔑᒷ

WORKS BY GIANNOZZO MANETTI

Das Corpus der Orationes. Edited by Heinz Willi Wittschier. Cologne-Graz: Böhlau, 1968.

Elogi dei Genovesi. Edited and translated by Giovanna Petti Balbi. Milan: Marzorati Editore, 1974.

De dignitate et excellentia hominis. Edited by Elizabeth R. Leonard. Padua: Antenore, 1975.

Vita Socratis et Senecae. Edited by Alfonso De Petris. Florence: Leo S. Olschki, 1979.

Apologeticus. Edited by Alfonso De Petris. Rome: Edizioni di Storia e Letteratura, 1981.

Dialogus consolatorius. Edited by Alfonso De Petris. Rome: Edizioni di Storia e Letteratura, 1983.

Vita di Nicolò V. Italian translation, introduction, and commentary by Anna Modigliani. Preface by Massimo Miglio. Rome: Roma nel Rinascimento, 1999.

Biographical Writings. Edited and translated by Stefano Ugo Baldassarri and Rolf Bagemihl. I Tatti Renaissance Library 9. Cambridge, MA: Harvard University Press, 2003.

De vita ac gestis Nicolai Quinti summi pontificis. Edited and translated by Anna Modigliani. Rome: Istituto storico italiano per il Medio Evo, 2005.

Adversus Iudaeos et Gentes liber VI. Edited by Stefano Ugo Baldassarri. In Baldassarri, "Scolastica e umanesimo nell' *Adversus Iudaeos et gentes*: edizione del VI libro." *Letteratura antica italiana* 7 (2006): 25–75.

Historia Pistoriensis. Edited by Stefano Ugo Baldassarri and Benedetta Aldi. Historical commentary by William J. Connell. Florence: SISMEL-Edizioni del Galluzzo, 2011.

De terremotu. Edited by Daniela Pagliara. Florence: SISMEL-Edizioni del Galluzzo, 2012.

A Translator's Defense. Edited by Myron McShane. English Translation by Mark Young. I Tatti Renaissance Library 71. Cambridge, MA: Harvard University Press, 2016. Latin text based on that of De Petris.

OTHER PRIMARY TEXTS

Platina, Bartolomeo. *Lives of the Popes*. Vol. 1. Edited and translated by Anthony F. D'Elia. I Tatti Renaissance Library 30. Cambridge, MA: Harvard University Press, 2008.

Vespasiano da Bisticci. *Le Vite*. Edited by Aulo Greco. 2 vols. Florence: Istituto Nazionale di Studi sul Rinascimento, 1970–76.

SECONDARY LITERATURE

Baldassarri, Stefano Ugo. "Riflessioni preliminari sulla traduzione manettiana del Nuovo Testamento." *Journal of Italian Translation* 8 (2013): 11–30.

———. "Conferme e novità sull'*Adversus Iudaeos et gentes* di Giannozzo Manetti." *Letteratura Italiana Antica* 25 (2014): 391–408.

Den Haan, Annet. *Giannozzo Manetti's New Testament: Translation Theory and Practice in Fifteenth-Century Italy*. Leiden: E. J. Brill, 2016. Contains a critical edition of Manetti's Latin translation of the New Testament.

De Petris, Alfonso. "L'*Adversus Judaeos et Gentes* di Giannozzo Manetti." *Rinascimento* 16 (1976): 193–205.

Dignitas et excellentia hominis: Atti del Convegno Internazionale di Studi su Giannozzo Manetti. Edited by Stefano Ugo Baldassarri. Florence: Le Lettere, 2008.

Dröge, Christoph. *Giannozzo Manetti als Denker und Hebraist*. Frankfurt: Peter Lang, 1987.

Fioravanti, Gianfranco. "L'apologetica anti-giudaica di Giannozzo Manetti." *Rinascimento* 23 (1983): 3–32.

Foà, Simona. "Manetti, Giannozzo." *Dizionario biografico degli italiani* 68 (2007): 613–17.

Fubini, Riccardo. "Ancora sul 'Testimento' di Niccolò V: modelli biblici e parabiblici nella 'vita' di G. Manetti. Echi di re Salomone e dei 'Testamenti dei dodici patriarche.'" In Baldassarri, *Dignitas et excellentia hominis*, 189–201.

Martelli, Mario. "Profilio ideologico di Giannozzo Manetti." *Studi Italiani* 1 (1989): 5–41.

Martines. Lauro. *The Social World of the Florentine Humanists, 1390–1460*. Princeton: Princeton University Press, 1963.

Smith, Christine, and Joseph F. O'Connor. *Building the Kingdom: Giannozzo Manetti on the Material and Spiritual Edifice*. Tempe, AZ: Medieval and Renaissance Texts and Studies, 2006.

Trinkaus, Charles. *In Our Image and Likeness: Humanity and Divinity in Italian Humanist Thought*. 2 vols. Chicago: University of Chicago, 1970.

Index

𝕭𝕾𝕻𝕾

Aaron (brother of Moses), 71–73, 101; daughters of, 123; sons of, 99, 101, 103

Abilene, 173

Abraham (patriarch), xii, xv, 5, 7, 9, 51, 55, 57, 119, 301, 305, 311, 313, 349, 385; daughter of, 239

Academic philosophers, 17, 19; New School, 19; Old School, 19

Acharon (demon), 269

Achiabus (grandson of Herod), 163

Achor (giant king), 61

Acts (biblical book): 1, 450n192; 7, 440n144

Adam (name), 3, 53, 437n93

Adam (first man), 9, 53, 111, 181, 385

Admetus (king), 37

Advent, 223

Aemilius Paullus (Lucius), 11

Aenon, 199

Aesculapius, 29, 37

Agamemnon (king of Argos), 43

Agathocles (king of Sicily), 43

Agenor (father of Cadmus), 25

Alberti, Leon Battista, x

Alcmaeon, 31

Alcmena (mother of Hercules), 37, 39

Alfonso of Aragon (king of Naples), x

Althea (queen of Calydon), 436n71

Amalekites, 89

Ambrose (saint), 181; *Commentary on Saint Luke*, 245, 457n379; *Exposition of Saint Luke*, 445n74, 446n90, 446n93, 448n152

Amos (biblical book): 1, 444n45

Amos the Teokite, 137

Anaxagoras, 15, 17, 31

Anaximander, 15, 31

Anaximenes, 15, 31

Andrew (saint, apostle), 187, 189, 195, 197, 207, 317

Androgeus (son of Minos), 43

Anna (mother of Mary), 117

Anna (daughter of Samuel; prophetess), 157

Annaeus Seneca, Lucius (the Younger), ix, 11; *Madness of Hercules*, 41, 437n81; *On Providence*, 13, 434n23

Annas (priest), 173, 369

Antipater of Ascalon, 147

Antisthenes, 31

Antony and Cleopatra, 131

Apis (Egyptian bull deity), 25

Apollo, 29, 35, 37, 43

Aquinas, Thomas: *Golden Chain, Continuous Gloss on the Gospels*, 445n60, 454n291, 461nn15–16,

469

Elijah (prophet), 141, 177, 179, 181,
235, 393
Elisha (prophet), 141
Elizabeth (cousin of Mary), 123,
129–31, 159, 191
Emmanuel (name), 121, 141,
444n54
Emmaus (Nicopolis), 409
Empedocles, 19, 31
Enoch (name), 53
Enoch (prophet), 53
Enos (name), 9, 53
Enos (son of Seth), 9, 53,
434n15
Ephesus, 365; Temple of Diana,
365
Epicurean philosophers, 19–21
Epicurus, 11, 17, 31
Erebus, 249
Esau (brother of Jacob), 57
Ethiopians, 75–79
Eudemus, 435n35
Eudoxus, 21
Europa, 25, 37, 39
Eurystheus, 37, 436n65
Eusebius of Caesarea, xii, 13, 215,
397, 444n44, 448n139; *Chroni-
cle*, 9, 433n8, 433n12, 434n17,
442n1, 463nn40–41; *Demonstra-
tion of the Gospel*, 437n92,
441n169, 441n185, 442n9,
445n61, 448n150; *Ecclesiastical
History*, 445n64, 445n66,
446n95, 446n102, 447n128,
452n248; *Preparation of the Gos-
pel*, xi, 434n25

Evangelical Law (Law of the Gospel), 7, 107, 113
Evangelista of Pisa (friar), viii
Exodus (biblical book), 69, 141;
1, 440n143; *2*, 440n150,
440nn157–58; *3*, 440n157;
5, 440nn159–60; *7*, 440n161;
12, 440n162, 447n113, 463n42;
13, 445n71; *14*, 440nn163–64;
15, 440n165; *19*, 440n166,
459n2; *28*, 440n149, 440n156;
34, 448n150; *39*, 444n56
Exodus (event), xii, 149
Ezra (biblical book), 1, 445n79

Faunus (Latin deity), 35
festivals, of Roman Catholic
Church: Annunciation, 129,
443n23, 443n30; Assumption,
444n42; Candlemas, xii,
446n82; Easter, 444n39;
Epiphany, xii, 151, 446n82; Na-
tivity of Virgin Mary, 444n42;
Purification, 155; Visitation, xii,
131, 443n34
Fioravanti, Gianfranco, xiv
Firmicus Maternus, *On the Error of
Profane Religion*, 436n56
Florea (Roman deity), 27
Florence, vii, viii, ix, x, xi,
443n30; Academy of Santo
Spirito, viii; *Arte del Cambio*
(banking guild), viii; *Arte della
Seta* (silk-making guild), viii;
cathedral, ix; church of Santo
Spirito, x; San Frediano dis-

475

Publication of this volume has been made possible by

The Myron and Sheila Gilmore Publication Fund at I Tatti
The Robert Lehman Endowment Fund
The Jean-François Malle Scholarly Programs and Publications Fund
The Andrew W. Mellon Scholarly Publications Fund
The Craig and Barbara Smyth Fund
for Scholarly Programs and Publications
The Lila Wallace–Reader's Digest Endowment Fund
The Malcolm Wiener Fund for Scholarly Programs and Publications